THE LETTERS OF ABELARD AND HELOISE

PETER ABELARD was a French scholastic philosopher and the greatest logician of the twelfth century. He taught mainly in Paris where his fame attracted students from all over Europe and laid the foundations of the University of Paris. HELOISE was his pupil, and after the tragic end of their love affair and marriage she became a nun, and Abelard a monk in the Abbey of St Denis. He continued to teach theology, but his unorthodoxy led to open conflict with St Bernard of Clairvaux and his condemnation by the Church. His last months were spent under the protection of Peter the Venerable, and he died in a Cluniac priory. Heloise became abbess of the convent of the Paraclete which Abelard founded, and was acclaimed for her learning, her poetry and her music.

Abelard and Heloise are shown on the front cover debating about love and marriage, as described by Jean de Meun in the *Roman de la Rose*. The contrast between them is stark. Abelard is dressed in the fine clothes of a layman, despite being a cleric and a master in the schools, whereas Heloise is garbed as a nun. This depicts the critical time when he removed her to the convent of Argenteuil and vested her as a nun, even though he continued to visit her and have sexual intercourse. As a consequence, her family believed that he had repudiated her and they took vengeance by castrating him.

The rubric, the two lines in red above the miniature, is explanatory. It reads: Comment Helouys labeesse / Entrodit Pierres Abalart (How Peter Abelard instructs Heloise). However, the hand gestures in the miniature show Abelard and Heloise engaged in debate rather than instruction. The two lines in black read: Pierres Abalart le confesse/Qui Suer Helouys labeesse (Peter Abelard confesses that Sister Heloise the abbess [never wished to agree to be his wedded wife]).

BETTY RADICE read classics at Oxford. She became joint editor of the Penguin Classics list in 1964. She translated Livy's *Rome and Italy*, the Latin comedies of Terence, Pliny's *Letters* and Erasmus's *Praise of Folly*, and wrote the Introduction to Horace's *The Complete Odes and Epodes* and *Propertius: The Poems*, all for Penguin

Classics. She also edited and introduced Edward Gibbon's *Memoirs of My Life* for the Penguin English Library. She collaborated as a translator in the Collected Works of Erasmus, and was the author of the Penguin Reference Book *Who's Who in the Ancient World*. Betty Radice was an honorary fellow of St Hilda's College, Oxford, and a vice-president of the Classical Association. She died in 1985.

MICHAEL CLANCHY is Professor Emeritus of Medieval History at the Institute of Historical Research, University of London, and a Fellow of the British Academy. He taught at the University of Glasgow 1964–85. He is the author of *From Memory to Written Record* (third edition, 2013), *England and its Rulers, 1066–1272* (second edition, 1998) and *Abelard: A Medieval Life* (1997), which has been translated into French and German.

The Letters of Abelard and Heloise

*Translated with an Introduction
and Notes by* BETTY RADICE
Revised by M.T. CLANCHY

PENGUIN BOOKS

PENGUIN BOOKS

UK | USA | Canada | Ireland | Australia
India | New Zealand | South Africa

Penguin Books is part of the Penguin Random House group of companies
whose addresses can be found at global.penguinrandomhouse.com.

Penguin
Random House
UK

Published in Penguin Books 1974
Revised edition published 2003

031

Set in 10.25/12.25 pt PostScript Adobe Sabon
Typeset by Rowland Phototypesetting Ltd, Bury St Edmunds, Suffolk
Printed in Great Britain by Clays Ltd, Elcograf S.p.A

www.greenpenguin.co.uk

MIX
Paper from
responsible sources
FSC® C018179

Penguin Random House is committed to a
sustainable future for our business, our readers
and our planet. This book is made from Forest
Stewardship Council® certified paper.

Contents

THE PERSONAL LETTERS

THE LETTERS OF DIRECTION

LETTERS OF PETER THE VENERABLE
AND HELOISE

TWO HYMNS BY ABELARD

MAPS

Acknowledgements

My grateful thanks are due to the many scholars, past and present, whose published works I have made use of, and to the Librarian and staff of the London Library who let me keep these books on loan for so long; to the late E. V. Rieu for entrusting me with the translation some years ago, and to friends and members of my family who have taken an interest in it, amongst them Elizabeth Stephenson for deftly typing much of the script and helping with proofs; and above all to those who have given me generous expert advice, Professor Lewis Thorpe, Professor David Luscombe, and Sister Benedicta Ward, SLG, whose experience and enthusiasm have given me necessary encouragement as her acute practical criticism has been a pleasure to receive. The remaining mistakes must lie where I did not ask for the further help I needed.

Highgate
February 1973

BETTY RADICE

Preface to the Revised Edition

Betty Radice's translation has itself become a classic, and this revised edition retains its substance. I have made the following changes:

The numbering of the letters has been altered to conform with standard practice: *Historia calamitatum* is now designated as 'Letter 1'.

Some revisions have been made in Radice's Introduction (particularly in updating the notes) and in the translations (mostly in *Historia calamitatum*).

The summary of Letter 7 on the origin and dignity of nuns has been considerably enlarged.

An update on 'The Letters of Abelard and Heloise in Today's Scholarship' has been appended to Radice's Introduction, and this is followed by a new 'Further Reading' section. A chronology for Abelard and Heloise has also been added.

I am grateful for advice to the following scholars (but all opinions expressed are my own): Alcuin Blamires, Brenda Cook, Stephen Jaeger, Gary Macy, Juanita Ruys, John Ward and David Wulstan. I have revised the Further Reading section and made other changes to take account of the new translations of the *Letters of Abelard and Heloise* by William Levitan (2007), Mary M. McLaughlin and Bonnie Wheeler (2009), and David Luscombe (2013).

November 2013

M. T.Clanchy
University of London

Chronology

Note: There are few firm dates in the lives of Abelard and Heloise because they give no dates for any events in their own writings and chroniclers' dates vary from one text to another.

1073–85 Pontificate of Pope Gregory VII, who aims to restore ecclesiastical authority and make the clergy celibate.

c. 1079 Birth of Peter Abelard at Le Pallet, near Nantes.

c. 1090 Possible date for the birth of Heloise, if she is assumed to be older than Peter the Venerable.

1092 or 1094 Birth of Peter the Venerable, abbot of Cluny (1122–56).

1092 The logician Roscelin is condemned for heresy concerning the Trinity at the Council of Soissons.

1093–9 At some time in this period Abelard is taught by Roscelin.

c. 1100 Abelard comes to Paris, where he is taught by William of Champeaux.

1100 or 1101 Traditional date for the birth of Heloise.

c. 1102–*c.* 1105 Abelard is master of his own school at Melun and then at Corbeil, probably under the protection of the king's minister, Stephen de Garlande.

c. 1105–*c.* 1108 Abelard 'fell ill through overwork and was obliged to return home' (Letter 1, p. 4).

c. 1108 Abelard returns to Paris and challenges William of Champeaux.

c. 1110–*c.* 1112 Abelard is master of his own school at the abbey of Mont-Sainte-Geneviève, on the left bank of the Seine in Paris.

c. 1112 Abelard again returns home, when his parents retire into monasteries.

1113 Abelard goes to Laon to study divinity with Anselm of Laon.

c. 1114 Abelard is established at Paris as master of the cathedral school of Notre-Dame.

c. 1115–*c.* 1117 Abelard seduces Heloise when he lodges at the house of Fulbert, her uncle. (It is not known how long Heloise had been living in Fulbert's house; as a girl, she had been at the convent of Argenteuil near Paris.)

c. 1118 Heloise bears Abelard a son, whom she names Astralabe. Under pressure from Fulbert, Abelard and Heloise are secretly married in Paris. Because Fulbert wants to make the marriage public, Abelard removes Heloise to the convent of Argenteuil. Believing that Abelard has repudiated the marriage, Fulbert has him castrated. Heloise becomes a nun at Argenteuil and Abelard a monk at the abbey of St Denis near Paris.

c. 1120 Abelard reopens the debate about the Trinity by complaining to the bishop of Paris that Roscelin has accused him of heresy.

c. 1121 Abelard's book on the Trinity, *Theologia*, is burned as heretical by the Council of Soissons. Abelard insults the abbey of St Denis and flees to the protection of Count Theobald of Champagne.

1122 With the permission of Suger, abbot of St Denis (1122–51), Abelard establishes a hermitage (dedicated to the Paraclete) near Troyes, where students join him.

c. 1123 Abelard publishes an enlarged edition of his book on the Trinity with the title *Theologia Christiana* (*Christian Theology*).

c. 1125–*c.* 1127 Allegedly because of the backbiting of St Bernard and St Norbert, Abelard abandons his hermitage and becomes abbot of St Gildas, on the west coast of Brittany.

1129 Heloise and her nuns are expelled from Argenteuil, when Suger wins possession of the convent for the abbey of St Denis.

1131 Abelard's gift of the convent of the Paraclete to Heloise and her nuns is confirmed by Pope Innocent II.

c. 1132 Abelard writes Letter 1 (*Historia calamitatum*) 'to a Friend'.

c. 1133 Abelard abandons the abbey of St Gildas and returns to Paris as a master.

c. 1133–*c.* 1138 Abelard and Heloise conduct the correspondence in Letters 2–8.

1140 or 1141 Abelard accused of heresy by St Bernard at the Council of Sens. He appeals to Rome. Pope Innocent II condemns him to perpetual silence. Berengar publishes Abelard's 'Confession of Faith' (p. 211). Abelard is protected by Peter the Venerable.

1142 or 1144 Abelard dies at the Cluniac priory of St Marcel near Chalon-sur-Saône.

c. 1144 Peter the Venerable writes to Heloise and brings her Abelard's body for burial at the convent of the Paraclete. Heloise asks him to obtain a prebend for Astralabe.

c. 1163 or *c.* 1164 Death of Heloise, abbess of the Paraclete.

Introduction

Most people have heard of Abelard and Heloise as a pair of lovers as famous as Dante and Beatrice or Romeo and Juliet, and many know that their story is told in the letters they exchanged. If we are interested in what is generally called the Twelfth-Century Renaissance we soon find that Abelard is a key figure, one of the most original minds of his day, that the medieval university of Paris arose out of his fame as a teacher and that his theological views brought him into conflict with St Bernard of Clairvaux. Heloise too was more than a girl deeply in love and a pupil avid for learning; she was the widely respected abbess of a famous convent and its daughter foundations. The two are representative of the best of their time in their classical knowledge and the way they express themselves, in their passionate interest in problems of faith and morality, and in their devotion to the Christian Church which ruled their lives. At the same time their dilemma is of timeless interest, created less by circumstances than by the relations between two highly complex personalities.

Peter Abelard was born into the minor Breton nobility in about 1079, and his career to the age of about fifty-four is set out in a remarkable piece of autobiographical writing, Letter 1, *Historia calamitatum* or *The Story of His Misfortunes*. His father may have served the duke of Brittany and wished his sons to have some education before following the same career. Abelard soon decided to renounce his rights as the eldest son and to become a scholar: 'I preferred the weapons of dialectic to all the other teachings of philosophy, and armed with these I chose the conflicts of disputation instead of the trophies of war.

I began to travel about in several provinces disputing, like a true peripatetic philosopher, wherever I had heard there was keen interest in the art of dialectic' (p. 3).

Abelard is writing rather formally in Latin and using semi-technical expressions which would be more readily understood by his contemporaries than they are today, but these two sentences take us straight into the intellectual ferment of the early twelfth century and the revolution in teaching in which Abelard played a leading part. The accepted course for higher education at this time (and for a long time to come) was that of the seven liberal arts: the *trivium*, consisting of grammar and rhetoric, which were the study of classical (Latin) language and literature, and logic, or dialectic as it was called, followed by the *quadrivium*, the sciences of geometry, arithmetic, astronomy and music. Beyond these lay the highest studies of theology, canon law and medicine. Abelard never shows much interest in science, and his knowledge of mathematics was elementary. He evidently decided at the start to concentrate on the *trivium* and, in particular, on logic (dialectic). The Greeks had been masters of logic, but at this time there was very little knowledge of their work. Abelard is not thought to have known any Greek, and what he knew of Aristotle was mainly from Porphyry's Introduction to Aristotle's *Categories* and Aristotle's *De Interpretatione*, both in a Latin translation by the sixth-century Roman scholar Boethius. Logic covered both linguistic logic, or theory of meaning of words and sentences, and formal logic, the theory of the correct manner to systemize known facts and to draw conclusions. It was 'an instrument of order in a chaotic world',[1] and in Abelard's hands it could provide a genuine intellectual education for his students. His unwavering determination to apply the rules of logic to all fields of thought was to dominate his life.

Abelard speaks of himself as moving from place to place wherever he heard that there was the teaching he wanted. This is the period of the 'wandering scholars'. All teaching was in the hands of the Church, in some form, but the Cathedral schools were becoming more prominent and beginning to replace the monastic schools such as those of Bec and Cluny; out of them would develop the medieval universities. Abelard's movements and his own career show that in these early days a teacher could set up a school of his own wherever he knew he could muster sufficient pupils, and the success or failure of a school rested on the teacher's popularity and skill. His own pupils sought him out wherever he settled, and were even prepared to camp out in the remote countryside to be near him. One tends today to think of logic as something dry and scholastic, perhaps by contrast with Renaissance humanism, but Abelard can make it sound new and invigorating, the opening of a door on to wider horizons.

Abelard also speaks of himself as 'disputing', and here again he shows himself in the vanguard of a new movement. By *disputatio* is meant a new technique to replace the traditional *lectio*, a lecture by a teacher on a selected passage of Scripture which was read aloud sentence by sentence and then expounded by glosses on the grammar and commentaries on the meaning drawn from the writings of the early Fathers of the Church. Disputation adopted a more conversational method, posing a problem and discussing it by means of question and answer, by setting out the difficulties and attempting to resolve conflicts. One method of teaching should not exclude the other, but Abelard was never anything but impatient with the orthodox lecture – witness his unjustified attack on Anselm of Laon (p. 7). He must have been a thorn in his teachers' flesh, conscious as he was of his own intellectual superiority, no respecter of persons and revelling in the cut-and-thrust of debate. So William of Champeaux found when Abelard arrived in Paris about 1100 and joined the Cloister School of Notre-Dame. Tension increased until Abelard set up his own school, first at Melun, then at Corbeil, with the intention of destroying William's reputation. There was a respite when his health broke down through overwork, and he spent three or four years in Brittany. How he spent the time he does not say, but he returned to the fray to find that William had joined the Order of Canons Regular, but was still teaching at the Abbey of St Victor. Abelard started to attend his lectures again, this time on the subject of rhetoric, and soon made his position impossible.

Letter 1, *Historia calamitatum*, then raises the question of universals, or general and abstract terms. It had been discussed by Plato and Aristotle, and mentioned though not fully examined by Porphyry, and it was now hotly debated. If you and I and all of us are human, i.e. we belong to the human species, does anything exist which is humanity independent of the individuals who belong to the species? Abelard never says which teachers he sought out when he was a wandering scholar, but he must have stopped at Loches on his way to Paris to hear Roscelin, the chief exponent of Nominalism. Roscelin held that universals or abstract terms were no more than names given to the individuals which alone existed. This was seen by the Church as endangering the doctrine of Unity in the Trinity, because Roscelin was thought to postulate three individual Gods and not one God. He had been tried for heresy and banished, but later allowed to return to France and resume his teaching. William of Champeaux headed the opposite faction, that known as Realism. Following Plato and the Neoplatonist Porphyry, the Realists believed in the actual existence outside awareness of abstract ideas – Plato's Forms or Ideas. Abelard is brief to the point of obscurity about what happened, but he seems to have forced William to modify his view by pointing out the absurdities of its logical development. William had taught that the essence of humanity was totally and essentially present in all human beings who are differentiated only by 'accidents' or local modifications outside their common nature. If this is so, it is hard to see how you and I can be genuinely different individuals. Under pressure from Abelard William modified 'essentially' to 'indifferently', meaning that you and I are united in the human species by non-difference or absence of difference. But William's lectures then fell into disrepute 'as if the whole subject rested solely on the question of universals' (p. 5).

For Abelard, logic meant more than the nature of universals and also something rather different. He distinguished clearly (as William and many of his contemporaries did not) between logic and physic or metaphysic, the one concerned with *words* and how we express concepts in words, the other with *things* (physic) or the ultimate reality (metaphysic). Logic for him was linguistic logic, an essential discipline for understanding, and the problem of universals was only one element in it. His was a critical approach to the meaning of words and concepts as the basis of rational understanding. He was not trying to develop a philosophy of nature nor a system of theology. But the Realists did not draw the same distinction between things which exist outside our awareness and the expression in words of our understanding of them, so that for them the nature of universals was crucial.

Abelard's triumph over William greatly increased his reputation, and a good many of William's pupils joined the rival school he set up on Mont-Sainte-Geneviève, from which the university of Paris was to grow. There was continued friction between the students as William did his best to prevent Abelard from succeeding him as head of the Cloister School. Once again Abelard was summoned to Brittany, this time to see his mother, who was preparing to take vows and follow her husband into the religious life. He was not away long, and returned to find that William was now installed as bishop of Châlons and there was no rival for the headship of the Cloister School. Yet Abelard says that he returned to France for the express purpose of studying theology – *maxime ut de divinitate addiscerem* – and he left at once for Laon, where he could hear Anselm, who had long been established there as the greatest teacher. He gives no reason; some have wondered if it was his mother's request that her brilliant eldest son should turn to more constructive thoughts of salvation. But this was a decision which was to have lasting and serious consequences.

Anselm's reputation was deserved, both as a lecturer and part-compiler of the *Glossa ordinaria* or commentary on the Bible, a standard work for theological students for a long time. According to Abelard, his teaching was conservative, and he made no use of disputation; his wonderful eloquence was confined to lecture and exposition. As a trained dialectician and one who valued ability more highly than seniority, Abelard had little use for him, and soon made this clear. He fell out with the other students and was easily provoked into offering to produce an exposition himself by the light of his natural intelligence and a close study of the text. He soon showed that he could beat Anselm at his own game and, to the indignation of the students, Anselm was incited by his two leading pupils to forbid Abelard to teach in Laon. Abelard then returned to Paris to be head of the Cloister School. To his fame for dialectic and rhetoric he could now add a growing reputation for theology, and Anselm's death soon afterwards left him supreme. Paris gained students from all over western Europe.

Abelard was then in his mid-thirties, at the peak of his powers. All accounts agree that he was a wonderful teacher, with a rare gift for kindling enthusiasm in his pupils and inspiring their devotion. He tells us himself that he had 'exceptional good looks', and Heloise adds that he had a talent for verse and song, though there is no mention of his enjoying the lighter side of student life as a young man but rather the suggestion that he kept himself aloof (p. 9). He had established himself as a logician by offering his own solution to the problem of universals, the middle way, which was to be known as Conceptualism: universals were neither realities nor mere names but the concepts formed by the intellect when abstracting the similarities between perceived individual things. It is remarkable that Abelard arrived independently at a solution much like that of Aristotle, in which we have perception of the particular and we know the universal, but we know it through the particular and perceive the particular in the universal. But he was already running personal risks as a professional dialectician who was now concerning himself with theology. The two pupils of Anselm, Alberic of Rheims and Lotulf of Lombardy, were his enemies from now on, and led the prosecution of Abelard for heresy at the Council of Soissons in 1121. This was not forgotten, and the final fateful clash between Abelard and St Bernard arose largely out of Abelard's application of dialectic to questions of theology.

By temperament Abelard was stimulated by controversy and one can imagine him bored by finding himself at the top without a rival. As he says:

But success always puffs up fools with pride, and worldly security weakens the spirit's resolution and easily destroys it through carnal temptations. I began to think myself the only philosopher in the world, with nothing to fear from anyone, and so I yielded to the lusts of the flesh . . . There was in Paris at the time a young girl named Heloise, the niece of Fulbert, one of the canons . . .' (pp. 9–10)

Abelard relates the opening stages of the story as a calculated seduction on his part, confident as he was of easy success, and there is never anything romantic or idealistic about his attitude to sexual love. To do him justice, he may have chosen this cool tone deliberately because the *Historia calamitatum* was written as a letter addressed to a third party, and omitted the painfully intimate details which emerge in his subsequent letters to Heloise. But however the relationship started, he was soon totally involved. Many years later Heloise accused him of feeling only lust for her, not love, and he admitted this (pp. 53, 86–7). Several of her modern champions have emphasized that he could never attain the heights of her selfless devotion. But in the modern idiom, they were passionately in love, their lovemaking was uninhibited and ecstatic, and Abelard was completely carried away and consequently quite reckless in his general behaviour. He neglected his pupils, abandoned all pretence of serious teaching, paid no attention to gossip and allowed his love songs which mentioned Heloise's name to be sung in public. When her uncle accepted the truth of what was common knowledge and tried to separate them, they took even greater risks and were found in bed together. Soon after, Heloise found she was pregnant and Abelard removed her to his people in Brittany where a son was born. From a later letter (p. 80) we know that he disguised her as a nun. Abelard returned to Paris and offered amends to Fulbert: he would marry Heloise so long as the marriage was kept secret so that his reputation did not suffer. Fulbert agreed, and Abelard returned to Brittany to fetch Heloise. It is at this point that she reveals her personality in an unexpected way.

Little is known of Heloise's parentage, though much has been conjectured.[2] She is thought to have been about seventeen at this time and born in 1100 or 1101. Fulbert's possessiveness has suggested to some that she was really his daughter, but taken with his brutal treatment of Abelard it would seem to have a strong sexual element, probably subconscious. Every credit is due to the nuns at Argenteuil for her early education, and to Fulbert for his encouragement of her remarkable gifts at a time when women were rarely educated at all. During the short time she was studying with Abelard they probably worked on philosophy; it was certainly a trained logical mind which argued so cogently against the marriage he proposed.

Heloise saw clearly, as Abelard would not, that a *secret* marriage was not going to satisfy Fulbert for a public scandal and, indeed, 'that no satisfaction could ever appease her uncle' (p. 13). She therefore opposed any form of marriage, first because of the risk to Abelard, secondly because it would disgrace them both. Both have a low view of marriage, derived from St Paul and St Jerome; they see it from the Christian monastic standpoint as no more than legalization of the weakness of the flesh. As a scholar Abelard was a clerk (*clericus*), and as master of the school of Notre-Dame he would be a member of the Chapter and a canon. Neither was a legal bar to marriage; though a married master might be unusual, one feels that his personality could have made the situation acceptable.[3] It is not known whether he was a priest in orders at this time: probably not. In any case, the Church forbade marriage only to the higher orders of the clergy. It is important to remember that there was no career open to an educated man at this time except in the Church, and that Abelard was prepared to sacrifice his ambitions for high office in order to secure Heloise for himself. He admits in a later letter that 'I desired to keep you whom I loved beyond measure for myself alone' (p. 83). Any marriage, open or secret, would be an effective bar. An open marriage would damage his reputation but might, just possibly, appease Fulbert, though Heloise who knew him well thought not. A secret marriage would not be damaging but would be dangerous in its effects on Fulbert.

All the authorities are now agreed that the question of reputation is crucial to Heloise's arguments and refers to something much deeper than self-interest on Abelard's part. If her arguments are read closely it is clear that she was much less concerned with the possible loss of Abelard's services to the Church than with the betrayal of the ideal which they both admired, that of the philosopher as a man who is set apart and above human ties. She argues from a classical rather than a Christian viewpoint, and she takes her illustrations from Theophrastus, Cicero, Seneca and Socrates as recorded by St Jerome. '[T]he great philosophers of the past have despised the world, not renouncing it so much as escaping from it, and have denied themselves every pleasure so as to find peace in the arms of philosophy alone' (p. 14). She points out the distractions and petty hindrances of domestic life which are inimical to philosophic contemplation, and compares the philosophers with 'those . . . who truly deserve the name of monks', that is, the dedicated solitaries such as John the Baptist or the ascetic sects of Jewish history. She concludes that 'the name of friend [*amica*] instead of wife would be dearer to her and more honourable for me' (p. 16), because then they would both be free from a permanent legal tie and Abelard would not incur the disgrace of renouncing the realization of his true self as a philosopher. They should be bound only by *gratia* – love freely given; marriage can add nothing of significance to an ideal relationship which is also classical in concept: that described in Cicero's *De amicitia*, a work they both knew, which sets the standard for true friendship in 'disinterested love' where physical love would be sublimated.

Heloise amplifies this point in her first letter (p. 51), in the well-known passage where she says that if the Emperor Augustus offered marriage she would still choose to be Abelard's whore; she says this in the context of preferring 'love to wedlock and freedom to chains'. She has loved Abelard only for himself, not for anything he could give her, and indeed, in her view, marriage for what either party could get from the other was no better than prostitution. By contrast, a lasting relationship should rest on the complete devotion of two persons; this is true disinterested love, based on what she calls 'chastity of spirit'. To such an ideal union a legal marriage could add nothing, and the presence or absence of an erotic element is, in a sense, irrelevant. The intention towards the ideal relationship is all-important. This is the 'ethic of pure intention' in which both Abelard and Heloise believed and to which she often returns. 'Wholly guilty though I am, I am also, as you know, wholly innocent. It is not the deed but the intention of the doer which makes the crime, and justice should weigh not what was done but the spirit in which it is done. What my intention towards you has always been, you alone who have known it can judge' (p. 53).

For Heloise the issue was clear and unequivocal, however difficult it is for us to follow her. Conventional morality would speak of a young woman who is willing to 'live in sin' with a man, so as not to stand in his path, as sacrificing herself, but for her living wholly for Abelard is self-realization. Abelard was torn by an impossible conflict between his desire for Heloise and all the jealous possessiveness which went with it, and his belief that his duty was to realize himself as a philosopher and to preserve his intention towards that ideal. It has been pointed out that the quotations used by Heloise all appear in a work of his own (Book II of his *Theologia Christiana*)[4] written after they parted but several years before Letter 1. It certainly seems likely that he filled in the outlines of her arguments with references to chapter and verse when he wrote his account for circulation. But there is no suggestion that he did not accept their validity; he simply refused to be persuaded. Perhaps it was too much to expect of an ardent lover and a proud and hypersensitive man.

> But at last she saw that her attempts to persuade or dissuade me were making no impression on my foolish obstinacy, and she could not bear to offend me; so amidst deep sighs and tears she ended in these words: 'We shall both be destroyed. All that is left us is suffering as great as our love has been.' In this, as the whole world knows, she showed herself a true prophet. (p. 16)

Heloise never reproaches Abelard for the *secrecy* of the marriage, which to her must have seemed an act of hypocrisy and another betrayal of the ideal. She was even ready to lie on

Abelard's behalf and deny it when Fulbert broke his promise and spread the news. Years later, however, in a bitter moment she pointed out the irony of the fact that they had been spared when guilty of fornication but punished 'through a marriage which you believed had made amends for all previous wrong doing' (p. 66). There were furtive meetings followed by scenes with Fulbert, which made Abelard decide to remove her from her uncle's house. The convent at Argenteuil where she had spent her childhood was the obvious place to take her, and it was near enough Paris for further meetings to be fairly easy. We know that Abelard could not keep away; he argues in one of his letters (p. 80) that they were more justly punished for their conduct when married than for anything they did before, because of their sacrilege in making love in a corner of the convent refectory, the only place where they could snatch a moment together alone. What he had in mind when he made her wear a postulant's habit no one can know, unless it was to give greater protection from Fulbert, but it was a disastrous thing to do. She could have stayed indefinitely with the nuns without it, and Fulbert very naturally assumed that Abelard was trying to get rid of her by making her a nun. This was the immediate cause of his horrible revenge: his kinsmen got into Abelard's room at night and castrated him.

Long afterwards Abelard could write of this to Heloise with hindsight as an act of God's mercy which rid him of his personal dilemma along with the torments of the flesh. But in Letter 1 what he vividly recalls is the pain and horror, his urge to escape and hide from the noisy sympathy of the crowds outside and the outcry of his pupils pushing into his room, his feelings of humiliation and disgust at being a eunuch, the unclean beast of Jewish law. He admits that 'it was shame and confusion in my remorse and misery rather than any devout wish for conversion which brought me to seek shelter in a monastery cloister' (p. 18).

His entry into the Abbey of St Denis must have been hurried on quickly (and the period of novitiate entirely waived), for Abelard says that his wound was scarcely healed when the clerks were clamouring for him to continue his teaching from the cloister. He accepted the challenge, by far the best thing he could have done, for teaching took him out of the retirement which was unsuited to his temperament and enabled him to get back into the company where he was happiest – that of eager, questioning young minds. He emerged from the crisis still the perfectionist, the uncompromising challenger of beliefs and practices which he judged to fall short of truth and honesty, and now single-minded in his purpose. And whatever his original motives were for entering the religious life, there is no reason to doubt that his subsequent conversion was completely sincere. In his way Abelard was as firm an upholder of the faith and the purity of monastic life as St Bernard, and to the end of his days he spoke out against the shortcomings of the Church wherever he detected them. He remained a dedicated humanist and scholar, seeing that he could use his knowledge of Greek philosophy to lead his pupils on to the 'true philosophy', as the great Origen had done (p. 19). There was a general interest amongst twelfth-century scholars in Origen's works through Latin translations, and Abelard had a close personal feeling for Origen, also a eunuch, though self-inflicted. He draws the comparison explicitly in a letter to Heloise (p. 82). Abelard's continued interest in Greek philosophy was one of the charges against him by St Bernard, who said that Abelard proved himself a pagan by attempting to turn Plato into a Christian.

The *Historia calamitatum* is a personal record of his life between his entry into St Denis in about 1118 and its conclusion sometime after 1132. It is not necessary here to recapitulate in detail all his tribulations: quarrels with the unreformed monks of St Denis, persecution by his old rivals and enemies leading to his condemnation at the Council of Soissons in about 1121, further trouble at St Denis and his flight to Champagne, retirement to a hermitage near Troyes to which his students followed him and built the oratory he named the Paraclete. He was certainly greatly helped and sustained by the devotion of these young people, and by the knowledge that his gifts as a teacher were unimpaired by calamity and what he saw as the jealousy of his contemporaries, but he is so vague when writing about his continued dangers and apprehensions of further charges of heresy that one wonders if he was developing a persecution complex. There must have been some foundation for his fears; at one point he seriously considered abandoning Christendom to seek refuge in Islamic Spain (p. 33). Instead he accepted an invitation perhaps in 1126 to be abbot of the remote monastery of St Gildas de Rhuys on the west coast of Brittany.

This time he could hardly have made a worse decision. According to Abelard, the monks were not only idle and dissolute but murderous in intent when he tried to reform them, and he felt himself isolated amongst illiterate savages.

> I used to weep as I thought of the wretched, useless life I led, as profitless to myself as to others; I had once done so much for the clerks, and now ... all I did for them and for the monks was equally fruitless. I had proved ineffective in all my attempts and undertakings, so that now above all men I justly merited the reproach, 'There is the man who started to build and could not finish.' (pp. 34–5)

He was tormented especially by the thought that the oratory of the Paraclete was deserted and neglected. It was not until 1129 that he heard that Suger, who had become abbot of St Denis in 1122 and was engaged in active and controversial reforms, had got documents establishing the abbey's claim to the convent of Argenteuil, and had expelled the nuns. Heloise was already prioress, and this is the first mention of her since she took her vows some nine years before.

She had taken them at his command and with no sense of vocation, as Abelard very well knew. She had had about eighteen months with him, and was probably in her twenties when she renounced any hope of further life outside the convent walls. Abelard says that she had refused to listen to those 'who in pity for her youth tried to dissuade her from submitting to the yoke of monastic rule as a penance too hard to bear' (p. 18); she had wept, and quoted from Lucan, a Stoic Roman poet whose works they both knew, Cornelia's last words before her suicide after the death of her husband Pompey. 'So saying she hurried to the altar, quickly took up (*confestim tulit* – almost 'snatched') the veil blessed by the bishop and publicly bound herself to the religious life.' Her mood was not one of Christian hope but of tragic despair. Abelard says nothing about her admission being as hurried and irregular as his own, and records only the bare fact that she took her vows before he did. From her letters we learn that this hurt and offended her more than anything, and the memory still rankled for years. Had he been afraid that she would turn back, like Lot's wife? She saw it as a sign of mistrust, though he knew that she would have followed him to the flames of Hell (p. 54). She may have guessed – and rightly – that jealous possessiveness prompted Abelard in this as in the secret marriage.

It is only from references in her letters that we know anything at all about her life as a nun at Argenteuil, and these are painful reading. Abelard was a changed man, physically and spiritually; she was not changed, she felt no vocation for convent life, and was tormented by frustrated sexual love. '[T]he pleasures of lovers which we shared have been too sweet – they cannot displease me, and can scarcely shift from my memory. Wherever I turn they are always there before my eyes, bringing with them awakened longings and fantasies which will not even let me sleep' (p. 68). Any meetings they had had after his mutilation to arrange her hurried reception into the convent had been impersonal, and very probably in the presence of the nuns. In her first letter she reproaches him for giving her no sympathy nor support in person or by letter. Yet though she evidently did not pretend to herself that love of God had supplanted love of Abelard, her good brains and strong character must have saved her from going to pieces. She would have social standing as the niece of a canon, but she would not have been chosen to be prioress of the convent unless her outward behaviour had been scrupulously correct. The prioress stood second to the abbess and had many responsibilities, one being the education of the nuns, novices and children brought up in the convent as Heloise had been herself.

Abelard writes defensively, in answer to her reproach, that he had not thought it necessary to write a letter of advice or sympathy, knowing her good sense (*prudentia*): 'God's grace has bestowed on you all essentials to enable you to instruct the erring, comfort the weak and encourage the faint-hearted, both by word and example, as, indeed, you have been doing since you first held the office of prioress under your abbess' (p. 56). It is arguable that Heloise was already prioress as early as 1123, though this is no more than a supposition based on a contemporary document, the obituary roll of the Blessed Vital, abbot and founder of the monastery of Savigny in the diocese of Avranches, who died in 1122. It was a monastic custom when a Church dignitary or benefactor died to inscribe the news of his death and a eulogy of his life on a parchment roll which a monk would then take round the monastic houses. Each of these would inscribe its full title and promises to pray for the departed, often with a request for similar prayers for members of its own community. The roll of the Blessed Vital contains the names of 207 religious houses in France and England, that of Ste Marie of Argenteuil being the fortieth. Beneath the title on the left is a Latin poem, while the conventional formulae for prayers are rather squeezed in on the right. There are other poems on the roll, four of them by convents of nuns, but this is written in correct Latin elegiacs (though the sentiments are not original in any way), and the handwriting is clear and well formed. It has therefore been supposed that this is the work and the writing of Heloise herself, and she would not have been entrusted with it had she not already been prioress.[5]

Abelard travelled from St Gildas to make arrangements to hand over the Paraclete to Heloise and some of the dispossessed nuns who stayed together, and there they met after a separation of ten years. Abbot Suger had made no provision at all for the nuns, and the *Historia calamitatum* records briefly that at first they suffered great hardship. The buildings could not have been more than the small church of wood or stone which the students had built to replace Abelard's original chapel and the primitive cells they had occupied, and the women were dependent on what they could get out of the stream and the fields, helped out by gifts from the neighbourhood, which were generous when their plight was known. In 1131 Pope Innocent the Second

visited Auxerre and granted a charter to the abbess Heloise
confirming the nuns' possession of the gifts they had received
and any subsequent gifts in perpetuity. There were further
meetings, all on an impersonal basis as the letters show, for
Letter 1 records that at first local opinion criticized Abelard
for not doing enough for the nuns, and then when he visited
them more often, there was malicious gossip about his former relations with Heloise and the fact that he still seemed
unable to keep away from her. It seems likely that he was absent
from St Gildas for some time, for he had installed them in
the Paraclete in 1129 and we know that on 20 January 1131,
during Innocent the Second's progress through France, Abelard
was present at a large gathering in the Benedictine abbey of
Morigny, near Etampes, where the pope consecrated the high
altar. He had gone to ask for a papal legate to be sent to St Gildas
for its reform (p. 41); there for the first time perhaps he met
St Bernard. The journey between St Gildas and the Paraclete
was some 360 miles and would take ten to fourteen days, so he
would hardly have travelled to and fro. He had indeed cherished
hopes of finding a haven of peace with the sisters, but the last
pages of the *Historia* show that he is back at St Gildas, feeling
himself an outcast and a wanderer like Cain, that he is recovering
from a painful fracture after a fall from his horse, and has
narrowly escaped from attempts to murder him by poison and
ambush, and sees no prospect of any improvement in his
position.

The *Historia calamitatum* was evidently written in 1132 or
soon after, and Heloise says in her first letter that by chance
someone brought it to her. If it was a genuine, personal letter of
consolation to an unnamed friend and fellow-monk, as Abelard
says, one wonders why it went further than him. It seems more
probable that Abelard intended it for circulation (there may
have been more than one copy) in order to win sympathy for
his predicament and to pave the way for release from St Gildas
so that he could return to his true vocation of teaching. He was
still remembered for this; in the account of his meeting with
Bernard he is described as 'monk and abbot and so himself of
the monastic order, the most distinguished master of the school

to which flocked the scholars of almost all the Latin world'.[6] It is known that he left St Gildas with his bishop's consent and the right to retain his rank of abbot, and that he was teaching in Paris in 1136 at Mont-Sainte-Geneviève when John of Salisbury heard him lecture on dialectic, though he left Paris before John did.[7] Perhaps this was only temporary; there are no other dates or indications of his whereabouts until 1140 or 1141 (the Council of Sens), but it is probable that most of the time he was in or near Paris and teaching, for this is the period of his greatest mental activity and output.

At first sight the *Historia calamitatum* looks as if it is written by a self-centred though not insensitive man, whose youthful years were ruled by self-assertion, pride and ambition. On reflection one sees it more as an attempt to put on record, from a detached standpoint, the facts of a life which the writer believed had often been misjudged and was now at risk. It has also been said that 'the writing of this letter became the act of catharsis that turned what might have been merely an apology into a true self-revelation'.[8] In this sense the *Historia* is a search for identity and a personal autobiography comparable with those of St Augustine, Cellini, St Teresa and Rousseau.

Heloise's reactions in her first letter (Letter 2) are dismay at his misfortunes, the details of which are unlikely to have reached her before, and horror at the idea of his life being in danger at St Gildas. She then points out that if he can write a long letter of consolation to a 'friend', he can also write to advise and encourage the community at the Paraclete, as is his duty as their founder. He is wasting himself on monks such as he describes, but would find her nuns receptive. He can also write to *her*, to whom he has a personal obligation. For twelve years or more she has brooded over his apparent indifference in never giving her a word of recognition for the sacrifice she made in entering monastic life. He knows very well that she did it only for love of him, but his neglect has forced her to the conclusion that what he had felt for her was no more than lust and, when physical desire had gone, any warmth of affection had gone with it. She virtually demands a letter of explanation from him as her right.

In Letter 3 Abelard defends himself on the charge of negligence: he had not supposed that Heloise any longer had need of him. Could he really have thought that? No one can be sure, but it cannot be dismissed as simple wishful thinking. Disgust with his mutilated person may have made him want to shut the past out of his mind; he was changed, and knowing she was prioress and now abbess he may have been all too ready to believe that she was changed too. And his own conversion had, at some point, been sincere and permanent, so that he was now dedicated to God. The tone of his letter is set by the superscription: he writes as abbot to abbess. If the community is anxious for his safety, he says, they should remember the power of prayer. She must know that the sacrament of marriage which binds them, as well as 'the integrity of our faith and . . . our profession of the same religious life' (p. 59), increases the effectiveness of her own prayers. I think one should not see this as a selfish refusal to be drawn on Abelard's part, but more as an attempt to put their relationship on a different basis because he knew this was in her best interests. But he certainly does not allow himself to enter imaginatively into Heloise's plight, and this prompts her to be more explicit.

In Letter 4 she writes of her sexual frustration and inability to forget their happiness as lovers. She puts her dilemma clearly: she took vows not for love of God but for love of Abelard. Taking vows meant that she ought to be a nun in the true sense, and that her life should be ruled by love of God, but how was that possible when she loved him alone? She is perpetually conscious of being a hypocrite, for when the world admires her piety it sees only her outward behaviour and this means nothing to her; the intention is all, and her intention is lacking. She looks for reward only from Abelard, and he has denied it to her. She can hope for nothing from God for she has denied him, and she cannot repent. 'How can it be called repentance for sins, however great the mortification of the flesh, if the mind still retains the will to sin and is on fire with its old desires?' (p. 68). She implores his help in resolving an intolerable situation.

This is a terrible picture of a soul in agony and of total human love which has brought only suffering. It is painful to contemplate how such intensity of feeling had been stoically concealed from the outside world for years of a young woman's life. It is characteristic of Heloise that she never compromises, and never wavers from the moral view she shared with Abelard, that of the ethic of intention.[9] Her keen intellect can analyse herself and her problem clearly, but the feeling behind the words is passionate and painful. Letter 4 jolts Abelard out of any suspected complacency. He replies at length, especially on the point of 'your old perpetual complaint against God concerning the manner of our entry into religious life and the cruelty of the act of treachery performed on me' (p. 72). The epithets (repeated later) imply that he had heard it before; the only time could have been when they met between his mutilation and her taking the veil. He sounds irritated by her raking it all up again, but perhaps that is reading too much into his words. He will not recall the past with nostalgia, as she does, but at least he shows he has not forgotten. He reminds her of certain events – their mockery of God when she dressed as a nun to go to Brittany, their overwhelming desire which led them to make love during the season of the Passion or in the refectory at Argenteuil – but he tries to make her see them as episodes which called for just punishment from God or, rather, for an act of God's mercy which freed them both from the flesh which can be only a barrier to divine love. He begs her to make a supreme effort to shake off bitterness and resentment and to think only of the love of Christ. 'It was he who truly loved you, not I. My love, which brought us both to sin, should be called lust, not love ... You say I suffered for you ... But he suffered truly for your salvation, on your behalf of his own free will ...' (p. 86). She must see herself as chosen to be the bride of Christ, and know that by surmounting her bodily suffering she can win the martyr's crown which can never be his, for where there is no battle there is no victory. All the time he is trying to make her see the whole story of their relationship from its start until their entry into religion from the Christian monastic point of view, knowing that they were at least agreed in believing that chastity was something higher than wedlock. The letter ends with a prayer that though parted on earth they may be forever united in heaven (pp. 88–9).

Heloise replies in Letter 6 with great dignity, and the first paragraph of her letter marks the turning point of the correspondence. She will not argue nor trouble him further with heartsearchings; she now asks only for his help in occupying her mind with more constructive thoughts. We are never to know if she was able to achieve a change of heart and reorientation of herself towards God. Time the healer would make the physical severance from Abelard less acutely felt, and one hopes that she found compensation in her service to the Paraclete. Perhaps later on she came to feel that this was a true form of devotion to God and more than outward works under a cloak of hypocritical piety – as everyone who has written about her has wanted to think. Meanwhile she asks on behalf of her community for information about the origin of the order of nuns and for advice on a Rule suitable for women.

Remembering what has gone before we can only admire Heloise's resolute self-control, and equally her intellectual and practical ability. She has lived under the Benedictine Rule for at least fourteen years, observing it, in a sense, from the outside. With her intelligence and erudition she is well equipped to offer criticism of what seems to her unsuitable if the Rule is to apply to women. She can appreciate that St Benedict was willing to temper his Rule to meet men's capacity to observe it, and suggests that women should not have too great demands made upon their physique. She also argues cogently that many details of observance can be categorized as outward 'works' and are unimportant in comparison with faith and spiritual intent. Accordingly she asks for guidance on questions such as manual labour, fasting, clothing and diet, as well as for suitable arrangements for the Divine Office and for the reading of the Gospel at night. The emphasis throughout is on reasonable demands, avoidance of extremes and sincerity of intent; it is better to promise what one is capable of doing and then do more than to break down under impossible demands. She would have a longer novitiate, a deeper personal commitment and a truly spiritual training; she wants a poorer and a simpler life – different perhaps from the one she had known at Argenteuil – for she sees that 'those who are true Christians are wholly occupied with the inner man ... but they have little or no concern for the outer man' (p. 107).

Abelard replies with two long treatises (Letters 7 and 8), one to answer Heloise's question about religious communities of women,[10] the other a detailed Rule for observance at the Paraclete. There is so little written about women's Orders that this is a document of intrinsic interest for convent life at this time, though it is not very well expressed nor logical in its arrangement, and despite its elaborate formal opening it breaks off with curious abruptness. It combines long passages of sermonizing and erudition with a down-to-earth approach to practical details: the nuns are to be sensibly dressed in underwear and habit which hangs clear of the dust, with a full change of clothing and necessary sanitary protection, to wear proper stockings and shoes and to have adequate bedding. Dirty hands and knives are not to be wiped on bread intended for the poor, to spare the tablecloths. There is to be no self-imposed fasting, no undue mortification of the flesh, and no cutting down of hours of sleep or the nuns will not be mentally alert for their prayers or studies. There is a characteristic emphasis on education; routine practical tasks are to be assigned to nuns with no aptitude for letters, but any nun with the ability to learn must be taught to read and write. As far as possible we should worship God with understanding, a statement which Abelard amplifies into an attack on current illiteracy in monasteries (pp. 201 ff.).

This letter seems to be the basis for a later set of rules[11] which were preserved in a manuscript at the Paraclete and were intended for the use of a mother foundation and its daughter houses; six of the latter were set up in Heloise's lifetime, and this rather later Rule has been thought to be by her, but it cannot be firmly dated. It differs from Abelard's recommendations in certain essentials and in a few less important points. There is no provision for the male superior ruling a double monastery such as he advocates (p. 155), but the abbess is to have authority over the monks and lay monks serving the convent, and the nuns are not strictly cloistered but may go outside the convent for necessary business. The blankets and pillows he specifies are not mentioned, and the nuns appear to sleep fully clothed instead of in their shifts as he wants; they may also eat pure wheat bread whereas he makes a point of one-third of the flour being of coarse grain. These are minor modifications, but a great deal has been read into the words '*in refectorio nostro cibi sine carnibus sunt legumina . . .*' If they are translated as 'in our refectory our meals are vegetables without meat . . .', this would accord with stricter monastic practice but directly contravene the founder's ruling (p. 189) that meat may be eaten three times a week and his expressed view that nothing except excess is forbidden. But if the words mean 'the meatless meals consist of vegetables' it is simply a reference to what Abelard goes on to say about the days when no meat is to be taken.

These long 'Letters of Direction', as they are called here, written in the rather stiff, formal style of contemporary scholarship, are also vital for an understanding of Abelard and Heloise. They provide the necessary depth of background to their relationship and show how this developed in the only way possible to them. In a sense Heloise has won her point; she has forced Abelard to look at her problem honestly and to renew contact with her, though not in the way she first hoped. Abelard has sincerely tried to show her that the only love which can now unite them is love of God, and that God has acted mercifully towards them, but he has had to learn something of what human love such as hers really means. She has agreed to try to put the past behind her, and from now on she has only to ask and Abelard will put all his learning and practical wisdom at the service of the Paraclete.

Abelard wrote a long letter addressed to the nuns on the importance of study and even urged them to apply themselves to Hebrew. In this he twice referred to Heloise as having knowledge of Greek and Hebrew as well as Latin[12] – a surprising statement, as Abelard himself showed no knowledge of Hebrew apart from an occasional word and had little or no Greek, and though Peter the Venerable had admired her learning and gift for logic when he was a young man (p. 217), no one else has said she knew any Hebrew except the monk William Godel, writing in 1173 (p. xlvi). She probably had enough Greek for liturgical purposes. Heloise wrote a short letter in which she addressed Abelard as 'loved by many but most dearly loved by us' to accompany what are known as the 'Problems of Heloise': forty-two difficulties of interpretation in the Scriptures, to each of which Abelard gives carefully reasoned answers.[13] Her request for hymns for the use of the nuns is lost, but his answer[14] accompanying the first batch he wrote gives the gist of it and shows how they now wrote to each other:

> At your urgent request, my sister Heloise, once dear to me in the world, now dearest in Christ, I have written what are called 'hymns' in Greek, 'tehillim' in Hebrew. When you and the sisters of your holy profession kept begging me to write these, I asked your purpose in doing so, for I thought it superfluous for me to compose new hymns when you had plenty of existing ones, and it seemed almost sacrilegious for new hymns by sinners to rank as high or higher than the ancient hymns of the saints. I received several different answers, among them this reasoned argument of your own: We know, you said, that the Latin Church in general and the French Church in particular follows customary usage rather than authority as regards both psalms and hymns. We still do not know for certain who was the author of the translation of the Psalter which our own French Church uses. If we want to reach a decision on the basis of the words of the variant translations, we shall still be a long way from a universally accepted interpretation and, in my opinion, this will carry no weight of authority. Customary practice has so long prevailed that although we have St Jerome's corrected text for the rest of the Scriptures, the translation of the Psalter, which we use so much, is of doubtful authority. Moreover, the hymns we use now are in considerable confusion; they are never or rarely distinguished by titles or names of the authors, and even when they appear to have definite authors, of whom Hilary and Ambrose are considered the best, and next to them Prudentius and several others, the words are often so irregular in scansion that it is hardly possible to fit them to the music: and without this there is no hymn at all, according to the definition that it is 'praise of God with song'. You went on to say that several of the feasts had no hymns of their own, those of the Innocents and the Evangelists, for example, or those for saintly

women who had been neither virgins nor martyrs, and there were also some feasts during which those who sang the hymns could not be truthful, either because these did not fit the occasion or because false material has been inserted . . .

The letter continues with a detailed discussion of certain hymns, and ends: 'And so as you beg this of me, brides or handmaids of Christ, in my turn I beg you through your prayers to relieve my shoulders of the burden you laid on them, so that the sower and the reaper of this harvest may rejoice in their work together.'

There are 133 extant Latin hymns by Abelard, evidently sent to the Paraclete in three batches, the second two with short accompanying letters addressed to the whole community, as well as some fine verse Laments. The most famous of these are included in this volume (pp. 230–35): 'Vespers: Saturday Evening' (*O quanta qualia sunt illa sabbata* – 'How mighty are the Sabbaths') and 'Good Friday: The Third Nocturn' (*Solus ad victimam procedis, Domine* – 'Alone to sacrifice thou goest, Lord').

Abelard also wrote thirty-four short sermons for the Paraclete, which were evidently sent with the following accompanying letter:

I recently completed at your request a little book of hymns or sequences, Heloise my sister whom I love and revere in Christ, and then, as you asked me, hastened to write as best I could (for it is not the kind of writing I am used to) several short sermons for you and your spiritual daughters gathered together in our oratory. As I was concerned with the written rather than the spoken word, I concentrated on clarity of exposition, not eloquence of style, literal sense rather than elaborate rhetoric. And it may be that plain wording instead of rhetorical speech will be easier for simple minds to understand as being more direct; moreover, for the type of person who will be listening, the simplicity of ordinary speech will seem like elegant refinement and will have a pleasant taste suitable for girls of limited understanding. In writing or, rather, arranging these, I have kept to the order of the feasts of the Church, beginning with the start of our redemption. Farewell in the Lord, you who are his handmaid, once dear to me in the world, now dearest in Christ, once in the flesh my wife, now in the spirit my sister and in profession of sacred purpose, my consort.[15]

This shows a side of Abelard we have not seen before: considerate, self-effacing and patient with the young. What he offers the nuns here seems decidedly more practical than advice to study Hebrew and Greek.

It was also at Heloise's request that he wrote the *Hexameron*, a commentary on the six days of the Creation, and this too is now generally thought to have been written during the 1130s.

Whether Abelard ever visited the convent or the Paraclete again is not known, but as all his writings for the nuns are introduced by letters to Heloise, it seems probable that they did not meet again. Apart from the bare fact that John of Salisbury heard him lecture in Paris in 1136, nothing is recorded of his movements until his confrontation with Bernard in 1140 or 1141, but as he was attacked then mainly for the corrupting influence of his theological teaching, it sounds as though he was mainly with his students in Paris.

Bernard was born in 1090 and entered the Cistercian foundation of Cîteaux in 1112.[16] In 1115 he was chosen to be abbot of the new foundation at Clairvaux, which by the end of his life in 1153 was famous throughout Europe, with sixty-eight daughter houses. Most monastic foundations hitherto had been based on the Rule of St Benedict of about 530, and the Cistercians preached 'The Rule to the last dot' (*Regula ad apicem literae*). But they also looked to the asceticism of the early Fathers of the Egyptian desert. Their return to the past was prompted by the desire to free themselves from the fetters of customary practice and an increasingly elaborate liturgy, in order to live a simpler life and thereby gain true spiritual freedom for meditation on the love of God. Many of the Benedictine houses at this time belonged to the congregation of Cluny, and from 1122 Cluny had its own outstanding leader in the person of Peter the Venerable. One of his most famous letters is addressed to Bernard[17] and is a reasoned defence of the Cluniac way of life and its interpretation of the Rule according to the spirit rather than the letter. But as Bernard permitted nothing either to the individual or to the community which could distract from the exacting demands of the Cistercian life, it follows that he was opposed to knowledge for its own sake and to any disinterested pursuit of learning, as a hindrance to the quest for perfection. Teaching in a Cistercian monastery was confined to its members, starting from the novitiate, and its purpose was salvation.

The clash between Abelard and Bernard was a *cause célèbre* of the twelfth century[18] and is in part an instance of the rivalry between two opposing systems of teaching, the traditional monastic instruction in the cloister and the greater freedom of the Cathedral schools. It rests still more on the conflicting temperaments of the two men, and the tragedy is that they had certain things in common. Abelard no less than Bernard criticizes insincerity, corruption and worldliness in the Church. He is as uncompromising with the licence he allegedly found at St Denis as with the flagrant immorality at St Gildas; he and Heloise exchange comments on precipitate entry into monastic life without proper preparation (p. 100), elaborate monastic building and luxurious living (p. 141), abbots who boast of the numbers in their care without being able to provide for them (p. 194), abbots who leave their monasteries (p. 196), ignorance and illiteracy (p. 201), 'the empty chatter of idleness, to which we see present-day monastic cloisters much addicted' (p. 206), and the prevalence of works instead of faith: 'They clean the outside of the pot or dish but pay little heed to cleanliness inside' (p. 183). But as a logician he believed in the importance of clear thinking, and as a Benedictine he taught that knowledge and understanding served faith, not hindered it.

For Bernard the mystery of faith transcends human knowledge and can be gained only through mystic contemplation. He sees himself as a preacher with a sacred duty to proclaim revealed truth and to defend it and, for all his reforming zeal, he stands against Abelard as a champion of tradition. He sees Abelard as a danger to the faith of young people and simple men, and Abelard's attempt to *understand* the Trinity as an evil example of intellectual arrogance and an insult to Christian belief. So he can write that 'the mysteries of God are forced open, the deepest things bandied about in discussion without reverence'.[19]

Abelard sees this attack on discussion as unjustified and personal, similar to those he suffered before. He maintains that he is defending Christian faith by making it as intelligible as possible. He always believes that the words of the sacred Scriptures and the testimony of the Fathers must be true, but we must examine the evidence we have (often in the form of corrupt texts and unreliable witnesses) to remove difficulties and contradictions. His famous *Sic et Non* (*Yes and No*) had been written with this purpose in mind, though more than anything it had given a false and damaging picture of him as a sceptic. There he had selected and set out 158 problems where there are conflicting authorities; no synthesis is offered nor conclusion drawn – it is a teaching manual, designed for disputation on the question of the manuscripts being faulty or misunderstood, prompted by the belief that by stating propositions and their opposites we can provoke enquiry and arrive at understanding. He says in his preface that his aim is to sharpen the wits of his young readers and incite them to seek for the truth.

It would be equally wrong to suppose Abelard a rationalist in any but the twelfth-century sense of wishing to use his mastery of logic for the better understanding of his faith. He writes sadly in his 'Confession of Faith' (p. 211) that logic has made him hated by the world through misrepresentation, though 'I do not wish to be a philosopher if it means conflicting with Paul, nor to be an Aristotle if it cuts me off from Christ.' And he makes it plain in his philosophical works that he has no use for popular dialecticians who display their expertise on empty topics; properly used, dialectic has a moral basis and examines real problems, and it demands courage and honesty on the part of the user in giving way neither to authority nor to shallow cleverness in argument. But one can see how his scrupulous search for the proper terms in which to discuss theological problems could lay him open to misinterpretation and the charge of tampering with the content of faith.

The earliest reference to contact between Abelard and Bernard is a letter addressed to Bernard by Abelard when Bernard had visited the Paraclete soon after Heloise was installed and before Abelard went to St Gildas.[20] He writes that on a recent visit to the convent Heloise had told him that Bernard had stayed there and had preached to the nuns 'like an angel'. However, she had also informed him privately (*secreto*) that Bernard had taken exception to their use of the Vulgate version of St Matthew, which refers to 'transubstantial' rather than 'daily' bread in the Lord's Prayer. The letter continues politely but firmly to defend Abelard's preference without yielding an inch. We do not know Bernard's reaction. The two men met at the gathering at the abbey of Morigny in 1131. Between 1132 and 1138 Bernard was travelling in France, Italy and Germany, preaching on behalf of Pope Innocent the Second, during the period of papal schism when many of the cardinals and important families in Italy recognized the rival claimant, Anacletus the Second. It was not until Anacletus died in 1138 that Innocent was able to live in Rome, and he must have left France deeply grateful for Bernard's campaigns to establish his legitimate claims. During this time Abelard was probably teaching, and certainly writing a great deal. After the burning of his book on the Trinity in 1121 he had started to rewrite and expand it in his *Theologia Christiana* and he planned a comprehensive *Theologia* (*Theology*) in three parts. He also wrote his *Ethica* (*Ethics*) or *Scito te ipsum* (*Know Yourself*), a commentary on St Paul's Epistle to the Romans, and the *Dialogue between a Philosopher, a Jew and a Christian*, as well as the hymns, sermons, answers to problems and the *Hexameron* for the nuns of the Paraclete.[21]

At some date in 1139 or 1140, a copy of Abelard's *Theologia* was read by William, the former abbot of St Thierry in the diocese of Rheims, who had resigned to join a remote Cistercian monastery at Signy in the Ardennes. He had known Abelard personally, perhaps when both had been students at Laon, and he was a close friend of Bernard. He was dismayed by what he read and by what he had heard of Abelard's teaching of 'new things' which would endanger the faith; he listed thirteen heretical points which he refuted, and sent the whole statement to

Bernard and to Bishop Geoffrey of Chartres, the papal legate in France at the time, who had supported Abelard at the Council of Soissons eighteen or nineteen years previously. We do not know if the bishop replied, but Bernard acted at once.

According to Bernard's biographer, Geoffrey of Auxerre, and other contemporary witnesses, Bernard twice met Abelard and suggested that he should modify his views and restrain his pupils, but to no effect. Bernard then approached first the bishop of Sens, and then the bishop of Paris to obtain permission to preach to the students. Abelard's reply seems to have been to bring out a fourth edition of his *Theologia*, unchanged in all essentials. Bernard then appealed to the Pope, enclosing his treatise against Abelard's heresies, and he also wrote to the cardinals at Rome. He links Abelard's name with the notorious Arnold of Brescia, and his violent abuse and intemperate language are startlingly disagreeable to an unprejudiced reader. Abelard then asked Archbishop Henry of Sens to arrange for a meeting between himself and Bernard on the Sunday after Whitsun, which should take the form of a public disputation on their disagreements. It was already to be a great occasion: the relics of the cathedral were to be shown to Louis VII and his court in the presence of the bishops and dignitaries of the diocese. Bernard at first refused to attend, on the grounds that he was no match for a skilled dialectician and he disapproved of arguing about matters of faith. His friends persuaded him to change his mind, so he proceeded to lobby the bishops both by letter and by meeting them at Sens, to explain what he intended to do and to enlist their support. He also preached publicly to the people assembled in the town.

In a letter addressed to his friends and pupils which Abelard wrote at this time, he made it clear that he looked upon Bernard's attack as yet another instance of misunderstanding and malice, this time from a monk who was greatly his inferior in intellectual capacity and training. He neither shared Bernard's burning conviction that the purity of the faith was jeopardized, nor was he likely to accept that he was 'a man who does not know his own limitations, making void the virtue of the Cross by the cleverness of his words'.[22] He asked his friends to support him at the Council of Sens, and they must have been confident that Bernard would be defeated in the promised disputation.

Instead, there was no disputation, but something much more like a court of inquisition at which Bernard produced a list of Abelard's heresies which he read aloud and called upon Abelard to defend, renounce or deny that they were his. Abelard refused to make any statement, on the grounds that he wished to appeal direct to the Pope, and left the Council. There has been much speculation why he did this. He may have felt that this was going to be another Council of Soissons, and that he could not face it again, or that a large social occasion with people like the king and Count Theobald of Champagne present was no place for subtle theological exposition and that no one would pay proper attention; this seems likely enough if we believe anything of the highly coloured satirical account of the Council given by Abelard's pupil, Berengar of Poitiers, who says that the bishops were half asleep and drunk after a heavy meal, mumbling *'namus'* (we swim) instead of *'damnamus'* (we condemn).[23] It has also been suggested that Abelard had long suffered from a progressive form of cancer, named as Hodgkin's disease, that he had felt exhausted and ill at Sens but had remission afterwards at Cluny.[24]

The Council condemned nineteen points in Bernard's statement as heretical, and Bernard sent off a letter describing the proceedings to the Pope. The archbishops of Sens and Rheims also wrote and Bernard wrote again to the cardinals. Six weeks later, on 16 July, the Pope sent his rescript to the archbishops and to Bernard condemning Abelard as a heretic, excommunicating his followers, ordering his books to be burned and himself to be confined in a monastery in perpetual silence. The news reached Abelard at Cluny, where he had stopped on the long journey to Rome and stayed on at the invitation of Peter the Venerable. Immediately after the Council of Sens (or possibly just before it) he had written his 'Confession of Faith', addressed to Heloise, a document of great dignity and restraint, which was probably the last personal message she had from him. If we accept an earlier dating, Peter the Venerable had already written to the Pope (p. 215) to report that he and the Abbot of Cîteaux had mediated between Abelard and Bernard, that the two men had met and were reconciled, and his letter asking permission for Abelard to remain as a monk of Cluny must have crossed the Pope's rescript; the sentence was afterwards lifted.

Abelard died some months later, in April 1142 or perhaps in 1144; Peter the Venerable's letter to Heloise (p. 217) describing his death in a daughter house of Cluny at St Marcel, near Chalon-sur-Saône, pays tribute to the simplicity and piety of his life and to his devotion to his studies, as far as his health permitted, right up to the end. It is uncertain if he actually wrote anything at Cluny and St Marcel. The long, rather platitudinous letter in verse giving advice to his son Astralabe is now generally dated to about 1135 rather than to this period, for the complete text[25] refers to 'the frequent complaint of our Heloise' (*nostrae Eloysae crebra querela*) that she can have no hope of salvation if she cannot repent of what she once did with Abelard, an echo of her second letter (pp. 67–8). Abelard is not likely to have brought this up again some six years later. The *Dialogue between a Philosopher, a Jew and a Christian* and the *Hexameron*, which used to be considered late works, are now also ascribed to the mid-1130s. The short general *Confession of Faith to Everyone* (not the one preserved by Berengar of Poitiers) which was Abelard's personal defence, may have been written before the Council of Sens, and an *Apologia* was planned but left unfinished – perhaps broken off when Abelard heard of the Pope's sentence.[26] There is no indication that he felt obliged to modify the theological views which he considered had been attacked in envy and ignorance, nor evidence that he put into writing the piety and humility to which Peter the Venerable testifies. He may well have been physically incapable of sustained creative effort.

Peter the Venerable is credited with a somewhat pedestrian verse epitaph which describes Abelard as 'The Socrates of the Gauls, Plato of the West, our Aristotle, prince of scholars ... the keen thinker and dialectician who won his greatest victory when he renounced all for the true philosophy of Christ.' One wonders what he had in mind in referring to Socrates – another opponent of self-deception and loose thinking who had been misrepresented as a corrupting influence on the minds of the young. Five anonymous epitaphs are also preserved, all of which emphasize Abelard's fame as a philosopher and scholar without reference to his chequered career as a teacher of theology.[27]

There remains an exchange of letters between Heloise and Peter the Venerable written sometime in 1144 (pp. 217 ff.), in which Heloise thanks Peter for visiting the Paraclete and bringing with him Abelard's body to rest in the care of the community he had founded. She asks him for a written absolution for Abelard to be hung over the tomb, and for help in getting her son Astralabe a benefice in one of the cathedrals. Peter sends the absolution (p. 228) along with a ratification of his verbal promise that Cluny will say thirty masses for Heloise after her death, and promises to do his best for Astralabe. This is the only time Heloise mentions him, and nothing definite is known about the young man who had played so small a part in his parents' lives.

Peter the Venerable died in 1156 or 1157, but Heloise outlived Abelard by some twenty-one years; she is recorded in the necrology of the Paraclete as dying on 16 May in 1163 or 1164. The romantics have liked to think that she died, like Abelard, at the age of sixty-three. In her competent hands the Paraclete grew to be one of the most distinguished religious houses in France. Six daughter houses were founded during her lifetime to receive the increasing numbers of postulants, and the Cartulary of the convent of the Paraclete lists twenty-nine documents which refer to the Paraclete when in her care, confirming privileges and registering deeds of gift. Eleven papal charters are among them; the one of Pope Eugenius of 1147 included arable land, meadows, woods, fish ponds, vineyards, farms, mills, tithes and money.[28] It is clear from Peter the Venerable's letter (p. 217) that Heloise was one of the Church's great abbesses, revered for her sanctity as well as for her learning.

It is impossible not to speculate about her inner thoughts and to wonder if she found her vocation, but of course there can be no answer. Human love such as hers does not end with separation or the death of the beloved, but it changes in quality as the physical pangs of severance are blunted; at least it seems unlikely that a woman of her character and common sense allowed herself the indulgence of brooding over the irrecoverable past. At a higher level one hopes that reconciliation with Abelard through their exchange of letters made it possible for her to love him on a different plane, as his 'sister in Christ'; at a lower level that her fine intelligence and administrative ability found full scope in what we should now call a rewarding career, and that with passage of time she achieved 'calm of mind, all passion spent'.[29]

Heloise is recorded in the Paraclete's burial record as having been buried alongside Abelard in the abbey church, which was later known as the chapel of St Denis or the Petit Moustier ('Little Monastery'). This was the small oratory built by Abelard's students many years before, to replace the simple reed and thatch structure he had first set up. In 1497 the abbess of the time had the bodies moved from what was described as a damp and watery position and placed on either side of the high altar in the new oratory which had been built further away from the Ardusson. They were moved again in 1621 to a crypt below an altar on which stood a stone representing the Three Persons of the Trinity, which was believed to have been carved under Abelard's direction. In 1701 this stone was moved to a better position in the choir, and in 1780 the bodies moved again to a new position, still in the crypt. When the convent was sold at the time of the Revolution and the buildings demolished, apart from the residence of the abbess (the present Château, dating from 1685), the bones were taken to the church of St Laurent in Nogent-sur-Seine, and in 1800 to Paris, to Alexandre Lenoir's Musée des Monuments Français. They were later moved to the cemetery of Mont Louis, now Père Lachaise. There they are still, in a sarcophagus brought from St Marcel which Lenoir believed to have been Abelard's original tomb, beneath a Gothic-style structure and surrounded by modern iron railings, through which flowers are still sometimes placed beside their effigies by tourists who know something of their history, and by Parisians on All Souls' Day.

Text and Translation

There are relatively few tributes to Abelard after his death, either as theologian or philosopher. People would remember or hear of the events at Sens who knew little or nothing of Abelard's last months at Cluny, and Bernard's influence was strong enough for Abelard's name to be virtually erased even if his theological teaching continued in the Cathedral schools where Bernard's traditionalism was not acceptable. The analytical and critical methods of the *Sic et Non* influenced such famous theological manuals as Peter the Lombard's *Books of the Sentences*, and Abelard stands as one of the creators of open-minded thinking which led to the birth of the medieval universities, but as a logician he suffered from the discovery of Aristotle's scientific works within a decade of his death. Once Aristotle's solution to the nature of Universals was known, Abelard's formulation of Conceptualism, which was remarkably Aristotelean, was no longer read.

There are, however, manuscripts of his logical works and his *Apologia* which date back to the late twelfth and early thirteenth century, as well as references to his teaching.[30] The case of the letters is very different. The occasional references we have to the lovers in the twelfth-century chroniclers are short and factual. William Godel, a monk of St Martin of Limoges, writing in 1173, says that Heloise or Helvisa was 'formerly Abelard's wife and truly his friend'[31] and a religious and learned woman well versed in both Latin and Hebrew. An allegorical poem, highlighting Abelard's struggle with Bernard, depicts Heloise searching for him in this time of crisis:

> The bride then asks where is her Palatine,
> He whose spirit showed itself totally divine?
> She asks why, like an exile, he has now withdrawn,
> He whom she had cherished at her breasts.[32]

From the early thirteenth century, the chronicle of Tours describes how Abelard had built the Paraclete and installed the nuns there with his former wife Heloise as abbess, how she 'who was truly his lover' had his body brought there for burial and prayed constantly for him after his death, and then adds: 'It is said that when she was lying in her last illness she gave instructions that when she was dead she should be laid in the tomb of her husband. And when her dead body was carried to the opened tomb, her husband, who had died long before her, raised his arms to receive her, and so clasped her closely in his embrace.'[33]

None of the nine known manuscripts of the letters can be dated before the late thirteenth century at the earliest, 150 years after the letters were written. There is no trace of an independent manuscript of Letter 1, *Historia calamitatum*, a copy of which Heloise herself (p. 47) says came into her hands. Jean de Meun must have had a manuscript when he translated the *Historia* and introduced the story of Abelard and Heloise into sixty-four lines of his continuation of the allegorical *Roman de la Rose* about 1280. It seems probable, as both J. Monfrin and R. W. Southern have suggested,[34] that the letters were kept by Heloise at the Paraclete, and that more than a century after her death they were brought to Paris and copied. It would be unlikely that anyone would know of her self-revelations during her lifetime. Peter the Venerable would hardly have thought so highly of her holiness and sense of vocation had he read of her sensual longings and self-reproach for hypocrisy. There seems no reason to suppose that Heloise 'edited' the personal letters in any way,[35] even if we accept that Abelard may have put words into her mouth in the *Historia calamitatum*. My own feeling is that once she had accepted that her relationship with Abelard must be re-established on a different basis and that henceforth she could look to him only for guidance as the founder of the institution of which she was a respected abbess, she would be unwilling to reread those painful outpourings of her heart. From the first paragraph of Letter 6 the correspondence takes on a different tone from which Heloise never wavers.

What became of Abelard's copies of the letters no one can know. It was current practice for medieval writers to keep copies of their own letters and even to revise them for later circulation as a letter-collection. This would be of general interest as showing the learning and expertise in the art of letter-writing of a single individual – such as St Bernard, Peter the Venerable or John of Salisbury – and its importance would be literary rather than historical, with the younger Pliny or Sidonius Apollinaris as models for variety of content and elegance of style. It was unusual for answers to be included: they could disturb the literary unity of the collection. Here is a further indication that the letters were not issued either in Heloise's lifetime or later as a literary letter-collection, but for their intrinsic personal interest when they came to light in the late thirteenth century.

Even after Jean de Meun, references remain scanty. Abelard and Heloise are not among the incontinent lovers in the Second Circle of Dante's *Inferno* (Canto 5), though their story has something in common with that of Paolo and Francesca da Rimini. Chaucer does no more than mention 'Helowys That was abbesse nat fer fro Parys' in the Wife of Bath's Prologue (lines 677–8), where she is one of an oddly assorted company in a satire on matrimony. He probably knew of her through the *Roman de la Rose*. The first genuine interest in the lovers was shown by Petrarch. One of the nine good manuscripts, dating from the early fourteenth century, belonged to him, and the marginal Latin notes to the *Historia calamitatum* and the personal letters are believed to be in his hand. It is certainly understandable that the author of the *Secretum* and of his own intensely personal letters should have read the manuscript closely. About a century later, *c.* 1461, François Villon included these lines in his *Ballade des Dames du Temps Jadis*, his theme being that death is inevitable for all mankind:

> Où est la très sage Hellois
> Pour qui fut chastré, puis moine
> Pierre Esbaillart à Saint-Denis?
> Pour son amour eut cette essoyne . . .
> Mais où sont les neiges d'antan?

('Where is that learned lady Heloise, for whose sake Pierre Abelard was first castrated, then became a monk at Saint-Denis? It was through love that he suffered such misfortune . . . But where are last year's snows?')

But this amounts to so little, especially at a time when romances like that of Tristan and Iseult or Aucassin and Nicolette were highly popular, that it seems likely that Abelard and Heloise could not be fitted into the current ideal of courtly love, with its emphasis on the lover's devotion to the chaste and unattainable lady. Abelard and Heloise speak a different language of sensuous frankness, of pagan realism in love and classical Stoic fortitude in adversity. Their relationship found physical expression, and Heloise is neither cold nor remote but loving and generous, eager to give service and not to demand it. By contrast with the cruel reality of their tragedy, courtly love as depicted in the romances of chivalry appears mannered and artificial.

The Latin text of the letters and of Abelard's major works was printed for the first time in Paris in 1616 in two practically identical editions, one of François d'Amboise, the other of André Duchesne. Why there were two editions has never been explained. The introductory material in the two differs, but the text is the same, and the notes on Letter 1 by Duchesne appear in both. This text remained standard for over two centuries.

In 1718 Richard Rawlinson brought out in London a new edition of the letters which adds nothing to the edition of 1616, and in 1841 John Caspar Orelli of Zurich published the *Historia* and the four personal letters. This was followed in 1849 by Victor Cousin's *Petri Abaelardi opera*, in two volumes, published in Paris, which became the standard edition. It includes Duchesne's notes, and the text is based on d'Amboise, plus Cousin's reading of four manuscripts. It is generally considered a better text than that of J.-P. Migne in Volume 178 of his *Patrologia Latina* (1855), though this too is mainly d'Amboise's text with Duchesne's notes.

Today the best edition for purposes of citation of the Latin text is that by David Luscombe, *The Letter Collection of Peter Abelard and Heloise* (Oxford, 2013).[36] This uses Betty Radice's translation and prints the Latin and English texts in parallel. Also useful is Eric Hicks's edition *La vie et les epistres Pierres Abaelart et Heloys sa fame* (Paris and Geneva, 1991). This has the medieval French translation (attributed to Jean de Meun) in parallel with the Latin text.

The d'Amboise–Duchesne text and the English edition by
Rawlinson gave rise to an extraordinary number of translations
and romantic paraphrases of the letters. The best translations
were the English one by the Reverend Joseph Berington
(London, 1787) and the French version by Dom Gervaise (Paris,
1723), but these were less influential than some of the wilder
flights of fancy. In 1687 Roger de Rabutin, Comte de Bussy,
sent Mme de Sévigné his own version of Heloise's two love-
letters and Abelard's reply to the first, in which he had inserted
fictitious incidents and reduced the whole story to a contemporary flirtatious intrigue. This continued to be reprinted until
the mid-nineteenth century. Another version paraphrased by
various hands and printed in Amsterdam in 1695 introduces
the name 'Philinthe' for the unknown recipient of Letter 1, and
a re-hash of this by F. N. Du Bois of the same year ran into
many editions. It was Du Bois's paraphrase which made the
romance generally known in England and inspired the version
by John Hughes, first published in London in 1714, and entitled
*Letters of Abelard and Heloise, to which is prefixed a particular
account of their lives, Amours and Misfortunes, extracted
chiefly from Monsieur Bayle, translated from the French.*

The fourth edition of this (1722) was reprinted in 1901 by
J. M. Dent in the Temple Classics series as *The Love Letters of
Abelard and Heloise*, and ran successfully through ten editions
until it went out of print in 1945. It is edited by Miss H. Morten,
who tells us in her short preface that 'It is rather a paraphrase
than a translation, but by its swiftness and sympathy best gives
the spirit of the original.' The *Historia calamitatum*, headed
'Abelard to Philintus', opens thus:

The last time we were together, Philintus, you gave me a melancholy account of your misfortunes; I was sensibly touched with
the relation, and like a true friend bore a share in your griefs.
What did I not say to stop your tears? I laid before you all the
reasons philosophy could furnish, which I thought might anyways
soften the strokes of fortune. But all these endeavours have proved
useless; grief, I perceive, has wholly seized your spirits, and your
prudence, far from assisting, seems to have forsaken you. But my

skilful friendship has found out an expedient to relieve you. Attend to me a moment, hear but the story of my misfortunes, and yours, Philintus, will be nothing as compared with those of the loving and unhappy Abelard.

And so it goes on. Heloise is given a maidservant, Agaton: 'She was brown, well-shaped, and a person superior to her rank; her features were regular and her eyes sparkling, fit to raise love in any man whose heart was not prepossessed by another passion.' She also has a singing-master who 'was excellently qualified for conveying a *billet* with the greatest dexterity and secrecy', and Abelard's sister Lucilla is persuaded to support her arguments against marriage. Typical of what flows from Heloise's pen is the following passage from Letter 2:

> Though I have lost my lover I still preserve my love. O vows! O convent! I have not lost my humanity under your inexorable discipline! You have not turned me to marble by changing my habit; my heart is not hardened by my imprisonment; I am still sensible to what has touched me, though, alas! I ought not to be! Without offending your commands permit a lover to exhort me to live in obedience to your rigorous rules.[37]

Hughes's travesty of the letters was apparently accepted as genuine even after Berington's translation of 1787. Its main interest now is that it is generally considered to be the source of Pope's *Eloisa to Abelard* which appeared among his works in 1717 (Rawlinson's Latin text did not appear until the following year). Pope's poem was immediately popular and frequently reprinted; it was also translated into French, German and Italian.[38] There were many other poetic versions of the lovers' story inspired by it, though none which showed the same imaginative intensity:

> The darksome pines that o'er yon rocks reclin'd
> Wave high, and murmur to the hollow wind,
> The wand'ring streams that shine between the hills,
> The grots that echo to the tinkling rills,

The dying gales that pant among the trees,
The lakes that quiver to the curling breeze;
No more these scenes my meditation aid,
Or lull to rest the visionary maid.
But o'er the twilight groves and dusky caves,
Long-sounding aisles, and intermingled graves,
Black Melancholy sits, and round her throws
A death-like silence, and a dead repose:
Her gloomy presence saddens all the scene,
Shades ev'ry flow'r, and darkens ev'ry green,
Deepens the murmur of the falling floods,
And breathes a browner horror on the woods.

But this is hardly the atmosphere of the gently undulating fields
and farmlands of Champagne, with the Ardusson quietly flowing through the rushes by the Paraclete. Pope conjures up something more like the crags and caverns and rushing torrents of
Clisson, already romantically associated with Heloise, and said
to have inspired some of Poussin's landscapes. It was there too
that Lamartine is said to have written his lines in memory of
Heloise. Nor does Pope's Eloisa recall the historic Heloise, but is
rather the neo-classical heroine painted by Angelica Kauffmann
and her contemporaries, languishing over Abelard's tomb or on
her own deathbed.

In 1925 *The Letters of Abelard and Heloise* translated by
C. K. Scott Moncrieff (the translator of Proust) from Migne's
text was published by the Cambridge University Press in an
edition limited to 750 copies and now out of print. Scott Moncrieff quotes from Hughes's translation but evidently knows
nothing of Berington's, as he claims to be the first to translate
from Latin and not to adapt a debased French version. There
are no explanatory notes, and as an introduction only a curious
and rather facetious exchange of letters with George Moore
querying the authenticity of the Letters. Moore's novel *Heloise
and Abelard* had appeared in 1921. The style of the translation
is idiosyncratic to the point of being sometimes barely intelligible; it wavers uneasily between the cadences of the Authorized
Version, a literal transcription of the original Latin sentence-

structure, and the underpunctuated sentences of Moore himself. Here is a passage from Heloise's first letter:

> There were two things, I confess, in thee especially, wherewith thou couldst at once captivate the heart of any woman; namely the arts of making songs and of singing them. Which we know that other philosophers have seldom followed. Wherewith as with a game, refreshing the labour of philosophic exercise, thou has left many songs composed in amatory measure or rhythm, which for the suavity both of words and of tune being oft repeated, have kept thy name without ceasing on the lips of all; since even illiterates the sweetness of thy melodies did not allow to forget thee. It was on this account chiefly that women sighed for love of thee. And as the greater part of thy songs descanted of our love, they spread my fame in a short time through many lands, and inflamed the jealousy of many women against me.[39]

Apart from Betty Radice in 1974, no other English translation of the letters of Abelard and Heloise appeared until 2007, when William Levitan produced his eloquent and accurate translation.[40] This was followed in 2009 by the excellent translation by Mary M. McLaughlin and Bonnie Wheeler.[41] In 2013 David Luscombe produced his revised version of Radice's translation in Oxford Medieval Texts. So there are now three reliable translations of the letters in addition to Radice's.

Abelard and Heloise do not write in the unsophisticated Latin of the previous century, and they have not the easy grace of an accomplished letter-writer such as Peter the Venerable. The composition and style of their letters follow the rules for correct letter-writing of the twelfth century. The elegance these sought in formal address, proper choice of words and arrangement of material seems to us excessive, and Scott Moncrieff has shown that the frequent use of connecting relative pronouns and elaborate antithesis of clauses have to be eschewed in translation. Abelard's *Historia calamitatum*, being largely narrative, is less rhetorical, and Heloise can write directly in her personal letters. But it was the convention of their day to overload a reasoned argument with strings of stock quotations from the Vulgate and the Christian Fathers, or to introduce a homily on an appropriate topic which reads like a set piece. Heloise, for example, has said something in Letter 6 about the evil of incontinence and the effect of strong drink (pp. 99 ff.) which Abelard elaborates on in Letter 8, repeating the same quotations (pp. 174 ff.). In addition, their intensive classical education leaves its mark both in quotation and choice of words. In this sense they are both learned clerks and write in 'a mood of literary showmanship'.[42] But they are also individuals who would be exceptional in any age, whose letters move through the widest range of emotions – devotion, disappointment, grief and indignation, self-confidence, ambition, impatience, self-reproach and resignation – all under the discipline of a keen critical intelligence which is as marked in Heloise as in Abelard. They deserve to be heard, even if imperfectly and at second-hand through a translation, in the words they wrote.

NOTES

1. R. W. Southern, *The Making of the Middle Ages* (London, 1953), p. 172.
2. See Enid McLeod, *Héloïse* (1938; reprinted, London, 1971), pp. 8–12, 253–5, and John O. Ward and N. Chiavaroli, 'The Young Heloise and Latin Rhetoric', in *Listening to Heloise*, ed. Bonnie Wheeler (New York, 2000), pp. 60–62. Heloise's birthdate is controversial: she may have been born in the 1090s rather than in 1100 or 1101: see M. T. Clanchy, *Abelard: A Medieval Life* (Oxford, 1997), pp. 173–4, and Constant J. Mews, *The Lost Love Letters of Heloise and Abelard* (New York, 1999), p. 32 and p. 302, note 11, and Mews in *Listening to Heloise*, ed. Wheeler, p. 37.
3. Radice is correct to say that no absolute legal bar stopped Abelard marrying, but he would not have been able to remain as master of the Paris school because his predecessor, William of Champeaux, had given it a reputation for celibacy and austerity. Abelard had to remain celibate, even if the other canons of Notre-Dame did not: see Clanchy, *Abelard*, pp. 188–9, 193–5.
4. J. T. Muckle, 'Abelard's Letter of Consolation to a Friend', *Mediaeval Studies* 12 (1950), pp. 173–4.
5. See McLeod, *Héloïse*, frontispiece and pp. 86–91, 265–6, and Mews, *Lost Love Letters*, pp. 161–3, 358–9.

6. *La Chronique de Morigny*, ed. L. Mirot (Paris, 1909), p. 54, and see Clanchy, *Abelard*, p. 207.

7. John of Salisbury, *Metalogicon*, 2.10. The date is precisely given as the year after the death of King Henry I of England.

8. Mary M. McLaughlin, 'Abelard as Autobiographer: The Motives and Meaning of his *Story of Calamities*', *Speculum* 42 (1967), pp. 463–88.

9. See Letter 2, p. 53.

10. See Letters 7 and 8.

11. This record of 'Our Statutes' (*Institutiones Nostrae*) is translated by Mary M. McLaughlin and Bonnie Wheeler, *The Letters of Heloise and Abelard* (New York, 2009), pp. 313–15.

12. Abelard, Letter Nine, is translated by Jan M. Ziolkowski, *Letters of Peter Abelard: Beyond the Personal* (Washington DC, 2008), pp. 10–33, and likewise by McLaughlin and Wheeler, *The Letters of Heloise and Abelard*, pp. 196–207.

13. Translated by McLaughlin and Wheeler, *The Letters of Heloise and Abelard*, pp. 211–67.

14. Translated by Sister Jane Patricia, *The Hymns of Abelard in English Verse* (Lanham, 1986), pp. 31–4. For a bibliography on Abelard's hymns, see David Luscombe, 'Peter Abelard and the Poets', in *Poetry and Philosophy in the Middle Ages: A Festschrift for Peter Dronke* (Leiden, 2001), p. 157, note 9, and Constant Mews, *Peter Abelard* (Aldershot, 1995), pp. 66–70.

15. *Petri Abaelardi Opera Omnia*, ed. J.-P. Migne, Patrologiae: Series Latina, Vol. 178 (Paris, 1855), pp. 379–80, and see Clanchy, *Abelard*, pp. 259–60, 263.

16. For Bernard, see G. R. Evans, *Bernard of Clairvaux* (Oxford, 2000) and *The Cistercian World*, ed. Pauline Matarasso (Harmondsworth, 1993).

17. For letter no. 28, see C. H. Lawrence, *Medieval Monasticism*, 2nd edn. (London, 1989), pp. 194–6.

18. For the issue between Bernard and Abelard, see D. E. Luscombe, *The School of Peter Abelard* (Cambridge, 1969), chapter 4; Clanchy, *Abelard*, chapter 13; John Marenbon, *The Philosophy of Peter Abelard* (Cambridge, 1997), pp. 25–34; Peter Godman, *The Silent Masters* (Princeton, 2000), chapter 3; and Constant J. Mews, 'The Council of Sens (1141): Abelard, Bernard and the Fear of Social Upheaval', *Speculum* 77 (2002), pp. 342–82.

19. Letter 238, in B. S. James, *The Letters of St Bernard of Clairvaux* (London, 1953; reprinted 1998).

20. Letter X, *Letters IX–XIV*, ed. Smits, pp. 239–47.

21. For English translations, see Further Reading, p. lxxxv.

22. Letter 241, in James, *Letters of St Bernard* (1953), p. 321.

23. See Clanchy, *Abelard*, p. 309. The 'Apologia' of Berengar of Poitiers is edited by R. M. Thomson, 'The Satirical Works of Berenger of Poitiers', *Mediaeval Studies* 42 (1980), pp. 111–33.

24. This is the hypothesis of Dr J. Jeannin, 'La dernière maladie d'Abelard', in *Mélanges St Bernard* (Dijon, 1952), pp. 109–15.

25. *Carmen ad Astralabium*, ed. J. Rubingh-Bosscher (Groningen, 1987), and comment in Marenbon, *Philosophy of Peter Abelard*, pp. 315–16.

26. See the chronology by Mews, 'The Council of Sens', p. 381.

27. Peter the Venerable's epitaph is translated in Elizabeth Hamilton, *Heloise* (New York, 1966), p. 156. The Latin text is in C. J. Mews and C. S. F. Burnett, 'Peter the Venerable's Epitaph for Abelard', *Studia Monastica* 27 (1985), p. 65. See comment by Clanchy, *Abelard*, p. 324.

28. Details in McLeod, *Héloïse*, pp. 216–19, and Mary M. McLaughlin, 'Heloise the Abbess', in *Listening to Heloise*, ed. Wheeler, pp. 1–17.

29. John Milton, *Samson Agonistes* (1671), line 1758.

30. For the manuscripts of Abelard's works, see Julia Barrow, Charles S. F. Burnett, David E. Luscombe, 'A Checklist of the MSS Containing the Writings of Abelard and Heloise', *Révue d'histoire des textes* 14–15 (1984–5), pp. 183–302.

31. Translated by Mews, *Lost Love Letters*, p. 38.

32. The text is in Peter Dronke, *Abelard and Heloise in Medieval Testimonies* (Glasgow, 1976), pp. 17–18, 36, and see Clanchy, *Abelard*, p. 146 and p. 365, note 103.

33. Dronke, *Abelard and Heloise in Medieval Testimonies*, pp. 50–51 and comment at p. 23. See McLeod, *Héloïse*, p. 290.

34. J. Monfrin, *Abelard – Historia Calamitatum* (Paris, 1959), p. 60, and R. W. Southern, 'The Letters of Heloise and Abelard', *Medieval Humanism and Other Studies* (Oxford, 1970), p. 103.

35. See below, 'The Letters of Abelard and Heloise in Today's Scholarship', p. lxvii. Heloise probably did edit the letters; Peter the Venerable may well have known of her sensual longings. See also Clanchy, *Abelard*, pp. 155–60.

36. The principal editions of the letters are listed by Luscombe, *The Letter Collection*, pp. civ–cxiv.

37. The passage comes near the end of the letter but there is nothing in the Radice text for comparison.

38. See C. Charrier, *Héloïse dans l'histoire et la légende* (Paris, 1933), pp. 470–71.

39. Compare pp. 52–3.

40. William Levitan, *Abelard and Heloise: the Letters and Other Writings* (Indianapolis, 2007).

41. McLaughlin and Wheeler, *The Letters of Heloise and Abelard* (New York, 2009).

42. Southern, *Medieval Humanism* (Oxford, 1970), p. 102.

The Letters of Abelard and Heloise in Today's Scholarship

by M. T. Clanchy

Betty Radice's translation of these letters has sold over 200,000 copies since its publication in 1974. It is by far the most widely read book on Abelard and Heloise in the English-speaking world. The proviso 'English-speaking' is important, as England was peripheral to Abelard's own milieu. He deliberately identified himself with France and in particular with Paris, which represented for him the capital of France and the centre of culture. As writers, he and Heloise have been famous in France at least since the publication of Jean de Meun's version of the *Romance of the Rose* in the early 1280s, which praised Heloise and quoted from her first letter. French enthusiasm for them remains very much alive and it is perhaps undergoing a revival. In 1996 Professor Jacques Verger published a new authoritative account for the general reader, *L'amour castré: l'histoire d'Héloïse et Abélard* and Jean Jolivet did the same for Abelard's theology in *La théologie d'Abélard*. A novel by Antoine Audouard, entitled *Adieu, mon unique* (echoing the final words of Heloise's first letter: 'Farewell, my only love'), was published in 2000 and an opera, *Héloïse et Abélard* by Ahmed Essyad, was staged at the Théâtre Musical du Châtelet in 2001. This Parisian theatre was an appropriate location to remember Abelard and Heloise, as the Châtelet was the fortified gate which gave access to the heart of Paris, the Île de la Cité, where their own drama had been played out nine centuries earlier.

Students came to Abelard from all over Latin Christendom and he described how he considered himself the greatest philosopher in the world. He knew nothing about China or India and very little about Islam or Byzantium. His 'world' was in fact confined to Catholic or Romanesque Europe, which regarded itself as the successor of the old Roman Empire. Through this cultural inheritance from the Middle Ages, European liberals of the eighteenth and nineteenth centuries identified with Abelard and Heloise as fellow free-spirits confronting persecution and prejudice. They were regarded as martyrs for love and heroes in the struggle against the Catholic Church. As models of enlightenment, Abelard was seen as the champion of reason opposing superstition, while Heloise was understood to challenge the doctrine of celibacy upon which the power of the Catholic clergy depended. She was also perceived as a proto-feminist, who opposed patriarchy by contradicting Abelard and ridiculing the pretensions of monks.

Throughout much of Western Europe Abelard and Heloise remained household names among educated people (particularly liberals) well into the first half of the twentieth century, as versions of their letters had been translated into the principal European languages. Their dilemmas were comprehensible and interesting to anyone with a Christian education, whether Catholic or Protestant. Catholics could be shocked – or inspired – by the irreverence of Abelard and Heloise towards ecclesiastical authority, while Protestants deplored the cruelty with which the Roman Church had treated them. The prestige of Abelard and Heloise as upstanding liberals made its way to the United States of America, the archetypal land of freedom and opportunity for Europeans in the nineteenth century. When the new state of Illinois (1818) recruited immigrants to populate Chicago, it advertised the city by declaring that 'Her men are all like Abelard, her women like Eloy' (this form of Heloise's name conveniently rhymed with Illinois).[1] In return, rich Americans made the pilgrimage to Paris to put flowers on the neo-Gothic tomb of Abelard and Heloise in Père-Lachaise cemetery. According to Mark Twain, writing under his real name of Samuel Clemens, in his travel book *Innocents Abroad* (1869), their tomb was more revered and more widely known than any other in Christendom save that of the Saviour himself.[2]

By contrast with all this, the popular reputations of Abelard and Heloise dwindled in the latter half of the twentieth century,

especially in the English-speaking world, almost in inverse ratio
to the volume of scholarship concerning them and the number
of students engaged with the humanities. (France is the obvious
exception to this rule, because French national feeling still identifies with Abelard and Heloise as famous French people.) It is
the success of Betty Radice's translation of the letters, in the face
of growing apathy and ignorance, which makes her achievement
so significant. Without her work, knowledge of Abelard and
Heloise in the English-speaking world might have dwindled
to miniscule proportions. The letters would of course have
continued to be known to experts in twelfth-century scholasti-
cism and monasticism, but they would no longer have been
accessible to a wider public. The story of Abelard and Heloise
had been sustained in the 1930s and 1940s through the success
of Helen Waddell's novel *Peter Abelard* (1933). This is a very
attractive book to any expert on Abelard and Heloise because
it is steeped in the original sources. However, its quotations
from the Latin and its theological rigour no longer appeal to the
young. When Chatto & Windus in 1971 reissued Enid McLeod's
biography of Heloise, which had sold well when it was first
published in 1938, it failed to make it into paperback. Similarly
Regine Pernoud's *Héloïse et Abélard*, which sold widely in
France, was limited to hardback when published in English
translation by Collins in 1973.

Explanations can only be speculative for the current decline in
knowledge of Abelard and Heloise among the English-speaking
educated public. The decline in didactic religious education is
probably one cause. Catholic children are no longer taught
the theology of celibacy and some Protestants have turned to
multiculturalism instead of attacking the pope. Furthermore,
the agonized sexual morality of Abelard and Heloise becomes
difficult for a new generation to understand, as contraception is
routine and abortion is argued to be a woman's right. Abelard
and Heloise are in danger of no longer being seen as liberal
icons or martyrs for love, but as ludicrous figures who could
not get a grip on their lives. So far from being courageous or
principled, they look like solipsists who dramatized their own
grotesque predicaments. After centuries of fame, time is at last

threatening to efface the memory of Abelard and Heloise. The honoured dead who are commemorated at Père-Lachaise cemetery now include the Communards of 1870, the soldiers of two World Wars, Oscar Wilde and Jim Morrison. So it is understandable that visitors only occasionally now lay flowers on the tomb of Abelard and Heloise at the entrance.

Betty Radice opens her Introduction with the generalization that 'Most people have heard of Abelard and Heloise as a pair of lovers as famous as Dante and Beatrice or Romeo and Juliet.' This reveals the generation to which Radice belonged, as many educated people now will not have heard of Dante and Beatrice, though they still know of Romeo and Juliet. In 1935 Cole Porter had indeed coupled Abelard and Heloise with Romeo and Juliet as free spirits in his popular song 'Just One of Those Things'.[3] Similarly with Dante and Beatrice, the Pre-Raphaelites had idealized them as icons of pure love, and reproductions of romanticized portraits of the couple were still common in the first half of the twentieth century. For the generations of students since 1960, however, who have been educated neither in the Bible nor in the Latin classics, the letters of Abelard and Heloise cannot have immediate appeal. Today's students know of the Middle Ages as the time of Robin Hood, King Arthur and Harry Potter's Hogwarts Castle. Despite their dramatic content and focus on sex and violence, the letters of Abelard and Heloise, with their formal structure and classical terms of reference, do not readily fit into this fairy-story view of the past.

Nevertheless, the continued success of Radice's translation of the letters, over the past twenty-five years and more, shows that she did succeed in producing a modern text which appeals to readers. At the end of her Introduction she explains why she rejected the literal but archaizing style of her predecessor C. K. Scott-Moncrieff. He was the translator of Proust and extraordinarily good at translation. But he chose for Abelard and Heloise an archaic style which is almost impossible to read, though it renders the Latin very accurately. The objection to Scott Moncrieff's translation of 1925 is that it gives the impression that Abelard and Heloise are old-fashioned pedants or members of some peculiar sect. They use 'thee' and 'thou', for example, to address each other. There is no warrant in the Latin text of the letters for this sort of archaizing in English. Abelard and Heloise thought of themselves as modern people and they wrote the most up-to-date Latin they knew.

A contentious modern element which Radice introduced into her translation is the distinction between 'Personal Letters' and 'Letters of Direction'. None of the manuscripts suggests any such distinction, nor is there a break in the correspondence between Letters 5 and 6. Radice derived these terms from J. T. Muckle's edition of the 'Personal Letters' in 1953 and Enid McLeod's biography of Heloise, which distinguished the 'Love Letters' from the 'Letters of Direction'. There is indeed a crucial turning point in the correspondence at the beginning of Letter 6, where Heloise ceases being concerned with herself and asks Abelard, on behalf of all her nuns, to counsel and direct them (which he duly does in Letters 7 and 8). Radice's distinction between 'Personal Letters' and 'Letters of Direction' remains a useful one, however, as long as it is understood to be an editorial explanation and not the work of Abelard or Heloise. Thenceforward, in her extant correspondence at least, Heloise always wrote to Abelard as the founder of her convent and not as her special lover. She may also have written more personal letters to him, but these have not been preserved. For example, she would have wanted to reply to his heart-rending 'Confession of Faith' (pp. 211–12), which was addressed to her and published by his student Berengar of Poitiers at the time of his condemnation at the Council of Sens in 1140 or 1141. But she may have judged it unwise to record any reply to him, as that might embroil both her and her nuns in accusations of heresy. Instead, she relied on the power of Peter the Venerable, abbot of Cluny, though he did not help her as much as he might have. (She had to remind him to send her a written absolution to hang on Abelard's tomb, and he was not enthusiastic about helping Astralabe, the son of Abelard and Heloise (p. 227).)

Allegations of Forgery

The greatest threat to the reputations of Abelard and Heloise over the past thirty years has come from allegations of forgery. Betty Radice underestimated these in her Introduction of 1974, though she had obtained a copy of the wide-ranging allegations made by John F. Benton at the international conference at Cluny in 1972.[4] She discussed Benton's arguments only in a footnote because she thought them ill founded (as indeed they were, on his own later admission), but she had no way of foreseeing the popularity of the forgery theory in America. It had a momentum of its own, particularly among academics and their students, for whom questions of disputed authorship and literary theory were the staple subject of seminars. Furthermore, Benton won the support of the leading expert, Giles Constable of Harvard University, who in his survey of medieval *Letters and Letter-Collections* (1976) agreed that 'the most celebrated exchange of love-letters in the Middle Ages, that of Abelard and Heloise, may not be authentic'.[5]

Radice had pointed out that Charlotte Charrier in 1933 (and others before her) had questioned the authenticity of the letters. Those of Heloise had been challenged in particular because she made such irreligious statements; how could any medieval woman, let alone a nun, have said such things? The editor of the Latin texts, J. T. Muckle, concluded that Heloise's first two letters had been forged, or at least reworked, because Heloise 'would not have desired to leave such a character sketch of herself' to posterity.[6] Benton went further than his predecessors, as he denied the authenticity of Letter 1, *Historia calamitatum*, as well as the subsequent letters, whereas *Historia calamitatum* had always been assumed to be a genuine autobiography and the crucial document in the study of Abelard. Benton concluded that Letter 1 was 'in large part a twelfth-century fiction' and that Heloise's letters had been composed in the thirteenth century.[7] His purpose in arguing for forgery, like that of Muckle who was a Catholic priest, was to controvert the conventional picture of Abelard and Heloise as liberals opposed to the authority of the Catholic Church. Benton and Muckle thought this anachronistic; it was a misrepresentation of Abelard and Heloise's dedicated lives as members of the monastic order. Heloise had been fulsomely praised by Peter the Venerable, abbot of Cluny, which she would not have been (according to the anti-liberal argument), if she had written the shocking letters attributed to her.

Eliminating Letter 1, *Historia calamitatum*, and the other letters of Abelard and Heloise from their literary corpus cuts the protagonists down to size and makes them more like other monks and nuns of their time. Abelard's academic writings on logic and theology survive in relative abundance, as does his poetry in the religious forms of hymns and liturgical laments. Similarly Heloise is documented as abbess of the convent of the Paraclete and as a correspondent of Peter the Venerable; she was also praised as a composer and poet by Hugh Metel. This material is confined to the intellectual and religious sphere, as is usual in medieval sources; these are the kind of things which clerics thought it appropriate to record. There is little personal information in all this; we are not told what Abelard and Heloise thought about themselves, still less what they felt. By contrast, it is the expression of their emotions which makes the allegedly forged letters of Abelard and Heloise so unusual and so precious. Abelard begins *Historia calamitatum* with an appeal to 'human feelings' and Heloise likewise opens her first letter to him with a description of her wounded feelings. It is because the letters of Abelard and Heloise address the emotions so deliberately that they arouse such strong reactions, of antagonism or enthusiasm, in their readers. As rhetorical works in a continuous Latin tradition stretching back to Cicero, this is exactly what they were intended to do.

By eliminating all eight letters, Benton aimed to recover a more truthful conception of Abelard and Heloise than that of the nineteenth-century liberal stereotype. We could now judge them, he argued, 'by standards which they themselves would have considered valid'.[8] Henceforward they could be seen 'in more positive terms': Heloise as a dutiful nun and Abelard as a respectable college professor. 'We can strike from the historical record [Benton wrote] the image of Abelard as a calculating seducer or as an arrogant and ungrateful student who could dismiss Anselm of Laon as a sterile and obfuscating teacher years after the death of that great scholar.[9] This was wishful thinking on Benton's part, however, as Abelard's contemporaries Fulk of Deuil and Roscelin described him as a seducer and Otto of Freising confirms that he mocked Anselm of Laon.[10] Abelard was not a *doctor* (a professor), another contemporary warned, he was a *joculator* (a jester).[11]

Much of the controversy about Abelard and Heloise arises from how we choose to characterize them. Ultimately this turns not on technical points of scholarship, but on each individual reader's reaction to what the sources say. There will never be agreement about them, because there was no agreement at the time. Was Abelard *Golias* – 'Goliath' (as St Bernard described him), the lord of misrule,[12] or was he 'Christ's philosopher' (as Peter the Venerable described him)? Was Heloise intellectually dependent on Abelard, as numerous scholars have assumed, or did she have a mind of her own? An epitaph for her (not known to Radice) declares that she was Abelard's equal in feeling, conduct and intellect; it then adds that she was without equal in her knowledge of all literature.[13] This implies that she was Abelard's superior in this respect. Heloise's level of education and knowledge can only be inferred from her letters. Judging from them, it is possible that she did have a better grounding in the Latin classics than Abelard, as he had specialized in logic (as distinct from literature) from boyhood.[14]

In 1980 Benton withdrew his allegation that Letter 1, *Historia calamitatum*, was mainly a work of fiction, admitting that his arguments had not been vindicated. But he did not abandon the theory of forgery as such, since he retreated to a fall-back position whereby Abelard became the author of the letters of Heloise. This hypothesis remained consistent with his aim to see Abelard and Heloise 'in more positive terms', as it meant that Abelard put words into Heloise's mouth in order to exemplify repentance and monastic peace.[15] Since John Benton's death in 1988, his position has been maintained by Chrysogonus Waddell in a modified form: 'The entire correspondence is from the pen of a single writer . . . There is one sole author at work and this author is Abelard. This in no way excludes the participation of Heloise, since the presentation of themes and exchange of ideas set forth in the letters probably correspond to actual discussions between them.'[16] This idea of a joint literary project between Abelard and Heloise had been first put forward by the Latinist Peter von Moos in 1980.[17] In 1988 David Luscombe in a lecture to the British Academy brought together the arguments as they then stood:

> The problem we are left with, and may never dispel, is that of knowing whether the letters were at first written for dispatch, separately and successively, with each provoking a reply and further correspondence until Abelard met Heloise's requests in full; or whether the collection arose from a compact to share, compose and exchange their thoughts, experiences and principles in fictive correspondence.[18]

In the latter case, Abelard and Heloise may be said to have forged the correspondence themselves. As Luscombe adds, 'the boundary between fact and fiction, between reality and art, is not firm in either case and cannot be certainly drawn'.

The forgery debate, which Benton had reopened in 1972 in terms of historical facts (about Abelard's life and about the transmission of manuscripts), had spread over in the 1980s into the broad post-modern question of 'What distinguishes History from Literature?'[19] The letters of Abelard and Heloise have been revalidated in factual terms (there are no anachronisms in them, as Benton had initially alleged). Nevertheless, they are not necessarily true, as any piece of writing is an artifice. Autobiography in particular has to be Literature as much as History. Abelard and Heloise were not even writing in their mother tongue, but in a learned language with a long and demanding rhetorical tradition. Abelard did not frame *Historia calamitatum* as a straightforward account of the facts of his life because there was no model for that in the Latin literature he knew. It purports to be a letter to a friend, who is a fellow monk, but to this day it is impossible to say whether this 'friend' is a literary fiction or a real person who has still to be identified. In other words, *Historia calamitatum* contains elements of fiction and ambiguity from its opening words addressed to Abelard's 'friend'.

A Single Author for All the Letters?

The reason why Benton and Waddell (and others) argued that the letters were all by a single author is that – so far at least – no one has succeeded in isolating stylistic traits which incontrovertibly distinguish the letters of Abelard from those of Heloise. Furthermore, they both made use of the same stock of quotations. If there were not a single author, there must at least have been an editor who made the letters into a book. Radice slipped up when she insisted that 'There seems no reason to suppose that Heloise "edited" the personal letters in any way' (p. xlvii). On the contrary, someone has edited these letters and Heloise is the most likely candidate. If not, then we have to presume a third party did it and that takes us back into arguments about forgery. In arguing that Abelard wrote all the letters, Benton worked on the premise that when Abelard and Heloise both use the same quotation, the initiative invariably comes from Abelard. This is what the textual evidence suggests, since some of the quotations in the letters are also found in Abelard's theological works. But Benton did not consider the possibility that many of the ideas (and perhaps the quotations also) in Abelard's theological works derived from Heloise and that she could therefore have been the initiator of the letters.[20]

If in the letters of Abelard and Heloise there is 'one sole author at work' (in the words of Waddell), that author is more likely to have been Heloise than Abelard. At the convent of the Paraclete she had the writing facilities, the stability, the time, the knowledge and the motive to write, whereas Abelard was repeatedly on the move as he engaged in a series of public controversies which culminated in his second trial for heresy at the Council of Sens in 1140 or 1141. For what it is worth, the manuscript tradition of the letters also suggests that Heloise rather than Abelard was their editor or author, as they are associated with her convent of the Paraclete and not with Paris or Cluny,

Abelard's homes in the last decades of his life. But the manuscript tradition is itself shaky and all the controversies about the authenticity of the letters originate from this.

There are no letters of Abelard and Heloise in the sense of actual documents written or sealed by them (there are no incontrovertible autograph writings of either of them at all). Their letters exist only as copies made up in book form and the earliest book of this sort dates from 1280, more than 150 years after the events they concern (as Radice points out). These facts in themselves do not prove, nor even suggest, that the correspondence is a forgery, as medieval letters were not usually kept any more than modern ones are. The only sorts of letters routinely preserved for posterity in the twelfth century were the charters documenting the property of monastic houses. In addition to that, exceptionally successful monks like St Bernard and Peter the Venerable had copies of their letters preserved in book form as spiritual reading for their successors. It is in such a monastic context that the letters of Abelard and Heloise are presumed to have been made up into a book at the convent of the Paraclete because they formed part of the foundation history of the convent. But this first twelfth-century copy of the letters has not been preserved (or it never actually existed, if we accept the forgery arguments). All we have now are the copies beginning around 1280 which are associated with Jean de Meun, who is credited with translating the letters into French and publishing them in Paris. Thenceforward the letters entered the literary canon and they were enjoyed by Petrarch and other intellectuals in the fourteenth and fifteenth centuries.

As Jean de Meun was undoubtedly the publicizer of the letters and there is no evidence of their existence before his time (no writer refers to them before 1280), Hubert Silvestre gave renewed life to the forgery controversy in 1985 by arguing that Jean himself was their author.[21] This hypothesis had the merit of naming a writer who might have been capable of such an imaginative feat, whereas Benton had never been as convincing or as specific about the motives of his unnamed forgers. On the other hand, Silvestre insisted that *Historia calamitatum* contained anachronisms and mistakes. As this is not the case, the argument for Jean's authorship is weakened, since it is hard to see how he could have been accurate about so many details of Abelard's life so long after his death. The failure of Benton's attempt to show that Letter 1, *Historia calamitatum* is a forgery has reinforced the authenticity of the letter collection as a whole, since all the manuscripts start with it and make the other letters depend on it.

Silvestre wanted Jean de Meun to be the author of the letters so that he could demonstrate that Heloise had been a good Catholic, who had never written a word to Abelard about being a harlot or an unbeliever. Just as Benton wanted Abelard to be a respectable college professor, Silvestre wanted Heloise to be an obedient old-fashioned nun. Like his fellow Catholic priest J. T. Muckle, Silvestre cited Peter the Venerable's letter to Heloise as 'irrefutable evidence' that Peter would never have praised her if he had known about her subversive letters. In Silvestre's view they are 'incompatible with morality and Christian doctrine'.[22] Whether Heloise was in fact a proud pagan, who derived her moral views from Seneca and the Roman Stoics rather than from Christ and his saints, is a question which will continue to be debated as long as her letters are read. There will always be differences of opinion about whether the Middle Ages were without exception an 'Age of Faith'.

It is impossible to be certain what Peter the Venerable knew about Heloise and her innermost thoughts. He probably knew more than his letters suggest. As abbot of Cluny, which controlled hundreds of monasteries across Latin Christendom, he headed the largest intelligence-gathering network in Europe. Silvestre's presumption that there is 'irrefutable evidence' that he would have condemned Heloise, if he had thought her immoral, has no factual basis. As abbot of Cluny, Peter the Venerable had all sorts of reasons for going out of his way to praise her, regardless of what his own personal opinion of her may have been. He was a master of ambiguity and diplomacy, as his letter to the pope in defence of Abelard demonstrates (pp. 215–16).[23] At the time Peter wrote this letter in 1141, Abelard was the most notorious heretic in Christendom. His books had been ceremonially burned by the pope himself in

St Peter's, Rome, and an order had gone out to arrest him on sight. Nevertheless, Peter the Venerable ignored all this and persisted in protecting Abelard by making him a monk of Cluny. He may have praised Heloise so fulsomely, just as he repeatedly praised Abelard, because all three had been slandered by St Bernard. In a series of letters to the pope in 1139 Bernard had called Peter the Venerable deceitful, arrogant and an enemy of God.[24] In this context of exaggeration and public abuse, the reputations of Abelard and Heloise became ammunition in the struggle for authority between Peter's Cluniac monks and Bernard's Cistercians.

After thirty years of controversy since Benton's reopening of the forgery question, the issues have now been set aside rather than resolved. The matter never will be decisively settled, as there is no way of proving that the letters of Abelard and Heloise were composed by them. On the other hand, the hypothesis that someone else wrote them has even less to commend it, as there is no evidence of forgery in the manuscripts and no convincing forger has been produced. These being the circumstances, most experts now accept that Abelard is the most likely author of the letters written in his name and Heloise of the letters in hers. Having granted that, these letters are none the less very unusual in being a series which goes back and forth between two correspondents. Furthermore *Historia calamitatum* is extraordinary in itself; there is nothing else like it, in either form or content. The model for autobiography was St Augustine's *Confessions*, which Abelard's contemporary, Guibert, abbot of Nogent, used in his account of his life. As for Heloise, the ideas she expresses are novel and disconcerting. Those who have argued for forgery, like Silvestre, have seen this most clearly. Jean de Meun commented that some people think her letters show that she was mad. But it should really cause no surprise if Abelard and Heloise produced some of the most extraordinary documents of the Middle Ages, as their contemporaries – whether they liked them or not – acknowledged them to be special.

The Identity of Heloise

In the 1990s the spotlight shifted from Abelard to Heloise. This was signalled by Barbara Newman's article of 1992 entitled 'Authority, Authenticity and the Repression of Heloise', which argued that she did indeed compose the letters to Abelard and that furthermore 'she came to Abelard with not only her mind but her imagination already well stocked'.[25] This refers to Abelard's description in Letter 1, *Historia calamitatum*, of how, even before he knew her, her literary knowledge had already 'made her most renowned throughout the realm' of France (p. 10). In a rare but revealing lapse Radice missed the force of the Latin superlative *nominatissima* ('*most* renowned'); her translation made the weaker statement that Heloise's knowledge 'had won her renown'.[26] This minor mistake reinforces Newman's argument that the reputation of Heloise has tended to get slighted by scholars, whether male or female, because a medieval woman intellectual is so unfamiliar a phenomenon. Peter the Venerable likewise commented on Heloise's extraordinary fame and he added that she could not be distracted 'from this useful plan to learn the arts'.[27]

For what literary achievements had Heloise won such precocious renown? Peter the Venerable drew attention to her musical compositions: 'Your skill sent new turns of melody to the very ears of God.'[28] Hugh Metel in his letter to her likewise began with her music: 'Sing praise to the Lord on harp and cymbal. Your fame, flying sounding through the void, has resounded with us.' (In medieval astronomical theory sound travels through space via the harmonies made by the crystal spheres which hold the stars in place.) By this means, Hugh explained, Heloise's fame had reached him and his fellow canons far away in Toul (on the border of France and Germany): 'You have surpassed the female sex. How? By composing [prose], by versifying, by [devising] new constructions and by renewing familiar words.'[29] These descriptions refer to later periods in Heloise's life and none of them is conclusive proof of her real fame, as each of these authors had an axe to grind. In *Historia calamitatum* Abelard wanted to show that Heloise was a good enough match for him: the greatest philosopher in the world would team up with the most brilliant woman in France. Peter the Venerable may have praised her so fulsomely because he wanted to draw her and her nuns into his Cluniac sphere of influence as against St Bernard's Cistercian. (In fact Heloise adopted Cistercian liturgical practices at the convent of the Paraclete.) As for Hugh Metel, he was an ally of St Bernard and a persistent self-publicist, who had attacked Abelard as a heretic on the basis of little evidence.[30]

Nevertheless these testimonies, despite their bias, do suggest that Heloise was famed for her mastery of Latin and her originality in composing prose, verse and music. The epitaph for her, stating that she was unequalled in her knowledge of all literature, confirms this image. If she was so renowned, among intellectuals at least, compositions of hers (in both oral and written forms) must have circulated widely in France, and beyond France as well according to Hugh Metel. Of her earliest work, which established her reputation before Abelard knew her, no information now survives. What sort of things might she have published? Not only poems presumably, as those who praise her all emphasize her outstanding knowledge of classical literature. This is displayed in the three letters to Abelard (Letters 2, 4 and 6) on which her reputation as a writer and thinker principally rests today. The best commentary on these letters is Peter Dronke's chapter on Heloise in *Women Writers of the Middle Ages* (1984).

Two additional letters by Heloise also survive. They emanate from manuscripts independent of those at her convent of the Paraclete: one is to Peter the Venerable (pp. 224–5) and the other to Abelard. The latter lacks its salutation and valediction and it was not translated by Radice, though she noted its description of Abelard as 'loved by many but most dearly loved by us' (p. xxxv). This letter introduces what Heloise calls 'baby questions' (*questinuculae*, a Ciceronian word) about passages in the Bible for Abelard to answer, which he duly does (often at length). Much of this work looks simplistic and it might have been ignored had it not been by Heloise and Abelard. For example, Enid McLeod in her biography of Heloise picked out question number 21: 'What does it mean when St Paul says "Pray without ceasing"?'[31] To which Abelard replies: 'Never neglect a moment when we should pray.' In fact Heloise was alluding here to a profound problem about the literal interpretation of Scripture: St Paul's words cannot be taken literally, as there would be no time for sleep or other essential needs. This is why Abelard explains that St Paul only means those times when we should be praying.

In commenting on these questions of Heloise's, McLeod says 'they afford notable evidence both of how attentively she was accustomed to read and of her profoundly critical attitude (largely the result, no doubt, of Abelard's influence)'.[32] McLeod's 'no doubt' is revealing. There is no evidence that Heloise derived her critical attitude from Abelard; on the contrary, it is more likely that she came to him with her mind 'already well stocked'. McLeod's underestimate of Heloise's abilities is comparable with Étienne Gilson's statement (likewise from the 1930s) that her ideas about love 'derived, probably through Abelard, from the writings of Cicero'. Gilson concedes that 'it is very difficult to say whether it was Heloise or Abelard who won the other over to these principles which they both ultimately held. It may well have been Abelard who first taught them to Heloise, but certainly it was she alone who really knew how to practise them.'[33] His assumptions here ('probably through Abelard' and 'It may well have been Abelard') bring his insight that it was Heloise who really mattered into line with the patriarchal presumption made over the centuries that she had to be Abelard's intellectual dependant. The extreme expression of this comes in Henry Adams's bestseller *From Mont-St-Michel to Chartres* (1905), which introduced generations of Americans to medieval culture. 'With infinite regret,' Adams wrote, 'Heloise must be left out of the story, because she was not a philosopher or a poet or an artist, but only a French woman to the last millimetre of her shadow.'[34]

It has taken a century to correct this ignorance. In 2000, fifteen essays, edited by Bonnie Wheeler, were published with the title: *Listening to Heloise: The Voice of a Twelfth-Century Woman*. 'By considering Heloise as a thinker and writer, and especially as an individual separate from Abelard,' Wheeler argues, 'this collection indicates how much more there was to Heloise's life than Abelard could have imagined.'[35] The title *Listening to Heloise* declares her to have had a distinct voice, different from Abelard's. By replacing the patriarchal presumptions of previous scholarship with a feminist ideology, today's students may recover the authentic voice of Heloise. This is the ideal to which these new studies aspire. *Listening to Heloise* gets off to a shaky start, however, by repeating the unfounded traditional presumption that Heloise was born around 1101, whereas some date in the 1090s is more likely.[36] Her date of birth is important for establishing what age she was when she married Abelard sometime around 1117 or 1118. Was she a teenage bride (which suits patriarchal interpretations of her), or was she a woman in her twenties?

From 'Listening *to* Heloise' it is a short step to 'Listening *for* Heloise'. This is done by combing through manuscripts and edited texts which are anonymous or ascribed to other authors, and reattributing them. For example, there is a poem from the *Carmina Burana* (the great thirteenth-century collection of medieval songs and poems) which F. J. E. Raby included in *The Oxford Book of Medieval Latin Verse* under the title 'Betrayed'.[37] The poem describes a woman's pregnancy, a most unusual theme for a twelfth-century Latin poet. But this woman is famous: she is 'on everyone's lips' (Latin *in ore omnium*). This phrase is likewise used by Heloise in her description of how Abelard's songs made every street resound with her name (p. 55). Furthermore, in the poem the woman's partner (Latin *amicus*, 'friend') has had to return 'into France from the ultimate limits' because of the ferocity of her father, much as Abelard needed to return from Brittany to Paris to placate Fulbert. These similarities do not prove that this poem is by Heloise, nor even that it concerns her. Nevertheless, this attribution is more convincing than Raby's explanation. He refused to admit that medieval women wrote Latin poems and so this poem could not describe a real experience, despite its being in his judgement one of the most moving poems in the *Carmina Burana*. To account for it, Raby fell back on what he called 'the hard truth' that this was a piece of school rhetoric, though the male writer succeeded in giving it 'a rather careless air of simplicity'. By 'hard truth' Raby meant that his interpretation, though laboured and implausible, conformed with the patriarchal rule that women did not write poems (like Gilson, he was writing in the 1930s).

The process of 'Listening *for* Heloise' may branch out in new directions in the coming years. There are thousands of medieval manuscripts which have never been thoroughly studied. Making a discovery is usually not a matter of finding some unknown book in a German castle or a monastery on a mountain top (shades of Umberto Eco's *The Name of the Rose*), but of looking again at well-known texts in the light of new questions. This is a painstaking business which few scholars undertake. In addition to a mastery of Latin and palaeography, researchers often need diplomatic skills in a variety of modern European languages to persuade archivists and librarians to allow them to see the documents in the first place. One area where 'Listening *for* Heloise' is already producing results is in music, where David Wulstan has argued that she is the author and composer of songs, liturgical drama and elegies previously attributed to Abelard or to unknown authors.[38] At the conference on Abelard held at Nantes (Abelard's family served the counts of Nantes) in 2001, the music and poetry of both Abelard and Heloise were highlighted.[39]

Newly Discovered Letters by Abelard and Heloise?

In 1974 Ewald Könsgen published a remarkable collection of 113 love letters in Latin between a master in France and a woman who is also well versed in philosophy.[40] The single manuscript containing these letters is entitled: 'From the letters of two lovers' (Latin *Ex epistolis duorum amantium*). This collection is therefore anonymous: it refers throughout to the two parties by an abbreviated V. (meaning *Vir*, 'Man') and M. (*Mulier*, 'Woman'). The 'From' (*Ex*) in the title is significant. Johannes de Vepria, the Cistercian monk who made this collection in the 1470s, was gathering examples of good style ('flowers' Latin masters called them) for teaching purposes. He began by excerpting only the salutations and valedictions.

Throughout all the 113 letters every salutation is different and many are very elaborate, which was useful for enlarging Latin vocabulary. Leafing through the series of letters, one can see Johannes getting interested in what the letters say as much as in their style. He begins to copy more and more of their contents including poems.

There is no way of knowing what the exemplar was like from which Johannes was copying, nor from which library his text came. He was himself a monk of Clairvaux (St Bernard's former abbey); but these letters might have originated from further afield, as it was the practice of monks to borrow books for copying. Heloise's convent of the Paraclete was only eighty miles away, so the exemplar could have come from there. Probably Johannes did not have the original letters in front of him, but some already edited version. As these letters exist only in this one manuscript, there is no way of knowing what he left out, though he was careful to indicate in his transcription whenever he did make an omission. In most of the letters he indicates no omissions, but we cannot know how many more documents in the series he ignored altogether. The text from which Johannes was copying may have contained the names of the writers and some details of their lives, which would have helped identify them. On the other hand, it is as likely that the letters were a fictitious or anonymous collection from the start. The Latin word *litterae* is ambiguous: it means 'letters' in the sense of missives, but it also means 'literature'. As in the preceding discussion of the alleged forgery of the later letters of Abelard and Heloise, it is often impossible to draw a firm line 'between fact and fiction, between reality and art'.[41]

The subtitle of Könsgen's edition asks: are these letters of Abelard and Heloise? In 1974 when this edition was published, Benton was just putting forward his argument that the later letters were forgeries. The experts were reluctant to engage in controversy on two fronts, and so Könsgen's edition was largely ignored, despite its interest in its own right – whether or not it concerned Abelard and Heloise. There the matter rested until 1999 when Constant Mews reissued the letters, together with an English translation, with the title: *The Lost Love Letters of*

Heloise and Abelard. In one of her later letters Heloise says Abelard sent her letters 'thick and fast' when he had first sought her out for sex (p. 54), and he describes in Letter 1, *Historia calamitatum*, how he had looked forward to their exchanging letters in which 'we could write many things more audaciously than we could say them' (p. 10). By entitling his edition '*The Lost Love Letters*', without Könsgen's question mark, Mews was declaring that these really were their earliest letters: 'I argue for the simplest solution, that they are indeed written by Abelard and Heloise.'[42] He and his publisher could not afford to express doubts in the title because that had consigned Könsgen's book to oblivion.

Mews's confidence in his identification stemmed from his unique knowledge. Unlike Könsgen, who had been at the start of his career, Mews had spent years editing Abelardian manuscripts, most notably the *Theologia* (published in 1987). He noticed similarities in vocabulary between the letters excerpted by Johannes de Vepria and Abelard's works. Most significantly, the Man interlocutor in the letters uses the philosophical term *indifferenter* ('indifferently') in a way that Abelard made his own.[43] (He was so proud of this that he devoted a long passage in *Historia calamitatum* to explaining it (p. 5).) Similarly the Woman interlocutor uses the novel word *scibilitas* ('knowability'), which is otherwise only known in the twelfth century in Abelard's works on logic.[44] (Possibly either Heloise or Abelard invented it.) Is the coincidental use of a few words really significant? The answer is 'Yes', when this common vocabulary is taken in conjunction with other similarities between the interlocutors and Abelard and Heloise. For example, the Man interlocutor is a great master who rouses envy in France and the Woman is addressed by him as 'the only disciple of philosophy among all the girls of our age'.[45]

Anyone challenging Mews's identification must produce a better explanation, in equal detail, for the numerous similarities between the Man and Woman interlocutors and Abelard and Heloise. The most likely counterargument is to say that these letters are a product of the schools: some teacher of the art of letter-writing invented them or adapted them; this would explain why their salutations are so elaborate and why they say so little about day-to-day life. But this argument would still have to explain how and why this hypothetical teacher of letter-writing included terms from Abelard's philosophical vocabulary. In other words, any effective challenge to Mews has to account for the positive evidence of *indifferenter* and *scibilitas* and the other words which he has highlighted. Abelard's works on logic rapidly went out of date and so these terms would only have been familiar to students during his lifetime. This hypothetical teacher of letter-writing has either therefore to be a contemporary of Abelard or someone later with a good knowledge of him – and of Heloise too. By Jean de Meun's time in 1300 some scholar in Paris might have been capable of confecting such a correspondence, not least Jean himself. But this takes us back to Silvestre's argument for John's authorship of the later letters of Abelard and Heloise, which has not proved convincing.

Instead of these alternative problematic hypotheses, it might seem best to accept Mews's 'simplest solution' that the letters excerpted by Johannes de Vepria were indeed written by Abelard and Heloise. But this is not really so simple, because there are no links between Johannes and the original missives of Abelard and Heloise. Mews likens the letters excerpted by Johannes to 'fragments of a mosaic of which only certain sections remain'.[46] One missing piece of the puzzle is: who put the letters together in the first place? Mews surmises it was Heloise and hence 'the manuscript which Johannes de Vepria transcribed appears to record Heloise's memories of her early relationship with Abelard'.[47] The idea that this manuscript records her memories is not the same as saying that it simply contains the letters of Abelard and Heloise, particularly when Mews adds: 'In a very real sense, it was a literary composition by Abelard's most distinguished student.' If these letters were a literary composition, how accurately did Heloise record them? 'We cannot say to what extent she may have edited the original messages.'[48]

Were Abelard's letters really like those of the Man interlocutor in Johannes de Vepria's version? He seems so priggish and relentlessly serious, whereas Abelard was famed as a jester. Into his lectures on logic he put the sentences 'Peter loves his girl' and 'May my girl friend come quick', presumably to get a laugh from his students at the time of his affair with Heloise.[49] Perhaps in copying his letters she left a good deal out, or even rewrote them, particularly anything that was sexually explicit (Abelard says in *Historia calamitatum* that writing would enable him to be more audacious). It does not follow from the special features of language (*indifferenter* and *scibilitas*, etc.) that 'these letters must have been written by Abelard and Heloise'.[50] As Abelard was a teacher of international renown, his philosophical vocabulary would have been familiar to a wide circle of students. He describes in *Historia calamitatum* how much they resented the deterioration in his lectures caused by his affair with Heloise (p. 11). If he could make jokes about it, so could they. Among his students later on were the satirists Berengar of Poitiers and Hilary of Orleans. Angry men like these, some of whom had already spent years in the schools, might readily have tapped into the antifeminist clerical discourse of their time to mock the love story of Abelard and Heloise. The language of the letters excerpted by Johannes de Vepria invites parody with its repeated references to honeycombs, spices, jewellery and stars. Nevertheless, when these letters are read as a whole, parody is not a sustainable explanation.

Medieval love letters in Latin are a peculiar genre of writing because it was only clerics and their dependants who wrote them. Because of clerical celibacy these were constrained relationships and they produced constrained Latin prose. Some aristocratic religious houses in France and Germany had schools connected with them, where young ladies boarded as well as boys. These women were surplus to the marriage market and were on their way to becoming nuns (where they performed a useful function for their families by controlling local religious houses). They were kept in reserve by their parents until it was clear where they were needed, either as wives and mothers or as nuns. In the interim these young people continued their education and they might even be taught by schoolmasters like male clerics. To their teachers, or to other clerical acquaintances real or imagined, the women addressed tentative letters or poems in Latin. Some of these texts may have begun in the classroom and they can read like hothouse products, straining a language which was nobody's mother tongue and which nobody spoke except in church or in the cloister. Copies of letters of this sort survive from the religious houses of Le Ronceray, Regensburg and Tegernsee:

> My mind is full of joy, my body is raised up from grief, because you – my teacher – have deigned to honour me with your love.

Some are more explicit:

> I implore you to come to the old chapel at dawn. Knock softly, for the minister stays in there. Then will the bed reveal what my heart now hides.[51]

Both parties in such relationships took considerable risks, because the girls had to remain virgins so that they kept their value in the marriage market, either as brides of noblemen or as brides of Christ. The girls' families enforced these rules even more effectively than the penalties of the Church, as the story of Abelard and Heloise amply illustrates.

The letters excerpted by Johannes de Vepria belong to this sort of clerical milieu and this genre of Latin writing. Their elaborate constructions and metaphors are consequences of writing in an alien language about feelings which clerics were not meant to articulate anyway. The Man and Woman interlocutors in the de Vepria letters may have been going through a learning process themselves: in writing Latin prose and verse, as well as in expressing their love. This matches the situation of Abelard and Heloise, as Fulbert wished him to advance her knowledge of literature. The style of the de Vepria letters may strike some modern readers as turgid, particularly on a first, cursory reading. Certainly they are different in feeling from the later correspondence of Abelard and Heloise, but the circumstances too were very different. Constant Mews has presented scholars and critics with a challenge. The evidence is strong for concluding that the de Vepria letters were originally composed by Abelard and Heloise. The considerable task that remains is to integrate this new evidence into our understanding of them both and of what really occurred when they first became lovers. The de Vepria letters will undoubtedly generate further controversy and speculation in the years to come.

It is not surprising that debates have continued over the centuries about the letters of Abelard and Heloise, nor that new ideas can emerge more than eight hundred years after their deaths. He has always been a controversial figure and she is rapidly becoming one. Perhaps he was, as St Bernard hissed, 'a man dissimilar even from himself'.[52] If so, we cannot say that anything is characteristic or uncharacteristic of him. He gave his great collection of citations from the Church Fathers the enigmatic title *Sic et Non* ('Yes and No'). Its prologue begins: 'Amid such a great mass of words, some of the statements even of the saints not only seem to differ from each other but actually to contradict one another.'[53] The bibliography on Abelard and Heloise has become comparably massive and bewildering, particularly because of the range of speculations about the identification and authenticity of their letters. Ultimately these are questions that experts cannot answer, as decisive proof – in the form of individual letters signed by them – is unlikely to come to light. The original copies of letters were usually thrown away or their parchment was recycled for other purposes. Some powerful letters from nuns from the convent of Admont in Bavaria, which are approximately contemporary with those by Heloise, have recently been recovered from fifteenth-century bookbinder's material. We should read these letters, their editor argues, 'as documents of practice that testify to the persistence of women's voices in the world beyond the cloister rather than as rhetorical exercises that echoed only within its walls'.[54]

In the prologue to *Sic et Non* Abelard proposed that his 'tender readers', by which he meant his students, should make every effort to question the contradictory sources for themselves without too much direction from their professors. He was optimistic of good results, for 'by doubting we come to inquiry and by inquiry we perceive the truth'.[55] The truth about the letters of Abelard and Heloise – and about the personalities and rich cultural heritage informing these letters – is something for their 'tender readers' today to discover.[56] Betty Radice's lively and accurate translation enables us to enter the Middle Ages and immerse ourselves in the thoughts of two remarkable people, who created a masterpiece of literature out of their suffering and injured feelings.

NOTES

1.   I owe this reference to Professor Robert Stein of the State University of New York at Purchase.

2.   D. W. Robertson, Jr, *Abelard and Heloise* (New York, 1972), pp. 216–17.

3.   M. T. Clanchy, *Abelard: A Medieval Life* (Oxford, 1997), p. 329.

4.   Radice, 1974 edition, p. 48, note 2.

5.   G. Constable, *Letters and Letter-Collections* (Turnhout, 1976), p. 34.

6.   J. T. Muckle, 'The Personal Letters Between Abelard and Heloise', *Mediaeval Studies* 15 (1953), p. 67.

7.   John F. Benton, 'Fraud, Fiction and Borrowing in the Correspondence of Abelard and Heloise', in *Pierre Abélard, Pierre le Vénérable* (Paris, 1975), p. 501; reprinted in *Culture, Power and Personality in Medieval France*, ed. T. N. Bisson (London, 1991), p. 448.

8.   Ibid. (1975), p. 501, (1991), p. 448.

9.   Ibid. (1975), p. 501, (1991), p. 448.

10.   Clanchy, *Abelard*, pp. 327–8.

11.   Ibid., pp. 18–19, 132.

12.   Ibid., pp. 133, 143.

13.   Peter Dronke, *Abelard and Heloise in Medieval Testimonies* (Glasgow, 1976), pp. 22, 49.

14.   Clanchy, *Abelard*, pp. 169–70, 277–9.

15.   Benton's arguments are set out in *Culture, Power and Personality*, chapters 24–5, pp. 475–512.

16.   C. Waddell, *The Paraclete Statutes: 'Institutiones Nostrae'* (Gethsemani Abbey, Ken., 1987), pp. 41, 53.

17.   P. von Moos, 'Post Festum', in *Petrus Abaelardus: Person, Werk und Wirkung*, ed. Rudolf Thomas (Trier, 1980), p. 84.

18.   D. E. Luscombe, 'The Correspondence of Abelard and Heloise', *Proceedings of the British Academy* 74 (1988), p. 278.

19. The current state of the forgery question is discussed by John Marenbon, 'Authenticity Revisited', in *Listening to Heloise*, ed. Bonnie Wheeler (New York, 2000), pp. 19–33.

20. Clanchy, *Abelard*, pp. 169–70, 277–80.

21. H. Silvestre, 'L'idylle d'Abélard et Héloïse: la part du roman', *Bulletin de la classe des lettres et des sciences morales et politiques* (Académie Royale de Belgique), 5th series, 71 (1985), pp. 157–200.

22. Ibid., p. 195 and note 96.

23. See Clanchy, *Abelard*, pp. 319–24.

24. St Bernard, Letters 166 and 168, in *Sancti Bernardi Opera*, ed. Jean Leclercq, C. H. Talbot, H. Rochais (Rome, 1975–7), Vol. 7, pp. 376–80, and see Clanchy, *Abelard*, p. 315.

25. Barbara Newman, 'Authority, Authenticity and the Repression of Heloise', *Journal of Medieval and Renaissance Studies* 22 (1992), p. 151.

26. Radice, 1974 edition, p. 66.

27. My translation of Peter the Venerable, Letter 115, *The Letters of Peter the Venerable*, ed. G. Constable, 2 vols. (1967), Vol. 1, p. 303, and see John O. Ward and N. Chiavaroli, 'The Young Heloise and Latin Rhetoric', in *Listening to Heloise*, ed. Wheeler, p. 60.

28. David Wulstan's translation of Peter the Venerable ('The Music of Heloise and Abelard', *Plainsong and Medieval Music* 11 (2002), p. 6), which is Letter 115, *The Letters of Peter the Venerable*, ed. Constable, Vol. 1, p. 304.

29. My translation of Hugh Metel, Letter 16, in Constant J. Mews (ed.), 'Hugh Metel, Heloise and Peter Abelard', *Viator* 32 (2001), p. 89.

30. Mews, 'Hugh Metel', pp. 67–8.

31. Enid McLeod, *Héloïse* (1938; reprinted, London, 1971), p. 184.

32. Ibid., p. 183.

33. Étienne Gilson, *Heloise and Abelard*, trans. L. K. Shook (Chicago, 1953), pp. 57, 58.

34. Henry Adams, *From Mont-St-Michel to Chartres* (1905; Harmondsworth, 1986), p. 270.

35. Bonnie Wheeler, *Listening to Heloise*, ed. Wheeler, p. xx.

36. Mary M. McLaughlin, 'Chronology', in *Listening to Heloise*, ed. Wheeler, p. xi; Constant Mews queries this birthdate, ibid., p. 37.

37. *The Oxford Book of Medieval Latin Verse* (Oxford, 1959), no. 223, pp. 330–32. Raby's comments are in *A History of Secular Latin Poetry in the Middle Ages*, 2nd edn. (Oxford,

1957), Vol. 2, pp. 274–5. I owe all this to Dr Juanita Ruys of the University of Sydney: 'Hearing Medieval Voices: Heloise and *Carmina Burana* 126', in *The Poetic and Musical Legacy of Heloise and Abelard*, ed. Marc Stewart and David Wulstan (Ottawa and Westhumble, 2003), pp. 91–9.

38. David Wulstan, '*Novi modulaminis melos*: The Music of Heloise and Abelard', *Plainsong and Medieval Music* 11 (2002), pp. 1–23, and see the articles in the same volume of this journal by Constant Mews and Juanita Ruys.

39. Jean Jolivet and Henri Habrias (eds.), *Pierre Abélard, Colloque international de Nantes* (Rennes, 2003).

40. Ewald Könsgen (ed.), *Epistolae Duorum Amantium: Briefe Abaelards und Heloises?* (Leiden, 1974).

41. Luscombe, 'The Correspondence of Abelard and Heloise', p. 278.

42. Constant J. Mews, *The Lost Love Letters of Heloise and Abelard* (New York, 1999), p. 6.

43. Ibid., pp. 124–8.

44. Ibid., pp. 129–30.

45. Ibid., p. 4, and Letter nos. 49 and 50.

46. Ibid., p. 114.

47. Ibid., p. 176.

48. Ibid., p. 143.

49. Clanchy, *Abelard*, pp. 112–13.

50. Mews, *Lost Love Letters*, p. 143.

51. Peter Dronke, *Medieval Latin and the Rise of the European Love-Lyric*, 2nd edn. (Oxford, 1968), pp. 424, 426, and see C. Stephen Jaeger, *Ennobling Love* (Philadelphia, 1999), pp. 74–8.

52. Clanchy, *Abelard*, p. 18.

53. The prologue to *Sic et Non*, in *Medieval Literary Theory and Criticism*, trans. by A. J. Minnis and A. B. Scott (Oxford, 1988), pp. 87–100.

54. Alison I. Beach, 'Voices from a Distant Land: Fragments of a Twelfth-Century Nuns' Letter Collection', *Speculum* 77 (2002), p. 52.

55. Prologue to *Sic et Non*, p. 99.

56. While this introduction was in the press, Peter von Moos published 'Die *Epistolae duorum amantium* und die säkulare Religion der Liebe', *Studi Medievali*, 3rd series, i (June 2003), pp. 1–115. He argues that the letters excerpted by Johannes de Vepria derive from the teaching of letter-writing in the schools and not from Abelard and Heloise. I am grateful to Professor von Moos for sending me a copy of this article.

Further Reading

STUDIES OF ABELARD AND HELOISE

Burge, James, *Heloise and Abelard* (London, 2003)

Dronke, Peter, *Abelard and Heloise in Medieval Testimonies* (Glasgow, 1976); reprinted in his *Intellectuals and Poets in Medieval Europe* (Rome, 1992), pp. 247–94

Gilson, Étienne, *Heloise and Abelard*, trans. L. K. Shook (Chicago, 1953)

Godman, Peter, *Paradoxes of Conscience in the High Middle Ages: Abelard, Heloise and the Archpoet* (Cambridge, 2009)

McLeod, Enid, *Héloïse: a Biography* (London, 1938, reprinted 1971)

Mews, Constant J., *Abelard and Heloise* (New York, 2005)

Mews, Constant J., *The Lost Love Letters of Heloise and Abelard*, second edition (New York, 2008)

Pernoud, Regine, *Heloise and Abelard*, trans. P. Wiles (London, 1973)

Stewart, Marc and Wulstan, David, (eds.), *The Poetic and Musical Legacy of Heloise and Abelard* (Ottawa and Westhumble, 2003)

Waddell, Helen, *Peter Abelard* [a novel] (London, 1933)

Wheeler, Bonnie, (ed.), *Listening to Heloise: the Voice of a Twelfth-Century Woman* (New York, 2000)

OTHER TRANSLATIONS OF THE LETTERS OF ABELARD AND HELOISE

Levitan, William, *Abelard and Heloise: the Letters and Other Writings* (Indianapolis, 2007)

Luscombe, David, *The Letter Collection of Peter Abelard and Heloise*, translation by Betty Radice revised by David Luscombe (Oxford, 2013)

McLaughlin, Mary M. and Wheeler, Bonnie, *The Letters of Heloise and Abelard* (New York, 2009)

[These three translations provide alternative readings and additional materials which supplement the Penguin Classics edition.]

THE DEBATE ABOUT THE 'LOST LOVE LETTERS' OF HELOISE AND ABELARD

Dronke, Peter and Orlandi, Giovanni, 'New Works by Abelard and Heloise?', *Filologia Mediolatina* 12 (2005), pp. 123–77

Marenbon, John, 'Lost Love Letters? A Controversy in Retrospect', *International Journal of the Classical Tradition* 15 (2008), pp. 267–80

Mews, Constant J., 'Discussing Love: the *Epistolae Duorum Amantium* and Abelard's *Sic et Non*', *Journal of Medieval Latin* 19 (2009), pp. 130–47

Newman, Barbara, *Making Love in the Twelfth Century: 'Letters of Two Lovers' in Context* (Philadelphia, 2016)

THE HISTORICAL AND LITERARY CONTEXT OF ABELARD AND HELOISE

Blamires, Alcuin, *The Case for Women in Medieval Culture* (Oxford, 1997)

Brooke, Christopher, *The Medieval Idea of Marriage* (Oxford, 1989)

Brower, Jeffrey E. and Guilfoy, Kevin (eds.), *The Cambridge Companion to Abelard* (Cambridge, 2004)

Cartlidge, Neil, *Medieval Marriage: Literary Approaches, 1100-1300* (Cambridge, 1997)

Cartwright, Steven R., *Peter Abelard, Commentary on the Epistle to the Romans* (Washington D.C., 2011)

Churchill, Laurie J., Brown, Phyllis R. and Jeffrey, Jane E.

(eds.), *Women Writing Latin: Vol. 2, Medieval Women Writing Latin* (New York, 2002)

Clanchy, Michael T., *Abelard: a Medieval Life* (Oxford, 1997)

Constable, Giles, *Letters and Letter Collections* (Turnhout, 1976)

Dronke, Peter, *Women Writers of the Middle Ages* (Cambridge, 1984)

Gurevich, Aaron, *The Origins of European Individualism* (Oxford, 1995)

Jaeger, C. Stephen, *Ennobling Love* (Philadelphia, 1999)

Luscombe, David, *Medieval Thought* (Oxford, 1997)

Luscombe, David, *The School of Peter Abelard* (Cambridge, 1969)

Marenbon, John, *Medieval Philosophy: an Historical and Philosophical Introduction* (London, 2007)

Marenbon, John, *The Philosophy of Peter Abelard* (Cambridge, 1997)

Mews, Constant J., Nederman Cary J. and Thomson, Rodney M., *Rhetoric and Renewal in the Latin West: Essays in Honour of John O. Ward* (Turnhout, 2003)

Moore, R. I., *The War on Heresy* (London, 2012)

Morris, Colin, *The Discovery of the Individual* 1050-1200 (Toronto, 1991)

Pelikan, Jaroslav, *The Growth of Medieval Theology, 600-1300* (Chicago, 1978)

Ruys, Juanita F., *The Repentant Abelard: Family, Gender and Ethics in Peter Abelard's* Carmen ad Astralabium *and* Planctus (New York, 2014).

Southern, R. W., *Scholastic Humanism and the Unification of Europe: Vol. 1, Foundations* (Oxford, 1995)

Spade, Paul V., *Peter Abelard, Ethical Writings* (Indianapolis, 1995)

Swanson, R. N., *The Twelfth-Century Renaissance* (Manchester, 1999)

Sweeney, Eileen C., *Logic, Theology and Poetry in Boethius, Abelard and Alan of Lille* (New York, 2006)

Ziolkowski, Jan M., *Letters of Peter Abelard, Beyond the Personal* (Washington D.C., 2008)

The Letters of
Abelard and Heloise

LETTER I

HISTORIA CALAMITATUM

Abelard to a Friend: *The Story of His Misfortunes*

There are times when example is better than precept for stirring or soothing human feelings; and so I propose to follow up the words of consolation I gave you in person with the history of my own misfortunes, hoping thereby to give you comfort in absence. In comparison with my trials you will see that your own are nothing, or only slight, and will find them easier to bear.[1]

I was born on the borders of Brittany, about eight miles I think to the east of Nantes, in a town called Le Pallet.[2] I owe my volatile temperament to my native soil and ancestry and also my natural ability for learning. My father had acquired some knowledge of letters before he was a knight, and later on his passion for learning was such that he intended all his sons to have instruction in letters before they were trained to arms. His purpose was fulfilled. I was his first-born,[3] and being specially dear to him had the greatest care taken over my education. For my part, the more rapid and easy my progress in my studies, the more eagerly I applied myself, until I was so carried away by my love of learning that I renounced the glory of a military life, made over my inheritance and rights of the eldest son to my brothers, and withdrew from the court of Mars in order to be educated in the lap of Minerva.[4] I preferred the weapons of dialectic to all the other teachings of philosophy, and armed with these I chose the conflicts of disputation instead of the trophies of war. I began to travel about in several provinces disputing, like a true peripatetic philosopher, wherever I had heard there was keen interest in the art of dialectic.[5]

At last I came to Paris, where dialectic had long been particularly flourishing, and joined William of Champeaux[6] who at the time was the supreme master of the subject, both in reputation and in fact. I stayed in his school for a time, but though he welcomed me at first he soon took a violent dislike to me because I set out to refute some of his arguments and frequently reasoned against him. On several occasions I proved myself his superior in debate. Those who were considered the leaders among my fellow-students were also annoyed, and the more so as they looked on me as the youngest and most recent pupil. This was the beginning of the misfortunes which have dogged me to this day, and as my reputation grew, so other men's jealousy was aroused.

It ended by my setting my heart on founding a school of my own, young as I was and estimating my capacities too highly for my years; and I had my eye on a site suited to my purpose – Melun, an important town at that time and a royal residence.[7] My master suspected my intentions, and in an attempt to remove my school as far as possible from his own, before I could leave him he secretly used every means he could to thwart my plans and keep me from the place I had chosen. But among the powers in the land he had several enemies, and these men helped me to obtain my desire. I also won considerable support simply through his unconcealed jealousy. Thus my school had its start and my reputation for dialectic began to spread, with the result that the fame of my old fellow-students and even that of the master himself gradually declined and came to an end. Consequently my self-confidence rose still higher, and I made haste to transfer my school to Corbeil, a town nearer Paris, where I could embarrass him through more frequent encounters in disputation.

However, I was not there long before I fell ill through over-work and was obliged to return home. For some years, being remote from France,[8] I was sought out more ardently by those eager for instruction in dialectic. A few years later, when I had long since recovered my health, my teacher William, archdeacon of Paris, changed his former status and joined the order of the Canons Regular,[9] with the intention, it was said, of gaining promotion to a higher prelacy through a reputation for increased piety. He was soon successful when he was made bishop of

Châlons. But this change in his way of life did not oblige him either to leave Paris or to give up his study of philosophy, and he soon resumed his public teaching in his usual manner in the very monastery to which he had retired to follow the religious life. I returned to him to hear his lectures on rhetoric, and in the course of our philosophic disputes I produced a sequence of clear logical arguments to make him amend, or rather abandon, his previous attitude to universals. He had maintained that in the common existence of universals, the whole species was essentially the same in each of its individuals, and among these there was no essential difference, but only variety due to multiplicity of accidents. Now he modified his view in order to say that it was the same not in essence but through non-difference.[10] This has always been the dialectician's chief problem concerning universals, so much so that even Porphyry did not venture to settle it when he deals with universals in his *Isagoge*,[11] but only mentioned it as a 'very serious difficulty'. Consequently, when William had modified or rather been forced to give up his original position, his lectures fell into such contempt that he was scarcely accepted on any other points of dialectic, as if the whole subject rested solely on the question of universals.

My own teaching gained so much prestige and authority from this that the strongest supporters of my master who had hitherto been the most violent among my attackers now flocked to join my school. Even William's successor[12] as head of the Paris school offered me his chair so that he could join the others as my pupil, in the place where his master and mine had won fame. Within a few days of my taking over the teaching of dialectic, William was eaten up with jealousy and consumed with anger to an extent it is difficult to convey, and, being unable to control the violence of his resentment for long, he made another artful attempt to banish me. I had done nothing to justify his acting openly against me, so he launched an infamous attack on the man who had put me in his chair, in order to remove the school from him and put it in the hands of one of my rivals. I then returned to Melun and set up my school there as before; and the more his jealousy pursued me, the more widely my reputation spread, for, as the poet says:

Envy seeks the heights, the winds sweep the summits.[13]

But not long after when he heard that there was considerable doubt about his piety amongst the majority of thoughtful men, and a good deal of gossip about his conversion, as it had not led to his departure from Paris, he removed himself and his little community, along with his school, to a village some distance from the city. I promptly returned to Paris from Melun, hoping for peace henceforth from him, but since he had filled my place there, as I said, by one of my rivals, I took my school outside the city to Mont-Sainte-Geneviève,[14] and set up camp there in order to lay siege to my usurper. The news brought William back to Paris in unseemly haste to restore such scholars as remained to him and his community to their former monastery, apparently to deliver from my siege the knight whom he had abandoned. But his good intentions did the man very serious harm. He had previously had a few pupils of a sort, largely because of his lectures on Priscian,[15] for which he had some reputation, but as soon as his master arrived he lost them all and had to retire from keeping a school. Soon afterwards he appeared to lose hope of future worldly fame, and he too was converted to the monastic life. The bouts of argument which followed William's return to the city between my pupils and him and his followers, and the successes in these battles which fortune gave my people (myself among them) are facts which you have long known. And I shall not go too far if I boldly say with Ajax that

If you demand the issue of this fight,
I was not vanquished by my enemy.[16]

Should I keep silence, the facts cry out and tell the outcome.

Meanwhile my dearest mother Lucie begged me to return home, for after my father Berengar's entry into monastic life she was preparing to do the same. When she had done so I returned to France, with the special purpose of studying divinity, to find my master William (whom I have often mentioned) already installed as bishop of Châlons. However, in this field his own master, Anselm of Laon,[17] was then the greatest authority because of his great age.

I therefore approached this old man, who owed his reputation more to long practice than to intelligence or memory. Anyone who knocked at his door to seek an answer to some question went away more uncertain than he came. Anselm could win the admiration of an audience, but he was useless when put to the question. He had a remarkable command of words but their meaning was worthless and devoid of all sense. The fire he kindled filled his house with smoke but did not light it up; he was a tree in full leaf which could be seen from afar, but on closer and more careful inspection proved to be barren. I had come to this tree to gather fruit, but I found it was the fig tree which the Lord cursed, or the ancient oak to which Lucan compares Pompey:

> There stands the shadow of a noble name,
> Like a tall oak in a field of corn.[18]

Once I discovered this I did not lie idle in his shade for long. My attendance at his lectures gradually became more and more irregular, to the annoyance of some of his leading pupils, who took it as a sign of contempt for so great a master. They began secretly to turn him against me, until their base insinuations succeeded in rousing his jealousy. One day it happened that after a session of Sentences[19] we students were joking amongst ourselves, when someone rounded on me and asked what I thought of the reading of the Holy Scriptures, when I had hitherto studied only philosophy. I replied that concentration on such reading was most beneficial for the salvation of the soul, but that I found it most surprising that for educated men the writings or glosses of the Fathers themselves were not sufficient for interpreting their commentaries without further instruction. There was general laughter, and I was asked by many of those present if I could or would venture to tackle this myself. I said I was ready to try if they wished. Still laughing, they shouted 'Right, that's settled! Take some commentary on a little-known text and we'll test what you say.' Then they all agreed on an extremely obscure prophecy of Ezekiel. I took the commentary and promptly invited them all to hear my interpretation the very next day. They then pressed unwanted advice on me, telling me not to hurry over something so important but to remember my inexperience and give longer thought to working out and confirming my exposition. I replied indignantly that it was not my custom to benefit by practice, but I relied on my own intelligence, and either they must come to my lecture at the time of my choosing or I should abandon it altogether.

At my first lecture there were certainly not many people present, for everyone thought it absurd that I could attempt this so soon, when up to now I had made no study at all of the Scriptures. But all those who came approved, so that they commended the lecture warmly, and urged me to comment on the text on the same lines as my lecture. The news brought people who had missed my first lecture flocking to the second and third ones, all alike most eager to make copies of the glosses which I had begun with on the first day.

Anselm was now wildly jealous, and being already set against me by the suggestions of some of his pupils, as I said before, he began to attack me for lecturing on the Scriptures in the same way as my master William had done previously over philosophy. There were at this time two outstanding students in the old man's school, Alberic of Rheims and Lotulf of Lombardy,[20] whose hostility to me was intensified by the good opinion they had of themselves. It was largely through their insinuations, as was afterwards proved, that Anselm lost his head and curtly forbade me to continue my work of interpretation in the place where he taught,[21] on the pretext that any mistake which I might write down through lack of training in the subject would be attributed to him. When this reached the ears of the students, their indignation knew no bounds – this was an act of sheer spite and calumny, such as had never been directed at anyone before; but the more open it was, the more it brought me renown, and through persecution my fame increased.

A few days after this I returned to Paris, to the school which had long ago been intended for and offered to me,[22] and from which I had been expelled at the start. I remained in possession there in peace for several years, and as soon as I began my course of teaching I set myself to complete the commentaries on Ezekiel which I had started at Laon. These proved so popular with their readers that they judged my reputation to stand as high for my interpretation of the Scriptures as it had previously done for philosophy. The numbers in the school increased enormously as the students gathered there eager for instruction in both subjects, and the wealth and fame this brought me must be well known to you.

But success always puffs up fools with pride, and worldly security weakens the spirit's resolution and easily destroys it through carnal temptations. I began to think myself the only philosopher in the world, with nothing to fear from anyone, and so I yielded to the lusts of the flesh. Hitherto I had been entirely continent, but now the further I advanced in philosophy and theology, the further I fell behind the philosophers and holy Fathers in the impurity of my life. It is well known that the philosophers, and still more the Fathers, by which is meant those who have devoted themselves to the teachings of Holy Scripture, were especially glorified by their chastity. Since therefore I was wholly enslaved to pride and lechery, God's grace provided a remedy for both these evils, though not one of my choosing: first for my lechery by depriving me of those organs with which I practised it, and then for the pride which had grown in me through my learning – for in the words of the Apostle, 'Knowledge breeds conceit' – when I was humiliated by the burning of the book[23] of which I was so proud.

The true story of both these episodes I now want you to know from the facts, in their proper order, instead of from hearsay. I had always held myself aloof from unclean association with prostitutes, and constant application to my studies had prevented me from frequenting the society of gentlewomen: indeed, I knew little of the secular way of life. Perverse Fortune flattered me, as the saying goes, and found an easy way to bring me toppling down from my pedestal, or rather, despite my overbearing pride and heedlessness of the grace granted me, God's compassion claimed me humbled for Himself.

There was in Paris at the time a young girl named Heloise,[24] the niece of Fulbert, one of the canons, and so much loved by him that he had done everything in his power to advance her education in letters. In looks she did not rank lowest, while in the extent of her learning she stood supreme. A gift for letters is so rare in women that it added greatly to her charm and had made her most renowned throughout the realm. I considered all the usual attractions for a lover and decided she was the one to bring to my bed, confident that I should have an easy success; for at that time I had youth and exceptional good looks as well as my great reputation to recommend me, and feared no rebuff from any woman I might choose to honour with my love. Knowing the girl's knowledge and love of letters I thought she would be all the more ready to consent, and that even when separated we could enjoy each other's presence by exchange of written messages in which we could write many things more audaciously than we could say them, and so need never lack the pleasures of conversation.

All on fire with desire for this girl I sought an opportunity of getting to know her through private daily meetings and so more easily winning her over; and with this end in view I came to an arrangement with her uncle, with the help of some of his friends, whereby he should take me into his house, which was very near my school, for whatever sum he liked to ask. As a pretext I said that my household cares were hindering my studies and the expense was more than I could afford. Fulbert dearly loved money, and was moreover always ambitious to further his niece's education in letters, two weaknesses which made it easy for me to gain his consent and obtain my desire: he was all eagerness for my money and confident that his niece would profit from my teaching. This led him to make an urgent request which furthered my love and fell in with my wishes more than I had dared to hope; he gave me complete charge over the girl, so that I could devote all the leisure time left me by my school to teaching her by day and night, and if I found her idle I was to punish her severely. I was amazed by his simplicity – if he had entrusted a tender lamb to a ravening wolf it would not have surprised me more. In handing her over to me to punish as well as to teach, what else was he doing but giving me complete freedom to realize my desires, and providing an opportunity, even if I did not make use of it, for me to bend her to my will by threats and blows if persuasion failed? But there were two special reasons for his freedom from base suspicion: his love for his niece and my previous reputation for continence.

Need I say more? We were united, first under one roof, then in heart; and so with our lessons as a pretext we abandoned ourselves entirely to love. Her studies allowed us to withdraw in private, as love desired, and then with our books open before us, more words of love than of our reading passed between us, and more kissing than teaching. My hands strayed oftener to her bosom than to the pages; love drew our eyes to look on each other more than reading kept them on our texts. To avert suspicion I sometimes struck her, but these blows were prompted by love and tender feeling rather than anger and irritation, and were sweeter than any balm could be. In short, our desires left no stage of lovemaking untried, and if love could devise something new, we welcomed it. We entered on each joy the more eagerly for our previous inexperience, and were the less easily sated.

Now the more I was taken up with these pleasures, the less time I could give to philosophy and the less attention I paid to my school. It was utterly boring for me to have to go to the school, and equally wearisome to remain there and to spend my days on study when my nights were sleepless with lovemaking. As my interest and concentration flagged, my lectures lacked all inspiration and were merely repetitive; I could do no more than repeat what had been said long ago, and when inspiration did come to me, it was for writing love songs, not the secrets of philosophy. A lot of these songs, as you know, are still popular and sung in many places,[25] particularly by those who enjoy the kind of life I led. But the grief and sorrow and laments of my students when they realized my preoccupation, or rather, distraction of mind are hard to realize. Few could have failed to notice something so obvious, in fact no one, I fancy, except the man whose honour was most involved – Heloise's uncle. Several people tried on more than one occasion to draw his attention to it, but he would not believe them; because, as I said, of his boundless love for his niece and my well-known reputation for chastity in my previous life. We do not easily think ill of those whom we love most, and the taint of suspicion cannot exist along with warm affection. Hence the remark of St Jerome in his letter to Sabinian: 'We are always the last to learn of evil in our own home, and the faults of our wife and children may be the talk of the town but do not reach our ears.'[26]

But what is last to be learned is somehow learned eventually, and common knowledge cannot easily be hidden from one individual. Several months passed and then this happened in our case. Imagine the uncle's grief at the discovery, and the lovers' grief too at being separated! How I blushed with shame and contrition for the girl's plight, and what sorrow she suffered at the thought of my disgrace! All our laments were for one another's troubles, and our distress was for each other, not for ourselves. Separation drew our hearts still closer while frustration inflamed our passion even more; then we became more abandoned as we lost all sense of shame and, indeed, shame diminished as we found more opportunities for lovemaking. And so we were caught in the act as the poet says happened to Mars and Venus.[27] Soon afterwards the girl found that she was pregnant, and immediately wrote me a letter full of rejoicing to ask what I thought she should do. One night then, when her uncle was away from home, I removed her secretly from his house, as we had planned, and sent her straight to my own country. There she stayed with my sister until she gave birth to a boy, whom she called Astralabe.[28]

On his return her uncle went almost out of his mind – one could appreciate only by experience his transports of grief and mortification. What action could he take against me? What traps could he set? He did not know. If he killed me or did me personal injury, there was the danger that his beloved niece might suffer for it in my country. It was useless to try to seize me or confine me anywhere against my will, especially as I was very much on guard against this very thing, knowing that he would not hesitate to assault me if he had the courage or the means.

In the end I took pity on his boundless misery and went to

him, accusing myself of the deceit love had made me commit as if it were the basest treachery. I begged his forgiveness and promised to make any amends he might think fit. I protested that I had done nothing unusual in the eyes of anyone who had known the power of love, and recalled how since the beginning of the human race women had brought the noblest men to ruin. Moreover, to conciliate him further, I offered him satisfaction in a form he could never have hoped for: I would marry the girl I had wronged. All I stipulated was that the marriage should be kept secret so as not to damage my reputation.[29] He agreed, pledged his word and that of his supporters, and sealed the reconciliation I desired with a kiss. But his intention was to make it easier to betray me.

I set off at once for Brittany and brought back my friend to make her my wife. But she was strongly opposed to the proposal, and argued hotly against it for two reasons: the risk involved and the disgrace to myself. She swore that no satisfaction could ever appease her uncle, as we subsequently found out. What honour could she win, she protested, from a marriage which would dishonour me and humiliate us both? The world would justly exact punishment from her if she removed such a light from its midst. Think of the curses, the loss to the Church and grief of philosophers which would greet such a marriage! Nature had created me for all mankind – it would be a sorry scandal if I should bind myself to a single woman and submit to such base servitude. She absolutely rejected this marriage; it would be nothing but a disgrace and a burden to me. Along with the loss to my reputation she put before me the difficulties of marriage, which the apostle Paul exhorts us to avoid when he says: 'Has your marriage been dissolved? Do not seek a wife. If, however, you do marry, there is nothing wrong in it; and if a virgin marries, she has done no wrong. But those who marry will have pain and grief in this bodily life, and my aim is to spare you.' And again: 'I want you to be free from anxious care.'[30]

But if I would accept neither the advice of the Apostle nor the exhortations of the Fathers on the heavy yoke of marriage, at least, she argued, I could listen to the philosophers, and pay regard to what had been written by them or concerning them on this subject – as for the most part the Fathers too have carefully done when they wish to rebuke us. For example, St Jerome in the first book of his *Against Jovinian* recalls how Theophrastus sets out in considerable detail the unbearable annoyances of marriage and its endless anxieties, in order to prove by the clearest possible arguments that a man should not take a wife; and he brings his reasoning from the exhortations of the philosophers to this conclusion: 'Can any Christian hear Theophrastus argue in this way without a blush?' In the same book Jerome goes on to say that 'After Cicero had divorced Terentia and was asked by Hirtius to marry his sister he firmly refused to do so, on the grounds that he could not devote his attention to a wife and philosophy alike. He does not simply say "devote attention", but adds "alike", not wishing to do anything which would be a rival to his study of philosophy.'[31]

But apart from the hindrances to such philosophic study, consider, she said, the true conditions for a dignified way of life. What harmony can there be between pupils and nursemaids, desks and cradles, books or tablets and distaffs, pen or stylus and spindles? Who can concentrate on thoughts of Scripture or philosophy and be able to endure babies crying, nurses soothing them with lullabies, and all the noisy coming and going of men and women about the house? Will he put up with the constant muddle and squalor which small children bring into the home? The wealthy can do so, you will say, for their mansions and large houses can provide privacy and, being rich, they do not have to count the cost nor be tormented by daily cares. But philosophers lead a very different life from rich men, and those who are concerned with wealth or are involved in mundane matters will not have time for the claims of Scripture or philosophy. Consequently, the great philosophers of the past have despised the world, not renouncing it so much as escaping from it, and have denied themselves every pleasure so as to find peace in the arms of philosophy alone. The greatest of them, Seneca, gives this advice to Lucilius: 'Philosophy is not a subject for idle moments. We must neglect everything else and concentrate on this, for no time is long enough for it. Put it aside for a moment, and you might as well give it up, for once interrupted it will not remain. We must resist all other occupations, not merely dispose of them but reject them.'[32]

This is the practice today through love of God of those among us who truly deserve the name of monks,[33] as it was of distinguished philosophers amongst the pagans in their pursuit of philosophy. For in every people, pagan, Jew or Christian, some men have always stood out for their faith or upright way of life, and have cut themselves off from their fellows because of their singular chastity or austerity. Amongst the Jews in times past there were the Nazirites,[34] who dedicated themselves to the Lord according to the Law, and the sons of the prophets, followers of Elijah or Elisha, whom the Old Testament calls monks, as St Jerome bears witness;[35] and in more recent times the three sects of philosophers described by Josephus in the eighteenth book of his *Antiquities*, the Pharisees, Sadducees and Essenes.[36] Today we have the monks who imitate either the communal life of the apostles or the earlier, solitary life of John. Among the pagans, as I said, are the philosophers: for the name of wisdom or philosophy used to be applied not so much to acquisition of learning as to a religious way of life, as we learn from the first use of the word itself and from the testimony of the saints themselves. And so St Augustine, in the eighth book of his *City of God*, distinguishes between types of philosopher:

> The Italian school was founded by Pythagoras of Samos, who is said to have been the first to use the term philosophy; before him men were called 'sages' if they seemed outstanding for some praiseworthy manner of life. But when Pythagoras was asked his profession, he replied that he was a philosopher, meaning a devotee or lover of wisdom, for he thought it too presumptuous to call himself a sage.[37]

So the phrase 'if they seemed outstanding for some praiseworthy manner of life' clearly proves that the sages of the pagans, that is, the philosophers, were so called as a tribute to their way of life, not to their learning. There is no need for me to give examples of their chaste and sober lives – I should seem to be teaching Minerva herself. But if pagans and laymen could live in this way, though bound by no profession of religion, is there not a greater obligation on you, as clerk and canon, not to put base pleasures before your sacred duties, and to guard against being sucked down headlong into this Charybdis,[38] there to lose all sense of shame and be plunged forever into a whirlpool of impurity? If you take no thought for the privilege of a clerk, you can at least uphold the dignity of the philosopher, and let a love of propriety curb your shamelessness if the reverence due to God means nothing to you. Remember Socrates' marriage and the sordid episode whereby he did at least remove the slur it cast on philosophy by providing an example to be a warning to his successors. This too was noted by Jerome, when he tells this tale of Socrates in the first book of his *Against Jovinian*: 'One day after he had withstood an endless stream of invective which Xanthippe poured out from a window above his head, he felt himself soaked with dirty water. All he did was to wipe his head and say: "I knew that thunderstorm would lead to rain."'[39]

Heloise went on to the risks I should run in bringing her back, and argued that the name of friend [*amica*] instead of wife would be dearer to her and more honourable for me – only love freely given should keep me for her, not the constriction of a marriage tie, and if we had to be parted for a time, we should find the joy of being together all the sweeter the rarer our meetings were. But at last she saw that her attempts to persuade or dissuade me were making no impression on my foolish obstinacy, and she could not bear to offend me; so amidst deep sighs and tears she ended in these words: 'We shall both be destroyed. All that is left us is suffering as great as our love has been.' In this, as the whole world knows, she showed herself a true prophet.

And so when our baby son was born we entrusted him to my sister's care and returned secretly to Paris. A few days later, after a night's private vigil of prayer in a certain church, at dawn we were joined in matrimony in the presence of Fulbert and some of his, and our, friends. Afterwards we parted secretly and went our ways unobserved. Subsequently our meetings were few and furtive, in order to conceal as far as possible what we had done. But Fulbert and his household, seeking satisfaction for the dishonour done to him, began to spread the news of the marriage and break the promise of secrecy they had given me. Heloise cursed them and swore that there was no truth in this, and in his exasperation Fulbert heaped abuse on her on several occasions. As soon as I discovered this I removed her to a convent of nuns in the town near Paris called Argenteuil, where she had been brought up and educated as a small girl, and I also had made for her a religious habit of the type worn by novices, with the exception of the veil, and made her put it on.[40]

At this news her uncle and his kinsmen and followers imagined that I had tricked them, and had found an easy way of ridding myself of Heloise by making her a nun. Wild with indignation they swore an oath against me, and one night as I slept peacefully in an inner room in my lodgings, they bribed one of my servants to admit them, and there they punished me with a most cruel and shameful vengeance of such appalling barbarity as to shock the whole world; they cut off the parts of my body whereby I had committed the wrong of which they complained. Then they fled, but the two who could be caught were blinded and castrated as I had been, one of them being the servant who had been led by greed while in my service to betray his master.

Next morning the whole city gathered before my house, and the scene of horror and amazement, mingled with lamentations, cries and groans which exasperated and distressed me, is difficult, no, impossible, to describe. In particular, the clerks and, most of all, my pupils tormented me with their unbearable weeping and wailing until I suffered more from their sympathy than from the pain of my wound, and felt the misery of my mutilation less than my shame and humiliation.[41] All sorts of thoughts filled my mind – how brightly my reputation had shone, and now how easily in an evil moment it had been dimmed or rather completely blotted out; how just a judgement of God had struck me in the parts of the body with which I had sinned, and how just a reprisal had been taken by the very man I had myself betrayed. I thought how my rivals would exult over my fitting punishment, how this bitter blow would bring lasting grief and misery to my friends and parents, and how fast the news of this unheard-of disgrace would spread over the whole

world. What road could I take now? How could I show my face
in public, to be pointed at by every finger, derided by every
tongue, a monstrous spectacle to all I met? I was also appalled
to remember that according to the cruel letter of the Law, a
eunuch is such an abomination to the Lord that men made
eunuchs by the amputation or mutilation of their members are
forbidden to enter a church as if they were stinking and unclean,
and even animals in that state are rejected for sacrifice. 'Ye shall
not present to the Lord any animal if its testicles have been
bruised or crushed, torn or cut.' 'No man whose testicles have
been crushed or whose organ has been severed shall become a
member of the assembly of the Lord.'[42]

I admit that it was shame and confusion in my remorse
and misery rather than any devout wish for conversion which
brought me to seek shelter in a monastery cloister. Heloise had
already agreed to take the veil in obedience to my wishes and
entered a convent. So we both put on the religious habit, I in
the abbey of St Denis,[43] and she in the convent of Argenteuil
which I spoke of before. There were many people, I remember,
who in pity for her youth tried to dissuade her from submitting
to the yoke of monastic rule as a penance too hard to bear, but
all in vain; she broke out as best she could through her tears and
sobs into Cornelia's famous lament:

> O noble husband,
> Too great for me to wed, was it my fate
> To bend that lofty head? What prompted me
> To marry you and bring about your fall?
> Now claim your due, and see me gladly pay . . .[44]

So saying she hurried to the altar, quickly took up the veil
blessed by the bishop and publicly bound herself to the religious
life.

I had still scarcely recovered from my wound when the clerks
came thronging round to pester the abbot and myself with
repeated demands that I should now for love of God continue
the studies which hitherto I had pursued only in desire for wealth
and fame. They urged me to consider that the talent entrusted

to me by God would be required of me with interest;[45] that instead of addressing myself to the rich as before I should devote myself to educating the poor, and recognize that the hand of the Lord had touched me for the express purpose of freeing me from the temptations of the flesh and the distractions of the world so that I could devote myself to learning, and thereby prove myself a true philosopher not of the world but of God.

But the abbey to which I had withdrawn was completely worldly and depraved, with an abbot whose pre-eminent position was matched by his evil living and notorious reputation. On several occasions I spoke out boldly in criticism of their intolerably foul practices, both in private and in public, and made myself such a burden and nuisance to them all that they gladly seized on the daily importunities of my pupils as a pretext for having me removed from their midst. As pressure continued for some time and these demands became insistent, my abbot and the monks intervened, and I retired to a cell[46] where I could devote myself to teaching as before; and there my pupils gathered in crowds until there were too many for the place to hold or the land to support.

I applied myself mainly to study of the Scriptures as being more suitable to my present calling, but I did not wholly abandon the instruction in the profane arts in which I was better practised and which was most expected of me. In fact I used it as a hook, baited with a taste of philosophy, to draw my listeners towards the study of the true philosophy – the practice of the greatest of Christian philosophers, Origen, as recorded by Eusebius in his *History of the Christian Church*.[47] When it became apparent that God had granted me the gift for interpreting the Scriptures as well as secular literature, the numbers in my school began to increase for both subjects, while elsewhere they diminished rapidly. This roused the envy and hatred of the other heads of schools against me; they set out to disparage me in whatever way they could, and two of them[48] especially were always attacking me behind my back for occupying myself with secular literature[49] in a manner totally unsuitable to my monastic calling, and for presuming to set up as a teacher of sacred learning when I had had no teacher myself. Their aim was for every form of teaching in a school to be forbidden me, and for this end they were always trying to win over bishops, archbishops, abbots, in fact anyone of account in the Church whom they could approach.

Now it happened that I first applied myself to lecturing on the basis of our faith by analogy with human reason, and composed a theological treatise on divine unity and trinity[50] for the use of my students who were asking for human and logical reasons on this subject, and demanded something intelligible rather than mere words. In fact they said that words were useless if the intelligence could not follow them, that nothing could be believed unless it was first understood, and that it was absurd for anyone to preach to others what neither he nor those he taught could grasp with the understanding: the Lord himself had criticized such 'blind guides of blind men'.[51] After the treatise had been seen and read by many people it began to please everyone, as it seemed to answer all questions alike on this subject. It was generally agreed that the questions were peculiarly difficult and the importance of the problem was matched by the subtlety of my solution.

My rivals were therefore much annoyed and convened a Council against me, prompted by my two old opponents, Alberic and Lotulf who, now that our former masters, William and Anselm, were dead, were trying to reign alone in their place and succeed them as their heirs. Both of them were heads of the school in Rheims, and there, by repeated insinuations, they were able to influence their archbishop, Ralph, to take action against me and, along with Conan, bishop of Palestrina, who held the office of papal legate in France at the time, to convene an assembly,[52] which they called a Council, in the city of Soissons, where I was to be invited to come bringing my treatise on the Trinity. This was done, but before I could make my appearance, my two rivals spread such evil rumours about me amongst the clerks and people that I and the few pupils who had accompanied me narrowly escaped being stoned by the people on the first day we arrived, for having preached and written (so they had been told) that there were three Gods.

I called on the legate as soon as I entered the town, handed him a copy of the treatise for him to read and form an opinion, and declared myself ready to receive correction and make amends if I had written anything contrary to the Catholic faith. But he told me at once to take the book to the archbishop and my opponents, so that my accusers could judge me themselves and the words 'Our enemies are judges'[53] be fulfilled in me. However, though they read and reread the book again and again they could find nothing they dared charge me with at an open hearing, so they adjourned the condemnation they were panting for until the final meeting of the Council. For my part, every day before the Council sat, I spoke in public on the Catholic faith in accordance with what I had written, and all who heard me were full of praise both for my exposition and for my interpretation. When the people and clerks saw this they began to say ' "Here he is, speaking openly,"[54] and no one utters a word against him. The Council which we were told was expressly convened against him is quickly coming to an end. Can the judges have found that the error is theirs, not his?' This went on every day and added fuel to my enemies' fury.

And so one day Alberic sought me out with some of his followers, intent on attacking me. After a few polite words he remarked that something he had noticed in the book had puzzled him very much; namely, that although God begat God, and there is only one God, I denied that God had begotten Himself. I said at once that if they wished I would offer an explanation on this point. 'We take no account of rational explanation,' he answered, 'nor of your interpretation in such matters; we recognize only the words of authority.' 'Turn the page,' I said, 'and you will find the authority.' There was a copy of the book at hand, which he had brought with him, so I looked up the passage which I knew but which he had failed to see – or else he looked only for what would damage me. By God's will I found what I wanted at once: a sentence headed 'Augustine, *On the Trinity*, Book One'. 'Whoever supposes that God has the power to beget Himself is in error, and the more so because it is not only God who lacks this power, but also any spiritual or corporeal creature. There is nothing whatsoever which can beget itself.'[55]

When his followers standing by heard this they blushed in embarrassment, but he tried to cover up his mistake as best he could by saying that this should be understood in the right way. To that I replied that it was nothing new, but was irrelevant at the moment as he was looking only for words, not interpretation. But if he was willing to hear an interpretation and a reasoned argument I was ready to prove to him that by his own words he had fallen into the heresy of supposing the Father to be His own Son. On hearing this he lost his temper and turned to threats, crying that neither my explanations nor my authorities would help me in this case. He then went off.

On the last day of the Council, before the session was resumed, the legate and the archbishop began to discuss at length with my opponents and other persons what decision to take about me and my book, as this was the chief reason for their being convened. They could find nothing to bring against me either in my words or in the treatise which was before them, and everyone stood silent for a while or began to retract his accusation, until Geoffrey, bishop of Chartres,[56] who was outstanding among the other bishops for his reputation for holiness and the importance of his see, spoke as follows:

All of you, Sirs, who are here today know that this man's teaching, whatever it is, and his intellectual ability have won him many followers and supporters wherever he has studied. He has greatly lessened the reputation both of his own teachers and of ours, and his vine has spread its branches from sea to sea.[57] If you injure him through prejudice, though I do not think you will, you must know that even if your judgement is deserved you will offend many people, and large numbers will rally to his defence; especially as in this treatise before us we can see nothing which deserves any public condemnation. Jerome has said that 'Courage which is unconcealed always attracts envy, and lightning strikes the mountain-peaks.'[58] Beware lest violent action on your part brings him even more renown, and we are more damaged ourselves for our envy than he is through the justice of the charge. Jerome also reminds us that 'A false rumour is soon stifled, and a man's later life passes judgement on his past.'[59] But if you are determined to act canonically against him, let his teaching or his writing be put before us, let him be questioned and allowed to give free reply, so that if he is convicted or confesses his error he can be totally silenced. This will at least be in accordance with the words of holy Nicodemus, when he wished to set free the Lord himself: 'Does our law permit us to pass judgement on a man unless we have first given him a hearing and learned the facts?'[60]

At once my rivals broke in with an outcry: 'Fine advice that is, to bid us compete with the ready tongue of a man whose arguments and sophistries could triumph over the whole world!' (But it was surely far harder to compete with Christ, and yet Nicodemus[61] asked for him to be given a hearing, as sanctioned by the law.) However, when the bishop could not persuade them to agree to his proposal, he tried to curb their hostility by other means, saying that the few people present were insufficient for discussing a matter of such importance, and this case needed longer consideration. His further advice was that my abbot, who was present, should take me back to my monastery, the Abbey of St Denis, and there a larger number of more learned men should be assembled to go into the case thoroughly and decide what was to be done. The legate agreed with this last suggestion, and so did everyone else. Soon after, the legate rose to celebrate Mass before he opened the Council. Through Bishop Geoffrey he sent me the permission agreed on: I was to return to my monastery and await a decision.

Then my rivals, thinking that they had achieved nothing if this matter were taken outside their diocese, where they would have no power to use force – it was plain that they had little confidence in the justice of their cause – convinced the archbishop that it would be an insult to his dignity if the case were transferred and heard elsewhere, and a serious danger if I were allowed to escape as a result. They hurried to the legate, made him reverse his decision and persuaded him against his better judgement to condemn the book without any inquiry, burn it immediately in the sight of all and condemn me to perpetual confinement in a different monastery. They said that the fact that I had dared to read the treatise in public and must have allowed many people to make copies without its being approved by the authority of the Pope[62] or the Church should be quite enough to condemn it, and that the Christian faith would greatly benefit if an example were made of me and similar presumption in many others were forestalled. As the legate was less of a scholar than he should have been, he relied largely on the advice of the archbishop, who in turn relied on theirs. When the bishop of Chartres saw what would happen he told me at once about their intrigues and strongly urged me not to take it too hard, as by now it was apparent to all that they were acting too harshly. He said I could be confident that such violence so clearly prompted by jealousy would discredit them and benefit me, and told me not to worry about being confined in a monastery as he knew that the papal legate was only acting under pressure, and would set me quite free within a few days of his leaving Soissons. So he gave me what comfort he could, both of us shedding tears.

I was then summoned and came at once before the Council. Without any questioning or discussion they compelled me to throw my book into the fire with my own hands, and so it was burnt. But so that they could appear to have something to say, one of my enemies muttered that he understood it was written in the book that only God the Father was Almighty. Overhearing this, the legate replied in great surprise that one would scarcely believe a small child could make such a mistake, seeing that it is a professed tenet of our common faith that there are three Almighties. Thereupon the head of a school, Thierry by name,[63] laughed and quoted the words of Athanasius: 'And yet there are not three Almighties, but one Almighty.'[64] His bishop spoke sharply to him and rebuked him for contempt of court, but he boldly stood his ground and, in the words of Daniel: ' "Are you such fools, you Israelites, thus to condemn a woman of Israel, without making careful inquiry and finding out the truth? Reopen the trial," '[65] he said, 'and judge the judge himself. You appointed this judge for the establishment of the Faith and the correction of error; but the person who should be doing the judging has condemned himself out of his own mouth. Today God in his mercy clearly acquits this innocent man as he delivered Susanna of old from the hands of her false accusers!'

Then the archbishop rose to his feet and confirmed the opinion of the legate, changing only the wording, as was needed. 'Truly, my lord,' he said, 'the Father is Almighty, the Son is Almighty and the Holy Spirit is Almighty, and whoever does not share this belief is clearly in error and should not be heard. And now, with your permission, it would be proper for our brother to profess his faith before us all, so that it may be duly approved or disapproved and corrected.' I then stood up to make a full profession of my faith and explain what I felt in my own words, but my enemies declared that it was only necessary for me to recite the Athanasian Creed[66] – as any boy could do. They even had the text put before me to read in case I should plead ignorance, as though I were not familiar with the words. I read it out as best I could through my tears, choked with sobs. Then I was handed over as if guilty and condemned to the abbot of St Médard,[67] who was present, and taken off to his cloister as if to prison. The Council then immediately dispersed.

The abbot and monks of St Médard welcomed me most warmly and treated me with every consideration, thinking that I should remain with them in future. They tried hard to comfort me, but in vain. God who judges equity, with what bitterness of spirit and anguish of mind did I reproach you in my madness and accuse you in my fury, constantly repeating the lament of St Antony[68] – 'Good Jesus, where were you?' All the grief and indignation, the blushes for shame, the agony of despair I suffered then I cannot put into words. I compared my present plight with my physical suffering in the past, and judged myself the unhappiest of men. My former betrayal seemed small in comparison with the wrongs I now had to endure, and I wept much more for the injury done to my reputation than for the damage to my body, for that I had brought upon myself through my own fault, but this open violence had come upon me only because of the purity of my intentions and love of our Faith which had compelled me to write.

But as the news spread and everyone who heard it began to condemn outright this wanton act of cruelty, the persons who had been present tried to shift the blame on to others; so much so that even my rivals denied it had been done on their advice, and the legate publicly denounced the jealousy of the French in this affair. He soon regretted his conduct and, some days later, feeling that he had satisfied their jealousy at a time when under constraint, he had me brought out of St Médard and sent back to my own monastery, where, as I said above, nearly all the monks who were there before were now my enemies; for their disgraceful way of life and scandalous practices made them deeply suspicious of a man whose criticisms they could ill endure.

A few months later chance gave them the opportunity to work for my downfall. It happened that one day in my reading I came across a statement of Bede, in his *Commentary on the Acts of the Apostles*,[69] which asserted that Dionysius the Areopagite was bishop of Corinth, not of Athens. This seemed in direct contradiction to their claim that their patron Denis is to be identified with the famous Areopagite[70] whose history shows him to have been bishop of Athens. I showed my discovery, by way of a joke, to some of the brothers who were standing by, as evidence from Bede which was against us. They were very much annoyed and said that Bede was a complete liar and they had a more truthful witness in their own abbot Hilduin,[71] who had spent a long time travelling in Greece to investigate the matter; he had found out the truth and removed all shadow of doubt in the history of the saint which he had compiled himself. Then one of them abruptly demanded my opinion on the discrepancy between Bede and Hilduin. I replied that the authority of Bede, whose writings are accepted by the entire Latin Church, carried more weight with me.[72]

In their fury at this answer they began to cry that now I had openly revealed myself as the enemy of the monastery, and was moreover a traitor to the whole country[73] in seeking to destroy the glory that was its special pride by denying that their patron was the Areopagite. I said that I had not denied it, nor did it much matter whether he was the Areopagite[74] or came from somewhere else, seeing that he had won so bright a crown in the eyes of God. However, they hurried straight to the abbot and told him what they accused me of. He was only too ready to listen and delighted to seize the opportunity to destroy me,[75] for he had the greater reason to fear me as his own life was even more scandalous than that of the rest. He summoned his council, and the chapter of the brethren, and denounced me severely, saying that he would send me straightaway to the king for punishment on the charge of having designs on the royal dignity and crown. Meanwhile he put me under close surveillance until I could be handed over to the king. I offered to submit myself to the discipline of the Rule if I had done wrong, but in vain.

I was so horrified by their wickedness and in such deep despair after having borne the blows of fortune so long, feeling that the whole world had conspired against me, that with the help of a few brothers who took pity on me and the support of some of my pupils I fled secretly in the night, and took refuge in the neighbouring territory of Count Theobald,[76] where once before I had stayed in a priory. I was slightly acquainted with the Count personally, and he had heard of my afflictions and took pity on me. There I began to live in the town of Provins,[77] in a community of monks from Troyes whose prior had long been my close friend and loved me dearly. He was overjoyed by my arrival and made every provision for me.

But one day it happened that the abbot of St Denis came to the town to see Count Theobald on some personal business; on hearing this, I approached the count, along with the prior, and begged him to intercede for me with the abbot and obtain his pardon and permission to live a monastic life wherever a suitable place could be found. The abbot and those with him took counsel together on the matter, so as to give the count their answer the same day, before they left. On deliberation they formed the opinion that my intention was to be transferred to another abbey and that this would be a great reproach to them, for they considered that I had brought them great glory when I entered the religious life by coming to them in preference to all other abbeys, and now it would be a serious disgrace if I cast them off and went elsewhere. Consequently they would not hear a word on the subject either from the count or from me. Moreover they threatened me with excommunication if I did not return quickly, and absolutely forbade the prior with whom I had taken refuge to keep me any longer, under penalty of sharing my excommunication.

Both the prior and I were very much alarmed at this. The abbot departed, still in the same mind, and a few days later he died. When his successor was appointed,[78] I met him with the bishop of Meaux, hoping that he would grant what I had sought from his predecessor. He too was unwilling to do so at first; but through the intervention of some of my friends I appealed to the king and his council, and so got what I wanted. A certain Stephen,[79] the king's seneschal at the time, summoned the abbot and his supporters and asked why they wished to hold me against my will when this could easily involve them in scandal and do no good, as my life and theirs could never possibly agree. I knew that the opinion of the king's council was that the more irregular an abbey was, the more reason why it should be subject to the king and bring him profit, at least as regards its worldly goods, and this made me think that I should easily win the consent of the king and his council – which I did. But so that the monastery should not lose the reputation gained from having me as a member, I was given permission to withdraw to any retreat I liked, provided that I did not come under the authority of any abbey. This was agreed and confirmed on both sides in the presence of the king and his council.

And so I took myself off to a lonely spot I had known before in the territory of Troyes, and there, on a piece of land given me, by leave of the local bishop, I built a sort of oratory[80] of reeds and thatch and dedicated it in the name of the Holy Trinity. Here I could stay hidden alone but for one of my clerks, and truly cry out to the Lord 'Lo, I escaped far away and found a refuge in the wilderness.'[81]

No sooner was this known than the students began to gather there from all parts, hurrying from cities and towns to inhabit the wilderness, leaving large mansions to build themselves little huts, eating wild herbs and coarse bread instead of delicate food, spreading reeds and straw in place of soft beds and using banks of turf for tables. They could rightly be thought of as imitating the early philosophers, of whom Jerome in the second book of his *Against Jovinian* says:

The senses are like windows through which the vices gain entry into the soul. The capital and citadel of the spirit cannot be taken except by a hostile army entering through the gates. If anyone takes pleasure in the circus and athletic contests, an actor's pantomime or a woman's beauty, the splendour of jewels and garments or anything of that sort, the liberty of his soul is captured through the window of the eye, and the word of the prophet is fulfilled: 'Death has climbed in through our windows.'[82] So when the marshalled forces of distraction have marched through these gates into the citadel of the soul, where will its liberty be and its fortitude? Where will be its thoughts of God? Especially when sensibility pictures for itself pleasures of the past and by recalling its vices compels the soul to take part in them and, as it were, to practise what it does not actually do. These are the considerations which have led many philosophers to leave crowded cities and the gardens outside them, where they find that water meadows and leafy trees, twittering of birds, reflections in spring waters and murmuring brooks are so many snares for eye and ear; they fear that amidst all this abundance of riches the strength of the soul will weaken and its purity be soiled. No good comes from looking often on what may one day seduce you, and in exposing yourself to the temptation of what you find it difficult to do without. Indeed, the Pythagoreans used to shun this kind of contact and lived in solitude in the desert. Plato himself was a wealthy man (and his couch was trampled on by Diogenes with muddy feet),[83] yet in order to give all his time to philosophy he chose to set up his Academy some way from the city on a site which was unhealthy as well as deserted, so that the perpetual preoccupation of sickness would break the assaults of lust, and his pupils would know no pleasures but what they had from their studies.[84]

Such too was the life that the sons of the prophets, the followers of Elisha, are said to have led, of whom (amongst other things)

Jerome writes to the monk Rusticus, as if they were the monks
of their time, that 'The sons of the prophets, who are called
monks in the Old Testament, built themselves huts by the river
Jordan, and abandoned city crowds to live on barley meal and
wild herbs.'[85] My pupils built themselves similar huts on the
banks of the Ardusson, and looked like hermits rather than
scholars.

But the greater the crowds of students who gathered there
and the harder the life they led under my teaching, the more my
rivals thought this brought honour to me and shame upon
themselves. They had done all they could to harm me, and now
they could not bear to see things turning out for my advantage;
and so, in the words of Jerome: 'Remote as I was from cities,
public affairs, law-courts and crowds, envy (as Quintilian says)
sought me out in my retreat.'[86] They brooded silently over their
wrongs, and then began to complain ' "Why, all the world has
gone after him" '[87] – we have gained nothing by persecuting him,
only increased his fame. We meant to extinguish the light of his
name but all we have done is make it shine still brighter. See
how the students have everything they need at hand in the cities,
but they scorn the comforts of civilization, flock to the barren
wilderness and choose this wretched life of their own accord.'

Now it was sheer pressure of poverty at the time which
determined me to open a school, since I was 'not strong enough
to dig and too proud to beg';[88] so I returned to the skill which I
knew, and made use of my tongue instead of working with my
hands. For their part, my pupils provided all I needed unasked,[89]
food, clothing, work on the land as well as building expenses,
so that I should not be kept from my studies by domestic cares
of any kind. As my oratory could not hold even a modest
proportion of their numbers, they were obliged to enlarge it,
and improved it by building in wood and stone. It had been
founded and dedicated in the name of the Holy Trinity, but
because I had come there as a fugitive and in the depths of my
despair had been granted some comfort by the grace of God, I
named it the Paraclete,[90] in memory of this gift. Many who
heard the name were astonished, and several people violently
attacked me, on the grounds that it was not permissible for my

church to be assigned specifically to the Holy Spirit any more than to God the Father, but that it must be dedicated according to ancient custom either to the Son alone or to the whole Trinity.

This false charge doubtless arose from their mistaken belief that there was no distinction between the Paraclete and the Holy Spirit as Paraclete. In fact, the whole Trinity or any member of the Trinity may be addressed as God and Protector and equally properly be addressed as Paraclete, that is, Comforter, according to the words of the Apostle: 'Praise be to the God and Father of our Lord Jesus Christ, the all-merciful Father and the God whose consolation never fails us. He comforts us in all our troubles; and as the Truth says, "And he shall give you another to be your Comforter." '[91] When the whole Church is consecrated in the name of the Father and of the Son and of the Holy Spirit, and is in their possession indivisibly, what is to prevent the house of the Lord from being ascribed to the Father or to the Holy Spirit just as much as to the Son? Who would presume to erase the owner's name from above his door? Or again, when the Son has offered himself as a sacrifice to the Father, and consequently, in celebrations of the Mass it is the Father to whom prayers are specially directed and the Host is offered, why should the altar not properly be particularly his to whom prayer and sacrifice are specially offered? Is it any better to say that the altar belongs to him who is sacrificed than to him to whom sacrifice is made? Would anyone claim that an altar is better named after the Lord's Cross, or the Sepulchre, St Michael, St John or St Peter, or any other saint who is neither sacrificed there nor receives sacrifice, nor has prayers addressed to him? Surely even amongst the idolators, altars and temples were said to belong only to those who received sacrifice and homage. Perhaps someone may say that neither churches nor altars should be dedicated to the Father because no deed of his exists which calls for a special feast in his honour. But this argument detracts from the entire Trinity, not from the Holy Spirit, since the Holy Spirit by its coming has its own feast of Pentecost,[92] just as the Son, by his, has the feast of the Nativity; for the Holy Spirit claims its own feast by coming among the disciples just as the Son came into the world.

In fact it seems more fitting that a temple should be ascribed to the Holy Spirit than to any other member of the Trinity, if we pay careful attention to apostolic authority and the workings of the Holy Spirit itself. To none of the three does the Apostle assign a special shrine except to the Holy Spirit, for he speaks neither of a shrine of the Father nor of the Son as he does of the Holy Spirit when he writes in the First Letter to the Corinthians: 'But he who links himself with Christ is one with him, spiritually,' and again, 'Do you not know that your body is a shrine of the in-dwelling Holy Spirit, and the spirit is God's gift to you? You do not belong to yourselves.'[93] Everyone knows too that the divine benefits of the sacraments administered in the Church are ascribed particularly to the effective power of divine Grace, by which is meant the Holy Spirit. For by water and the Holy Spirit we are reborn in baptism, after which we first become a special temple for God; and in the sacrament of confirmation the sevenfold grace of the Holy Spirit is conferred on us whereby the temple of God is adorned and dedicated. Is it then surprising that we dedicate a material temple to the one to whom the Apostle has specially ascribed a spiritual one? To whom can a church be more fittingly consecrated than to the one to whose effective power all the benefits of the Church sacraments are particularly ascribed? However, in first giving my oratory the name of Paraclete I had no thought of declaring its dedication to a single person; my reason was simply what I said above – it was in memory of the comfort I had found there. But even if I had done so with the intention that was generally believed, it would not have been unreasonable, though unknown to general custom.

Meanwhile, though my person lay hidden in this place, my fame travelled all over the world, resounding everywhere like that poetic creation Echo, so called because she has so large a voice but no substance.[94] My former rivals could do nothing by themselves, and therefore stirred up against me some new apostles in whom the world had great faith.[95] One of these boasted that he had reformed the life of the Canons Regular,[96] the other the life of the monks.[97] They went up and down the country, slandering me shamelessly in their preaching as much as they could, and for a while brought me into considerable disrepute in the eyes of the ecclesiastical as well as of the secular authorities; and they spread such evil reports of my faith and of my way of life that they also turned some of my chief friends against me, while any who up till now had retained some of their old affection for me took fright and tried to conceal this as best they could. God is my witness that I never heard that an assembly of ecclesiastics had met without thinking this was convened to condemn me. I waited like one in terror of being struck by lightning to be brought before a council or synod and charged with heresy or profanity, and, if I may compare the flea with the lion, the ant with the elephant, my rivals persecuted me with the same cruelty as the heretics in the past did St Athanasius. Often, God knows, I fell into such a state of despair that I thought of quitting the realm of Christendom and going over to the heathen,[98] there to live a quiet Christian life amongst the enemies of Christ at the cost of what tribute was asked. I told myself they would receive me more kindly for having no suspicion that I was a Christian on account of the charges against me, and they would therefore believe I could more easily be won over to their pagan beliefs.

While I was continuously harassed by these anxieties and as a last resort had thought of taking refuge with Christ among Christ's enemies, an opportunity was offered me which I believed would bring me some respite from the plots against me; but in taking it I fell among Christians and monks who were far more savage and wicked than the heathen. There was in Brittany, in the diocese of Vannes, the Abbey of St Gildas de Rhuys, which the death of its abbot had left without a superior. I was invited there by the unanimous choice of the monks, with the approval of the lord of the district,[99] and permission from the abbot and brothers of my monastery was easily obtained. Thus the jealousy of the French drove me West as that of the Romans once drove St Jerome East.[100] God knows, I should never have accepted this offer had I not hoped to find some escape from the attacks which, as I said, I had perpetually to endure. The country was wild and the language unknown to me,[101] the natives were brutal and barbarous, the monks were beyond control and led a dissolute life which was well known to all. Like a man who rushes at a precipice in terror at the sword hanging over him, and at the very moment he escapes one death, meets another, I wilfully took myself from one danger to another, and there by the fearful roar of the waves of the Ocean, at the far ends of the earth where I could flee no further, I used to repeat in my prayers the words of the Psalmist: 'From the end of the earth I have called to thee when my heart was in anguish.'[102]

Everyone knows now, I think, of this anguish which my tormented heart suffered night and day at the hands of that undisciplined community I had undertaken to direct, while I thought of the dangers to my soul as well as to my body. I was certain at any rate that if I tried to bring them back to the life of Rule for which they had taken their vows it would cost me my own life; yet if I did not do my utmost to achieve this, I should be damned. In addition, the abbey had long been subject to a certain very powerful tyrant in that land who had taken advantage of the disorder in the monastery to appropriate all its adjoining lands for his own use, and was exacting heavier taxes from the monks than he would have done from Jews subject to tribute.[103] The monks beset me with demands for their daily needs, though there was no common allowance for me to distribute, but each one of them provided for himself, his concubine and his sons and daughters from his own purse. They took delight in distressing me over this, and they also stole and carried off what they could, so that when I had reached the end of my resources I should be forced to abandon my attempt at enforcing discipline or leave them altogether. The entire savage population of the area was similarly lawless and out of control; there was no one I could turn to for help since I disapproved equally of the morals of them all. Outside the monastery wall that tyrant and his minions never ceased to harry me, inside it the monks were always setting traps for me, until it seemed that the words of the Apostle applied especially to my case: 'Quarrels all round us, forebodings in our heart.'[104]

I used to weep as I thought of the wretched, useless life I led, as profitless to myself as to others; I had once done so much for the clerks, and now that I had abandoned them for the monastery, all I did for them and for the monks was equally fruitless. I had proved ineffective in all my attempts and undertakings, so that now above all men I justly merited the reproach, 'There is the man who started to build and could not finish.'[105] I was in deep despair when I remembered what I had fled from and considered what I had met with now; my former troubles were as nothing in retrospect, and I often used to groan and tell myself that I deserved my present sufferings for deserting the Paraclete, the Comforter, and plunging myself into certain desolation – in my eagerness to escape from threats I had run into actual dangers.

What tormented me most of all was the thought that in abandoning my oratory I had been unable to make proper provision for celebrating the Divine Office, since the place was so poor that it could barely provide for the needs of one man. But then again the true Paraclete himself brought me true comfort in my great distress, and provided for the oratory as was fitting, for it was his own. It happened that my abbot of St Denis by some means took possession of the Abbey of Argenteuil where Heloise – now my sister in Christ rather than my wife – had taken the veil. He claimed that it belonged to his monastery by ancient right,[106] and forcibly expelled the community of nuns, of which she was prioress, so that they were now scattered as exiles in various places. I realized that this was an opportunity sent me by the Lord for providing for my oratory, and so I returned and invited her, along with some other nuns from the same convent who would not leave her, to come to the Paraclete; and once they had gathered there,[107] I handed it over to them as a gift, and also everything that went with it. Subsequently, with the approval of the local bishop acting as intermediary, my deed of gift was confirmed by Pope Innocent the Second by charter[108] in perpetuity to them and their successors.

Their life there was full of hardship at first and for a while they suffered the greatest deprivation, but soon God, whom they served devoutly, in his mercy brought them comfort; he showed himself a true Paraclete to them too in making the local people sympathetic and kindly disposed towards them. Indeed,

I fancy that their worldly goods were multiplied more in a single year than mine would have been in a hundred, had I remained there, for a woman, being the weaker sex, is the more pitiable in a state of need, easily rousing human sympathy, and her virtue is the more pleasing to God as it is to man. And such favour in the eyes of all did God bestow on that sister of mine who was in charge of the other nuns, that bishops loved her as a daughter, abbots as a sister, the laity as a mother; while all alike admired her piety and wisdom, and her unequalled gentleness and patience in every situation. The more rarely she allowed herself to be seen (so that she could devote herself without distraction to prayer and meditation on holy things in a closed cell), the more eagerly did those outside demand her presence and her spiritual conversation for their guidance.

But then all the people in the neighbourhood began attacking me violently for doing less than I could and should to minister to the needs of the women, as (they said) I was certainly well able to do, if only through my preaching; so I started to visit them more often to see how I could help them. This provoked malicious insinuations, and my detractors, with their usual perverseness, had the effrontery to accuse me of doing what genuine charity prompted because I was still a slave to the pleasures of carnal desire and could rarely or never bear the absence of the woman I had once loved. I often repeated to myself the lament of St Jerome in his letter to Asella about false friends: 'The only fault found in me is my sex, and that only when Paula comes to Jerusalem.' And again: 'Before I knew the house of saintly Paula, my praises were sung throughout the city, and nearly everyone judged me worthy of the highest office of the Church. But I know well that it is through good and evil report that we make our way to the kingdom of heaven.'[109]

When, as I say, I recalled the injustice of such a calumny against so great a man, I took no small comfort from it. 'If my rivals,' said I, 'were to find such strong grounds for suspicion in my case, how I should suffer from their slander! But now that I have been freed from such suspicion by God's mercy, and the power to commit this sin is taken from me, how can the suspicion remain? What is the meaning of this latest monstrous accusation? My present condition removes suspicion of evil-doing so completely from everyone's mind that men who wish to keep close watch on their wives employ eunuchs, as sacred history tells us in the case of Esther and the other concubines of King Ahasuerus.[110] We also read that it was a eunuch of the Ethiopian Queen Candace, a man of authority in charge of all her treasure, whom the apostle Philip was directed by the angel to convert and baptize.[111] Such men have always held positions of responsibility and familiarity in the homes of modest and honourable women simply because they are far removed from suspicions of this kind, and it was to rid himself of it entirely, when planning to include women in his teaching of sacred learning, that the great Christian philosopher Origen laid violent hands on himself, as Book Six of the *History of the Church* relates.'[112] However, I thought that in this God's mercy had been kinder to me than to him, for he is believed to have acted on impulse and been strongly censured as a result, whereas it had happened to me through no fault of mine, but so that I might be set free for a similar work; and with all the less pain for being quick and sudden, for I was asleep when attacked and felt practically nothing.

Yet though perhaps I suffered less physical pain at the time, I am now the more distressed for the calumny I must endure. My agony is less for the mutilation of my body than for the damage to my reputation, for it is written that 'A good name is more to be desired than great riches.'[113] In his sermon *On the Life and Morals of Clerics* St Augustine remarks that 'He who relies on his conscience to the neglect of his reputation is cruel to himself,' and earlier on says: '"For our aims," as the Apostle says, "are honourable not only in God's sight but also in the eyes of men."'[114] For ourselves, our conscience within us is sufficient. For your sake, our reputation should not be sullied but should be powerful amongst you. Conscience and reputation are two different things; conscience concerns yourself, reputation your neighbour.'[115] But what would my enemies in their malice have said to Christ himself and his followers, to the prophets, the apostles or the other holy Fathers, had they lived in their times, when these men were seen with their manhood intact consorting with women on the friendliest terms? Here also St Augustine in his book *On the Work of Monks* proves that women too were the inseparable companions of our Lord Jesus Christ and the apostles, even to the extent of accompanying them on their preaching:

> To this end, faithful women who had worldly goods went with them and made provision for them so that they should lack none of the necessities of this life. If anyone does not believe that it was the practice of the apostles to take with them women of holy life wherever they preached the Gospel, he has only to hear the Gospel to know that they did this following the example of the Lord himself. For there it is written: 'After this he went journeying from town to town and village to village, proclaiming the good news of God. With him were the Twelve and a number of women who had been set free from evil spirits and infirmities: Mary, known as Mary of Magdala ... Joanna, the wife of Chuza, Herod's steward, and Susanna, and many others. These women provided for them out of their own resources.'[116]

Leo the Ninth too, in answer to a letter of Parmenian, of the monastery of Studius, says:

> We declare absolutely that no bishop, presbyter, deacon or sub-deacon may give up the care of his wife in the name of religion, so as not to provide her with food and clothing, though he may not lie with her carnally. This was the practice of the holy apostles, as we read in St Paul: 'Have I no right to take a Christian wife about with me, like the rest of the apostles and the Lord's brothers and Cephas?' Take note, you fool, that he did not say 'Have I no right to embrace a wife' but 'to take about', meaning that they should support their wives on the profit from their preaching, not that they should have further carnal intercourse with them.[117]

Certainly that Pharisee who said to himself of the Lord, 'If this man were a real prophet he would know who this woman is who touches him, and what sort of woman she is, a sinner,'[118] could have supposed far more easily, as far as human judgement goes, that the Lord was guilty of evil-living than my enemies could imagine the same of me; while anyone who saw the Lord's mother entrusted to the care of a young man or the prophets enjoying the hospitality and conversation of widows[119] would entertain far more probable suspicions. And what would my detractors have said if they had seen Malchus, the captive monk of whom St Jerome writes, living in the same home with his wife?[120] In their eyes it would have been a great crime, though the famous doctor had nothing but high praise for what he saw: 'There was an old man named Malchus there . . . a native of the place, and an old woman living in his cottage . . . Both of them were so eager for the faith, for ever wearing down the threshold of the church, that you would have thought them Zacharias and Elizabeth in the Gospel but for the fact that John was not with them.'

Finally, why do they refrain from accusing the holy Fathers themselves, when we have often read or seen how they founded monasteries for women too and ministered to them there, following the example of the seven deacons, who were appointed to wait at table and look after the women?[121] The weaker sex needs the help of the stronger, so much so that the Apostle lays down that the man must always be over the woman, as her head, and as a sign of this he orders her always to have her head covered.[122] And so I am much surprised that the custom should have been long established in convents of putting abbesses in charge of women just as abbots are set over men, and of binding women by profession according to the same rule, for there is so much in the Rule which cannot be carried out by women, whether in authority or subordinate. In several places too, the natural order is overthrown to the extent that we see abbesses and nuns ruling the clergy[123] who have authority over the people, with opportunities of leading them on to evil desires in proportion to their dominance, holding them as they do beneath a heavy yoke. The satirist has this in mind when he says that 'Nothing is more intolerable than a rich woman.'[124]

After much reflection I decided to do all I could to provide for the sisters of the Paraclete, to manage their affairs, to watch over them in person too, so that they would revere me the more, and thus to minister better to their needs. The persecution I was now suffering at the hands of the monks who were my sons was even more persistent and distressing than what I had endured previously from my brothers, so I thought I could turn to the sisters as a haven of peace and safety from the raging storms, find repose there for a while, and at least achieve something amongst them though I had failed with the monks. Indeed, the more they needed me in their weakness, the more it would benefit me.

But now Satan has put so many obstacles in my path that I can find nowhere to rest or even to live; a fugitive and wanderer I carry everywhere the curse of Cain,[125] forever tormented (as I said above) by 'quarrels all round us, forebodings in our heart', or rather, quarrels and forebodings without and within. The hostility of my sons here is far more relentless and dangerous than that of my enemies, for I have them always with me and must be forever on my guard against their treachery. I can see my enemies' violence as a danger to my person if I go outside the cloister; but it is within the cloister that I have to face the incessant assaults – as crafty as they are violent – of my sons, that is, of the monks entrusted to my care, as their abbot and father. How many times have they tried to poison me – as happened to St Benedict![126] The same reason which led him to abandon his depraved sons might well have encouraged me to follow the example of so great a Father of the Church, lest in exposing myself to certain dangers I should be thought a rash tempter rather than a true lover of God, or even appear to be my own destroyer. And while I guarded as well as I could against their daily assaults by providing my own food and drink, they tried to destroy me during the very sacrifice of the altar[127] by putting poison in the chalice. On another day, when I had gone into Nantes to visit the count who was ill, and was staying there in the home of one of my brothers in the flesh, they tried to poison me by the hand of one of the servants accompanying me, supposing, no doubt, that I should be less on my guard against a plot of that kind. By God's intervention it happened that I did not touch any of the food prepared for me. But one of the monks I had brought from the abbey, who knew nothing of their intentions, ate it and dropped dead; and the servant who had dared to do this fled in terror, as much through consciousness of his guilt as because of the evidence of his crime.

From then on their villainy was known to all, and I began to make no secret of the fact that I was avoiding their snares as well as I could; I even removed myself from the abbey and lived in small cells with a few companions. But whenever the monks heard that I was travelling anywhere they would bribe robbers and station them on the roads and byways to murder me. I was still struggling against all these perils when one day the hand of the Lord struck me sharply and I fell from my saddle, breaking my collar-bone. This fracture caused me far greater pain and weakened me more than my previous injury. Sometimes I tried to put a stop to their lawless insubordination by excommunication, and compelled those of them I most feared to promise me either on their honour or on oath taken before the rest that they would leave the abbey altogether and trouble me no more. But then they would openly and shamelessly violate both the word they had given and the oaths they had sworn, until in the end they were forced to renew their oaths on this and many other things in the presence of the count and the bishops, by authority of the Roman Pope Innocent, through his special legate[128] sent for this purpose.

Even then they would not live in peace. After those mentioned had been expelled, I recently came back to the abbey and entrusted myself to the remaining brothers from whom I thought I had less to fear. I found them even worse than the others. They did not deal with poison but with a dagger held to my throat, and it was only under the protection of a certain lord of the land that I managed to escape. I am still in danger, and every day I imagine a sword hanging over my head, so that at meals I dare scarcely breathe: like the man we read about, who supposed the power and wealth of the tyrant Dionysius to constitute the greatest happiness, until he looked up and saw a sword suspended by a thread over Dionysius's head.[129] Then he learned what sort of joy it is which accompanies earthly power. This is my experience all the time; a poor monk raised to be an abbot, the more wretched as I have become more wealthy, in order that my example may curb the ambition of those who have deliberately chosen a similar course.

Dearly beloved brother in Christ, close friend and long-standing companion, this is the story of my misfortunes which have dogged me almost since I left my cradle; let the fact that I have written it with your own affliction and the injury you have suffered in mind suffice to enable you (as I said at the beginning of this letter) to think of your trouble as little or nothing in comparison with mine, and to bear it with more patience when you can see it in proportion. Take comfort from what the Lord told his followers about the followers of the Devil: 'As they persecuted me they will persecute you. If the world hates you, it hated me first, as you know well. If you belonged to the world, the world would love its own.'[130] And the Apostle says: 'Persecution will come to all who want to live a godly life as Christians,' and elsewhere, 'Do you think I am currying favour with men? If I still sought men's favour I should be no servant of Christ.'[131] The Psalmist says that 'They are destroyed who seek to please men, since God has rejected them.'[132] It was with this particularly in mind that St Jerome, whose heir I consider myself as regards slanders and false accusations, wrote in his letter to Nepotian: ' "If I still sought men's favour," says the Apostle, "I should be no servant of Christ." He has ceased to seek men's favour and is become the servant of Christ.'[133] He also wrote to Asella, concerning false friends, 'Thank God I have deserved the hatred of the world,' and to the monk Heliodorus: 'You are wrong, brother, wrong if you think that the Christian can ever be free of persecution. Our adversary "like a roaring lion, prowls around, seeking someone to devour", and do you think of peace? "He sits in ambush with the rich." '[134]

Let us then take heart from these proofs and examples, and bear our wrongs the more cheerfully the more we know they are undeserved. Let us not doubt that if they add nothing to our merit, at least they contribute to the expiation of our sins. And since everything is managed by divine ordinance, each one of the faithful, when it comes to the test, must take comfort at least from the knowledge that God's supreme goodness allows nothing to be done outside his plan, and whatever is started wrongly, he himself brings it to the best conclusion. Hence in all things it is right to say to him, 'Thy will be done.'[135] Finally, think what consolation comes to those who love God on the authority of the Apostle, who says: 'As we know, all things work together for good for those who love God.'[136] This is what the wisest of mankind had in mind when he said in his *Proverbs*: 'Whatever befalls the righteous man it shall not sadden him.'[137] Here he clearly shows that those who are angered by some personal injury, though they well know it has been laid on them by divine dispensation, leave the path of righteousness and follow their own will rather than God's; they rebel in their secret hearts against the meaning of the words 'Thy will be done', and set their own will above the will of God. Farewell.

THE PERSONAL LETTERS

LETTER 2
HELOISE TO ABELARD

To her lord, or rather father; to her husband, or rather brother; from his handmaid, or rather daughter; from his wife, or rather sister: to Abelard, from Heloise.

Not long ago, my beloved, by chance someone brought me the letter of consolation you had sent to a friend. I saw at once from the superscription that it was yours, and was all the more eager to read it since the writer is so dear to my heart. I hoped for renewal of strength, at least from the writer's words which would picture for me the reality I have lost. But nearly every line of this letter was filled, I remember, with gall and wormwood, as it told the pitiful story of our entry into religion and the cross of unending suffering which you, my only love, continue to bear.

In that letter you did indeed carry out the promise you made your friend at the beginning, that he would think his own troubles insignificant or nothing, in comparison with your own. First you revealed the persecution you suffered from your teachers, then the supreme treachery of the mutilation of your person, and then described the abominable jealousy and violent attacks of your fellow-students, Alberic of Rheims and Lotulf of Lombardy. You did not gloss over what at their instigation was done to your distinguished theological work or what amounted to a prison sentence passed on yourself. Then you went on to the plotting against you by your abbot and false brethren, the serious slanders from those two pseudo-apostles, spread against you by the same rivals, and the scandal stirred up among many people because you had acted contrary to custom in naming your oratory after the Paraclete. You went on to the incessant, intolerable persecutions which you still endure at the hands of that cruel tyrant and the evil monks you call your sons, and so brought your sad story to an end.

No one, I think, could read or hear it dry-eyed; my own sorrows are renewed by the detail in which you have told it, and redoubled because you say your perils are still increasing. All of us here are driven to despair of your life, and every day we await in fear and trembling the final word of your death. And so in the name of Christ, who is still giving you some protection for his service, we beseech you to write as often as you think fit to us who are his handmaids and yours, with news of the perils in which you are still storm-tossed. We are all that are left you, so at least you should let us share your sorrow or your joy.

It is always some consolation in sorrow to feel that it is shared, and any burden laid on several is carried more lightly or removed. And if this storm has quietened down for a while, you must be all the more prompt to send us a letter which will be the more gladly received. But whatever you write about will bring us no small relief in the mere proof that you have us in mind. Letters from absent friends are welcome indeed, as Seneca himself shows us by his own example when he writes these words in a passage of a letter to his friend Lucilius:

> Thank you for writing to me often, the one way in which you can make your presence felt, for I never have a letter from you without the immediate feeling that we are together. If pictures of absent friends give us pleasure, renewing our memories and relieving the pain of separation even if they cheat us with empty comfort, how much more welcome is a letter which comes to us in the very handwriting of an absent friend.[1]

Thank God that here at least is a way of restoring your presence to us which no malice can prevent, nor any obstacle hinder; then do not, I beseech you, allow any negligence to hold you back.

You wrote your friend a long letter of consolation, prompted no doubt by his misfortunes, but really telling of your own. The detailed account you gave of these may have been intended for his comfort, but it also greatly increased our own feeling of desolation; in your desire to heal his wounds you have dealt us fresh wounds of grief as well as re-opening the old. I beg you, then, as you set about tending the wounds which others have dealt, heal the wounds you have yourself inflicted. You have done your duty to a friend and comrade, discharged your debt to friendship and comradeship, but you have bound yourself by a greater debt to us who can properly be called not friends so much as dearest friends, not comrades but daughters, or any other conceivable name more tender and holy. How great the debt by which you have bound yourself to us needs neither proof nor witness, were it in any doubt; if everyone kept silent, the facts themselves would cry out.[2] For you after God are the sole founder of this place, the sole builder of this oratory, the sole creator of this community. You have built nothing here upon another man's foundation.[3] Everything here is your own creation. This was a wilderness open to wild beasts and brigands, a place which had known no home nor habitation of men. In the very lairs of wild beasts and lurking-places of robbers, where the name of God was never heard, you built a sanctuary to God and dedicated a shrine in the name of the Holy Spirit. To build it you drew nothing from the riches of kings and princes, though their wealth was great and could have been yours for the asking: whatever was done, the credit was to be yours alone. Clerks and scholars came flocking here, eager for your teaching, and ministered to all your needs; and even those who had lived on the benefices of the Church and knew only how to receive offerings, not to make them, whose hands were held out to take but not to give, became pressing in their lavish offers of assistance.

And so it is yours, truly your own, this new plantation for God's purpose, but it is sown with plants which are still very tender and need watering if they are to thrive. Through its feminine nature this plantation would be weak and frail even if it were not new; and so it needs a more careful and regular cultivation, according to the words of the Apostle: 'I planted the seed and Apollos watered it; but God made it grow.'[4] The

Apostle through the doctrine that he preached had planted and established in the faith the Corinthians, to whom he was writing. Afterwards the Apostle's own disciple, Apollos, had watered them with his holy exhortations and so God's grace bestowed on them growth in the virtues. You cultivate a vineyard of another's vines which you did not plant yourself and which has now turned to bitterness against you,[5] so that often your advice brings no result and your holy words are uttered in vain. You devote your care to another's vineyard; think what you owe to your own. You teach and admonish rebels to no purpose, and in vain you cast pearls of divine eloquence before swine.[6] While you spend so much on the stubborn, consider what you owe to the obedient; you are so generous to your enemies but should reflect on how you are indebted to your daughters. Apart from everything else, consider the close tie by which you have bound yourself to me, and repay the debt you owe a whole community of devoted women by discharging it the more dutifully to her who is yours alone.

Your superior wisdom knows better than our humble learning of the many serious treatises which the holy Fathers compiled for the instruction or exhortation or even the consolation of holy women, and of the care with which these were composed. And so in the precarious early days of our conversion long ago I was not a little surprised and troubled by your forgetfulness, when neither reverence for God nor our mutual love nor the example of the holy Fathers made you think of trying to comfort me, wavering and exhausted as I was by prolonged grief, either by word when I was with you or by letter when we had parted.[7] Yet you must know that you are bound to me by an obligation which is all the greater for the further close tie of the marriage sacrament uniting us, and are the deeper in my debt because of the love I have always borne you, as everyone knows, a love which is beyond all bounds.

You know, beloved, as everyone knows, how much I have lost in you, how at one wretched stroke of fortune that supreme act of flagrant treachery robbed me of my very self in robbing me of you; and how my sorrow for my loss is nothing compared with what I feel for the manner in which I lost you. Surely the greater the cause for grief the greater the need for the help of consolation, and this no one can bring but you; you are the sole cause of my sorrow, and you alone can grant me the grace of consolation. You alone have the power to make me sad, to bring me happiness or comfort; you alone have so great a debt to repay me, particularly now when I have carried out all your orders so implicitly that when I was powerless to oppose you in anything, I found strength at your command to destroy myself. I did more, strange to say – my love rose to such heights of madness that it robbed itself of what it most desired beyond hope of recovery, when immediately at your bidding I changed my clothing along with my mind, in order to prove you the sole possessor of my body and my will alike.

God knows I never sought anything in you except yourself; I wanted simply you, nothing of yours. I looked for no marriage-bond, no marriage portion, and it was not my own pleasures and wishes I sought to gratify, as you well know, but yours. The name of wife may seem more sacred or more binding, but sweeter for me will always be the word friend [*amica*], or, if you will permit me, that of concubine or whore. I believed that the more I humbled myself on your account, the more gratitude I should win from you, and also the less damage I should do to the brightness of your reputation.

You yourself on your own account did not altogether forget this in the letter of consolation I have spoken of which you wrote to a friend; there you thought fit to set out some of the reasons I gave in trying to dissuade you from binding us together in an ill-starred marriage. But you kept silent about most of my arguments for preferring love to wedlock and freedom to chains. God is my witness that if Augustus, Emperor of the whole world, thought fit to honour me with marriage and conferred all the earth on me to possess for ever, it would be dearer and more honourable to me to be called not his Empress but your whore.

For a person's worth does not rest on wealth or power; these depend on fortune, but worth on its merits. And a woman should realize that if she marries a rich man more readily than a poor one, and desires her husband more for his possessions than for himself, she is offering herself for sale. Certainly any woman who comes to marry through desires of this kind deserves wages, not gratitude, for clearly her mind is on the man's property, not himself, and she would be ready to prostitute herself to a richer man, if she could. This is evident from the argument put forward, in the dialogue of Aeschines Socraticus, by the philosopher Aspasia to Xenophon and his wife. When she had expounded it in an effort to bring about a reconciliation between them, this philosopher ended with these words: 'Unless you come to believe that there is no better man nor worthier woman on earth you will always still be looking for what you judge the best thing of all – to be the husband of the best of wives and the wife of the best of husbands.'[8]

These are saintly words which are more than philosophic; indeed, they deserve the name of wisdom, not philosophy. It is a holy error and a blessed delusion between man and wife that perfect love can keep the ties of marriage unbroken not so much through bodily continence as chastity of spirit. But what error permitted other women, plain truth permitted me, and what they thought of their husbands, the world in general believed, or rather, knew to be true of yourself; so that my love for you was the more genuine for being further removed from error. What king or philosopher could match your fame? What district, town or village did not long to see you? When you appeared in public, who – I ask – did not hurry to catch a glimpse of you, or crane her neck and strain her eyes to follow your departure? Every wife, every young girl desired you in absence and was on fire in your presence; queens and great ladies envied me my joys and my bed.

In you, I readily admit, there were two things especially, with which you could immediately win the heart of any woman – the gift of composing and the gift of singing.[9] We know that the other philosophers achieved no success in these things, whereas for you they served as a kind of game, as a recreation from the labour and exertion of philosophy. You have left many songs composed in amatory verse or rhyme. Because of the great sweetness of their poetry as much as of their tunes, they have been frequently sung and they kept your name unceasingly on everyone's lips. The beauty of the melodies ensured that even those who knew no Latin did not forget you; more than anything this made women sigh for love of you. And as most of these songs told of our love, they soon made me widely known and roused the envy of many women against me. For your manhood was adorned by every grace of mind and body, and among the women who envied me then, could there be one now who does not feel compelled by my misfortune to sympathize with my loss of such joys? Who is there who was once my enemy, whether man or woman, who is not moved now by the compassion which is my due? Wholly guilty though I am, I am also, as you know, wholly innocent. It is not the deed but the intention of the doer which makes the crime, and justice should weigh not what was done but the spirit in which it is done.[10] What my intention towards you has always been, you alone who have known it can judge. I submit all to your scrutiny, yield to your testimony in all things.

Tell me one thing, if you can. Why, after our entry into religion, which was your decision alone, have I been so neglected and forgotten by you that I have neither a word from you when you are here to give me strength nor the consolation of a letter in absence?[11] Tell me, I say, if you can – or I will tell you what I think and indeed everyone suspects. It was desire, not affection which bound you to me, the flame of lust rather than love. So when the end came to what you desired, any show of feeling you used to make went with it. This is not merely my own opinion, beloved, it is everyone's. There is nothing personal or private about it; it is the general view which is widely held. I only wish that it *were* mine alone, and that the love you professed could find someone to defend it and so comfort me in my grief for a while. I wish I could think of some explanation which would excuse you and somehow cover up the way you hold me cheap.

I beg you then to listen to what I ask – you will see that it is a small favour which you can easily grant. While I am denied your presence, give me at least through your words – of which you have enough and to spare – some sweet semblance of yourself. It is no use my hoping for generosity in deeds if you are grudging in words. Up to now I had thought I deserved much of you, seeing that I carried out everything for your sake and continue up to the present moment in complete obedience to you. It was not any sense of vocation which brought me as a young girl to accept the austerities of the cloister, but your bidding alone, and if I deserve no gratitude from you, you may judge for yourself how my labours are in vain. I can expect no reward for this from God, for it is certain that I have done nothing as yet for love of him. When you hurried towards God I followed you, indeed, I went first to take the veil – perhaps you were thinking how Lot's wife turned back[12] when you made me put on the religious habit and take my vows before you gave yourself to God. Your lack of trust in me over this one thing, I confess, overwhelmed me with grief and shame. I would have had no hesitation, God knows, in following you or going ahead at your bidding to the flames of Hell.[13] My heart was not in me but with you, and now, even more, if it is not with you it is nowhere; truly, without you it cannot exist. See that it fares well with you, I beg, as it will if it finds you kind, if you give grace in return for grace,[14] small for great, words for deeds. If only your love had less confidence in me, my dear, so that you would be more concerned on my behalf! But as it is, the more I have made you feel secure in me, the more I have to bear with your neglect.

Remember, I implore you, what I have done, and think how much you owe me. While I enjoyed with you the pleasures of the flesh, many were uncertain whether I was prompted by love or lust; but now the end is proof of the beginning. I have finally denied myself every pleasure in obedience to your will, kept nothing for myself except to prove that now, even more, I am yours. Consider then your injustice, if when I deserve more you give me less, or rather, nothing at all, especially when it is a small thing I ask of you and one you could so easily grant. And so, in the name of that God to whom you have dedicated yourself, I beg you to restore your presence to me in the way you can – by writing me some word of comfort, so that in this at least I may find increased strength and readiness to serve God. When in the past you sought me out for sinful pleasures your letters came to me thick and fast, and your many songs put your Heloise on everyone's lips, so that every street and house resounded with my name. Is it not far better now to summon me to God than it was then to satisfy our lust? I beg you, think what you owe me, give ear to my pleas, and I will finish a long letter with a brief ending: farewell, my only love.

LETTER 3
ABELARD TO HELOISE

To Heloise, his dearly beloved sister in Christ, from Abelard her brother in Him.

If since our conversion from the world to God I have not yet written you any word of comfort or advice, it must not be attributed to indifference on my part but to your own good sense, in which I have always had such confidence that I did not think anything was needed; God's grace has bestowed on you all essentials to enable you to instruct the erring, comfort the weak and encourage the faint-hearted, both by word and example, as, indeed, you have been doing since you first held the office of prioress under your abbess. So if you still watch over your daughters as carefully as you did previously over your sisters, it is sufficient to make me believe that any teaching or exhortation from me would now be wholly superfluous. If, on the other hand, in your humility you think differently, and you feel that you have need of my instruction and writings in matters pertaining to God, write to me what you want, so that I may answer as God permits me. Meanwhile thanks be to God who has filled all your hearts with anxiety for my desperate, unceasing perils, and made you share in my affliction; may divine mercy protect me through the support of your prayers and quickly crush Satan beneath our feet. To this end in particular, I hasten to send the Psalter you earnestly begged from me,[1] my sister once dear in the world and now dearest in Christ, so that you may offer a perpetual sacrifice of prayers to the Lord for our many great aberrations, and for the dangers which daily threaten me.

We have indeed many examples as evidence of the high position in the eyes of God and his saints which has been won by the prayers of the faithful, especially those of women on behalf of their dear ones and of wives for their husbands. The Apostle observes this closely when he bids us pray continually.[2] We read that the Lord said to Moses 'Let me alone, to vent my anger upon them,' and to Jeremiah 'Therefore offer no prayer for these people nor stand in my path.'[3] By these words the Lord himself makes it clear that the prayers of the devout set a kind of bridle on his wrath and check it from raging against sinners as fully as they deserve; just as a man who is willingly moved by his sense of justice to take vengeance can be turned aside by the entreaties of his friends and forcibly restrained, as it were, against his will. Thus when the Lord says to one who is praying or about to pray, 'Let me alone and do not stand in my path,' he forbids prayers to be offered to him on behalf of the impious; yet the just man prays though the Lord forbids, obtains his requests and alters the sentence of the angry judge. And so the passage about Moses continues: 'And the Lord repented and spared his people the evil with which he had threatened them.'[4] Elsewhere it is written about the universal works of God, 'He spoke, and it was.'[5] But in this passage it is also recorded that he had said the people deserved affliction, but he had been prevented by the power of prayer from carrying out his words.

Consider then the great power of prayer, if we pray as we are bidden, seeing that the prophet won by prayer what he was forbidden to pray for, and turned God aside from his declared intention. And another prophet says to God: 'In thy wrath remember mercy.'[6] The lords of the earth should listen and take note, for they are found obstinate rather than just in the execution of the justice they have decreed and pronounced; they blush to appear lax if they are merciful, and untruthful if they change a pronouncement or do not carry out a decision which lacked foresight, even if they can emend their words by their actions. Such men could properly be compared with Jephtha, who made a foolish vow and in carrying it out even more foolishly, killed his only daughter.[7] But he who desires to be a 'member of his body' says with the Psalmist 'I will sing of mercy and justice unto thee, O Lord.'[8] Mercy, it is written, exalts judgement, in accordance with the threat elsewhere in the Scriptures: 'In that judgement there will be no mercy for the man who has shown no mercy.'[9] The Psalmist himself considered this carefully when, at the entreaty of the wife of Nabal the Carmelite, as an act of mercy he broke the oath he had justly sworn concerning her husband and the destruction of his house.[10] Thus he set prayer above justice, and the man's wrongdoing was wiped out by the entreaties of his wife.

Here you have an example, sister, and an assurance how much your prayers for me may prevail on God, if this woman's did so much for her husband, seeing that God who is our father loves his children more than David did a suppliant woman. David was indeed considered a pious and merciful man, but God is piety and mercy itself. And the woman whose entreaties David heard then was an ordinary lay person, in no way bound to God by the profession of holy devotion; whereas if you alone are not enough to win an answer to your prayer, the holy convent of widows and virgins which is with you will succeed where you cannot by yourself. For when the Truth says to the disciples, 'When two or three have met together in my name, I am there among them,' and again, 'If two of you agree about any request you have to make, it shall be granted by my Father,'[11] we can all see how the communal prayer of a holy congregation must prevail upon God. If, as the apostle James says, 'A good man's prayer is powerful and effective,'[12] what should we hope for from the large numbers of a holy congregation? You know, dearest sister, from the thirty-eighth homily of St Gregory[13] how much support the prayers of his fellow brethren quickly brought a brother, although he was unwilling and resisted. The depths of his misery, the fear of peril which tormented his unhappy soul, the utter despair and weariness of life which made him try to call his brethren from their prayers – all the details set out there cannot have escaped your understanding.

May this example give you and your convent of holy sisters greater confidence in prayer, so that I may be preserved alive for you all, through him, from whom, as Paul bears witness, women have even received back their dead raised to life.[14] For if you turn the pages of the Old and New Testaments you will find that the greatest miracles of resurrection were shown only, or mostly, to women, and were performed for them or on them. The Old Testament records two instances of men raised from the dead at the entreaties of their mothers, by Elijah and his disciple Elisha. The Gospel, it is true, has three instances only of the dead being raised by the Lord but, as they were shown to women only, they provide factual confirmation of the Apostle's words I quoted above: 'Women received back their dead raised to life.' It was to a widow at the gate of the city of Nain that the Lord restored her son, moved by compassion for her, and he also raised Lazarus his own friend at the entreaty of his sisters Mary and Martha. And when he granted this same favour to the daughter of the ruler of the synagogue at her father's petition,[15] again 'women received back their dead raised to life,' for in being brought back to life she received her own body from death just as those other women received the bodies of their dead.

Now these resurrections were performed with only a few interceding; and so the multiplied prayers of your shared devotion should easily win the preservation of my own life. The more God is pleased by the abstinence and continence which women have dedicated to him, the more willing he will be to grant their prayers. Moreover, it may well be that the majority of those raised from the dead were not of the faith, for we do not read that the widow mentioned above whose son was raised without her asking was a believer. But in our case we are bound together by the integrity of our faith and united in our profession of the same religious life.

Let me now pass from the holy convent of your community, where so many virgins and widows are dedicated to continual service of the Lord, and come to you alone, you whose sanctity must surely have the greatest influence in the eyes of God, and who are bound to do everything possible on my behalf, especially now when I am in the toils of such adversity. Always remember then in your prayers him who is especially yours; watch and pray the more confidently as you recognize your cause is just, and so more acceptable to him to whom you pray. Listen, I beg you, with the ear of your heart to what you have so often heard with your bodily ear. In the book of Proverbs it is written that 'A capable wife is her husband's crown,' and again, 'Find a wife and you find a good thing; so you will earn the favour of the Lord'; yet again, 'Home and wealth may come down from ancestors; but an intelligent wife is a gift from the Lord.'[16] In Ecclesiasticus too it says that 'A good wife makes a happy husband,' and a little later, 'A good wife means a good life.'[17] And we have it on the Apostle's authority that 'the unbelieving husband now belongs to God through his wife'.[18] A special instance of this was granted by God's grace in our own country of France, when Clovis the king was converted to the Christian faith more by the prayers of his wife than by the preaching of holy men;[19] his entire kingdom was then placed under divine law so that humbler men should be encouraged by the example of their betters to persevere in prayer. Indeed, such perseverance is warmly recommended to us in a parable of the Lord which says: 'If the man perseveres in his knocking, though he will not provide for him out of friendship, the very shamelessness of the request will make him get up and give him all he needs.'[20] It was certainly by what I might call this shamelessness in prayer that Moses (as I said above) softened the harshness of divine justice and changed its sentence.

You know, beloved, the warmth of charity your convent once used to show me in their prayers at the times I could be with you. At the conclusion of each of the Hours every day they would offer this special prayer to the Lord on my behalf; after the proper response and versicle were pronounced and sung they added prayers and a collect, as follows:

RESPONSE: Forsake me not, O Lord: Keep not far from me, my God.

VERSICLE: Make haste, O Lord, to help me.

PRAYER: Save thy servant, O my God, whose hope is in thee; Lord hear my prayer, and let my cry for help reach thee.[21]

(LET US PRAY) O God, who through thy servant hast been pleased to gather together thy handmaidens in thy name, we beseech thee to grant both to him and to us that we persevere in thy will. Through our Lord, etc.

But now that I am not with you, there is all the more need for the support of your prayers, the more I am gripped by fear of greater peril. And so I ask of you in entreaty, and entreat you in asking, particularly now that I am absent from you, to show me how truly your charity extends to the absent by adding this form of special prayer at the conclusion of each hour:

RESPONSE: O Lord, Father and Ruler of my life, do not desert me, lest I fall before my adversaries and my enemy gloats over me.

VERSICLE: Grasp shield and buckler and rise up to help me, lest my enemy gloats.[22]

PRAYER: Save thy servant, O my God, whose hope is in thee. Send him help, O Lord, from thy holy place, and watch over him from Zion. Be a tower of strength to him, O Lord, in the face of his enemy. Lord hear my prayer, and let my cry for help reach thee.

(LET US PRAY) O God, who through thy servant hast been pleased to gather together thy handmaidens in thy name, we beseech thee to protect him in all adversity and restore him in safety to thy handmaidens. Through our Lord, etc.

But if the Lord shall deliver me into the hands of my enemies so that they overcome and kill me, or by whatever chance I enter upon the way of all flesh while absent from you, wherever my body may lie, buried or unburied, I beg you to have it brought to your burial-ground, where our daughters, or rather, our sisters in Christ may see my tomb more often and thereby be encouraged to pour out their prayers more fully to the Lord on my behalf. There is no place, I think, so safe and salutary for a soul grieving for its sins and desolated by its transgressions than that which is specially consecrated to the true Paraclete, the Comforter, and which is particularly designated by his name. Nor do I believe that there is any place more fitting for Christian burial among the faithful than one amongst women dedicated to Christ. Women were concerned for the tomb of our Lord Jesus Christ, they came ahead and followed after, bringing precious ointments,[23] keeping close watch around this tomb, weeping for the death of the Bridegroom, as it is written: 'The women sitting at the tomb wept and lamented for the Lord.'[24] And there they were first reassured about his resurrection by the appearance of an angel and the words he spoke to them; later on they were found worthy both to taste the joy of his resurrection when he twice appeared to them, and also to touch him with their hands.

Finally, I ask this of you above all else: at present you are over-anxious about the danger to my body, but then your chief concern must be for the salvation of my soul, and you must show the dead man how much you loved the living by the special support of prayers chosen for him.

Live, fare you well, yourself and your sisters with you,
Live, but I pray, in Christ be mindful of me.

LETTER 4
HELOISE TO ABELARD

To her only one after Christ, from his only one in Christ.

I am surprised, my only love, that contrary to custom in letter-writing and, indeed, to the natural order, you have thought fit to put my name before yours in the greeting which heads your letter, so that we have the woman before the man, wife before husband, handmaid before lord, nun before monk, deaconess[1] before priest and abbess before abbot. Surely the right and proper order is for those who write to their superiors or equals to put their names before their own, but in letters to inferiors, precedence in order of address follows precedence in rank.[2]

We were also greatly surprised when instead of bringing us the healing balm of comfort as you should have, you increased our desolation and made the tears to flow which you should have dried. For which of us could remain dry-eyed on hearing the words you wrote towards the end of your letter: 'But if the Lord shall deliver me into the hands of my enemies so that they overcome and kill me . . .'? My dearest, how could you think such a thought? How could you give voice to it? Never may God be so forgetful of his humble handmaids as to let them outlive you; never may he grant us a life which would be harder to bear than any form of death. The proper course would be for you to perform our funeral rites, for you to commend our souls to God, and to send ahead of you those whom you assembled for God's service – so that you need no longer be troubled by worries for us, and follow after us the more gladly because freed from concern for our salvation. Spare us, I implore you, my lord, spare us words such as these which can only intensify our existing unhappiness; do not deny us, before death, the one thing by which we live. 'Sufficient unto the day is the evil thereof,'[3] and that day, shrouded in bitterness, will bring with it distress enough to all it comes upon. 'Why is it necessary,' says Seneca, 'to summon up evil'[4] and to destroy life before death?

You ask us, my only one, if you chance to die when absent from us, to have your body brought to our burial-ground so that you may reap a fuller harvest from the prayers we shall offer in constant memory of you. But how could you suppose that our memory of you could ever fade? Besides, what time will there be then which will be fitting for prayer, when extreme distress will allow us no peace, when the soul will lose its power of reason and the tongue its use of speech? Or when the frantic mind, far from being resigned, may even (if I may say so) rage against God himself, and provoke him with complaints instead of placating him with prayers? In our misery then we shall have time only for tears and no power to pray; we shall be hurrying to follow, not to bury you, so that we may share your grave instead of laying you in it. If we lose our life in you, we shall not be able to go on living when you leave us. I would not even have us live to see that day, for if the mere mention of your death is death for us, what will the reality be if it finds us still alive? God grant we may never live on to perform this duty, to render you the service which we look for from you alone; in this may we go before, not after you!

And so, I beg you, spare us – spare her at least, who is your only one – by refraining from words like these. They pierce our hearts with swords of death, so that what comes before is more painful than death itself. A heart which is exhausted with grief cannot find peace, nor can a mind preoccupied with anxieties genuinely devote itself to God. I beseech you not to hinder God's service to which you specially committed us. Whatever has to come to us bringing with it total grief we must hope will come suddenly, without torturing us far in advance with useless apprehension which no foresight can relieve. This is what the poet has in mind when he prays to God:

> May it be sudden, whatever you plan for us; may man's mind
> Be blind to the future. Let him hope on in his fears.[5]

But if I lose you, what is left for me to hope for? What reason for continuing on life's pilgrimage, for which I have no support but you, and none in you save the knowledge that you are alive, now that I am forbidden all other pleasures in you and denied even the joy of your presence which from time to time could restore me to myself? O God – if it is lawful to say it – cruel to me in everything! O merciless mercy! O Fortune who is only ill-fortune, who has already spent on me so many of the shafts she uses in her battle against mankind that she has none left with which to vent her anger on others. She has emptied a full quiver on me, so that henceforth no one else need fear her onslaughts, and if she still had a single arrow she could find no place in me to take a wound. Her only dread is that through my many wounds death may end my sufferings; and though she does not cease to destroy me, she still fears the destruction which she hurries on.

Of all wretched women I am the most wretched, and amongst the unhappy I am unhappiest. The higher I was exalted when you preferred me to all other women, the greater my suffering over my own fall and yours, when equally I was flung down; for the higher the ascent, the heavier the fall. Has Fortune ever set any great or noble woman above me or made her my equal, only to be similarly cast down and crushed with grief? What glory she gave me in you, what ruin she brought upon me through you! Violent in either extreme, she showed no moderation in good or evil. To make me the saddest of all women she first made me blessed above all, so that when I thought how much I had lost, my consuming grief would match my crushing loss, and my sorrow for what was taken from me would be the greater for the fuller joy of possession which had gone before; and so that the happiness of supreme ecstasy would end in the supreme bitterness of sorrow.

Moreover, to add to my indignation at the outrage, all the laws of equity in our case were reversed. For while we enjoyed the pleasures of an uneasy love and abandoned ourselves to fornication (if I may use an ugly but expressive word) we were spared God's severity. But when we amended our unlawful conduct by what was lawful, and atoned for the shame of fornication by an honourable marriage, then the Lord in his anger laid his hand heavily upon us, and would not permit a chaste union though he had long tolerated one which was unchaste. The punishment you suffered would have been proper vengeance for men caught in open adultery. But what others deserve for adultery came upon you through a marriage which you believed had made amends for all previous wrongdoing; what adulterous women have brought upon their lovers, your own wife brought on you. Nor was this at the time when we abandoned ourselves to our former delights, but when we had already parted and were living more chastely, you presiding over the school in Paris and I at your command living with the nuns at Argenteuil. Thus we were separated, to give you more time to devote yourself to your pupils, and me more freedom for prayer and meditation on the Scriptures, both of us leading a life which was more holy as well as more chaste. It was then that you alone paid the penalty in your body for what we had both done equally. You alone were punished though we were both to blame, and you paid all, though you had deserved less, for you had made more than necessary reparation by humbling yourself on my account and had raised me and all my kind to your own level – so much less then, in the eyes of God and of your betrayers, should you have been thought deserving of such punishment.

What misery for me – born as I was to be the cause of such a crime! Is it the general lot of women to bring total ruin on great men? Hence the warning about women in Proverbs: 'But now, my son, listen to me, attend to what I say: do not let your heart entice you into her ways, do not stray down her paths; she has wounded and laid low so many, and the strongest have all been her victims. Her house is the way to hell, and leads down to the halls of death.'[6] And in Ecclesiastes: 'I put all to the test ... I find woman more bitter than death; she is a snare, her heart a net, her arms are chains. He who is pleasing to God eludes her, but the sinner is her captive.'[7]

It was the first woman in the beginning who lured man from Paradise, and she who had been created by the Lord as his helpmate became the instrument of his total downfall. And that mighty man of the Lord, [Samson] the Nazirite whose conception was announced by an angel,[8] Delilah alone overcame; betrayed to his enemies and robbed of his sight, he was driven by his suffering to destroy himself along with his enemies. Only the woman he had had sex with could infatuate Solomon, wisest of all men; she drove him to such a pitch of madness that although he was the man whom the Lord had chosen to build the temple in preference to his father David, who was a righteous man, she plunged him into idolatry until the end of his life, so that he abandoned the worship of God which he had preached and taught in word and writing.[9] Job, holiest of men, fought his last and hardest battle against his wife, who urged him to curse God.[10] The cunning arch-tempter well knew from repeated experience that men are most easily brought to ruin through their wives, and so he directed his usual malice against us too, and tempted you through marriage when he could not destroy you through fornication. Denied the power to do evil through evil, he effected evil through good.

At least I can thank God for this: the tempter did not prevail on me to do wrong of my own consent, like the women I have mentioned, though in the outcome he made me the instrument of his malice. But even if my conscience is clear through innocence, and no consent of mine makes me guilty of this crime, too many earlier sins were committed to allow me to be wholly free from guilt. I yielded long before to the pleasures of carnal desires, and merited then what I weep for now. The sequel is a fitting punishment for my former sins, and an evil beginning must be expected to come to a bad end. For this offence, above all, may I have strength to do proper penance, so that at least by long contrition I can make some amends for your pain from the wound inflicted on you; and what you suffered in the body for a time, I may suffer, as is right, throughout my life in contrition of mind, and thus make reparation to you at least, if not to God.

For if I truthfully admit to the weakness of my most wretched soul, I can find no penitence whereby to appease God, whom I always accuse of the greatest cruelty in regard to this outrage. By rebelling against his ordinance, I offend him more by my indignation than I placate him by making amends through penitence. How can it be called repentance for sins, however great the mortification of the flesh, if the mind still retains the will to sin and is on fire with its old desires? It is easy enough for anyone to confess his sins, to accuse himself, or even to mortify his body in outward show of penance, but it is very difficult to tear the heart away from hankering after its dearest pleasures. Quite rightly then, when the saintly Job said, 'I will speak out against myself,' that is, 'I will loose my tongue and open my mouth in confession to accuse myself of my sins,' he added at once, 'I will speak out in bitterness of soul.'[11] St Gregory comments on this: 'There are some who confess their faults aloud but in doing so do not know how to groan over them – they speak cheerfully of what should be lamented. And so whoever hates his faults and confesses them must still confess them in bitterness of spirit, so that this bitterness may punish him for what his tongue, at his mind's bidding, accuses him.'[12] But this bitterness of true repentance is very rare, as St Ambrose observes, when he says: 'I have more easily found men who have preserved their innocence than men who have known repentance.'[13]

In my case, the pleasures of lovers which we shared have been too sweet – they cannot displease me, and can scarcely shift from my memory. Wherever I turn they are always there before my eyes, bringing with them awakened longings and fantasies which will not even let me sleep. Even during the celebration of the Mass, when our prayers should be purer, lewd visions of those pleasures take such a hold upon my unhappy soul that my thoughts are on their wantonness instead of on prayers. I should be groaning over the sins I have committed, but I can only sigh for what I have lost. Everything we did and also the times and places where we did it are stamped on my heart along with your image, so that I live through them all again with you. Even in sleep I know no respite. Sometimes my thoughts are betrayed in a movement of my body, or they break out in an unguarded word. In my utter wretchedness, that cry from a suffering soul could well be mine: 'Miserable creature that I am, who is there to rescue me out of the body doomed to this death?'[14] Would that I could truthfully answer: 'The grace of God through Jesus Christ our Lord.' This grace, my dearest, came upon you unsought – a single wound of the body by freeing you from these torments has healed many wounds in your soul. Where God may seem to you an adversary, he has in fact proved himself kind: like an honest doctor who does not shrink from giving pain if it will bring about a cure. But for me, youth and passion and experience of pleasures which were so delightful intensify the torments of the flesh and longings of desire, and the assault is the more overwhelming as the nature they attack is the weaker.

Men call me chaste; they do not know the hypocrite I am. They consider purity of the flesh a virtue, though virtue belongs not to the body but to the soul. I can win praise in the eyes of men but deserve none before God, who searches our hearts and loins[15] and sees in our darkness. I am judged religious at a time when there is little in religion which is not hypocrisy, when whoever does not offend the opinions of men receives the highest praise. And yet perhaps there is some merit and it seems somehow acceptable to God, if a person whatever her intention gives no offence to the Church in her outward behaviour, if the name of the Lord is not blasphemed among the infidels because of her nor if she does not disgrace the Order of her profession amongst the worldly. And this too is a gift of God's grace and comes through his bounty – not only to do good but to abstain from evil – though the latter is vain if the former does not follow from it, as it is written: 'Turn from evil and do good.'[16] Both are vain if not done for love of God.

At every stage of my life up to now, as God knows, I have feared to offend you rather than God, and tried to please you more than him. It was your command, not love of God, which made me take the veil. Look at the unhappy life I lead, pitiable beyond any other, if in this world I must endure so much in vain, with no hope of future reward. For a long time my pretence deceived you, as it did many, so that you mistook hypocrisy for piety; and therefore you commend yourself to our prayers and ask me for what I expect from you. I beg you, do not feel so sure of me that you cease to help me by your own prayers. Do not suppose me healthy and so withdraw the grace of your healing. Do not believe I want for nothing and delay helping me in my hour of need. Do not think me strong, lest I fall before you can sustain me. False praise has harmed many and taken from them the support they needed. The Lord cries out through Isaiah: 'O my people! Those who call you happy lead you astray and confuse the path you should take.'[17] And through Ezekiel he says: 'Woe to them that sew cushions under every elbow and make pillows for the heads of people of every age in order to catch souls.'[18] On the other hand, through Solomon it is said that 'The sayings of the wise are sharp as goads, like nails driven home.'[19] That is to say, nails which cannot touch wounds gently, but only pierce through them.

Cease praising me, I beg you, lest you acquire the base stigma of being a flatterer or the charge of telling lies, or the breath of my vanity blows away any merit you saw in me to praise. No one with medical knowledge diagnoses an internal illness by examining only outward appearance. What is common to the damned and the elect can win no favour in the eyes of God: of such a kind are the outward actions which are performed more eagerly by hypocrites than by saints. 'The heart of man is deceitful and inscrutable; who can fathom it?' And: 'A road may seem straightforward to a man, yet may end as the way to death.'[20] It is rash for man to pass judgement on what is reserved for God's scrutiny, and so it is also written: 'Do not praise a man in his lifetime.'[21] By this is meant, do not praise a man while in doing so you can make him no longer praiseworthy.

To me your praise is the more dangerous because I welcome it. The more anxious I am to please you in everything, the more I am won over and delighted by it. I beg you, be fearful for me always, instead of feeling confidence in me, so that I may always find help in your solicitude. Now particularly you should fear, now when I no longer have in you an outlet for my incontinence. I do not wish you to exhort me to virtue or summon me to battle. You say: 'Power comes to its full strength in weakness' and 'He cannot win a crown unless he has kept the rules.'[22] I do not seek a crown of victory; it is sufficient for me to avoid danger, and this is safer than engaging in war. In whatever corner of heaven God shall place me, it will be enough for me. No one will envy one another there, and what each one has will suffice. So that I might add the strength of authority to this our counsel, let us hear St Jerome: 'I confess my weakness, I do not wish to fight in hope of victory, lest the day comes when I lose the battle. What need is there to forsake what is certain and pursue uncertainty?'[23]

LETTER 5
ABELARD TO HELOISE

To the bride of Christ, from His servant.

The whole of your last letter is given up to a recital of your misery over the wrongs you suffer, and these, I note, are on four counts. First, you complain that contrary to custom in letter-writing, or indeed against the natural order of the world, my letter to you put your name before mine in its greeting. Secondly, that when I ought to have offered you some remedy for your comfort I actually increased your sense of desolation and made the tears flow which I should have checked. This I did by writing, 'But if the Lord shall deliver me into the hands of my enemies, so that they overcome and kill me . . .' Thirdly, you went on to your old perpetual complaint against God concerning the manner of our entry into religious life and the cruelty of the act of treachery performed on me. Lastly, you set your self-accusations against my praise of you, and implored me with some urgency not to praise you again.

I have decided to answer you on each point in turn, not so much in self-justification as for your own enlightenment and encouragement, so that you will more willingly grant my own requests when you understand that they have a basis of reason, listen to me more attentively on the subject of your own pleas as you find me less to blame in my own and be less ready to refuse me when you see me less deserving of reproach.

What you call the unnatural order of my greeting, if you consider it carefully, was in accordance with your own view as well as mine. For it is common knowledge, as you yourself have shown, that in writing to superiors one puts their name first, and you must realize that you became my superior from the day when you began to be my lady on becoming the bride of my Lord; witness St Jerome, who writes to Eustochium 'This is my reason for writing "my lady Eustochium". Surely I must address as "my lady" her who is the bride of my Lord.'[1] It was a fortunate trading of your married state: as you were previously the wife of a poor mortal and now you are raised to the bed of the high king. By the privilege of this honour you are set not only over your former husband but over every servant of that king. So you should not be surprised if I commend myself in life as in death to the prayers of your community, seeing that in common law it is accepted that wives are better able than their households to intercede with their husbands, being ladies rather than servants. As an illustration of this, the Psalmist says of the queen and bride of the high king: 'On your right stands the queen,'[2] as if it were clearly stated that she is nearest to her husband and closest to his side, and proceeds as an equal, while all the rest stand apart or follow behind. The bride in the Canticles, an Ethiopian (such as the one Moses took as a wife) rejoices in the glory of her privileged position and says: 'I am black but lovely, daughters of Jerusalem; therefore the king has loved me and brought me into his chamber.' And again, 'Take no notice of my darkness, because the sun has discoloured me.'[3] Allegorically it is the contemplative soul which is described in these words and specifically called the bride of Christ. Your outer habit indicates that these words have particular application to you. For your outer garb of coarse black clothing, like the mourning worn by good widows who weep for the dead husbands they had loved, shows you to be, in the words of the Apostle, truly widowed and desolate and such as the Church should be charged to support.[4] The Scriptures also record the grief of these widows for their spouse who was slain, in the words: 'The women sitting at the tomb wept and lamented for the Lord.'[5]

The Ethiopian woman is black in the outer part of her flesh and as regards exterior appearance looks less lovely than other women; yet she is not unlike them within, but in several respects she is whiter and lovelier, in her bones, for instance, or her teeth. Indeed, whiteness of teeth is also praised in the bridegroom, in reference to 'his teeth whiter than milk'.[6] And so she is black outside but lovely within; for she is blackened outside in the flesh because in this life she suffers bodily affliction through the repeated tribulations of adversity, according to the saying of the Apostle: 'Persecution will come to all who want to live a godly life as Christians.'[7] As prosperity is marked by white, so adversity may properly be indicated by black, and she is white within in her bones because her soul is strong in virtues, as it is written that 'All the glory of the king's daughter is within.'[8] For the bones within, surrounded by the flesh without, are the strength and support of the very flesh they wear or sustain, and can properly stand for the soul which gives life and sustenance to the flesh itself in which it is, and to which it gives movement and direction and provision for all its well-being. Its whiteness or beauty is the sum of the virtues which adorn it.

She is black too in outward things because while she is still an exile on life's pilgrimage, she keeps herself humble and abject in this life so that she may be exalted in the next, where she is hidden with Christ in God, once she has reached her homeland. So indeed the true sun changes her colour because the heavenly love of the bridegroom humbles her like this, or torments her with tribulations lest prosperity raises her up. He changes her colour, that is, he makes her different from other women who thirst for earthly things and seek worldly glory, so that she may truly become through her humility a lily of the valley, and not a lily of the heights like those foolish virgins who pride themselves on purity of the flesh or an outward show of self-denial, and then wither in the fire of temptation. And she rightly told the daughters of Jerusalem, that is, the weaker amongst the faithful who deserve to be called daughters rather than sons, 'Take no notice of my darkness, because the sun has discoloured me.' She might say more openly: 'The fact that I humble myself in this way or bear adversity so bravely is due to no virtue of mine but to the grace of him whom I serve.' This is not the way of heretics and hypocrites who (at any rate when others are present) humiliate themselves to excess in hopes of earthly glory, and endure much to no purpose. The sort of abjection or tribulation they put up with is indeed surprising, and they are the most pitiable of men, enjoying the good things neither of this life nor of the life to come. It is with this in mind that the bride says, 'Do not wonder that I do so'; but we must wonder at those who vainly burn with desire for worldly praise and deny themselves advantages on earth so that they are as unhappy in their present life as they will be in the next. Such self-denial is that of the foolish virgins who found the door shut against them.[9]

And she did well to say that, because she is black, as we said, and lovely, she is chosen and taken into the king's bedchamber, that is, to that secret place of peace and contemplation, and into the bed, of which she says elsewhere, 'Night after night on my bed I have sought my true love.'[10] Indeed, the disfigurement of her blackness makes her love what is hidden rather than open, what is secret rather than public. Such a wife desires private, not public delights with her husband, and would rather be experienced in bed than seen at table. Moreover it often happens that the flesh of black women is all the softer to touch though it is less attractive to look at, and for this reason the pleasure they give is greater and more suitable for private than for public gratification. Their husbands take them into a bedroom to enjoy them rather than parade them in public. Following this metaphor, when that spiritual bride said, 'I am black but lovely,' she rightly added at once, 'Therefore the king has loved me and brought me into his chamber.' She relates each point to the other: because she was lovely he loved her, and because she was black he brought her into his chamber. She is lovely, as we said before, with virtues within which the bridegroom loves, and black outside from the adversity of bodily tribulation. Such blackness of bodily tribulation easily turns the minds of the faithful away from love of earthly things and attaches them to the desire for eternal life, often leading them from the stormy life of the world to retirement for contemplation. Thus St Jerome writes that our own, that is, the monastic life, took its beginning from Paul [of Thebes].[11]

The humiliation of coarse garments also looks to retirement rather than to public life, and is to be preserved as being most suitable for the life of humility and withdrawal which especially befits our profession. The greatest encouragement to public display is costly clothing, which is sought by none except for empty display and worldly ceremony, as St Gregory clearly shows in saying that 'No one adorns himself in private, only where he can be seen.'[12] As for the chamber of the bride, it is the one to which the bridegroom himself in the Gospel invites anyone who prays, saying 'But when you pray, go into a room by yourself, shut the door and pray to your Father.'[13] He could have added 'not like the hypocrites, at street corners and in public places'. By a room he means a place that is secluded from the tumult and sight of the world, where prayer can be offered more purely and quietly, such as the seclusion of monastic solitude, a place where we are told to shut the door, that is, to close up every approach, lest something happen to hinder the purity of prayer and what we see distract the unfortunate soul.

Yet there are many wearing our habit who despise this counsel, or rather, this divine precept, and we find them hard to tolerate when they celebrate the divine offices with cloister or choir wide open and conduct themselves shamelessly in full view of both men and women, especially during the Mass when they are decked out in precious ornaments like those of the worldly men to whom they display them. In their view a feast is best celebrated if it is rich in external display and lavish in food and drink. Better to keep silence, as it is shameful to speak of their wretched blindness that is wholly contrary to the religion of Christ's poor. At heart they are like Jews, following their own custom instead of a rule, making a mockery of God's command in their practices, looking to usage, not duty; although, as St Augustine reminds us, the Lord said, 'I am truth'[14] not 'I am custom.' Anyone who cares to may entrust himself to the prayers of these men, which are offered with doors open, but you who have been led by the king of heaven himself into his chamber and rest in his embrace, and with the door always shut are wholly given up to him, are more intimately joined to him, in the Apostle's words, 'But anyone who is joined to the Lord is one spirit with him.'[15] So much the more confidence, then, have I in the purity and effectiveness of your prayers, and the more urgently I demand your help. And I believe these prayers are offered more devoutly on my behalf because we are bound together in such great mutual love.

But if I have distressed you by mentioning the dangers which beset me or the death I fear, it was done in accordance with your own request, or rather, entreaty. For the first letter you wrote me has a passage which says:

> And so in the name of Christ, who is still giving you some protection for his service, we beseech you to write as often as you think fit to us who are his handmaids and yours, with news of the perils in which you are still storm-tossed. We are all that are left you, so at least you should let us share your sorrow or your joy. It is always some consolation in sorrow to feel that it is shared, and any burden laid on several is carried more lightly or removed.[16]

Why then do you accuse me of making you share my anxiety when I was forced to do so at your own behest? When I am suffering in despair of my life, would it be fitting for you to be joyous? Would you want to be partners only in joy, not grief, to join in rejoicing without weeping with those who weep?[17] There is no wider distinction between true friends and false than the fact that the former share adversity, the latter only prosperity.

Say no more, I beg you, and cease from complaints like these which are so far removed from the true depths of love! Yet even if you are still offended by this, I am so critically placed in danger and daily despair of life that it is proper for me to take thought for the welfare of my soul, and to provide for it while I may. Nor will you, if you truly love me, take exception to my forethought. Indeed, had you any hope of divine mercy being shown me, you would be all the more anxious for me to be freed from the troubles of this life as you see them to be intolerable. At least you must know that whoever frees me from life will deliver me from the greatest suffering. What I may afterwards incur is uncertain, but from what I shall be set free is not in question. Every unhappy life is happy in its ending, and those who feel true sympathy and pain for the anxieties of others want to see these ended, even to their own loss, if they really love those they see suffer and think more of their friends' advantage than of their own. So when a son has long been ill a mother wants his illness to end even in death, for she finds it unbearable, and can more easily face bereavement than have him share her misery. And anyone who takes special pleasure in the presence of a friend would rather have him happy in absence than present and unhappy, for he finds suffering intolerable if he cannot relieve it. In your case, you are not even permitted to enjoy my presence, unhappy though it is, and so, when any provision you are able to make for me is to your own advantage, I cannot see why you should prefer me to live on in great misery rather than be happier in death. If you see your advantage in prolonging my miseries, you are proved an enemy rather than a friend. But if you hesitate to appear in such a guise, I beg you, as I said before, to cease your complaints.

However, I approve of your rejection of praise, for in this very thing you show yourself more praiseworthy. It is written that 'He who is first in accusing himself is just' and 'Whoever humbles himself will be exalted.'[18] May your written words be reflected in your heart! If they are, yours is true humility and will not vanish with anything I say. But be careful, I beg you, not to seek praise when you appear to shun it, and not to reject with your lips what you desire in your heart. St Jerome writes to the virgin Eustochium on this point, amongst others: 'We are led on by our natural evil. We give willing ear to our flatterers, and though we may answer that we are unworthy and an artful blush suffuses our cheeks, the soul inwardly delights in its own praise.'[19] Such artfulness Virgil describes in the wanton Galatea, who sought what she wanted by flight, and by feigning rejection led on her lover more surely towards her:

She flees to the willows and wishes first to be seen.[20]

Before she hides she wants to be seen fleeing, so that the very flight whereby she appears to reject the youth's company ensures that she obtains it. Similarly, when we seem to shun men's praise we are directing it towards ourselves, and when we pretend that we wish to hide lest anyone discovers what to praise in us, we are leading the unwary[21] on to give us praise because in this way we appear to deserve it. I mention this because it is a common occurrence, not because I suspect such things of you; I have no doubts about your humility. But I want you to refrain from speaking like this, so that you do not appear to those who do not know you so well to be seeking fame by shunning it, as Jerome says. My praise will never make you proud, but will summon you to higher things, and the more eager you are to please me, the more anxious you will be to embrace what I praise. My praise is not a tribute to your piety which is intended to bolster up your pride, and we ought not in fact to believe in our friends' approval any more than in our enemies' abuse.

I come at last to your old perpetual complaint,[22] as we have called it, in which you presume to blame God for the manner of our entry into religion instead of wishing to glorify him as you justly should. I had thought that this bitterness of heart at what was so clear an act of divine mercy had long since disappeared. The more dangerous such bitterness is to you in wearing out body and soul alike, the more pitiful it is and distressing to me. If you are anxious to please me in everything, as you claim, and in this at least would end my torment, or even give me the greatest pleasure, you must rid yourself of it. If it persists you can neither please me nor attain bliss with me. Can you bear me to come to this without you – I whom you declare yourself ready to follow to the very fires of hell? Seek piety in this at least, lest you cut yourself off from me who am hastening, you believe, towards God; be the readier to do so because the goal we must come to will be blessed, and our companionship the more welcome for being happier. Remember what you have said, recall what you have written, namely that in the manner of our conversion, when God seems to have been more my adversary, he has clearly shown himself kinder.[23] For this reason at least you must accept his will, that it is most salutary for me, and for you too, if your transports of grief will see reason. You should not grieve because you are the cause of so great a good, for which you must not doubt you were specially created by God. Nor should you weep because I have to bear this, except when our blessings through the martyrs in their sufferings and the

Lord's death sadden you. If it had befallen me justly, would you find it easier to bear? Would it distress you less? In fact if it had been so, the result would have been greater disgrace for me and more credit to my enemies, since justice would have won them approval while my guilt would have brought me into contempt. And no one would be stirred by pity for me to condemn what was done.

However, it may relieve the bitterness of your grief if I prove that this came upon us justly, as well as to our advantage, and that God's punishment was more properly directed against us when we were married than when we were living in sin. After our marriage, when you were living in the cloister with the nuns at Argenteuil and I came one day to visit you privately, you know what my uncontrollable desire did with you there, actually in a corner of the refectory, since we had nowhere else to go. I repeat, you know how shamelessly we behaved on that occasion in so hallowed a place, dedicated to the most holy Virgin. Even if our other shameful behaviour was ended, this alone would deserve far heavier punishment. Need I recall our previous fornication and the wanton impurities which preceded our marriage, or my supreme act of betrayal, when I deceived your uncle about you so disgracefully, at a time when I was continuously living with him in his own house? Who would not judge me justly betrayed by the man whom I had first shamelessly betrayed? Do you think that the momentary pain of that wound is sufficient punishment for such crimes? Or rather, that so great an advantage was fitting for such great wickedness? What wound do you suppose would satisfy God's justice for the profanation such as I described of a place so sacred to his own Mother? Surely, unless I am much mistaken, not that wound which was wholly beneficial was intended as a punishment for this, but rather the daily unending torment I now endure.

You know too how when you were pregnant and I took you to my own country you disguised yourself in the sacred habit of a nun, a pretence which was an irreverent mockery of the religion you now profess. Consider, then, how fittingly divine justice, or rather, divine grace brought you against your will to the religion which you did not hesitate to mock, so that you should willingly expiate your profanation in the same habit, and the truth of reality should remedy the lie of your pretence and correct your falsity. And if you would allow consideration of our advantage to be an element in divine justice, you would be able to call what God did to us then an act not of justice, but of grace.

See then, my beloved, see how with the dragnets of his mercy the Lord has fished us up from the depth of this dangerous sea, and from the abyss of what a Charybdis he has saved our shipwrecked selves, although we were unwilling, so that each of us may justly break out in that cry: 'The Lord takes thought for me.'[24] Think and think again of the great perils in which we were and from which the Lord rescued us; tell always with the deepest gratitude how much the Lord has done for our souls. Comfort by our example any unrighteous who despair of God's goodness, so that all may know what may be done for those who ask with prayer, when such benefits are granted sinners even against their will. Consider the magnanimous design of God's mercy for us, the compassion with which the Lord directed his judgement towards our chastisement, the wisdom whereby he made use of evil itself and mercifully set aside our impiety, so that by a wholly justified wound in a single part of my body he might heal two souls. Compare our danger and manner of deliverance, compare the sickness and the medicine. Examine the cause, our deserts, and marvel at the effect, his pity.

You know the depths of shame to which my unbridled lust had consigned our bodies, until no reverence for decency or for God even during the days of Our Lord's Passion, or of the greater sacraments[25] could keep me from wallowing in this mire. Even when you were unwilling, resisted to the utmost of your power and tried to dissuade me, as yours was the weaker nature I often forced you to consent with threats and blows. So intense were the fires of lust which bound me to you that I set those wretched, obscene pleasures, which we blush even to name, above God as above myself; nor would it seem that divine mercy could have taken action except by forbidding me these pleasures altogether, without future hope. And so it was wholly just and merciful, although by means of the supreme treachery of your uncle, for me to be reduced in that part of my body which was the seat of lust and sole reason for those desires, so that I could increase in many ways; in order that this member should justly be punished for all its wrongdoing in us, expiate in suffering the sins committed for its amusement and cut me off from the slough of filth in which I had been wholly immersed in mind as in body. Only thus could I become more fit to approach the holy altars, now that no contagion of carnal impurity would ever again call me from them. How mercifully did he want me to suffer so much only in that member, the privation of which would also further the salvation of my soul without defiling my body nor preventing any performance of my duties! Indeed, it would make me readier to perform whatever can be honourably done by setting me wholly free from the heavy yoke of carnal desire.

So when divine grace cleansed rather than deprived me of those vilest members which from their practice of utmost indecency are called 'the parts of shame' and have no proper name of their own, what else did it do but remove a foul imperfection in order to preserve perfect purity? Such purity, as we have heard, certain sages have desired so eagerly that they have mutilated themselves, so as to remove entirely the shame of desire. The Apostle too is recorded as having besought the Lord to rid him of this thorn in the flesh, but was not heard.[26] The great Christian philosopher Origen provides an example, for he was not afraid to mutilate himself in order to quench completely this fire within him, as if he understood literally the words that those men were truly blessed who castrated themselves for the Kingdom of Heaven's sake, and believed them to be truthfully carrying out the bidding of the Lord about offending members, that we should cut them off and throw them away;[27] and as if he interpreted as historic fact, not as a hidden symbol, that prophecy of Isaiah in which the Lord prefers eunuchs to the rest of the faithful: 'The eunuchs who keep my sabbaths, and choose to do my will I will give a place in my own house and within my walls and a name better than sons and daughters. I will give them an everlasting name which shall not perish.'[28] Yet Origen is seriously to be blamed because he sought a remedy for blame in punishment of his body. True, he has zeal for God, but an ill-informed zeal,[29] and the charge of homicide can be made against him for his self-mutilation. People think he did this either at the suggestion of the devil or in grave error but, in my case, through God's compassion, it was done by another's hand. I do not incur blame, I escape it. I deserve death and gain life. I am summoned and reprieved; I persist in crime and am pardoned against my will. The Apostle prays and is not heard, he persists in prayer and is not answered. Truly the Lord takes thought for me. I will go then and declare how much the Lord has done for my soul.[30]

Come too, my inseparable companion, and join me in thanksgiving, you who were made my partner both in guilt and in grace. For the Lord is not unmindful also of your own salvation, indeed, he has you much in mind, for by a kind of holy presage of his name he marked you out to be especially his when he named you Heloise, after his own name, Elohim.[31] In his mercy, I say, he intended to provide for two people in one, the two whom the devil sought to destroy in one; since a short while before this happening he had bound us together by the indissoluble bond of the marriage sacrament. At the time I desired to keep you whom I loved beyond measure for myself alone for ever, but he was already planning to use this opportunity for our joint conversion to himself. Had you not been previously joined to me in wedlock, you might easily have clung to the world when I withdrew from it, either at the suggestion of your relatives or in enjoyment of carnal delights. See then, how greatly the Lord was concerned for us, as if he were reserving us for some great ends, and was indignant or grieved because our knowledge of letters, the talents which he had entrusted to us, were not being used to glorify his name; or as if he feared for his humble and incontinent servant, because it is written 'Women make even the wise forsake their faith.'[32] Indeed, this is proved in the case of the wisest of men, Solomon.[33]

How great an interest the talent of your own wisdom pays daily to the Lord in the many spiritual daughters you have born for him, while I remain totally barren and labour in vain amongst the sons of perdition! What a hateful loss and grievous misfortune if you had abandoned yourself to the defilement of carnal pleasures only to bear in suffering a few children for the world, when now you are delivered in exultation of numerous progeny for heaven! Nor would you have been more than a woman, whereas now you rise even above men, and have turned the curse of Eve into the blessing of Mary. How unseemly for those holy hands which now turn the pages of sacred books to have to do the obscene degradations of women's work! God himself has thought fit to raise us up from the contamination of this filth and the pleasures of this mire and draw us to him by force – the same force whereby he chose to strike and convert Paul[34] – and by our example perhaps to deter from our audacity others who are also trained in letters.

I beg you then, sister, do not be aggrieved, do not vex the Father who corrects us in fatherly wise; pay heed to what is written: 'Whom the Lord loves he reproves' and 'He lays the rod on every son whom he acknowledges.' And elsewhere: 'A father who spares the rod hates his son.'[35] This punishment is momentary, not eternal, and for our purification, not damnation. Hear the prophet and take heart: 'The Lord will not judge twice on the same issue and no second tribulation shall arise.'[36] Listen too to that supreme and mighty exhortation of the Truth: 'By your endurance you will possess your souls.'[37] Solomon, too: 'Better be slow to anger than be a fighter; and master one's heart rather than storm a city.'[38] Are you not moved to tears or remorse by the only begotten Son of God who, for you and for all mankind, in his innocence was seized by the hands of impious men, dragged along and scourged, blindfolded, mocked at, buffeted, spat upon, crowned with thorns, finally hanged between thieves on the Cross, at the time so shameful a gibbet, to die a horrible and accursed form of death? Have this man always, sister, as your true spouse and the spouse of all the Church. Keep him in mind. Look at him going to be crucified for your sake, carrying his own cross. Be one of the crowd, one of the women who wept and lamented over him, as Luke tells: 'A great crowd of people followed, many women among them, who wept and lamented over him.' To these he graciously turned and mercifully foretold the destruction which would come to avenge his death, against which they could provide, if they understood. 'Daughters of Jerusalem,' he said, 'do not weep for me; no, weep for yourselves and your children. For the days are surely coming when they will say, "Happy are the barren, the wombs that never bore a child, the breasts that never fed one." Then they will start saying to the mountains, "Fall on us," and to the hills, "Cover us." For if these things are done when the wood is green, what will happen when it is dry?'[39]

Have compassion on him who suffered willingly for your redemption, and look with remorse on him who was crucified for you. In your mind be always present at his tomb, weep and wail with the faithful women, of whom it is written, as I said, 'The women sitting at the tomb wept and lamented for the Lord.' Prepare with them the perfumes for his burial, but better perfumes, which are of the spirit, not of the body, for this is the fragrance he needs though he rejected the other. Be remorseful over this with all your powers of devotion, for he exhorts the faithful to this remorse and compassion in the words of Jeremiah: 'All you who pass by, look and see if there is any sorrow like my sorrow.'[40] That is, if there is some sufferer for whom you should sorrow in compassion when I alone, for no guilt of mine, atone for the sins of others. He himself is the way whereby the faithful pass from exile to their own country. He too has set up the Cross, from which he summons us, as a ladder for us to use. On this, for you, the only begotten Son of God was killed; he was made an offering because he wished it. Grieve with compassion over him alone and share his suffering in your grief. Fulfil what was foretold of devout souls through the prophet Zachariah: 'They shall wail for him as over an only child, and shall grieve for him as for the death of a first-born son.'[41]

See, sister, what great mourning there is amongst those who love their king over the death of his only and first begotten son. Behold the lamentation and grief with which the whole household and court are consumed; and when you come to the bride of the only son who is dead, you will find her wailing intolerable and more than you can bear. This mourning, sister, should be yours and also the wailing, for you were joined to this bridegroom in blissful matrimony. He bought you not with his wealth, but with himself. He bought and redeemed you with his own blood. See what right he has over you, and know how precious you are. This is the price which the Apostle has in mind when he considers how little he is worth for whom the price was paid, and what return he should make for such a gift: 'God forbid that I should boast of anything but the Cross of our Lord Jesus Christ, through whom the world is crucified to me and I to the world!'[42] You are greater than heaven, greater than the world, for the Creator of the world himself became the price for you. What has he seen in you, I ask you, when he lacks nothing, to make him seek even the agonies of a fearful and inglorious death in order to purchase you? What, I repeat, does he seek in you except yourself? He is the true friend who desires yourself and nothing that is yours, the true friend who said when he was about to die for you: 'There is no greater love than this, that a man should lay down his life for his friends.'[43]

It was he who truly loved you, not I. My love, which brought us both to sin, should be called lust, not love. I took my fill of my wretched pleasures in you, and this was the sum total of my love. You say I suffered for you, and perhaps that is true, but it was really through you, and even this, unwillingly; not for love of you but under compulsion, and to bring you not salvation but sorrow. But he suffered truly for your salvation, on your behalf of his own free will, and by his suffering he cures all sickness and removes all suffering. To him, I beseech you, not to me, should be directed all your devotion, all your compassion, all your remorse. Weep for the injustice of the great cruelty inflicted on him, not for the just and righteous payment demanded of me, or rather, as I said, the supreme grace granted us both. For you are unrighteous if you do not love righteousness, and most unrighteous if you consciously oppose the will, or more truly, the boundless grace of God. Mourn for your Saviour and Redeemer, not for your corrupter and fornicator; wail for the Lord who died for you, not for the servant who lives and, indeed, for the first time is truly freed from death. I beg you, beware lest Pompey's reproach to weeping Cornelia is applied to you, to your shame:

> The battle ended, Pompey the Great
> Lives, but his fortune died. It is this you now mourn
> And loved.[44]

Take this to heart, I pray, and blush for shame, unless you would commend the wanton vileness of our former ways. And so I ask you, sister, to accept patiently what mercifully befell us. This is a father's rod, not a persecutor's sword. The father strikes to correct, and to forestall the enemy who strikes to kill. By a wound he prevents death, he does not deal it; he thrusts in the steel to cut out disease. He wounds the body, and heals the soul; he makes to live what he should have destroyed, cuts out impurity to leave what is pure. He punishes once so that he need not punish forever. One suffers the wound so that two may be spared death; two were guilty, one pays the penalty. That, too, was granted by divine mercy to your weaker nature and, in a way, with justice, for you were naturally weaker in sex and stronger in continence, and so the less deserving of punishment. For this I give thanks to the Lord, who both spared you punishment then and reserved you for a crown to come, and who also by a moment of suffering in my body cooled once and for all the fires of that lust in which I had been wholly absorbed through my excessive incontinence, lest I be consumed. The many greater sufferings of the heart through the continual prompting of the flesh of your own youth he has reserved for a martyr's crown. Though you may weary of hearing this and forbid it to be said, the truth of it is clear. For the one who must always strive there is also a crown; and the athlete cannot win his crown unless he has kept to the rules.[45] But no crown is waiting for me, because no cause for striving remains. The matter for strife is lacking in him from whom the thorn of desire is pulled out.

Yet I think it is something, even though I may receive no crown, if I can escape further punishment, and by the pain of a single momentary punishment may perhaps be let off much that would be eternal. For it is written of the men, or rather, the beasts of this wretched life, 'The beasts have rotted in their dung.'[46] Then too, I complain less that my own merit is diminished when I am confident that yours is increasing; for we are one in Christ, one flesh according to the law of matrimony. Whatever is yours cannot, I think, fail to be mine, and Christ is yours because you have become his bride. Now, as I said before, you have as a servant me whom in the past you recognized as your lord, more your own now when bound to you by spiritual love than one subjected by fear. And so I have increasing confidence that you will plead for us both before him and, through your prayer, I may be granted what I cannot obtain through my own; especially now, when the daily pressure of dangers and disturbances threaten my life and give me no time for prayer. Nor can I imitate that blessed eunuch, the high official of Candace, Queen of Ethiopia, who had charge of all her wealth, and had come from so far to worship in Jerusalem. He was on his way home when the apostle Philip was sent by the angel to convert him to the faith, as he had already deserved by his prayers and his assiduous reading of the Scriptures. Because he did not want to take time from this even on his journey, although he was a man of great wealth and a gentile, it came about through the great goodness of providence that the passage of Scripture was before him which gave the apostle the perfect opportunity for his conversion.[47]

So that nothing may delay my petition nor defer its fulfilment, I hasten to compose and send to you this prayer, which you may offer to the Lord in supplication on our behalf:

God, who at the beginning of human creation, in forming woman from a rib of man didst especially sanctify the sacrament of the marriage bond, and who didst glorify marriage with boundless honours both by being born of one given in marriage and by the first of thy miracles; thou who moreover didst grant this remedy for the incontinence of my frailty, in such manner as pleased thee, despise not the prayers of thy humble handmaid which I pour out as a suppliant in the presence of thy majesty for my own excesses and those of my beloved. Pardon, O most gracious, who art rather graciousness itself, pardon our many great offences, and let the ineffable immensity of thy mercy test the multitude of our faults. Punish the guilty now, I beseech thee, that thou mayst spare them hereafter. Punish now, lest thou punish in eternity. Take to thy servants the rod of correction, not the sword of wrath. Afflict their flesh that thou mayst preserve their souls. Come as a redeemer, not an avenger; gracious rather than just; the merciful Father, not the stern Lord. Prove us, Lord, and test us,[48] in the manner in which the prophet asks for himself, as if he said openly: First consider my strength and measure accordingly the burden of my testing. This is what St Paul promises to the faithful, when he says 'God keeps faith, and he will not allow you to be tested beyond your powers, but when the test comes he will also provide a way out, so that you are able to sustain it.'[49] Thou hast joined us, Lord, and thou hast parted us, when and in what manner it pleased thee. Now, Lord, what thou hast mercifully begun, most mercifully end, and those whom thou hast parted for a time on earth, unite forever to thyself in heaven: thou who art our hope, our portion, our expectation and our consolation, O Lord, who art blessed world without end. Amen.

Farewell in Christ, bride of Christ; in Christ fare well and live in Christ.

THE LETTERS OF
DIRECTION

LETTER 6
HELOISE TO ABELARD

To him who is specially hers, she who is singularly his.

Or: *To the lord especially, she who is singularly his.*[1]

I would not want to give you cause for finding me disobedient in anything, so I have set the bridle of your injunction on the words which issue from my unbounded grief; thus in writing at least I may moderate what it is difficult or rather impossible to forestall in speech. For nothing is less under our control than the heart – having no power to command it we are forced to obey. And so when its impulses move us, none of us can stop their sudden promptings from easily breaking out, and even more easily overflowing into words which are the every-ready indications of the heart's emotions: as it is written, 'A man's words are spoken from the overflowing of the heart.'[2] I will therefore hold my hand from writing words which I cannot restrain my tongue from speaking; would that a grieving heart would be as ready to obey as a writer's hand! And yet you have it in your power to remedy my grief, even if you cannot entirely remove it. As one nail drives out another hammered in,[3] a new thought expels an old, when the mind is intent on other things and forced to dismiss or interrupt its recollection of the past. But the more fully any thought occupies the mind and distracts it from other things, the more worthy should be the subject of such a thought and the more important it is where we direct our minds.

And so all we handmaids of Christ, who are your daughters in Christ, come as suppliants to demand of your paternal interest two things which we see to be very necessary for ourselves. One is that you will teach us how the order of nuns began and what authority there is for our profession. The other, that you will prescribe some Rule for us and write it down, a Rule which shall be suitable for women, and also describe fully the manner and habit of our way of life, which we find was never done by the holy Fathers. Through lack and need of this it is the practice today for men and women alike to be received into monasteries to profess the same Rule, and the same yoke of monastic ordinance is laid on the weaker sex as on the stronger.

At present the one Rule of St Benedict[4] is professed in the Latin Church by women equally with men, although, as it was clearly written for men alone, it can only be fully obeyed by men, whether subordinates or superiors. Leaving aside for the moment the other articles of the Rule: how can women be concerned with what is written there about cowls, drawers or scapulars?[5] Or indeed, with tunics or woollen garments worn next to the skin, when the monthly purging of their superfluous humours must avoid such things? How are they affected by the ruling for the abbot, that he shall read aloud the Gospel himself and afterwards start the hymn?[6] What about the abbot's table, set apart for him with pilgrims and guests? Which is more fitting for our religious life: for an abbess never to offer hospitality to men, or for her to eat with men she has allowed in? It is all too easy for the souls of men and women to be destroyed if they live together in one place, and especially at table, where gluttony and drunkenness are rife, and wine which leads to lechery[7] is drunk with enjoyment. St Jerome warns us of this when he writes to remind a mother and daughter that 'It is difficult to preserve modesty at table.'[8] And the poet himself, that master of sensuality and shame, in his book called *The Art of Love* describes in detail what an opportunity for fornication is provided especially by banquets:

> When wine has sprinkled Cupid's thirsty wings
> He stays and stands weighed down in his chosen place . . .
> Then laughter comes, then even the poor find plenty,
> Then sorrow and care and wrinkles leave the brow . . .
> That is the time when girls bewitch men's hearts,
> And Venus in the wine adds fire to fire.[9]

And even if they admit to their table only women to whom they have given hospitality, is there no lurking danger there? Surely nothing is so conducive to a woman's seduction as woman's flattery, nor does a woman pass on the foulness of a corrupted mind so readily to any but another woman; which is why St Jerome particularly exhorts women of a sacred calling to avoid contact with women of the world.[10] Finally, if we exclude men from our hospitality and admit women only, it is obvious that we shall offend and annoy the men whose services are needed by a convent of the weaker sex, especially if little or no return seems to be made to those from whom most is received.

But if we cannot observe the tenor of this Rule, I am afraid that the words of the apostle James may be quoted to condemn us also: 'For if a man keeps the whole law but for one single point, he is guilty of breaking all of it.' That is to say, although he carries out much of the law he is held guilty simply because he fails to carry out all of it, and he is turned into a law-breaker by the one thing he did not keep unless he fulfilled all the law's precepts. The apostle is careful to explain this at once by adding: 'For the One who said "Thou shalt not commit adultery" said also "Thou shalt not commit murder." You may not be an adulterer, but if you commit murder you are a law-breaker all the same.'[11] Here he says openly that a man becomes guilty by breaking any one of the law's commandments, for the Lord himself who laid down one also laid down the other, and whatever commandment of the law is violated, it shows disregard of him who laid down the law in all its commandments, not in one alone.

However, to pass over those provisions of the Rule which we are unable to observe in every detail, or cannot observe without danger to ourselves: what about gathering in the harvest – has it ever been the custom for convents of nuns to go out to do this, or to tackle the work of the fields? Again, are we to test the constancy of the women we receive during the space of a single year, and instruct them by three readings of the Rule,[12] as it says there? What could be so foolish as to set out on an unknown path, not yet defined, or so presumptuous as to choose and profess a way of life of which you know nothing, or to take a vow you are not capable of keeping? And since discretion is the mother of all the virtues and reason the mediator of all that is good, who will judge anything virtuous or good which is seen to conflict with discretion and reason? For the virtues which exceed all bounds and measure are, as Jerome says, to be counted among vices.[13] It is clearly contrary to reason and discretion if burdens are imposed without previous investigation into the strength of those who are to bear them, to ensure that human industry may depend on natural constitution. No one would lay on an ass a burden suitable for an elephant, or expect the same from children and old people as from men, the same, that is, from the weak as from the strong, from the sick as from the healthy, from women, the weaker sex, as from men, the stronger one. The Pope St Gregory was careful to make this distinction as regards both admonition and precept in the twenty-fourth chapter of his *Pastoral Rule*:[14] 'Therefore men are to be admonished in one way, women in another; for heavy burdens may be laid on men and great matters exercise them, but lighter burdens on women, who should be gently converted by less exacting means.'

Certainly those who laid down rules for monks were not only completely silent about women but also prescribed regulations which they knew to be quite unsuitable for them, and this showed plainly enough that the necks of bullock and heifer should in no sense be brought under the same yoke of a common Rule, since those whom nature created unequal cannot properly be made equal in labour. St Benedict, who is imbued with the spirit of justice in everything, has this discretion in mind when he moderates everything in the Rule according to the quality of men or the times, so that, as he says himself at one point, all may be done in moderation.[15] And so first of all, starting with the abbot himself, he lays down that he shall preside over his subordinates in such a way that (he says)

he will accommodate and adapt himself to them all in accordance with the disposition and intelligence of each individual. In this way he will suffer no loss in the flock entrusted to him but will even rejoice to see a good flock increase ... At the same time he must always be conscious of his own frailty and remember that the bruised reed must not be broken . . . He must also be prudent and considerate, bearing in mind the good sense of holy Jacob when he said: 'If I drive my herds too hard on the road they will all die in a single day.' Acting on this, and on other examples of discretion, the mother of the virtues, he must arrange everything so that there is always what the strong desire and the weak do not shrink from.[16]

Such modification of regulations is the basis of the concessions granted to children, and the old and the weak in general, of the feeding of the lector or weekly server in the kitchen before the rest,[17] and in the monastery itself, the provision of food and drink in quality or quantity adapted to the diversity of the people there. All these matters are precisely set out in the Rule. He also relaxes the set times for fasting according to the season or the amount of work to be done, to meet the needs of natural infirmity. What, I wonder, when he adapts everything to the quality of men and seasons, so that all his regulations can be carried out by everyone without complaint – what provision would he make for women if he laid down a Rule for them like that for men? For if in certain respects he is obliged to modify the strictness of the Rule for the young, the old and weak, according to their natural frailty or infirmity, what would he provide for the weaker sex whose frailty and infirmity is generally known?

Consider then how far removed it is from all reason and good sense if both women and men are bound by profession of a common Rule, and the same burden is laid on the weak as on the strong. I think it should be sufficient for our infirmity if the virtue of continence and also of abstinence makes us the equals of the rulers of the Church themselves and of the clergy who are confirmed in holy orders, especially when the Truth says: 'Everyone will be fully trained if he reaches his teacher's level.'[18] It would also be thought a great thing if we could equal religious laymen; for what is judged unimportant in the strong is admired in the weak. In the words of the Apostle: 'My strength is made perfect in weakness.'[19] But lest we should underestimate the religion of the laity, of men like Abraham, David and Job, although they had wives, Chrysostom reminds us[20] in his seventh sermon on the Letter to the Hebrews:

There are many ways whereby a man may struggle to charm that beast. What are they? Toil, study, vigils. 'But what concern are they of ours, when we are not monks?' Do you ask me that? Rather, ask Paul, when he says: 'Be watchful in all tribulation and persevere in prayer' and 'Give no more thought to satisfying the bodily appetites.'[21] For he wrote these things not only for monks but for all who were in the cities, and the layman should not have greater freedom than the monk, apart from sleeping with his wife. He has permission for this, but not for other things; and in everything he must conduct himself like a monk. The Beatitudes too, which are the actual words of Christ, were not addressed to monks alone, otherwise the whole world must perish . . . and he would have confined the things which belong to virtue within narrow limits. And how can marriage be honourable[22] when it weighs so heavily on us?

From these words it can easily be inferred that anyone who adds the virtue of continence to the precepts of the Gospel will achieve monastic perfection. Would that our religion could rise to this height – to carry out the Gospel, not to go beyond it, lest we attempt to be more than Christians! Surely this is the reason (if I am not mistaken) why the holy Fathers decided not to lay down a general Rule for us as for men, like a new law, nor to burden our weakness with a great number of vows; they looked to the words of the Apostle: 'Because law can bring only retribution; but where there is no law there can be no breach of law.' And again, 'Law intruded to multiply law-breaking.'[23] The same great preacher of continence also shows great consideration for our weakness and appears to urge the younger widows to a second marriage, when he says: 'It is my wish, therefore, that young widows shall marry again, have children and preside over a home. Then they will give no opponent occasion for slander.'[24] St Jerome also believes this to be salutary advice, and tells Eustochium of the rash vows taken by women, in these words:

'But if those who are virgins are still not saved, because of other faults, what will become of those who have prostituted the members of Christ and turned the temple of the Holy Spirit into a brothel? It were better for a man to have entered matrimony and walked on the level than to strain after the heights and fall into the depths of hell.'[25] St Augustine too has women's rashness in taking vows in mind when he writes to Julian in his book *On the Continence of Widows*: 'Let her who has not begun, think it over, and her who has made a start, continue. No opportunity must be given to the enemy, no offering taken from Christ.'[26]

Consequently, canon law has taken our weakness into account, and laid down that deaconesses must not be ordained before the age of forty, and only then after thorough probation, while deacons may be promoted from the age of twenty. And in the monasteries there are those called the Canons Regular of St Augustine who claim to profess a certain rule and think themselves in no way inferior to monks although we see them eating meat and wearing linen. If our weakness can match their virtue, it should be considered no small thing. And Nature herself has made provision for our being safely granted a mild indulgence in any kind of food, for our sex is protected by greater sobriety. It is well known that women can be sustained on less nourishment and at less cost than men, and medicine teaches that they are not so easily intoxicated. And so Macrobius Theodosius in the seventh book of his *Saturnalia* notes that:

> Aristotle says that women are rarely intoxicated, but old men often. Woman has an extremely humid body, as can be known from her smooth and glossy skin, and especially from her regular purgations which rid the body of superfluous moisture. So when wine is drunk and merged with so general a humidity, it loses its power and does not easily strike the seat of the brain when its strength is extinguished.

Again:

> A woman's body which is destined for frequent purgations is pierced with several holes, so that it opens into channels and

provides outlets for the moisture draining away to be dispersed. Through these holes the fumes of wine are quickly released. By contrast, in old men the body is dry, as is shown by their rough and wrinkled skin.[27]

From this it can be inferred how much more safely and properly our nature and weakness can be allowed any sort of food and drink; in fact we cannot easily fall victims to gluttony and drunkenness, seeing that our moderation in food protects us from the one and the nature of the female body as described from the other. It should be sufficient for our infirmity, and indeed, a high tribute to it, if we live continently and without possessions, wholly occupied by service of God, and in doing so equal the leaders of the Church themselves in our way of life or religious laymen or even those who are called Canons Regular and profess especially to follow the apostolic life.

Finally, it is a great sign of forethought in those who bind themselves by vow to God if they perform more than they vow, so that they add something by grace to what they owe. For the Truth says in his own words: 'When you have carried out all your orders, say "We are useless servants and have only done our duty." '[28] Or, in plain words, 'We are useless and good for nothing, and deserve no credit, just because we were content only to pay what we owed and added nothing extra as a gift.' The Lord himself, speaking in a parable, says of what should be freely added: 'But if you give more in addition, I will repay you on my return.'[29]

If indeed many of those who rashly profess monastic observance today would pay more careful attention to this, would consider beforehand what it is that they profess in their vows, and study closely the actual tenor of the Rule, they would offend less through ignorance, and sin less through negligence. As things are, they all hurry almost equally indiscriminately to enter monastic life: they are received without proper discipline and live with even less, they profess a Rule they do not know and are equally ready to despise it and set up as law the customs they prefer. We must therefore be careful not to impose on a woman a burden under which we see nearly all men stagger and even fall.

We see that the world has now grown old, and that with all other living creatures men too have lost their former natural vigour: and, in the words of the Truth, amongst many or indeed almost all men love itself has grown cold.[30] And so it would seem necessary today to change or to modify those Rules which were written for men in accordance with men's present nature.

St Benedict himself was also well aware of this need to discriminate, and admits that he has so tempered the rigour of monastic strictness that he regards the Rule he has set out, in comparison with earlier institutes, as no more than a basis for virtuous living and the beginning of a monastic life. He says that 'We have written down this Rule in order that by practising it we may show that we have attained some degree of virtue and the rudiments of monastic observance. But for anyone who would hasten towards perfection of the monastic life, there are the teachings of the holy Fathers, observance of which may lead a man to the summit of perfection.' And again, 'Whoever you are, then, who hasten to the heavenly kingdom, observe, with Christ's help, this minimum Rule as a beginning, and then you will come finally to the higher peaks of doctrine and virtue, under the protection of God.'[31] He also says specifically that whereas we read that the holy Fathers of old used to complete the psalter in a single day, he has modified psalmody for the lukewarm so as to spread the psalms over a week; the monks may then be content with a smaller number of them, as the clergy are.[32]

Moreover, what is so contrary to the religious life and peace of the monastery as the thing which most encourages sensuality and starts up disturbances, which destroys our reason, the very image of God in us, whereby we are raised above the rest of creation? That thing is wine, which the Scriptures declare to be the most harmful of any form of nourishment, warning us to beware of it. The wisest of wise men refers to it in Proverbs in these words:

Wine is reckless and strong drink quarrelsome; no one who delights in it grows wise ... Who will know woe, as his father will, and quarrels, brawls, bruises without cause and bloodshot eyes? Those who linger late over their wine, and look for ready-mixed wine. Do not look at the wine when it glows and sparkles in the glass. It goes down smoothly, but in the end it will bite like a snake and spread venom like a serpent. Then your eyes will see strange sights, and your mind utter distorted words; you will be like a man sleeping in mid-ocean, like a drowsy helmsman who has lost his rudder, and you will say: 'They struck me and it did not hurt, dragged me off and I felt nothing. When I wake up I shall turn to wine again . . .'[33]

And again:

Do not give wine to kings, O Lemuel, never to kings, for there is no privy council where drinking prevails. If they drink they may forget what they have decreed and neglect the pleas of the poor for their sons.[34]

In Ecclesiasticus too it is written: 'Wine and women rob the wise of their wits and are a hard test for good sense.'[35] Jerome himself also, when writing to Nepotian about the life of the clergy, and apparently highly indignant because the priests of the Law abstain from anything which could intoxicate them and surpass our own priests in such abstinence, says:

Never smell of wine, lest you hear said of you those words of the philosopher: 'This is not offering a kiss but proffering a cup.' The Apostle equally condemns priests who are given to drink, and the Old Law forbids it: 'Those who serve the altar shall not drink wine nor strong drink.' By 'strong drink' in Hebrew is understood any drink which can intoxicate, whether produced by fermentation, or from apple juice, or from honey-comb which has been distilled into a sweet, rough drink, or when the fruit of the date palm is pressed into liquid, or water is enriched with boiled grain. Whatever intoxicates and upsets the balance of the mind, shun it like wine.[36]

See how what is forbidden kings to enjoy is wholly denied to priests, and is known to be more dangerous than any food. And yet so spiritual a man as St Benedict himself is compelled to allow it to monks as a sort of concession to the times in which he lived. 'Although,' he says, 'we read that wine is no drink for monks, yet because nowadays monks cannot be persuaded of this, etc.'[37] He had read, if I am not mistaken, these passages in the *Lives of the Fathers*:

Certain people told abba Pastor that a particular monk drank no wine, to which he replied that wine was not for monks.

And further on:

There was once a celebration of the Mass on the Mount of abba Antony, and a jar of wine was found there. One of the elders took a small vessel, carried a cupful to abba Sisoi and gave it to him. He drank once, and a second time he took it and drank, but when it was offered a third time he refused, saying 'Peace, brother, do you not know it is Satan?'

It is also said of abba Sisoi:

His disciple Abraham then asked, 'If this happens on the Sabbath and the Lord's Day in church, and he drinks three cups, is that too much?' 'If it were not Satan,' the old man replied, 'it would not be much.'[38]

On the question of meat: where, I ask you, has this ever been condemned by God or forbidden to monks? Look, pray, and mark how of necessity St Benedict modifies the Rule on this point too (though it is more dangerous for monks and he knew it was not for them), because in his day it was impossible to persuade monks to abstain from meat. I would like to see the same dispensation granted in our own times, with a similar modification regarding matters which fall between good and evil and are called indifferent, so that vows would not compel what cannot now be gained by persuasion. If concession were made without scandal on neutral points, it would be enough to forbid only what is sinful. Thus the same dispensations could be made for food as for clothing, so that provision could be made of what can be purchased more cheaply, and, in everything, necessity not superfluity could be our consideration. For things which do not prepare us for the Kingdom of God or commend us least to God call for no special attention. These are all outward works which are common to the damned and elect alike, as much to hypocrites as to the religious.[39] For nothing so divides Jew from Christian as the distinction between outward and inner works, especially since between the children of God and those of the devil love alone distinguishes: what the Apostle calls the sum of the law and the object of what is commanded.[40] And so he also disparages pride in works in order to set above it the righteousness of faith, and thus addresses Jewry:

> What room then is left for human pride? It is excluded. And on what principle? Of works? No, but through the principle of faith. For our argument is that a man is justified by faith without observances of the law.

And again:

> For if Abraham was justified by works, then he has a ground for pride, but not before God: for what does Scripture say? 'Abraham put his faith in the Lord and that faith was counted to him as righteousness.'

Once more:

> But if without any work he simply puts his faith in him who makes a just man of the sinner, then his faith is indeed 'counted as righteousness' according to God's gracious plan.[41]

The Apostle also allows Christians to eat all kinds of food and distinguishes from it those things which count as righteous. 'The Kingdom of God,' he says, 'is not eating and drinking, but justice, peace, and joy in the Holy Spirit . . . Everything is pure in itself, but anything is bad for the man who gives offence by his eating. It is a good thing not to eat meat and not to drink wine, nor to do anything which may offend or scandalize or weaken your brother.'[42] In this passage there is no eating of food forbidden, only the giving of offence by eating, because certain converted Jews were scandalized when they saw things being eaten which the Law had forbidden. The apostle Peter was also trying to avoid giving such offence when he was seriously rebuked and wholesomely corrected, as Paul himself recounts in his letter to the Galatians.[43] Paul also writes to the Corinthians: 'Certainly food does not commend us to God,' and again: 'You may eat anything sold in the meat market ... The earth is the Lord's and all that is in it.'[44] To the Colossians he says: 'Allow no one therefore to take you to task about what you eat or drink,' and later on, 'If you died with Christ and passed beyond the elements of this world, why do you behave as though still living the life of the world? "Do not touch this, do not taste that, do not handle the other" – these are all things which perish as we use them, all based on the injunctions and teaching of men.'[45] The elements of the world are what he calls the first rudiments of the law dealing with carnal observances, in the practice of which, as in learning the rudiments of letters, the world, that is, a people still carnal, was engaged. But those who are Christ's own are dead as regards these rudiments or carnal observances, for they owe them nothing, as they no longer live in this world among carnal people who pay heed to forms and distinguish or discriminate between certain foods and similar things, and so say 'Do not touch this or that.' For such things when touched or tasted or handled, says the Apostle, are destructive to the soul in the act of using them for some purpose only in accordance with the precepts and teaching of men, that is, of carnal beings who interpret the law in a worldly sense and not in the way of Christ or of his own.

When Christ sent his apostles out to preach, at a time when it was even more necessary to avoid any scandal, he allowed them to eat any kind of food, so that wherever they might be shown hospitality they could live like their hosts, eating and drinking what was in the house.[46] Paul certainly foresaw through the Holy Spirit that they would fall away from this, the Lord's teaching and his own, and wrote on the subject to Timothy:

The Spirit says expressly that in after-times some will desert from the faith and give their minds to subversive doctrines inspired by devils who speak lies in hypocrisy . . . They forbid marriage and demand abstinence from certain foods, though God created them to be enjoyed with thanksgiving by believers who have inward knowledge of the truth. For everything that God created is good, and nothing is to be rejected when it is taken with thanksgiving, since it is hallowed by God's own word and by prayer. By offering such advice as this to the brotherhood you will prove a good servant of Jesus Christ, bred in the precepts of our faith and of the sound instruction which you have followed.[47]

But if anyone turns his bodily eye to the display of outward abstinence, he would then prefer John and John's disciples wasting away through excessive fasting, to Christ and his disciples: and indeed, John's disciples who were apparently still following Jewish custom in outward matters grumbled against Christ and his disciples, and even questioned the Lord himself: 'Why is it that John's disciples and the disciples of the Pharisees are fasting but yours are not?'[48] In examining this passage and determining the difference between virtue and exhibition of virtue, St Augustine concludes that as regards outward matters, works add nothing to merit. In his book *On the Good of Marriage* he says that:

Continence is a virtue not of the body but of the soul. But the virtues of the spirit are displayed sometimes in works, sometimes in natural habit, as when the virtue of martyrs has been seen in their endurance of suffering. Also, patience was already in Job; the Lord knew this and gave proof of knowing it, but he made it known to men through the ordeal of Job's testing.[49]

And again:

So that it may truly be better understood how virtue may be in natural habit though not in works, I will quote an example of which no Catholic is in doubt. That the Lord Jesus, in the truth of the flesh, was hungry and thirsty and ate and drank, no one can fail to know who is faithful to his Gospel. Yet surely the virtue of continence was as great in him as in John the Baptist? 'For John came neither eating nor drinking and men said he was possessed. The Son of man came eating and drinking and they said, "Look at him, a glutton and a drinker, a friend of taxgatherers and sinners!"' After which he added, 'And yet God's wisdom is proved right by its own children,'[50] for they see that the virtue of continence ought always to exist in natural habit but is shown in practice only in appropriate times and seasons, as was the virtue of endurance in the holy martyrs ... And so just as the merit of endurance is not greater in the case of Peter who suffered martyrdom than in John who did not, so John who never married wins no greater merit for continence than Abraham who fathered children, for the celibacy of the one and the marriage of the other both fought for Christ in accordance with the difference of their times. Yet John was continent in practice as well, Abraham only as a habit. At the time after the days of the Patriarchs, when the Law declared a man to be accursed if he did not perpetuate his race in Israel, a man who could have continence did not reveal himself, but even so, he had it.[51] Afterwards 'the term was completed' when it could be said, 'Let the man accept it who can';[52] and if he can, put it into practice, but if he does not wish to do so, he must not claim it untruthfully.[53]

From these words it is clear that virtues alone win merit in the eyes of God, and that those who are equal in virtue, however different in works, deserve equally of him.

Consequently, those who are true Christians are wholly occupied with the inner man, so that they may adorn him with virtues and purify him of vices, but they have little or no concern for the outer man. We read that the apostles themselves were so simple and almost rough in their manner even when in the company of the Lord, that they were apparently forgetful of respect and propriety, and when walking through the cornfields were not ashamed to pick the ears of corn[54] and strip and eat them like children. Nor were they careful about washing their hands before taking food; but when they were rebuked by some for what was thought an unclean habit, the Lord made excuses for them, saying that 'To eat without first washing his hands does not defile a man.' He then added the general ruling that the soul is not defiled by any outward thing but only by what proceeds from the heart, 'wicked thoughts, adultery, murder'[55] and so on. For unless the spirit be first corrupted by evil intention, whatever is done outwardly in the body cannot be a sin. He also rightly says that even adultery or murder proceed from the heart and can be perpetrated without bodily contact, as in the words: 'If a man looks upon a woman with a lustful eye he has already committed adultery with her in his heart,' and 'Everyone who hates his brother is a murderer.' Such acts are not necessarily committed by contact with or injury to the body, as when, for instance, a woman is violently assaulted or a judge compelled in justice to kill a man. 'No murderer', it is written, 'has a place in the Kingdom of Christ and of God.'[56]

And so it is not so much what things are done as the spirit in which they are done that we must consider, if we wish to please him who tests the heart and the loins and sees in hidden places, 'who will judge the secrets of men', says Paul, 'in accordance with my gospel',[57] that is, according to the doctrine of his preaching. Consequently, the modest offering of the widow, which was two tiny coins worth a farthing,[58] was preferred to the lavish offerings of all the rich by him of whom it is said that he has no need of any possessions, and who takes pleasure in the offering because of the giver, rather than in the giver because of his offering: as it is written 'The Lord received Abel and his gift with favour,'[59] that is, he looked first at the devotion of the giver and was pleased with the gift offered because of him. Such devotion of the heart is valued the more highly by God the less it is concerned with outward things, and we serve him with greater humility and think more of our duty to him the less we put our trust in outward things. The Apostle too, after writing to Timothy on the subject of a general indulgence about food, as I said above, went on to speak of training the body: 'Keep yourself in training for the practice of religion. The training of the body brings limited benefit, but the benefits of religion are without limit, since it holds promise not only for this life but for the life to come.'[60] For the pious devotion of the mind to

God wins from him both what is necessary in this life and things eternal in the life to come. By these examples are we not surely taught to think as Christians, and like Jacob to provide for our Father a meal from domestic animals and not go after wild game with Esau,[61] and act the Jew in outward things? Hence the verse of the Psalmist: 'I have bound myself with vows to thee, O God, and will redeem them with due thank-offerings.'[62] To this add the words of the poet: 'Do not look outside yourself.'[63]

There are many, indeed innumerable testimonies from the learned, both secular and ecclesiastic, to teach us that we should care little for what is performed outwardly and called indifferent, otherwise the works of the Law and the insupportable yoke of its bondage, as Peter calls it,[64] would be preferable to the freedom of the Gospel and the easy yoke and light burden of Christ. Christ himself invites us to this easy yoke and light burden in the words: 'Come to me, all you whose work is hard, whose load is heavy . . .'[65] The apostle Peter also sharply rebuked certain people who were already converted to Christ but believed they should still keep to the works of the Law, as it is recorded in the Acts of the Apostles: 'My brothers . . . why do you provoke God by laying on the shoulders of these converts a yoke which neither we nor our fathers were able to bear? No, we believe that it is by the grace of the Lord Jesus that we are saved, and so are they.'[66]

Do you then also, I beg you, who seek to imitate not only Christ but also this apostle, in discrimination as in name, modify your instructions for works to suit our weak nature, so that we can be free to devote ourselves to the offices of praising God. This is the offering which the Lord commends, rejecting all outward sacrifices, when he says: 'If I am hungry I will not tell you, for the world and all that is in it are mine. Shall I eat the flesh of your bulls or drink the blood of he-goats? Offer to God the sacrifice of thanksgiving and pay your vows to the Most High. Call upon me in time of trouble and I will come to your rescue, and you shall honour me.'[67]

We do not speak like this with the intention of rejecting physical labour when necessity demands it, but so as not to attach importance to things which serve bodily needs and obstruct the celebration of the divine office, particularly when on apostolic authority the special concession was granted to devout women of being supported by services provided by others rather than on the result of their own labour. Thus Paul writes to Timothy: 'If any among the faithful has widows in the family, he must support them himself: the Church must be relieved of the burden, so that it may be free to support those who are widows in the full sense.'[68] By widows in the full sense he means all women devoted to Christ, for whom not only are their husbands dead but the world is crucified and they too to the world. It is right and proper that they should be supported from the funds of the Church as if from the personal resources of their husbands. Hence the Lord provided his mother with an apostle to care for her instead of her own husband, and the apostles appointed seven deacons, or ministers of the Church, to minister to devout women.[69]

We know of course that when writing to the Thessalonians the Apostle sharply rebuked certain idle busybodies by saying that 'A man who will not work shall not eat', and that St Benedict instituted manual labour for the express purpose of preventing idleness.[70] But was not Mary sitting idle in order to listen to the words of Christ, while Martha was working for her as much as for the Lord and grumbling rather enviously about her sister's repose, as if she had to bear the burden and heat of the day alone?[71] Similarly today we see those who work on external things often complaining as they serve the earthly needs of those who are occupied with divine offices. Indeed, people often protest less about what tyrants seize from them than about what they are compelled to pay to those whom they call lazy and idle, although they observe them not only listening to Christ's words but also busily occupied in reading and chanting them. They do not see that it is no great matter, as the Apostle says, if they have to make material provision for those to whom they look for things of the spirit,[72] nor is it unbecoming for men occupied with earthly matters to serve those who are devoted to the spiritual. That is why the ministers of the Church were also granted by the sanction of the Law this salutary concession of freedom through leisure, whereby the tribe of Levi should have no patrimony in the land, the better to serve the Lord, but should receive tithes and offerings from the labour of others.[73]

As regards fasts, which Christians hold to be abstinence from vices rather than from food, you must consider whether anything should be added to what the Church has instituted, and order what is suitable for us.

But it is chiefly in connection with the offices of the Church and ordering of the psalms that provision is needed, so that here at least, if you think fit, you may allow some concession to our weakness, and when we recite the psalter in full within a week it shall not be necessary to repeat the same psalms. When St Benedict divided up the week according to his view, he left instructions that others could order the psalms differently, if it seemed better to do so,[74] for he expected that with passage of time the ceremonies of the Church would become more elaborate, and from a rough foundation would arise a splendid edifice.

Above all, we want you to decide what we ought to do about reading the Gospel in the Night Office.[75] It seems to us hazardous if priests and deacons, who should perform the reading, are allowed among us at such hours, when we should be especially segregated from the approach and sight of men in order to devote ourselves more sincerely to God and to be safer from temptation.

It is for you then, master, while you live, to lay down for us what Rule we are to follow for all time, for after God you are the founder of this place, through God you are the creator of our community,[76] with God you should be the director of our religious life. After you we may perhaps have another to guide us, one who will build something upon another's foundation, and so, we fear, he may be less likely to feel concern for us, or be less readily heard by us; or indeed, he may be no less willing, but less able. Speak to us then, and we shall hear. Farewell.

LETTER 7

ABELARD TO HELOISE

This long letter is Abelard's answer to Heloise's first question about the origin of nuns. To us it seems prolix and not very logical in the arrangement of the many examples it gives of the specially favoured position of women among the followers of Christ and in the early Church. It also draws comparisons between Christian women and the heroines of the Old Testament and classical antiquity. (BR) A fuller summary than that supplied by Radice follows, including quotations from Abelard.[1] (MTC)

'Out of love, dearest sister, you and your spiritual daughters have sought to know about the origin of your profession and how the religion of nuns began. I will reply as succinctly and shortly as I can. The order of monks and also of nuns has taken the form of its religion most fully from our Lord Jesus Christ.' Even before Christ, the germ of this idea already existed. The widow Anna, mentioned in St Luke's Gospel,[2] 'equally with Simeon, was held worthy to receive the Lord in the temple and to be filled with the spirit of prophecy'. As the embodiment of justice and the fulfilment of all good things, Christ comes in the fullness of time to perfect what is incomplete and to manifest what is unknown. 'As he came to call and redeem both sexes, he deigned to unite them in the true monkhood of his congregation, so that the authority of this profession is therefore granted to men and women alike and the perfection of the life he proposed is to be imitated by everybody.' Along with the male apostles and disciples, we read in the gospels of 'the convent of holy women who renounced the world and gave up all property so they might possess Christ only'. Scripture records 'how devoutly these most blessed women and true nuns followed Christ, and with what gratitude and honour both Christ himself and the apostles after him showed their devotion to them'.

The principal examples are the sisters Martha who served Christ within the house and Mary who anointed his feet. 'The Gospels record that it was only women who ministered to the Lord. They even devoted their own resources to his daily sustenance and provided the necessities of life especially for him.' Who does not know that Mary Magdalene anointed the head of Christ with the oil spilling over from her alabaster box? 'What, I ask, is this bounty of the Lord? What is this dignity of women, by which he should offer his head as well as his feet for anointing by none but women? What, I ask, is this privilege of the weaker sex by which a woman should anoint the supreme Christ, who was already anointed from conception with all the ointments of the Holy Spirit? As if by consecrating him as king and priest with bodily sacraments, she makes him "the Christ" meaning "the anointed one".' There are examples of anointing by patriarchs and priests in the Old Testament. But these show that 'men imprint the sacraments by figures, whereas the woman (Mary Magdalene) worked on the very truth itself, as the Truth actually attests, saying: "She has wrought a good work on me." '[3] Thus Christ himself, who is the head, was anointed by a woman, whereas Christians now, who are the members, are anointed by men.

'Consider therefore the dignity of this woman by whom the living Christ was twice anointed, on his feet and also on his head, and from whom he received the sacraments of kingship and priesthood.' These anointings by a woman demonstrate the unique dignity of Christ's kingship and priesthood. 'Look at how he received the sacrament of kingship from a woman, although he refused to accept the kingdom offered to him by men and he fled from those who wanted to force him to be a king. The woman conferred the sacrament of a heavenly kingdom and not an earthly one, for he said later of himself: "My kingdom is not of this world." '[4]

When bishops anoint kings and priests today, they strut

around in gilded vestments, even though those whom they bless are often cursed by God. Yet it was a humble woman, with no special clothing or ceremonial, 'who conferred these sacraments on Christ, not by the office of prelacy but by the merit of her devotion'. He held this action in such high esteem 'that he decided it should be included in the Gospel itself, so that the praise of the woman who had done this should be preached everywhere where the Gospel is preached as a memorial of her.[5] Nowhere else do we read of the services of any other persons whatsoever being commended and sanctioned by the Lord's authority in this way. Likewise he preferred the alms of the poor widow to all the other offerings in the temple. This exactly demonstrates how acceptable the devotion of women is to him.' Peter and his fellow apostles had the temerity to say that they gave up everything for Christ and many others too incurred great expenses, and yet they did not win the Lord's commendation in the way the women did.

'The outcome of the Lord's life also clearly demonstrates how great indeed the devotion of the women towards him always was. For they stood fearless even when Peter, the prince of the apostles, denied him and John, the beloved of the Lord, fled with the rest of the runaway apostles. Nor could any fear or desperation separate the women from Christ, either in his passion or in his death.' John tells how he returned and stood by the cross, even though he had previously fled. But, in telling this in his Gospel, 'he puts the perseverence of the women in first place, as if he had been inspired and called back by their example, saying: "There stood by the cross of Jesus his mother and his mother's sister, Mary the wife of Cleophas, and Mary Magdalene." '[6] This constancy of the holy women and the failure of the disciples had been prophesied long before by Job[7] in the Old Testament.

'By their faithfulness at the Lord's death the women showed, by actions rather than words, how much they had loved him in life. By that same solicitude, which they had for his passion and death, they were the first to rejoice in his resurrection.' It was they who received the angelic vision of the resurrection, they who first saw and held the Lord and they who told the apostles that Christ was risen. He appeared first of all to Mary Magdalene and said to her: 'Go to my brethren and say to them: I ascend unto my father.'[8] 'From this we infer that these holy women were constituted as if they were female apostles superior to the male ones, since they were sent to the male apostles either by the Lord himself or by angels. These women announced the highest joy of the resurrection, which everybody awaited, so that the male apostles might first learn through women what they should preach thereafter to the whole world.'

After the Lord's Ascension, 'the Acts of the Apostles diligently describe the religious life of that sacred convent, not omitting the perseverence of the devotion of the holy women, when the text says: "These all continued with one accord in prayer, with the women, and Mary the mother of Jesus."[9] The Acts of the Apostles also show concern both for the Jewish women converted during the life of Christ and for the Greeks converted subsequently. The ministries of Stephen, the first martyr, and of St Paul attest this. Paul 'seems openly to declare: is it not permissible for us to have convents of holy women and to take them with us on our preaching, just as the rest of the apostles are ministered to in their preaching by the necessary support of women?' Hence St Augustine says that faithful women accompanied the apostles and ministered to them from their substance, so that none of them might lack anything needed for the sustenance of life. He also says: 'Is there anyone who does not think that what was done by the apostles was that women of holy life went around with them, wherever they preached the Gospel, following the example of the Lord himself?'[10] For in the Gospel it is written: 'And it came to pass that he went throughout every city and village, preaching and showing the glad tidings of the kingdom of God, and the twelve were with him, and certain women who had been healed of evil spirits and infirmities: Mary called Magdalene, and Joanna, the wife of Chuza the steward of Herod, and Susanna and many others, who ministered to him from their substance.'[11] 'From this it is clear that the Lord also in his preaching was sustained in bodily things by the ministry of women and they, equally with the apostles, stayed with him as inseparable companions . . .

'Later on, in the very beginning of the nascent Church, the religious life of this profession multiplied among women equally with men, so that women – equally with men – possessed their own monasteries to live in.' This is attested by Philo of Alexandria, Cassiodorus and St Jerome.[12] 'If we turn to the old histories, we find in them that women were not separated from men in the things that pertain to God or to any feature of religion whatsoever. Equally with men, they not only sang sacred chants but also composed them, as Holy Scripture attests.' The canticle celebrating the liberation of the children of Israel from Egypt was sung by Miriam the prophetess; the Scripture makes no mention of Moses in this context. This woman's song expresses mystically but accurately the form of spiritual chant in monastic congregations.[13] We also have the hymns of Deborah and Hannah and Judith, and in the New Testament the 'Magnificat' of Mary the mother of God.

In the Old Testament it is clear that the daughters of Aaron belonged to the sanctuary and to the hereditary priestly office of the Levites equally with their brothers. 'Hence it appears that the religion of women was not separated from the order of clerics (the Levites), as it is agreed that the women also were conjoined with them by name, since we speak of "deaconesses" as well as of "deacons", as if in both we recognized the tribe of Levi and its female "Levitesses".'[14] Similarly in the consecration of the Nazarites, the Lord commanded Moses that women and men might equally be instituted into this order. The holy widow Anna mentioned by St Luke was like a Nazirite. Equally with Simeon, she was held worthy to receive the Lord in the temple and to be filled with the spirit of prophecy. She is praised for her public preaching of the promised birth of the Saviour, whereas St Luke does not mention anything about Simeon preaching to others.

Widowhood as a religious profession and vocation is honoured by St Paul and St Jerome, though they both distrusted young widows. In the choice of women for the ministry of the diaconate, Paul writes: 'A widow should not be put on the roll under sixty years of age. She must have been faithful in marriage to one man.'[15] And Jerome explains: 'Beware in the ministry of the diaconate lest a bad example be furnished in place of a good':[16] that is, younger women should not be chosen, as they are more prone to temptation and are lighter by nature. Concerning this provision of St Paul on the election of deaconesses, Pope Gregory the Great prohibited youthful abbesses.

Those whom we now call abbesses they called deaconesses in former times, as if they were servants rather than mothers. For 'deacon' means 'servant' (or 'minister') in Greek and they considered that deaconesses should be named from their ministry rather than from their rank, just as Christ said: 'The Son of Man came not to be ministered unto, but to minister.'[17] St Jerome argues that no one in monasteries should be called an abbot because the name 'Abba' means 'Father' and belongs only to God. Among the first deaconesses was Phebe of the church of Cenchrea, whom St Paul commends in his epistle to the Romans.[18] In their commentaries on this, both Cassiodorus and Claudius describe her as a 'deaconess' of that church. Claudius adds that this passage teaches that women are duly constituted in the ministry of the Church by apostolic authority. 'Not only in instituting deaconesses was the care of St Paul most watchful, but in general it is clear how concerned he was regarding widows of holy profession, so that he might cut off every occasion of temptation.' He accorded them honour as well as necessities: 'Honour widows,' he says, 'that are widows indeed.'[19]

The honour due to women from reverence for their holy profession is shown by the way they are addressed. St Paul writes: 'Salute Rufus chosen in the Lord, and his mother and mine.'[20] St John writes: 'Unto the elect lady and her children', and he asks to be loved, adding: 'And now I beseech thee, lady, that we love one another.'[21] On this scriptural authority, when writing to the virgin Eustochium, St Jerome did not blush to address her as 'my lady Eustochium'. He explained: 'Surely I must address as "my lady" her who is the bride of my Lord.' Virginity is a very special grace, as Jerome also shows. The consecration of virgins is reserved for the chief festivals of the Church. Speaking of the Church, the Psalmist says: 'After her shall virgins be brought to the king; they shall be brought with gladness and rejoicing, they shall be brought into the temple of the king.'[22] The apostles have left us in writing no authorized blessing for either clerics or monks. 'Only the religion of women is distinguished by the name of sanctity, since they are called "sanctimoniales" (nuns) from the word "sanctimonia" meaning sanctity.'

Although women are the weaker sex, their virtue is more pleasing to God and more perfect.[23] 'Who could have said there was in anything such complete fulfilment – by the dispensation of divine grace – as in the very weakness of the female sex, which the fault (of Eve) as well as nature has made contemptible? Look at the range of status in this sex: not only are there virgins and widows and wives, there are also foul harlots. Then you will see that the grace of Christ is fuller in the female sex, for the Lord said: "The last shall be first and the first shall be last." '[24]

We can see the benefits of divine grace and the honour shown to women from the very beginning of the world. 'We immediately find the creation of woman surpasses that of man in dignity, as she was created in paradise whereas man was made outside.[25] So women are advised to be specially aware that paradise is their native homeland and that it therefore becomes them all the more to follow the celibate life of paradise.' St Ambrose notes the paradox that woman, the inferior sex, was made within paradise whereas man, the better part, was made outside.[26] This priority of women is shown also in the way the Lord rectified the root of all evil, which Eve represented, through the birth of Mary before he put right Adam's sin through the birth of Christ. Just as sin began with a woman (Eve), so did grace begin with a woman (Mary) and the privilege of virginity flowered again in her. In the persons of Anna and Mary the form of the holy profession (of nuns) was shown to widows and virgins before any models of monastic religion were set before men through the examples of John the Baptist and the apostles.

'After Eve, we should look at the courage of Deborah, Judith and Esther.'[27] By comparison with them we should be ashamed at the weakness of the 'manly' sex. When the men had failed, it was Deborah who set the Lord's people free. Judith cut off the head of Holofernes and defeated the enemy entirely by herself. Esther, who was married to a Gentile king, reversed his decree to destroy her people. Great virtue is ascribed to David who overcame Goliath with a sling and a stone. But Judith went against a hostile army without either a sling or a stone, without indeed any arms at all, and Esther by speech alone liberated her people and caught her enemies in the trap which they had made. The memory of this famous deed is celebrated every year among the Jews to this day. No deeds of any man – however splendid – have merited a tribute like this.

'Who does not marvel at the incomparable determination of the mother of seven sons whom, as the Book of Maccabees relates, the wicked king Antiochus tried in vain to force to eat pig meat in contravention of the Law?[28] This woman endured the loss of everything, including her own life and that of her sons, rather than commit a single offence against the Law. What is this transgression, I ask, to which she was being driven? Was it to renounce God or to offer incense to idols? Nothing, I say, was demanded of her and her sons except that they eat the meat which the Law prohibited ... O brothers and fellow monks, who so shamelessly crave meat day after day in contravention of the institution of the Rule and of your profession, what have you to say about the constancy of this woman? Are you so shameless that you are not even confounded with blushing when you hear this? The constancy of this woman should be much more of a reproach to you, because she did much greater things than you, and also because you are the more strictly bound to religion by the vow of your profession.'

In praise of heroic virgins who would not choose Jephtha's daughter? What would she have done, I ask, if she had faced martyrdom? Would she have denied God? Would she, when asked about Christ, have replied like Peter the prince of the apostles: 'I know him not.'[29] By her death Jephtha's daughter liberated her father from perjuring himself. The great fortitude of this girl is deservedly celebrated every year by the daughters of Israel with solemn hymns for the obsequies of virgins.

'Let us pass over all the other instances and ask: What has been as necessary to our redemption and to the salvation of the whole world as the female sex, which brought forth for us the Saviour himself? . . . What glory can be compared to what this sex has achieved in the mother of the Lord? Our redeemer could, if he chose, have assumed his body through a man, just as he chose to form the first woman from the body of a man. Instead he transferred the singular grace of his humility to the honour of the weaker sex. He could similarly have been born of another and more worthy part of the female body than the rest of mankind are, who are born of that vilest member by which they are conceived. But, to the incomparable honour of the weaker body, the Lord has sanctified the female genitals by his birth more amply than he did the male sex by circumcision[30] . . .

'I will omit, for the present, the singular honour of virgins and turn my pen to the rest of women.' Consider how great was the grace that Christ's coming brought to Elizabeth the married woman and to Anna the widow. The gift of prophecy is more amply fulfilled in Elizabeth, who prophesied concerning Mary's miraculous conception,[31] than in John the Baptist, who announced Jesus long after he was born. 'Therefore, just as we call Mary Magdalene the female apostle of the apostles, let us not hesitate to call Elizabeth the prophetess of the prophets, and the same applies to the holy widow Anna, who has been discussed more fully above.'

If we extend the gift of prophecy to the Gentiles as well, then the Sibyl should take centre stage[32] and propound the revelations made to her about Christ. If we compare her with all the prophets, including even Isaiah, we will see that this woman far outstrips the men. St Augustine in the eighteenth book of *The City of God* (chapter 23) says that in some of the verses of the Erythraean Sibyl the initial letters of each line make an acrostic which reads: 'Jesus Christ, Son of God, the Saviour'. Augustine also cites Lactantius' account of the Sibylline prophecies concerning the suffering, crucifixion, descent into Hell and resurrection of Christ. This is the prophecy of the Sibyl which, if I am not mistaken, Virgil our greatest poet heard and used in the fourth book of his *Eclogues*. He foretold the miraculous birth, which would shortly happen under Augustus Caesar in the time of Pollio's consulate,[33] of a boy sent from heaven to earth who would take away the sins of the world and establish a new age on earth.

'Look at every word of the Sibyl and see how completely and openly she embraces the totality of Christian belief concerning Christ. Neither in prophesying nor in writing does she overlook either his divinity or his humanity.' She takes account of the first coming of Christ, when he was unjustly judged through the crucifixion, and equally of his second coming, when in majesty he will justly judge the world. She omits neither his descent into Hell nor the glory of his resurrection. In all this 'she seems to surpass not only the prophets of the Old Testament but even the Evangelists, who wrote very little about the descent into Hell ...

'Is there anyone who does not marvel also at that familiar and profound conversation which Christ had all alone with a Gentile woman: that is, with the Samaritan whom he deigned to instruct so diligently? The apostles themselves were absolutely outraged at this.' He asked her for drink, even though she was an infidel and guilty of having many husbands. 'What is this grace, I ask, which he shows to the weaker sex? Why ask for water from this woman, when he has bestowed the water of life on everybody?' What explanation can there be, I ask, except that he clearly demonstrates through this that the virtue of women is the more pleasing to him because their nature is weaker. He thirsts the more for their salvation because their virtue is known to be more admirable. When he asked for drink from a woman, he meant that he thirsted especially for the salvation of women. The Samaritan woman was filled with the spirit of prophecy, saying: 'I know that the Messiah cometh, who is called Christ: when he is come, he will tell us all things.'[34] With her, Christ's preaching to the Gentiles is seen to have begun, as he won over not only her but many others through her. It is clear what great grace for the Gentiles this woman gained from Christ, as she ran to the city to announce his coming, said what she had heard and quickly won over many of her people.

'If we turn over the pages of the Old Testament and the Gospels, we shall see that divine grace bestowed the highest gifts of the raising of the dead especially on women. These miracles were done either to them or for them.' Sons were raised to life through the intercession of their mothers by Elijah and his disciple Elisha. Then the Lord himself bestowed the gift of this immense miracle particularly on women, as is shown by the raising of the widow's son, of the daughter of the ruler of the synagogue and the bringing back to life of Lazarus at the request of his sisters. This is why St Paul, writing of Jewish history, says: 'Women received back their dead raised to life.' From all this it is clear how great is the grace which the Lord has always shown to women. He has raised them and their dear ones to life, and finally he has exalted them most greatly through his own resurrection, since he appeared to them first (as has already been pointed out).

'This sex is also seen to have won merit because it was affected by its natural compassion towards the Lord, when he faced persecution from the people. This is why St Luke recalled that the women cried and wept when the men were taking Christ to be crucified.' Similarly St Matthew notes that it was Pilate's wife who told him to have nothing to do with this just man.[35] We read also that once when Christ was preaching, a solitary woman raised her voice from the crowd in great praise of him, saying that the womb was blessed which bore him and the breasts that gave him suck. To which she was immediately privileged to hear the pious correction of her confession, when he replied: 'Yea rather, blessed are they that hear the word of God and keep it.'[36] 'Concerning the privilege of love, only John among Christ's apostles obtained this, as he is called the beloved of the Lord. Nevertheless, John himself writes of how Christ loved Martha and Mary, saying: "Now Jesus loved Martha, and her sister, and Lazarus."[37] This apostle, who records that he alone was loved by the Lord, ascribed this privilege of love to none of the other apostles. It is only the women whom he distinguished with this privilege.' It is true that he seems to associate their brother Lazarus with this honour; but John placed the women's names before Lazarus' because he believed that they took precedence in love.

Let us return now to the subject of faithful Christian women and marvel at the respect paid by God's mercy even to the abjectness of public prostitutes. What could be more abject than the original state of life of Mary Magdalene or Mary the Egyptian?[38] Yet divine grace raised them by honour or merit to sublime heights: 'I say unto you that the harlots go into the kingdom of God before you.'[39] 'Who does not know that women have embraced the exhortation of Christ and the counsel of the apostles with such great zeal for their chastity that they have offered themselves to God as a burnt sacrifice through martyrdom? Preserving equally the wholeness of the body and the mind, they triumph with a double crown. They strive to follow the Bridegroom of virgins, "the Lamb of God whithersoever he goeth".[40] We know that such perfection of virtue is rare in men but common in women.' We even read that some women have not hesitated to lay hands on themselves, rather than lose the virtue which they had vowed to God, so that they might come as virgins to the virgin Bridegroom.

'The Lord showed in what regard he held the devotion of holy virgins when a crowd of pagan people ran to the protection of St Agatha and spread out her veil against the terrible fire erupting from Mount Etna. The Lord saved them from the fire in both body and soul. We do not know of any monk's cowl which has won the grace of so great a benefit. We read that at a touch of Elijah's mantle the river Jordan parted, so that he and Elisha were able to cross over on dry land.[41] By the veil of a virgin, on the other hand, an immense multitude of a still pagan people were saved in both body and soul, as the road to heaven was opened to them when they converted.' Another thing which considerably commends the dignity of women is that when they are consecrated, they do so with these words: 'With his ring he has espoused me' and 'I am betrothed to him.' These are in fact the words of St Agnes, by which virgins who make their profession as nuns are betrothed to Christ.

If anyone wants to know about the form and dignity of women's dedication to religion among the pagans, it is easy to show that some institution for this purpose already existed among them – with the exception of what pertains to the faith – just as it existed too among the Jews. The Church has collected together these precedents from both Jews and Gentiles and changed them for the better. 'Who does not know that all the orders of clerics from doorkeeper to bishop, together with seasons of fasting, unleavened bread, the pomp of priests' vestments and some dedications and other sacraments were taken over by the Church from the Synagogue? Is there anyone likewise who does not know that by a most beneficial arrangement the ranks of secular dignities among kings and princes were retained in the converted nations, together with some rules of law and the teachings of the discipline of philosophy?' Likewise the Church took over from the pagans some of the grades of ecclesiastical dignities, along with the ideal of sexual continence and religious dedication to bodily purity. 'It is well known too that bishops and archbishops now preside where once there were "flamens"⁴² and "archflamens". What began as temples erected to demons were later consecrated to the Lord and dedicated to the memories of saints . . .

'We know too that the privilege of virginity shone especially among the pagans, when the curse of their law forced the Jews into marriage. This virtue or purity of the flesh was valued so highly among the pagans that in their temples great convents of women dedicated themselves to the celibate life.' St Jerome refers to the 'uni-virae' of Juno, the 'uni-virgines' of Vesta and the continent women dedicated to other pagan deities.⁴³ By 'uni-virae' and 'uni-virgines' he means nuns, 'monkesses' as it were ('monachae' in Latin), who have either known only one man or have remained single as virgins. 'Monachus' meaning 'monk' comes from 'monos' in Greek: that is to say, 'alone' or 'single'. St Jerome too in his book *Against Jovinian* gives many examples of the chastity or continence of pagan women. He shows how the Lord seems to have especially approved purity of the flesh among every people and he has exalted not a few pagans also, either by the conferring of merits or by the manifestation of miracles. 'What am I to say,' Jerome asks, 'about the Erythraean Sibyl or the Cumaean one or about the other eight? For Varro asserts that there were ten in all. They were distinguished by their virginity and the reward of their virginity was the power of divination.'⁴⁴ Jerome also mentions the Vestal

Virgin, Claudia, who – in order to prove herself innocent of fornication – is said to have drawn along by her girdle a vessel which thousands of men had been unable to move. Similarly St Augustine in the twenty-second book of *The City of God* (chapter 11) cites Varro's statement that an accused Vestal Virgin carried water from the Tiber in a sieve, without spilling any, in order to prove her innocence to her judges.

'It is not surprising if in these and other instances God should have exalted the chastity of unbelievers, or if he should have allowed it to be exalted by the agency of demons, in order that the faithful now might be inspired all the more, when they learn that unbelievers also have been so greatly exalted.' We know that grace was conferred on the prelacy of the high priest Caiphas and not on his person; likewise false apostles have sometimes been distinguished by miracles. So is it really to be wondered at if the Lord should have granted miraculous powers not to the persons of the unbelieving women themselves but to their virtue of continence, so that an innocent virgin should be set free and a false accusation of improbity be destroyed? 'For it is clear that a love of continence is a good thing even among unbelievers, as is also respect for the pact of marriage, which is a gift of God among all peoples.'

Through his gifts God honours not the error of infidelity but the example of virtue. The pagan emperor Vespasian is said to have healed the sick and St Gregory prayed for the soul of the emperor Trajan.[45] 'God cannot be ignorant of his gifts being linked to infidelity and neither can he hate any of the things which he has made. The more brightly they shine as signs, the more strongly he demonstrates them to be his; they cannot be polluted by man's depravity. He reveals himself to unbelievers so that believers may see where their hope lies.' The greatness of the dignity in which the pagans held the purity of the women devoted to temples is shown by the penalties for violation. Juvenal in his fourth satire (8–9) against Crispinus speaks of a defiled priestess being buried beneath the ground while her blood was still warm. St Augustine confirms in the third book of *The City of God* (chapter 5) that the ancient Romans used to bury alive the priestesses of Vesta detected in fornication. He comments that, as the Romans did not kill adulterous women, this shows how much more highly they rated the divine marriage-bed than the human one.

'This is also the case with us: the more the care of Christian princes provides for the protection of chastity, the more its holiness is not to be doubted.' This is why the emperor Justinian legislated that anyone who even contemplates marriage with holy virgins incurs the death penalty. Pope Innocent I wrote to Vitricius, Bishop of Rouen, that women who marry Christ and are veiled by a priest, if they subsequently get publicly married or are corrupted in secret, are not to be reconciled by the doing of penance unless the man to whom they have joined themselves has departed this life. 'There are those also who have not yet been clothed with the sacred veil, but who have always given the impression that they intended to remain in the virginal state even though they were not veiled.' If these women marry, a penance for some period is required because their bridal vow was held by Christ. For if in secular life contracts made in good faith are not to be broken for any reason, how much the more can this promise to God not be dissolved without penalty? St Paul says that those who depart from the state of widowhood have condemned themselves 'because they have cast off their first faith'.[46] This is even more true of those virgins who have in no way preserved the good faith of their previous undertakings. The famous Pelagius declared that an adulteress against Christ is more guilty than one against a husband because she has violated her body which is sanctified to God.

'If we wish to examine with what great care, diligence and love the holy Doctors, inspired by the examples of the Lord himself and the apostles, have shown to devout women, we shall find them to have embraced and cherished the devotion of these women with the utmost zeal and love. They constantly instructed them and augmented their religious life with frequent teaching and attentive exhortation. I will pass over the others and produce as evidence the principal Doctors of the Church, namely Origen, Ambrose and Jerome.' The first of these is that greatest Christian philosopher, who embraced the religion of women with such zeal that he castrated himself (according to

Eusebius' *History of the Christian Church*) so that no suspicion might take him away from the instruction and exhortation of women.

'Who can be ignorant of the great harvest of books of divinity, asked for by Paula and Eustochium, which St Jerome has left to the Church?' We know that some of the greatest Doctors of the Church wrote to Jerome often asking for a few words from him, but they got nothing. St Augustine reports that Jerome said he had no time to reply to him. 'Think of such a great man as Augustine[47] having to wait so long for a short little answer and still not getting it!' At these women's request, on the other hand, we know that Jerome sweated over numerous great volumes produced either by copying or by dictation. He showed much more reverence for them than he did for Augustine, even though he was a bishop. Perhaps he embraced the virtue of these women with such great enthusiasm because he thought their nature was frailer, and neither could he bear to disappoint them. Often the zeal of his charity towards them is so great that he seems to go beyond the bounds of truth in his praise of them. At the very beginning of his life of St Paula, as if he wished to direct the reader's attention towards himself, Jerome says: 'If all the members of my body were turned into tongues and every joint sounded like a human voice, I could say nothing worthy of the virtues of the saintly and venerable Paula.'[48] He had already written about the distinguished lives – shining with miracles – of many holy Fathers of the Church, in which far more marvellous things are reported than in Paula's life. Yet he seems to have extolled no one with such praise as he does this widow.

He writes in a similar way to the virgin Demetrias, praising her so much at the start of the letter that he seems to fall into immoderate adulation. It had evidently been very precious to this holy man to apply whatever skill in words he had to inspiring a fragile nature to virtue. Nevertheless, the charity which Jerome cultivated towards pious women was so great that his boundless sanctity imprinted a blot on his own reputation. Concerning false friends and detractors, he wrote to Asella from Rome, saying: 'There is no objection to me except my sex . . . Before I came to know the house of the holy Paula, my praises sounded throughout the city. In the opinion of almost everybody I was deemed worthy of the Supreme Pontificate. But once I began to venerate and tend her and to look after her – for the merit of her sanctity – my whole virtuous reputation deserted me.'[49]

We read of how the Lord himself showed such great familiarity to the blessed harlot (Mary Magdalene) that the Pharisee who was entertaining him said: 'This man, if he were a prophet, would have known who and what manner of woman this is who touches him.'[50] Is it surprising then if the members of Christ's Church, inspired by his example to gain such souls, are prepared to risk damage to their own reputations? For this cause Origen (as has been pointed out) sustained serious harm to his own body. The charity of the holy Fathers in the teaching and exhortation of women sometimes expressed itself so forcefully that their admirable compassion seems to promise things contrary to the faith. To console the sisters of the emperor Valentinian, St Ambrose implied that he was saved, even though he died as a catechumen.[51] This view seems a long way from the Catholic faith and the truth of the Gospel.

Numerous virgins have followed the Mother of the Lord in the pursuit of virtue, whereas we know of few men who have won the grace to follow 'the Lamb of God whithersoever he goeth'. Some women have killed themselves to preserve the integrity of the flesh which they had vowed to God. Not only is this not blameworthy, but these martyrs have merited many dedications of churches to them. 'Virgins who are also betrothed, if they decide to choose the monastic life before they have had sexual intercourse, may repudiate the man and make God their husband. They have legal freedom to do this, whereas we do not read anywhere that such a licence is granted to men.' Some women too have gone against the law by wearing male clothing in order to guard their chastity. These have excelled even among monks by such great virtues that they have merited to be made abbots. Thus we read of St Eugenia, who was actually ordered by her bishop St Helenus to put on male clothing. She was baptized by him and became a member of a community of monks.

'Dearest sister in Christ, I think I have written enough in answer to the first of your most recent requests, concerning the authority of your order and – over and above that – in commendation of its special dignity, so that you may more warmly embrace the calling of your profession through better understanding of its excellence. Now let me have the support of your merits and your prayers so that, God willing, I may also fulfil the second request. Farewell.'

LETTER 8
ABELARD TO HELOISE

Some part of your request has already been answered, as far as I was able, and it remains, God willing, for me to turn my attention to the rest of it by fulfilling the wishes of your spiritual daughters and yourself. For I still have to meet the second part of your demand by writing out some regulations to be a kind of Rule for your calling and to deliver this to you, so that the written word may give you more certainty than custom about what you should follow. Relying, therefore, partly on good practices and partly on the testimony of the Scriptures with the support of reason, I have decided to put all these together, in order to adorn the spiritual temple of God which you are[1] by embellishing it with certain choice pictures, and from several imperfect elements, to create as far as I can a single, complete work. In this I intend to imitate the painter Zeuxis, and work on the spiritual temple as he planned his achievement on a material one. For, as Tully records in his *Rhetoric*,[2] the people of Crotona appointed him to decorate with the best possible pictures a certain temple for which they had the highest veneration. So that he might do so more surely he chose from the people the five most beautiful maidens and looked at them as they sat by him while he worked, so that he could copy their beauty in his painting. This was probably done for two reasons: first, as the philosopher I quoted above remarks, Zeuxis had developed his greatest skill in portraying women, secondly, because maidenly beauty is naturally considered more refined and delicate than the male figure. Moreover, Tully says that he chose several girls because he did not believe he could find all the members of a single one equally lovely, since so much grace and beauty had never been conferred by nature on any one so as to give her equal beauty in every feature; for nature in creating bodies produces nothing which is perfect in every detail, as though she would have nothing left to bestow on the rest if she conferred all her advantages on one.

I too, then, in wishing to depict the beauty of the soul and describe the perfection of the bride of Christ, in which you may discover your own beauty or blemish as in the mirror of one spiritual virgin always held before your eyes, propose to instruct your way of life through the many documents of the holy Fathers and the best customs of monasteries, gathering each blossom as it comes to mind and collecting in a single bunch what I shall see will accord with the sanctity of your calling; and choosing what was instituted not only for nuns but also for monks. For as in name and profession of continence you are one with us, so nearly all our institutions are suitable for you. Gathering from these then, as I said, many things as if they were flowers with which to adorn the lilies of your chastity, I must describe the virgin of Christ with far greater care than that which Zeuxis applied to painting the likeness of an idol. Indeed, he believed that five maidens were sufficient for him to copy their beauty; but I have abundant riches in the records of the Fathers and, trusting in God's aid, do not despair of leaving you a more finished work, whereby you may be able to attain to the lot or description of those five wise virgins whom the Lord sets before us in the Gospel in depicting the virgin of Christ. May I be granted the power to achieve this through your prayers. Greetings[3] to you in Christ, Brides of Christ.

I have decided that in describing and fortifying your religion and arranging the celebration of divine service, the treatise for your instruction shall be divided into three parts, in which I believe the sum of monastic faith to rest: that is, a life of continence and one without personal possessions and, above all, the observance of silence. This is, in accordance with the Lord's teaching in the commandments of the Gospel, to be ready with belts fastened, to forsake everything and to avoid idle talk.[4]

Continence is indeed the practice of chastity which the Apostle enjoins when he says: 'The unmarried woman cares for the

Lord's business and her aim is to be dedicated to him in body as in spirit.'[5] In body, he says, as a whole, and not in one member, so that none of her members may fall into lasciviousness in deed or word. She is dedicated in spirit when her mind is neither defiled by compliance nor puffed up with pride, like the minds of those five foolish virgins who ran back to the oil-sellers and then were left outside the door. They beat vainly upon the door which was already shut and cried 'Lord, Lord, open to us,' but the bridegroom himself gave a terrible reply: 'Truly I know you not.'

Then too, in forsaking everything we follow naked a naked Christ, as the holy apostles did, when for his sake we put behind us not only our earthly possessions and affection for our kindred in the flesh, but also our own wishes, so that we may not live by our own will but be ruled by the command of our superior, and may wholly submit ourselves for Christ to him who presides over us in the place of Christ, as if to Christ. For Christ himself says that 'Whoever listens to you, listens to me; whoever rejects you, rejects me.'[6] Even if he lives an evil life (which God forbid), so long as his precepts are good, God's utterance must not be rejected because of the vice of the man. God himself enjoins this, saying: 'What they tell you, observe and do; but do not follow their practices.'[7] This spiritual conversion from the world to God he also describes accurately himself, saying that 'Unless a man part with all his possessions he cannot be a disciple of mine'; and again, 'If anyone comes to me and does not hate his father and mother, wife and children, brothers and sisters, even his own life, he cannot be a disciple of mine.'[8] Now, to hate father or mother etc. is to refuse to yield to affection for kindred in the flesh, just as to hate one's own life is to renounce one's own will. This too he enjoins elsewhere, saying: 'If anyone wishes to be a follower of mine, he must leave self behind, take up his cross and come with me.'[9] For in thus drawing near to him we are his followers, that is, by closely imitating him we follow him, who says: 'I have come not to do my own will but the will of him who sent me.'[10] It is as if he said, let everything be done under obedience.

For what is 'renouncing self' if not for a man to put behind him carnal affections and his own will and commit himself to being ruled by another's judgement and not his own? And so he does not receive his cross from another but takes it up himself, so that through it the world may be crucified to him and he to the world,[11] when by the voluntary offering of his own profession he denies himself worldly and earthly desires: which is a renunciation of his own will. For what else do the carnal seek, except to carry out their will, and what is earthly pleasure if not the fulfilment of our will, even when we attain our desires only with the greatest risk or effort? What is bearing a cross, that is, enduring some form of suffering, if not doing something against our will, however easy or profitable it seems to us? The other Jesus, who was by far the lesser, warns us of this in Ecclesiasticus when he says: 'Do not let your passions be your guide, but restrain your desires. If you indulge yourself with all that passion fancies, it will make you the butt of your enemies.'[12]

It is only when we wholly renounce both our possessions and ourselves that all that we own is cast away and we truly enter into the apostolic life which reduces everything to a common store; as it is written: 'The whole body of believers was united in heart and soul. Not a man of them claimed any of his possessions as his own, but everything was held in common ... It was distributed to each according to his need.'[13] For they were not equally in want, and so it was not distributed in equal shares to all, but in accordance with each man's need. They were united in heart through faith, because it is through the heart that we believe; and united in soul because there was one mutual will through love, since each man wished the same for his neighbour as for himself and did not seek his own advantage rather than another's, or because everything was brought together by all for the common good, and no one sought or pursued what was his but what was of Jesus Christ. Otherwise they could never have lived without property, which consists in ambition rather than possession.

An idle or superfluous word and too much talk are the same thing. Hence St Augustine says in the first book of his *Retractions*: 'Far be it from me to hold that there is too much talk when necessary words are spoken, however long-winded and prolix they may be.'[14] And in the person of Solomon it is also said that 'Where men talk too much sin is not far away; the man who holds his tongue is wise.'[15] We must therefore guard against what is sinful and take all the greater precautions against this evil, the more dangerous and difficult it is to avoid. St Benedict provides for this when he says that 'At all times monks ought to practise silence.'[16] Evidently to practise or study silence means more than to keep silence, for study is the intense concentration of the mind on doing something. We do many things carelessly or unwillingly, but nothing studiously unless we are willing and apply ourselves.

Just how difficult it is to bridle the tongue, but how beneficial, the apostle James carefully considers when he says that 'All of us often go wrong: the man who never says a wrong thing is perfect.' Again, he says: 'Beasts and birds of every kind, creatures that crawl on the ground and all others are tamed and have been tamed by mankind.' Between these two statements, when he considers how much matter for evil there is in the tongue and destruction of all that is good, he says: 'The tongue is a small member of the body, but how great a fire! How vast a forest it can set alight! ... It is a world of wickedness, an intractable evil, charged with deadly venom.'[17] What is more dangerous than venom or more to be shunned? As venom destroys life, so idle talk means the complete destruction of religion. And so James says earlier on: 'A man may think he is religious, but if he has no control over his tongue he is deceiving himself, and his religion is futile.'[18] Hence it is said in Proverbs: 'Like a city that is breached and left unwalled is a man who cannot control his temper in speech.'[19] This is what the old man had in mind when he made the following reply to Antony who had asked about the talkative brethren accompanying him on his way: 'Have you found good brethren to be with you, Father?' 'No doubt they are good but their dwelling has no door. Anyone who likes can go into the stable and untie the ass.'[20] It is as though our soul were tethered to the manger of the Lord, refreshing itself there by ruminating on sacred thoughts, but once untied from the manger it runs here and there all over the world in its thought, unless the bar of silence keeps it in. Words do indeed impart understanding to the soul, so that it may direct itself towards what it understands and adhere to this by thinking; and by thinking we speak to God as we do in words to men. While we tend towards the words of men it is necessary for us to be led from there, for we cannot tend towards God and man at the same time.

Not only idle words but also those which seem to have some purpose should be avoided, because it is easy to pass from the necessary to the idle, and from the idle to the harmful. The tongue, as James says, is an intractable evil, and being smaller and more sensitive than all the other parts of the body it is the more mobile, so that whereas the others are wearied by movement, it does not tire when moving and finds inactivity a burden. The more sensitive it is in you, and the more flexible from your softness of body, the more mobile and given to words it is, and can be seen to be the seedbed of all evil. The Apostle marks this vice especially in you when he absolutely forbids women to speak in church, and even on matters which concern God he permits them only to question their husbands at home. In learning such things, or whatever things are to be done, he particularly subjects them to silence, writing thus to Timothy on the point: 'A woman must be a learner, listening quietly and with due submission. I do not permit a woman to be a teacher, nor must woman domineer over man; she should be quiet.'[21]

If he has made these provisions for silence in the case of lay and married women, what ought you to do? Again, in showing Timothy why he has ordered this, he explains that women are gossips and speak when they should not.[22] So, to provide a remedy for so great a plague, let us subdue the tongue by perpetual silence, at least in these places or times: at prayer, in the cloister, the dormitory, refectory, and during all eating and cooking, and from Compline onwards let this be specially observed by all. If necessary in these places or times let us use signs instead of words. Careful attention must be paid to teaching and learning these signs, and if words are also needed for this, the speaker must be asked to speak in a suitable place chosen for the purpose. Once the necessary words are briefly said, she should return to her former duties or the next suitable task.

Any excess of words or signs must be firmly corrected, words especially, in which lies the greater danger – a frequent and serious danger which St Gregory was most anxious to forestall when he instructs us in the seventh book of his *Morals*:

> When we are careless about guarding against idle words, we come on to harmful ones. By these provocation is sown, quarrels arise, the torches of hatred are set alight and the whole peace of the heart is destroyed. And so it is well said through Solomon: 'Letting out water starts quarrels.' To let out water is to let loose the tongue in a flood of eloquence. On the other hand he says approvingly that 'Man's utterance is like water which runs deep.' So he who lets out water is a source of quarrels because he does not bridle his tongue and breaks up concord. Thus it is written that 'He who makes a fool keep silence softens anger.'[23]

This is a clear warning that we should employ the strictest censure to correct this vice above all, lest its punishment be deferred and religion thereby greatly endangered. From this spring slander, litigation and abuse, and often conspiracies and plots which do not so much undermine the whole structure of religion as overthrow it. Once this vice has been cut out, evil thoughts may not perhaps be wholly extinguished but they will cease to corrupt others. Abba Macharius told his brethren to shun this one vice as though he thought that was sufficient for their religion, as it is written in these words:

> Abba Macharius the elder in Scythia said to his brethren 'After Mass, brothers, flee from the churches.' One of them said to him, 'Father, where can we flee further than this wilderness?' He put his finger on his lips and answered 'That is what I say you are to flee.' So saying he went into his cell, shut the door and sat down alone.[24]

This virtue of silence which, as James says, makes a man perfect, and of which Isaiah prophesied that 'The harvest of righteousness is quietness,' was seized on so eagerly by the holy Fathers that (it is written) abba Agatho carried a stone in his mouth for three years until he should learn to keep silence.[25]

Although a place cannot bring salvation, it still provides many opportunities for easier observance and safeguarding of religion, and many aids or impediments to religion depend on the place. And so the sons of the prophets, whom, as Jerome says, we read of as monks in the Old Testament, removed themselves to the secret places of the wilderness and set up huts by the waters of the Jordan.[26] John also and his disciples, whom we regard as the first of our calling, and after them Paul, Antony, Macharius and all those who have been pre-eminent among us, fled from the tumult of their times and the world full of temptations, and carried the bed of their contemplation to the peace of the wilderness, so that they could devote themselves to God more sincerely. The Lord himself also, whom no stirrings of temptation could ever have touched, teaches us by his example, for he sought hidden places particularly and avoided the clamour of the crowd whenever he had something special to do. Thus he consecrated the desert for us by his forty days' fasting, refreshed the crowds in the desert, and for purity of prayer withdrew not only from the crowds of people but even from the apostles. The apostles too he set apart on a mountain to receive instruction and appointment; he honoured the wilderness by the glory of his transfiguration and gladdened the apostles assembled on a mountain by the revelation of his resurrection; he ascended from a mountain into heaven, and all his miracles were performed either in lonely or in hidden places.[27] He also appeared to Moses or the patriarchs of old in the wilderness, and through the wilderness he led his people to the promised land; there too he delivered the Law to the people long held captive, rained manna, brought out water from a rock and comforted them with frequent apparitions and the miracles he worked. In this he plainly taught them how much his wish to be alone desires a lonely place for us, where we can more purely devote ourselves to him.

He also takes pains to describe symbolically the freedom of the wild ass which loves the wilderness, and warmly approves of it, saying to holy Job: 'Who has let the wild ass of Syria range at will and given the wild ass of Arabia its freedom? – whose home I have made in the wilderness and its lair in the saltings. It disdains the noise of the city and is deaf to the driver's shouting; it roams the hills as its pasture and searches for anything green.'[28] It is as though he says openly, 'Who has done this, if not I?' Now the wild ass, which we call the ass of the woods, is the monk, who is freed from the chains of worldly things and has taken himself off to the peace and freedom of the solitary life; he has fled from the world and not remained in it. And so he 'lives in the saltings of the land' and his members through abstinence are parched and dry. He is deaf to the driver's shouting but hears his voice, because he provides for his stomach not what is superfluous but what is needed; for who is so demanding and unremitting a driver as the stomach? It shouts when it makes its immoderate demands for superfluous foods and delicacies, and this is when it should least be heard. The hills for his pasture are the lives and teachings of the sublime Fathers, by reading and meditating on which we are refreshed. By 'anything green' is meant the entire Scriptures on the heavenly and unfading life.

In specially exhorting us on this St Jerome writes as follows to the monk Heliodorus: 'Consider the meaning of the word "monk", your name. What are you doing in a crowd, when you are a solitary?'[29] And in drawing the distinction between our life and that of the clergy, he also writes to the priest Paul:

If you want to perform the duties of a priest, if the work – or burden – of the episcopate happens to please you, then live in cities and towns and make the salvation of others a profit to your soul. If you desire to be, as you say, a monk, that is, a solitary, what are you doing in cities, the homes not of solitaries but of crowds? Every calling has its leaders, and to come to our own way of life, bishops and priests should take as their example the apostles and apostolic men, whose positions they occupy and to whose merit they should try to attain. For us, the leaders of our calling should be the Pauls, Antonies, Hilaries and Macharius, and, to return to the Scriptures, let our leaders be Elijah and Elisha, the chief of the prophets, who lived in fields and the wilderness and made themselves huts by the river Jordan. Amongst these too are the sons of Rechab who drank neither wine nor cider, who lived in tents and are praised by the voice of God through Jeremiah saying that they shall not lack a descendant to stand before the Lord.[30]

Let us therefore set up huts for ourselves in the wilderness, so that we may be better able to stand before the Lord and, being prepared, take part in serving him, and so that the society of men will not jolt the bed of our repose, disturb our rest, breed temptations and distract our minds from our holy calling.

When the Lord directed holy Arsenius to this freedom and peace in life we were all given a clear example in this one man. It is written that:

When abba Arsenius was still in the palace he prayed to the Lord, saying 'Lord, guide me to salvation.' And a voice came to him, saying, 'Arsenius, flee from men and you will be saved.' He retired to the monastic life and prayed again, in the same words, 'Lord, guide me to salvation.' He heard a voice say to him, 'Arsenius, flee, be silent, be at peace, for these are the roots of not sinning.' And so, acting on this one rule of the divine command, he not only fled from men but even drove them from him. One day his archbishop came to him, along with a certain judge, and asked him for a sermon of edification. 'If I give you one,' said Arsenius, 'will you follow it?' They promised that they would. Then he said to them, 'Wherever you hear of Arsenius, do not go there.' On another occasion the archbishop was visiting him and sent first to see if he would open his door. He sent back word: 'If you come, I will open to you, but if I open to you I am opening to all, and then I can stay here no longer.' Hearing this, the archbishop said: 'If my coming will persecute him, I will never go to this holy man.' To a certain Roman matron who came to visit his holiness, Arsenius said: 'Why have you presumed to undertake such a voyage? You must know you are a woman and should not travel at all. Or do you intend to return to Rome and tell other women that you have seen Arsenius, so that they will make the sea a highway for women coming to see me?' 'If the Lord wishes me to return to Rome,' she replied, 'I shall not allow anyone to come here. Only pray for me, and remember me always.' But he answered: 'I pray God to wipe out the memory of you from my heart.' Hearing this she went away dismayed.[31]

It is also recorded that when Arsenius was asked by abba Mark why he fled from men, he replied: 'God knows that I love men, but I cannot be equally with men and with God.'[32]

The holy Fathers did indeed so shun the conversation and attention of men that many of them feigned madness, in order to drive men from them, and, remarkable to relate, even professed to be heretics. Anyone who likes may read in the *Lives of the Fathers* about abba Simon, and how he prepared himself for a visit from the judge of the province; he covered himself with a sack and, holding bread and cheese in his hand, sat at the door of his cell and started eating.[33] He may read too of the hermit who, when he saw people coming towards him with lanterns, pulled off his clothes, threw them into the river, and standing there naked began to wash them. His acolyte blushed for shame at the sight and asked the men to go away, saying 'Our old man has lost his senses.' Then he went to him, and said: 'Why did you do this, father? All who saw you said that "The old man is possessed."' 'That is what I wanted to hear,' he replied.[34] Let him read also of abba Moses, who in order to keep a judge of the province well away from him, got up and fled into a marsh. The judge and his followers came along and called, 'Tell us, old man, where is the cell of abba Moses?' 'Why do you want to look for him?' he replied. 'The man is crazy and a heretic.'[35] And what of abba Pastor, who even refused to be seen by the judge of the province in order to free from prison the son of his own sister, in answer to her plea?[36]

You see then how the presence of the saints is sought by the powerful in the world with great veneration and devotion, while their aim is to keep people at a distance, even at the loss of their own dignity.

Now, so that you may know the virtue of your own sex in this matter, could anyone adequately tell of that virgin who refused a visit even from the holy saint Martin, so that she could devote herself to contemplation? Jerome writes of this to the monk Oceanus:

> In the *Life of St Martin*, we read that Sulpicius relates how St Martin when travelling wished to call on a certain virgin who was outstanding for her morals and chastity. She refused, but sent him a gift, and looking from her window said to the holy man: 'Offer prayer where you are, father, for I have never been visited by a man.' Hearing this St Martin thanked God that a woman of such morals had kept her desire for chastity. He blessed her and departed, filled with joy.[37]

This woman in fact disdained or feared to rise from the bed of her contemplation, and was prepared to say to a friend knocking at her door: 'I have washed my feet, how shall I defile them?'[38]

O what an insult to themselves would the bishops or priests of our day consider it, if they received such a rebuff from Arsenius or this virgin! If any monks still remain in solitude, let them blush for such things, whenever they delight in the society of bishops and build them special houses for their entertainment, when they do not shun worldly potentates whom a crowd accompanies or gathers round but rather invite them, and by multiplying their buildings on the pretext of hospitality, change the solitary place they sought into a city. Indeed, by the craft and cunning of the old tempter, nearly all the monasteries of today which were formerly founded in solitude so that men could be avoided, now that religious fervour has subsided, have subsequently invited men to them, have assembled manservants and maidservants and built great villages on monastic sites; and thus they have returned to the world, or rather, have brought the world to them. By involving themselves in such great inconvenience and binding themselves in total slavery both to ecclesiastical and secular powers, while they seek to live at ease and enjoy the fruits of another's labour, they have lost the very name of monk, that is, of solitary, as well as their monastic life. They also often fall a victim to other misfortunes: while struggling to protect the persons and possessions of their followers they lose their own, and in the frequent fires which break out in adjoining buildings the monasteries are burned down as well. Yet not even this checks their ambition.

There are those too who will not submit to monastic restriction of any kind, but are scattered in twos and threes amongst the villages, towns and cities, or even live alone, without observance of a rule, and are thereby worse than men of the world the more they fall away from their profession. They also make misuse of the places where their people dwell as much they do their own, calling these Obedientaries,[39] though no rule is kept there and no obedience shown except to the belly and the flesh, and there they live with relatives and friends, behaving as freely as they wish, as they have so little to fear from their own consciences. There can be no doubt that in shameless apostates such as these, excesses are criminal which in other men are venial. You should not permit yourselves to take example from such lives nor even to hear of them.

Solitude is indeed all the more necessary for your woman's frailty, inasmuch as for our part we are less attacked by the conflicts of carnal temptations and less likely to stray towards bodily things through the senses. Hence St Antony says: 'Whoever sits in solitude and is at peace is rescued from three wars, that is, wars of hearing, speech and sight; he shall have only one thing to fight against, the heart.'[40] These and all the other advantages of the desert the famous Doctor of the Church Jerome has particularly in mind in giving urgent counsel to the monk Heliodorus: 'O desert rejoicing in the presence of God! What are you doing in the world, brother, when you are greater than the world?'[41]

Now that we have discussed where monasteries should be set up, let us show what the layout of the site should be. In planning the site of the actual monastery, also in accordance with St Benedict's Rule, provision should be made if possible for those things which are particularly necessary for monasteries to be contained within its precincts, that is, a garden, water, a mill, a bakehouse with oven and places where the sisters may carry out their daily tasks without any need for straying outside.[42]

As in the army camps of the world, so in the camp of the Lord, that is, in monastic communities, people must be appointed to be in authority over the rest. In an army there is one commander over all, at whose bidding everything is carried out, but because of the size of his army and complexity of his duties he shares his burdens with several others, and appoints subordinate officers to be responsible for various duties or companies of men. Similarly in convents it is also necessary for one matron to preside over all; the others must do everything in accordance with her decision and judgement, and no one must presume to oppose her in anything or even to grumble at any of her instructions. No community of people nor even a small household in a single house can continue as a whole unless unity is preserved in it, and complete control rests on the authority of a single person. And so the Ark, as a model for the Church, was many cubits long and wide but rose to a single point. It is written in Proverbs that 'For its sins a land has many rulers,'[43] and on the death of Alexander, when kings were multiplied, evils were multiplied too. Rome could not maintain concord when authority was shared amongst many rulers. Lucan reminds us in his first book:

> You, Rome, have been the cause of your own ills,
> Shared in three masters' hands; the pacts spell death
> Of power that never should devolve on many.

A little later he says:

> So long as earth supports the sea and is itself
> Poised in the air, the sun rolls on its course,
> Night follows day throughout the zodiac's signs,
> No trust binds fellow-rulers, every power
> Rejects a partner . . .[44]

Such, surely, were those disciples of the abbot St Frontonius, whom he had assembled to the number of seventy in the city where he was born. He had won great favour there in the eyes of God and men, but then he left the monastery in the city, and with their portable goods took them naked with him into the desert. After a while, like the Israelites complaining against Moses because he had led them out of Egypt into the wilderness, abandoning their fleshpots and wealth in the land, they started grumbling foolishly. 'Is chastity only to be found in the desert and not in town?' they asked. 'Why can't we go back to the city we have left? Will God hear our prayers only in the desert? Who can live by the bread of angels? Who wants to have cattle and wild beasts for company? Why do we have to stay here? Why can't we return and bless the Lord in the place where we were born?'[45]

Hence the apostle James gives warning: 'My brothers, not many of you should try to teach others; be sure that if you do, you will be judged with greater severity.'[46] Similarly, Jerome in writing to the monk Rusticus on the conduct of his life says:

> No skill is learned without a teacher. Even dumb animals and herds of wild beasts follow their leaders; amongst bees, one goes first and the rest follow, and cranes follow one of their number in regular order. There is one emperor, one judge of a province. When Rome was founded there could not be two brothers as kings at the same time, and this was settled by fratricide. Esau and Jacob fought in Rebecca's womb. The churches each have one bishop, one dean and one archdeacon, and every order in the Church depends on its rulers. In a ship there is one helmsman, in a house one master; in an army, however large, men look to the standard of one man. By all these examples my discourse aims at teaching you that you must not be left to your own will, but must live in a monastery under the discipline of one Father and in the company of many of your fellows.[47]

So that concord may therefore be maintained in all things, it is proper for one sister to be over all, and all to obey her in everything. Several other sisters should also be appointed, as she herself decides, to serve under her, like officers. They shall preside over the duties she has ordered and as far as she wishes, as though they were dukes or counts serving in their lord's army, while all the rest are the soldiers or infantry who are under the direction of the others and shall fight freely against the evil one and his hordes.

Seven persons only out of your number I think are all that are needed for the entire administration of the convent: portress, cellaress, wardrober, infirmarian, chantress, sacristan and lastly the deaconess, who is now called the abbess.[48] And so in this camp, and in this kind of service in the Lord's army, as it is written that 'Man's life on earth is like service,' and elsewhere, 'Awesome as a regimented army,'[49] the abbess takes the place of the commander who is obeyed by all in everything. The six under her, the officers as we call them, hold the position of duke or count; while all the other nuns, whom we call the cloistral sisters, perform their service for God promptly, like soldiers, and the lay sisters, who have renounced the world and dedicated themselves to serving the nuns, wear a kind of religious (though not a monastic) habit and, like infantry, hold a lower rank.

Now, under the Lord's inspiration, it remains to marshal the several ranks of this army so it may truly be what is called 'a regimented army' to meet the assaults of demons. And so, starting at the head of this institution, with the deaconess, as we'll call her, let us first dispose of her through whom all must be disposed. First of all, her sanctity: as I said in my preceding letter, St Paul in writing to Timothy describes in detail how outstanding and proved this must be:

A widow should not be put on the roll under sixty years of age. She must have been faithful in marriage to one man, and must produce evidence of good deeds performed, showing whether she has had the care of children, or given hospitality, or washed the feet of God's people, or supported those in distress – in short, whether she has taken every opportunity of doing good. Avoid younger widows, etc.[50]

And earlier on, when he was laying down rules for the life of deacons, he says about deaconesses: 'Their wives, equally, must be high-principled, not given to talking scandal, sober and trustworthy in every way.'[51] I have said enough in my last letter to show how highly I value the meaning and reasoning behind all these words, especially the reason why the Apostle wishes her to be the wife of one husband alone and to be advanced in age.

And so I am much surprised that the pernicious practice has

arisen in the Church of appointing virgins to this office rather than women who have known men, and often of putting younger over older women. Yet Ecclesiastes says: 'Woe betide the land where a boy is king,' and we all approve the saying of holy Job: 'There is wisdom in age and long life brings understanding.'[52] It is also written in Proverbs: 'Grey hair is a crown of glory if it shall be won by a virtuous life,' and in Ecclesiasticus:

> How beautiful is the judgement of grey hairs and counsel taken from the old! How beautiful the wisdom of the aged, how glorious their understanding and counsel! Long experience is the old man's crown and his pride is the fear of the Lord.[53]

Again:

> Speak, if you are old, for it is your privilege . . . If you are young, speak in your own case, but not much. If you are asked twice, let your reply be brief . . . For the most part be like a man who knows and can keep silence while making enquiries . . . Do not be familiar among the great, nor talk much before your elders.[54]

So the presbyters who have authority over the people in the Church are understood to be Elders, so that their very name may teach what they ought to be. And the men who wrote the *Lives of the Saints* gave the name of Elder to those whom we now call abbas or Fathers.[55]

Thus in every way care must be taken when electing or consecrating an abbess to follow the advice of the Apostle,[56] and to elect one who must be above all the rest in her life and learning, and of an age to promise maturity in conduct; by obedience she should be worthy of giving orders, and through practising the Rule rather than hearing it she should have learned it and know it well. If she is not lettered let her know that she should accustom herself not to philosophic studies nor dialectical disputations but to teaching of life and performance of works: as it is written of the Lord, he 'set out to do and teach',[57] that is, he taught afterwards what he did first, for teaching through works rather than speech, the deed before the word, is better and more thorough. Let us pay careful heed to what abba Ipitius is recorded to have said: 'He is truly wise who teaches others by deed, not by words.'[58] He gives us no little comfort and encouragement thereby.

We should listen too to the argument of St Antony which confounded the wordy philosophers who laughed at his authority as being that of a foolish and illiterate man: 'Tell me,' he said, 'which comes first, understanding or letters? Which is the beginning of the other – does understanding come from letters or letters from understanding?' When they declared that understanding was the author and inventor of letters, he said: 'So if a man's understanding is sound, he has no need of letters.'[59] We should hear too the words of the Apostle, and be strengthened in the Lord: 'Has not God made the wisdom of this world look foolish?' And again, 'To shame the wise, God has chosen what the world counts weakness. God has chosen the base and contemptible things of the world so as to bring to nothing what is now in being; then no human pride may boast in his presence.'[60] For the kingdom of God, as he says later, is not a matter of talk but of power.

But if to gain better understanding of some things the abbess thinks she should have recourse to the Scriptures, she should not be ashamed to ask and learn from the lettered, nor despise the evidence of their education in these matters, but accept it devoutly and thoughtfully, just as the foremost himself of the apostles thoughtfully accepted public correction from his fellow-apostle Paul.[61] For, as St Benedict also remarks, the Lord often reveals what is better to the lesser man.[62]

So that we may better follow the Lord's injunction which the Apostle recorded above, we should never let this election be made from the nobility or the powerful in the world except under pressure of great necessity and for sound reason. Such women, from their easy confidence in their breeding, become boastful or presumptuous or proud, and especially when they are native to the district, their authority becomes damaging to the convent. Precautions must be taken against the abbess becoming presumptuous because of the proximity of her kindred, and the convent's being burdened or disturbed by their numbers, so that religion suffers harm through her people and she comes under contempt from others: in accordance with the Truth: 'A prophet will always be held in honour except in his native place.'[63] St Jerome also made provision for this when he wrote to Heliodorus and enumerated several things which stand in the path of monks who stay in their native place. 'The conclusion of these considerations,' he says, 'is that a monk cannot be perfect in his native place; and not to wish to be perfect is a sin.'[64]

But what damage to souls will there be if she who is the authority over religion is lacking in religion herself? For it is sufficient for her subordinates if each of them displays a single virtue, but in her examples of all the virtues should shine out, so that she can be a living example of all she enjoins on the others, and not contradict her precepts by her morals, nor destroy by her own deeds what she builds in words; in order that the word of correction may not fall away from her lips when she is ashamed to correct in others the errors she is known to commit herself. The Psalmist prays to the Lord lest this happens to him: 'Rob not my mouth of the power to tell the truth,'[65] he says, for he was expecting that stern rebuke of the Lord to which he refers elsewhere. 'God's word to the wicked man is this: What right have you to recite my laws and make so free with the words of my covenant, you who hate correction and turn your back when I am speaking?'[66] The Apostle too was careful to provide against this: 'I punish my own body,' he says, 'and make it know its master, for fear that after preaching to others I should find myself rejected.'[67] For anyone whose life is despised must see his preaching or teaching condemned as well, and a man who should heal another but suffers from the same infirmity is rightly reproached by the sick man: 'Physician, heal yourself.'[68]

Whoever is seen to have authority in the Church must think carefully what ruin his own fall will bring about when he takes his subjects along with him to the precipice. 'If any man,' says the Truth, 'breaks even the lowest of the Lord's command-ments and teaches others to do the same, he will be the least in the kingdom of Heaven.'[69] He breaks a commandment who infringes it by acting against it, and if he corrupts others by his example he sits in his chair as a teacher of pestilence. But if anyone acting thus is to be called the least in the kingdom of Heaven, that is in the Church here on earth, what are we to call a superior who is utterly vile, and because of whose negligence the Lord demands the life-blood not only of his own soul but of all the souls subject to him? And so the Book of Wisdom rightly curses such men:

> It is the Lord who gave you your authority, and your power comes from the Most High. He will put your actions to the test and scrutinize your intentions. Though you are viceroys of his kingly power, you have not been upright judges; you do not stand up for the law of justice. Swiftly and terribly will he descend on you, for judgement falls relentlessly on those in high places. The small man may find pardon, but the powerful will be powerfully tormented, and a cruel trial awaits the mighty.[70]

It is sufficient for each of the subject souls to provide for itself against its own misdeed, but death hangs over those who also have responsibility for the sins of others for, when gifts are increased, the reasons for gifts are also multiplied, and more is expected of him to whom more is committed. We are warned in Proverbs to guard against so great a danger, when it says: 'My son, if you pledge yourself to a friend and stand surety for a stranger, if you are caught by your promise, trapped by some words you have said, do what I now tell you and save yourself, my son, when you fall into another man's power. Run, hurry, rouse your friend, let not your eyes sleep nor your eyelids slumber.'[71] For we pledge ourselves to a friend when our charity admits someone into the life of our community; we promise him the care of our supervision, as he promises his obedience to us. So too we stand surety for him by joining hands when we confirm our willingness to work on his behalf; and we fall into his power because unless we make provision for ourselves against him, we shall find that he is the slayer of our soul. It is against this danger that the advice is given 'Go, hurry etc.'

And so now here, now there, like a watchful and tireless

captain, let our abbess go carefully round her camp and watch lest through any negligence a way is opened to him who, like a roaring lion, prowls around looking for someone to devour.[72] She must be the first to know all the evils of her house, so that she may correct them before they are known to the rest and taken as a precedent. Let her beware too of the charge St Jerome lays against the foolish or negligent: 'We are always the last to learn of the evils of our own home, and are ignorant of the faults of our wives and children when they are the talk of the neighbourhood.'

She who thus presides must remember that she has taken on the care of bodies as well as of souls, and concerning the former there is advice for her in the words of Ecclesiasticus: 'Have you daughters? See that they are chaste, and do not be too lenient with them.' Again, 'A daughter is a secret anxiety to her father, and the worry of her takes away his sleep for fear she may be defiled.'[73] But we defile our bodies not only by fornication but by doing anything improper with them, as much by the tongue as by any other member, or by abusing the bodily senses in any member for some idle whim. So it is written, 'Death comes in through our windows,'[74] that is, sin enters the soul by means of the five senses.

What death is more grievous or care more perilous than that of souls? 'Do not fear those who kill the body but cannot kill the soul,'[75] says the Truth. But if anyone hears this, does he not still fear the death of the body rather than of the soul? Who would not avoid a sword rather than a lie? And yet it is written that 'A lying tongue is death to the soul.'[76] What can be destroyed so easily as the soul? What arrow can be fashioned so speedily as a lie? Who can safeguard himself, if only against a thought? Who is able to watch out for his own sins but not those of others? What shepherd in the flesh has the power to protect spiritual sheep from spiritual wolves, both alike invisible? Who would not fear the robber who never ceases to lie in wait, whom no wall can shut out, no sword can kill or wound? He is forever plotting and persecuting, with the religious as his chosen victims, for, in the words of Habakkuk, they 'enjoy rich fare',[77] and it is against him that the apostle Peter urges us to be on our guard, saying: 'Your enemy the devil, like a roaring lion, prowls around looking for someone to devour.' How confident he is of devouring us the Lord himself says to holy Job: 'The flooded river he drinks unconcerned: he is confident he can draw up Jordan into his mouth.'[78] For what would he not be bold enough to try, when he tried to test the Lord himself? It was he who took our first parents straight from Paradise to captivity, and even snatched an apostle whom the Lord had chosen from the apostles' company. What place is safe from him, what doors are not unbarred to him? Who can take action against his plots or stand up to his strength? It was he who struck with a single stroke the four corners of the house of holy Job, and crushed and killed his innocent sons and daughters.[79]

What then can the weaker sex do against him? Who but women have his seductive ways so much to fear? It was a woman he first seduced, and through her her husband too, and so made captive all their descendants. His desire for a greater good robbed her of her possession of a lesser good, and by the same wiles he can still easily seduce a woman when her desire is for authority, not for service, and she is brought to this through her ambition for wealth or status. Which of the two mattered more to her, the sequel will show. For if she lives more luxuriously when in authority than she did as a subordinate, or claims any special privilege for herself beyond what is necessary, there can be no doubt that she coveted this. If she seeks more costly ornaments after than before, it is certain that she is swollen with vainglory. What she was before will afterwards appear, and her office will reveal whether what she displayed before was true virtue or pretence.

She should be brought to office, not come to it herself, in accordance with the Lord's words: 'Those who have come of themselves are all thieves and robbers,'[80] on which Jerome comments '"Who have come", not "who were sent."' She should be raised to the honour, not take it on herself, for 'Nobody,' as the Apostle says, 'takes the honour on himself; he is called by God, as Aaron was.'[81] If called she should mourn as though led to her death; if rejected, rejoice as though delivered from death. When we are said to be better than the rest we blush to hear the words, but when this is proved by the fact of our election, we shamelessly lose all shame. For who does not know that the better are preferable to the rest? So in the twenty-fourth book of *Morals* it is said that 'No one should undertake the leadership of men if he does not know how to rebuke men properly by admonition. Nor should the one chosen for this purpose of correcting the faults of others commit himself what ought to have been rooted out.'[82] But if in this election we try to avoid this shamelessness by some light verbal refusal, and only to the ear reject the position offered us, we immediately incur the charge of trying to appear more righteous and worthy than we are.

How many have we seen at their election weeping with their eyes while laughing in their hearts, accusing themselves of unworthiness and thereby courting more approval and human support for themselves! They had in mind the words: 'The just man is the first to accuse himself,'[83] but afterwards when they were blamed and given a chance to retire they were completely shameless and persistent in their efforts to defend the position which they had declared themselves unwilling to accept, with feigned tears and well-founded accusations of themselves. In how many churches have we seen canons resisting their bishops when compelled by them to take holy orders, professing themselves unworthy of such priestly offices and quite unwilling to comply! Yet should the clergy subsequently elect them to the episcopate they are given only a frivolous refusal or none at all. And those who yesterday were avoiding a diaconate to escape endangering their souls, so they said, apparently find justification overnight, and have no fears of downfall from a higher office. In the same book of Proverbs it is written of such people: 'A foolish man applauds when he stands as surety for a friend';[84] for the poor wretch rejoices though he should rather mourn when he assumed authority over others, and binds himself by his own declaration to caring for his subordinates, by whom he ought to be loved rather than feared.

We can provide against this evil as far as we can by absolutely forbidding the abbess to live in greater luxury and comfort than her subordinates. She must not have private apartments for eating or sleeping, but should do everything along with the flock entrusted to her, and be better able to make provision for them the more she is present in their midst. We know of course that St Benedict was greatly concerned about pilgrims and guests and set a table apart for the abbot to entertain them.[85] Though this was a pious provision at the time, it was afterwards amended by a dispensation which is highly beneficial to monasteries, whereby the abbot does not leave the monks but provides a faithful steward for the pilgrims; for it is easy for discipline to be relaxed at table, and that is the time when it should be more strictly observed. There are many too who use hospitality as an opportunity to think of themselves rather than of their guests, so that those who are not present are troubled by the gravest suspicions and make complaints. The authority of a superior is weakened the less his way of life is known to his people; moreover, any shortage there may be can be more easily accepted by all when it is shared by all, and especially by superiors. This we have learned from the example of Cato, who, it is written, 'when the people with him were thirsty', rejected and poured away the few drops of water offered him 'so that all were satisfied'.[86]

Since therefore sobriety is so necessary for those in authority, they must live sparingly, and the more so as provision for the others rests with them. And lest they turn the gift of God, that is, the authority conferred on them, into pride, and so show themselves insolent to their subjects, let them hear what is written: 'Do not play the lion in your house, upsetting your household and oppressing your servants ... Pride is hateful to God and man.'[87] The beginning of pride in man is renunciation of God, since the heart withdraws from God who made him, just as pride in any form is the beginning of sin. 'The Lord has overturned the seats of proud princes and enthroned the gentle in their place ... Have they chosen you to preside? Do not put on airs; behave to them as one of themselves.'[88] And the Apostle in giving instructions to Timothy about his subordinates says: 'Never be harsh to an elder; appeal to him as though he were your father. Treat the younger men as brothers, the older women as mothers and the young as your sisters.'[89] 'You did not choose me,' says the Lord, 'I chose you.'[90] All others in authority are elected by their subjects and are created and set up by them, because they are chosen not to lord over men but to serve them. God alone is truly Lord and has the power to choose his subjects for his service. Yet he did not show himself as a lord but as a servant, and when his disciples were already aspiring to high seats of power he rebuked them by his own example, saying: 'You know that in the world rulers lord it over their subjects, and those in authority are called benefactors; but it shall not be so with you.'[91] Whoever seeks dominion over his subjects rather than service to them, who works to be feared, not loved, and being swollen with pride in his authority likes to have 'places of honour at feasts and the chief seats in the synagogue, to be greeted respectfully in the street and to be addressed as "Rabbi"', imitates the princes of the world. As for the honour of this title, we should not take pride in names but look to humility in everything. 'But you,' says the Lord, 'must not be called "Rabbi" and do not call any man on earth "father".' And afterwards he forbade self-glorification altogether, saying 'Whoever exalts himself shall be humbled.'[92]

We must also make sure that the flock is not imperilled by the absence of its shepherds, and discipline slacken within when authority strays from its duties. And so we rule that the abbess, whose care is for spiritual rather than material matters, must not leave her convent for any external concern, but be the more solicitous for her subordinates the more active she is. Thus her appearances in public will be more highly valued for their rarity, as it is written: 'If a great man invites you, keep away, and he will be the more pressing in his invitation.'[93] But if the convent needs emissaries, the monks or their lay monks[94] should supply them, for it is always men's duty to provide for women's needs, and the greater the religious devotion of the nuns, the more they give themselves up to God and have need of men's protection. And so Joseph was bidden by the angel to care for the mother of the Lord, though he was not allowed to sleep with her.[95] The Lord himself at his death chose for his mother a second son who should take care of her in material things. There is no doubt either, as I have said elsewhere, that the apostles paid great attention to devout women and appointed the seven deacons for their service. We too, then, acting on this authority and in accordance with the demands of the situation, have decided that monks and lay monks, like the apostles and deacons, shall perform for convents of women such duties as call for outside assistance; the monks are necessary especially to celebrate Mass, the lay monks for other services.

It is therefore essential as we read was the practice in Alexandria under Mark the Evangelist in the early days of the infant Church, that monasteries of men should be near at hand for convents of women, and that all external affairs should be conducted for the women through men of the same religious life. And indeed we believe that convents then maintain the religion of their calling more firmly, if they are ruled by the guidance of spiritual men, and the same shepherd is set over the ewes as well as the rams: that is, that women shall come under the same authority as men, and always, as the Apostle ruled, 'Woman's head is man, as man's head is Christ and Christ's is God.'[96] And so the convent of St Scholastica which was situated on land belonging to a monastery was also under the supervision of one of the brothers, and took both instruction and comfort from frequent visits by him or the other brothers. The Rule of St Basil also instructs us on this kind of supervision, in the following passage:

QUESTION: Shall the brother who presides, apart from the sister who presides over the nuns, say anything for their instruction?

ANSWER: How else shall the precept of the Apostle be observed, which says, 'Let all be done decently and in order'?

QUESTION: Is it seemly for him who presides to converse frequently with her who presides over the sisters, especially if some of the brethren are offended by this?

ANSWER: Although the Apostle asks, 'Is my freedom to be called in question by another man's conscience?', it is good to follow him when he says 'But I have availed myself of no such right, lest I should offer any hindrance to the gospel of Christ.' As far as possible the sisters should be seldom seen and preaching kept brief.[97]

On this there is also the decision of the Council of Seville:

By common consent we have decreed that the convents of nuns in the Baetic province shall be ruled through the ministration and authority of monks. For we can best provide what is salutary for virgins dedicated to Christ by choosing for them spiritual fathers whose guidance can give them protection and whose teaching provide edification. But proper precautions must be taken so that the monks do not intrude on the privacy of the nuns, nor have general permission even to approach the vestibule. Neither the abbot nor anyone in authority over them shall be permitted, apart from their superior, to say anything to the virgins of Christ concerning regulations for their moral life; nor should he speak often with the superior alone, but in the presence of two or three sisters. Access should be rare and speech brief. God forbid the unmentionable – that we should wish the monks to be familiar with the virgins of Christ; they must be kept separate and far apart, as the statutes of the Rule and the canons lay down. We commit the nuns to their charge in the sense that one man, the best proved of the monks, shall be chosen to take over the management of their lands in the country, or town, and also the erection of buildings, or provision of whatever else is needed by the convent, so that the handmaids of Christ may be concerned only with the welfare of their souls, may live only for divine worship and performance of their own works. Of course the one proposed by his abbot must have the approval of his bishop. The sisters for their part should make clothing for the monasteries to which they look for guidance, since they will receive in return, as I said, the fruits of the monks' labour and support of their protection.[98]

In accordance with this provision, then, we want convents of women always to be subject to monasteries of men, so that the brothers may take care of the sisters and one man preside over both like a father whose authority each community shall recognize, and thus for both in the Lord 'there will be one flock and one shepherd'.[99] Such a society of spiritual brotherhood should be the more pleasing to God as it is to man, the more perfectly it is able to meet the needs of either sex coming for conversion, the monks taking in the men and the nuns the women, so that it can provide for every soul seeking its own salvation. And whoever wishes to be converted along with a mother, sister, daughter or any other woman for whom he is responsible will be able to find complete fulfilment there, and the two monasteries should be joined by a greater mutual affection and feel a warmer concern for each other the more closely their inmates are united by some kinship or connection.

The Superior of the monks, whom they call Abbot, we want to preside over the nuns too in such a way that he regards those who are the brides of the Lord whose servant he is as his own mistresses, and so be glad to serve rather than rule them. He should be like a steward in a king's palace who does not oppress the queen by his powers but treats her wisely, so that he obeys her at once in necessary matters but pays no heed to what might be harmful, and performs all his services outside the bedchamber without ever penetrating its privacy unbidden. In this way, then, we want the servant of Christ to provide for the brides of Christ, to take charge of them faithfully for Christ, and to discuss everything necessary with the abbess, so that he makes no decisions about the handmaids of Christ and their concerns without consulting her and issues no instructions or presumes to speak to any of them except through her. But whenever the abbess summons him he should be prompt to come, and not delay carrying out as far as he is able whatever she advises him about the needs of herself or her subordinates. When summoned by her he should speak to her openly, in the presence of approved persons, and not approach too near nor detain her with prolonged talk.

Anything to do with food or clothing, and money too, if there is any, shall be collected amongst the handmaids of Christ, or set aside so that what is surplus to the sisters' requirements can be made over to the brothers. And so the brothers shall attend to everything outside the buildings, and sisters confine themselves to what can suitably be done indoors by women, such as making clothes for themselves and the brothers, doing the washing, kneading bread and putting it to bake, and handling it when baked. They shall also take charge of the milk and its products, and of feeding hens or geese, and whatever women can do more conveniently than men.

The abbot himself on his appointment shall swear in the presence of the bishop and the sisters that he will be to them a faithful steward in the Lord, and will carefully keep their bodies from carnal contamination. If by chance (which God forbid) the bishop finds him negligent in this, he must depose him at once as guilty of perjury. All the brothers too, in making their profession, shall bind themselves by oath to the sisters not to consent to their oppression in any form, and to guarantee their bodily purity as far as they can. None of the men, therefore, except with the abbot's permission, shall have access to the sisters, nor receive anything sent by them except through the hands of the abbot. None of the sisters shall ever leave the precincts of the convent, but everything outside, as was said above, shall be the brothers' concern, for men should sweat over men's work. None of the brothers shall ever enter these precincts, unless he has obtained leave from the abbot and abbess for some necessary or worthy reason. If anyone ventures to do so, he shall be expelled from the monastery immediately.

But so that the men, being stronger than the women, shall not make too heavy demands on them, we make it a rule that they shall impose nothing against the will of the abbess, but do everything at her bidding and, all alike, men and women, shall make profession to her and promise obedience; for peace will be more soundly based and harmony better preserved the less freedom is allowed to the stronger, while the men will be less burdened by obedience to the weaker women the less they have to fear violence from them. The more a man has humbled himself before God, the higher he will certainly be exalted. Let this be enough for the moment about the abbess. Now let us write of the officers under her.

The Sacristan, who is also the Treasurer, shall provide for the whole oratory; and she herself must keep all the keys that belong to it and everything necessary to it. If there are any offerings she shall receive them, and she shall have charge of making or remaking whatever is needed in the oratory and caring for all its furnishings. It is her duty too to see to the hosts, the vessels, the books for the altar and all its fittings, the relics, incense, lights, clock and striking of the bells. If possible the nuns should prepare the hosts themselves and purify the flour they are made from, and wash the altar-cloths. But neither the sacristan nor any of the sisters shall ever be allowed to touch the relics or the altar-vessels, nor even the altar-cloths except when these are given them to be washed. They must summon the monks or the lay monks for this and await their coming. If necessary, some of them may be appointed to serve under the sacristan for this duty, who shall be thought fit to touch these things when the need arises, and take them out or replace them when she has unlocked the chests. The sister in charge of the sanctuary must be outstanding in purity of life, whole in mind as in body, if possible, and her abstinence and continence must be proved. She must be particularly well taught to calculate the phases of the moon, so that she can provide for the oratory according to the order of the seasons.

The Chantress shall be responsible for the whole choir, and shall arrange the divine offices and direct the teaching of singing and reading, and of everything to do with writing or composition. She shall also take charge of the book-cupboard, shall hand books out from it and receive them back, undertake the task of copying or binding them, or see that this is done. She shall decide how the sisters are to sit in choir and assign the seats, arrange who are to read or sing, and shall draw up the list, to be recited on Saturdays in Chapter, in which all the duties of the week are set out. Hence it is most important for her to be lettered, and especially to have some knowledge of music. She shall also see to all matters of discipline after the abbess, and if she happens to be busy with other affairs, the Infirmarian shall take her place.[100]

The Infirmarian shall take care of the sick, and shall protect them from sin as well as from want. Whatever their sickness requires, baths, food or anything else, is to be allowed them; for there is a well-known saying, 'The law was not made for the sick.' Meat is not to be denied them on any account, except on the sixth day of the week or on the chief vigils or the fasts of the

Ember Days or of Lent. But they should all the more be restrained from sin the more it is incumbent on them to think of their departure. That is the time when they should most observe silence, as they are very near their end, and concentrate on prayer, as it is written: 'My son, if you have an illness, do not neglect it but pray to the Lord, and he will heal you. Renounce your sin, amend your ways, and cleanse your heart from all sin.'[101] There must also be a watchful nurse always with the sick to answer their call at once when needed, and the infirmary must be equipped with everything necessary for their illness. Medicaments too must be provided, according to the resources of the convent, and this can more easily be done if the sister in charge of the sick has some knowledge of medicine. Those who have a period of bleeding shall also be in her care. And there should be someone with experience of blood-letting, or it would be necessary for a man to come in amongst the women for this purpose. Provision must also be made for the sick not to miss the offices of the Hours and communion; on the Lord's Day at least they should communicate, as far as possible always after confession and penance. For the anointing of the sick, the precept of St James the apostle[102] is to be carefully observed, and in order to perform this, especially when the sick woman's life is despaired of, two of the older priests with a deacon must be brought in from the monks, bringing with them the holy oil; then they must administer the sacrament in the presence of the whole convent, though divided off by a screen. Communion shall be celebrated when needed in the same way. It is therefore essential for the infirmary to be so arranged that the monks can easily come and go to perform these sacraments without seeing the sisters or being seen by them.

Once at least every day the abbess and the Cellaress should visit the sick woman as if she were Christ, so that they may carefully provide for her bodily as well as her spiritual needs, and show themselves worthy to hear the words of the Lord: 'I was sick and you visited me.'[103] But if the sick woman is near her end and has reached her death-agony, someone who is with her must run at once through the convent beating on a wooden board to give warning of the sister's departure. The whole convent, whatever the hour of day or night, must then hurry to the dying, unless prevented by the offices of the Church. Should this happen, as nothing must come before the work of God, it is enough if the abbess and a few others she has chosen shall go there quickly and the convent follow later. Whoever comes running at the beating of the board should start at once on the Litany, until the invocation of the saints, male and female, is completed, and then the psalms should follow or the other offices of the dead. How salutary it is to go to the sick or the dead Ecclesiastes points out, when he says: 'It is better to visit the house of mourning than the house of feasting; for to be mourned is the lot of every man, and the living should take this to heart.' Similarly, 'The wise man's heart is where there is grief, and the fool's heart where there is joy.'[104]

The body of the dead woman must then be washed at once by the sisters, clad in some cheap but clean garment and stockings, and laid on a bier, the head covered by the veil. These coverings must be firmly stitched or bound to the body and not afterwards removed. The body shall be carried into the church by the sisters for the monks to give it proper burial, and the sisters meanwhile shall devote themselves to psalm-singing and prayer in the oratory. The burial of an abbess shall have only one feature to distinguish it from that of others: her entire body shall be wrapped only in a hair-shirt and sewn up in this as in a sack.

The Wardrober shall be in charge of everything to do with clothing, and this includes shoes. She shall have the sheep shorn and receive the hides for shoes, spin and card flax or wool, take entire charge of weaving, and supply everyone with needle, thread and scissors. She shall also be personally responsible for the dormitory and provide bedding for all, and also for tablecloths, towels and cloths of every kind, and shall see to cutting and sewing and also washing them. To her especially the words apply: 'She seeks wool and flax and works by the skill of her hands ... She sets her hand to the distaff and her fingers grasp the spindle ... She will have no fear for her household when it snows, for all her servants are wrapped in two cloaks and she can laugh at tomorrow. She keeps her eye on the ways of her household and does not eat the bread of idleness. Her sons rise up and call her blessed.'[105] She shall keep the tools necessary for her work, and shall arrange what part of it to assign to which of the sisters, for she will have charge of the novices until they are admitted into the community.

The Cellaress shall be responsible for everything connected with food, for the cellar, refectory, kitchen, mill, bakehouse and its oven, and also the gardens, woods and entire cultivation of the fields. She shall also take charge of bees, herds and flocks, and all necessary poultry. She shall be expected to provide all essentials to do with food, and it is most important that she should not be grudging but ready and willing to provide everything required, 'For God loves a cheerful giver.'[106] We absolutely forbid her to favour herself above the others in dispensing her stores; she must neither prepare private dishes for herself nor keep anything for herself by defrauding the others of it. 'The best steward', says Jerome, 'is one who keeps nothing for himself.' Judas abused his office of steward when he had charge of the common purse and left the company of the apostles. Ananias too and Sapphira his wife were condemned to death for keeping money back.[107]

The Portress or Doorkeeper (which means the same) has the duty of receiving guests and all comers, announcing them or bringing them to the proper place, and dispensing hospitality. She should be discreet in years and mind, so that she will know how to receive and give an answer, and to decide who and who not to admit, and in what way. She especially, as if she were the vestibule of the Lord, should be an ornament for the religious life of the convent, since knowledge of it starts with her. She should therefore be gentle of speech and mild in manner, and should try by giving a suitable reason to establish a friendly relationship even with those she has to turn away. For it is written that 'A soft answer turns away anger, but a sharp word makes tempers hot.' And elsewhere: 'Pleasant words win many friends and soothe enemies.'[108] She also, as she sees the poor more regularly and knows them better, should share out what food and clothing there is for distribution; but if she or any of the officials need support or assistance, the abbess should appoint deputies for them, taking these generally from the lay sisters, lest some of the nuns are absent from the divine offices or from Chapter and the refectory.

The Portress should have a lodge by the gate, where she or her deputy can always be ready for all comers; they must not sit idle and, as their talk may easily be heard outside, they should be careful to observe silence. Indeed, her duty is not only to deny entrance to people who must be kept out but also to exclude entirely any rumours, so that they are not carelessly allowed into the convent, and she must be called to account for any failure in this matter. But if she hears what ought to be known, she should report it privately to the abbess so that she may think it over if she wishes. As soon as there is any knocking or clamour at the gate the Portress must ask the newcomers who they are and what they want and, if necessary, open the gate at once to admit them. Only women shall be entertained inside; men must be directed to the monks. Thus no man may be admitted for any reason, unless the abbess has been previously consulted and has issued instructions, but entrance shall be granted to women at once. The women when admitted, or the men allowed to enter on some occasion, must be made to wait by the Portress in her cell, until the abbess or the sisters, if it is necessary or fitting, shall come to them. In the case of poor women whose feet need to be washed, the abbess herself or the sisters shall duly perform this charitable act of hospitality. For the Lord too was called deacon by the apostles chiefly for this service to humanity, as someone has recorded in the *Lives of the Fathers*, saying: 'For you, O men, the Saviour became a deacon, girding himself with a towel and washing the disciples' feet, and telling them to wash their brothers' feet.'[109] And so the Apostle says of the deaconess, 'if she has given hospitality and washed the feet of God's people'. And the Lord himself says: 'I was a stranger, and you took me in.'[110]

All the officials (except the Chantress) should be chosen from the sisters who do not study letters, if there are others better fitted to make use of greater freedom for their studies.

The ornaments for the oratory should be necessary, not superfluous, and clean rather than costly. There should be nothing made of gold or silver in it apart from one silver chalice, or more than one if needed. There must be no furnishings of silk, apart from the stoles or maniples, and no carved images. Nothing but a wooden cross shall be set up on the altar there, though if the sisters like to paint the statue of the Saviour, that is not forbidden. But the altars must have no other statues. The convent must be content with a pair of bells. A vessel of holy water should be set outside the entrance to the oratory, for the sisters to bless themselves with when they go in in the morning and come out after Compline.

None of the nuns may be absent from the Canonical Hours, but as soon as the bell is rung, everything must be put down and each sister go quickly, with modest gait, to the divine office. As they come into the oratory unobserved, let all who can, say: 'Through thy great love I will come into thy house, and bow low towards thy holy temple in awe of thee.'[111] No book is to be kept in the choir except the one needed for the office at the time. The psalms should be repeated clearly and distinctly so as to be understood, and any chanting or singing must be pitched so that anyone with a weak voice can sustain the note. Nothing may be said or sung in church which is not taken from authentic scripture, and chiefly from the Old or New Testament. These are to be divided amongst the lessons so that they are read in their entirety in the course of the year. But exposition of the Scriptures or sermons of the Doctors of the Church or any other writings of an edifying nature shall be read aloud in the refectory or in Chapter; the reading of all these is permitted where the need is felt. No one must presume to read or sing without previous preparation, and if anyone happens to mispronounce something in the oratory, she must make amends on the spot by prayer in the presence of all, saying softly to herself: 'Yet again, Lord, forgive my carelessness.'

They must rise at midnight for the Night Office as the prophet enjoins, and so they must retire to bed early, so that their weak nature can sustain these vigils, and all the matters for the day can be done in daylight as St Benedict also laid down.'[112] After the Office they should return to the dormitory until the hour is struck for morning Lauds. If any of the night still remains, sleep should not be denied their weakness, for sleep more than anything refreshes weary nature, makes it able to endure toil, and keeps it equable and alert. However, if any of them feel a need to meditate on the Psalter or the lessons, as St Benedict also says,[113] they must concentrate without disturbing those who are asleep, for in this passage he refers to meditation rather than reading, lest the reading of some disturb the sleep of others. And when he spoke of 'the brothers who feel a need', he was certainly not compelling anyone to meditate in this way. But if there is sometimes also a need for instruction in chanting, this will also have to be met for those for whom it is necessary.

The morning Hour should be celebrated as soon as day dawns, and, if it can be arranged, the bell should be rung at sunrise. When it is ended the sisters should return to the dormitory, and, if it is summer, and the night is short and the morning long, we are willing for them to sleep a little before Prime, until they are waked by the bell. Such sleep after morning Lauds is mentioned by St Gregory in the second chapter of his *Dialogues* in speaking of the venerable Libertinus: 'But on the second day there was a case to be heard for the benefit of the monastery. And so, after morning hymns had been sung, Libertinus came to the abbot's bedside and humbly sought a prayer for himself . . .' This morning sleep shall accordingly be permitted from Easter until the autumn equinox, after which the night begins to exceed the day.

On coming out of the dormitory they must wash and then take books and sit in the cloister reading or chanting until Prime is rung. After Prime they should go to Chapter, and when all are seated there, a lesson from the Martyrology should be read, after the day of the month is given out. After this there should either be some edifying words or some of the Rule should be read and expounded. Then if there are matters to correct or arrange they should go on to these.

But it must be understood that neither a monastery nor some particular house should be called irregular if some irregularities occur there, but only if they are not afterwards carefully corrected. For is there any place which is wholly faultless? St Augustine took due note of this in a certain passage when he was instructing his clergy:

However strict the discipline in my house, I am a man and live among men. I would not venture to claim that my house is better than Noah's Ark, where one amongst eight persons was found to be a reprobate, or better than the house of Abraham where it was said 'Drive out this slave-girl and her son,' or better than the house of Isaac of which the Lord said, 'I love Jacob, I hate Esau,' or better than the house of Jacob where a son defiled his father's bed, or better than the house of David, where one son slept with his sister and another rebelled against the holy mildness of his father; or better than the company of the apostle Paul, who, had he lived among good men would not have said 'Quarrels all round us, forebodings within.' Nor if he had been living among good men would he have said, 'There is no one here who takes a genuine interest in your concerns; they are all bent on their own ends.' It is not better than the company of Christ himself, in which eleven good men had to endure the thief and traitor Judas, nor better, lastly, than heaven from which angels fell.[114]

Augustine also, in pressing us to seek the discipline of the monastery, added: 'I confess before God, from the day on which I began to serve God, I have had difficulty in finding better men than those who have made progress in monasteries, but equally I have found none worse than those in monasteries who have fallen.' Hence, I think, it is written in the Apocalypse, 'Let the good man persevere in his goodness and the filthy man continue in his filth.'[115]

Correction must therefore be rigorous, to the extent that any sister who has seen something to be corrected in another and concealed it shall be subjected to a harsher discipline than the offender. No one then should put off denouncing her own or another's wrongdoing. Whoever anticipates the others in accusing herself, as it is written that 'The just man is the first to accuse himself,' deserves a milder punishment, if her negligence has ceased. But no one shall presume to make excuses for another unless the abbess happens to question her about the truth of a matter which is unknown to the rest. No one shall ever presume to strike another for any fault unless she has been ordered to do so by the abbess. Concerning the discipline of correction, it is written: 'My son, do not spurn the Lord's correction nor be cast down at his reproof; for those whom he loves the Lord reproves, as a father punishes a favourite son.' Again, 'A father who spares the rod hates his son, but one who loves him keeps him in order.' 'Strike a scornful man and a fool will be wiser.' 'Punish a scornful man and the simple will be wiser.' 'A whip for the horse, a halter for the ass and a rod for the back of fools.' 'Who takes a man to task will in the end win more thanks than the man with a flattering tongue.' 'Discipline is never pleasant, at the time it seems painful, but later, for those trained by it, it yields a harvest of peace and goodness.' 'There is shame in being the father of a spoilt son, and the birth of a foolish daughter will bring loss.' 'A man who loves his son will whip him often so that he may have joy in him in the end.' 'An unbroken horse turns out stubborn, and an unchecked son turns out headstrong. Pamper your son and he will shock you; play with him and he will grieve you.'[116]

In a discussion on what counsel to take, it shall be open to anyone to offer her opinion, but whatever everyone else thinks, the abbess's decision must not be swayed, for everything depends on her will, even if (which God forbid) she may be mistaken and decide on a worse course. For as St Augustine says in his *Confessions*, 'He who disobeys his superiors in anything sins greatly, even if he chooses what is better than what is commanded him.'[117] It is indeed far better for us to do well than to do good, and we must think less of what should be done and more of the manner and spirit in which to do it. A thing is well done which is done obediently, even if it seems the least good thing to have done. And so superiors must be obeyed in everything, whatever the material harm, if there is no apparent danger to the soul. The superior must take care that he orders well since it is sufficient for his subjects to obey well and not to follow their own will but, as they professed, that of their superiors. For we absolutely forbid that custom should ever be set above reason; a practice must never be defended on grounds of custom but only of reason, not because it is usual but because it is good, and it should be more readily accepted the better it is shown to be. Otherwise like the Jews we should set the antiquity of the Law before the Gospel.

On this point St Augustine several times gives proof from the counsel of Cyprian, and says in one passage: 'Whoever despises truth and presumes to follow custom is either ill-disposed and hostile towards his fellow-men, to whom truth is revealed, or he is ungrateful to God on whose inspiration his Church is founded.' Again, 'In the Gospel the Lord says "I am Truth." He did not say "I am custom." And so as truth was made manifest, custom must yield to truth.' Again, 'Since the truth was revealed, error must yield to truth, just as Peter, who was previously circumcised, yielded to Paul who preached truth.' Similarly, in the fourth book *On Baptism* he writes: 'In vain do those who are vanquished by reason plead custom against us, as though custom were greater than truth, or in spiritual matters we should not follow what was revealed for the better by the Holy Spirit. This is clearly true because reason and truth must be set before custom.'[118]

Gregory the Seventh writes to Bishop Wimund: 'And certainly, in the words of St Cyprian, any custom, however long established and widespread, must stand second to truth and practice which is contrary to truth must be abolished.'[119] And we are told how lovingly we should adhere to the truth in speech by Ecclesiasticus when he says 'Do not be ashamed to speak the truth for your soul's sake,' and 'Do not contradict the truth in any way,' and again, 'A true word should come before every enterprise and steady counsel before every deed.'[120] Nothing must be taken as a precedent because it is done by many but because it is approved by the wise and good. As Solomon says, 'The number of fools cannot be counted,' and, in accordance with the assertion of the Truth, 'Many are summoned but few are chosen.'[121] Valuable things are rare, and multiplication of numbers diminishes value. In taking counsel no one should follow the larger number of men but the better men; it is not a man's years which should be considered but his wisdom, and regard paid not to friendship but to truth. Hence also the words of the poet:

Even from a foe it is right to learn.[122]

But whenever there is need for counsel it must not be postponed and, if important matters are to be debated, the whole convent should be assembled. For discussing minor affairs it will be enough for the abbess to meet a few of the senior nuns. It is also written concerning counsel that 'The people fares ill that has no guidance, but safety reigns where counsel abounds.' 'The fool is right in his own eyes, but the wise man listens to counsel.' 'Do nothing, my son, except with counsel, and afterwards you will have no regrets.'[123] If something done without taking counsel happens to have a successful outcome, fortune's kindness does not excuse the doer's presumption. But if after taking counsel men sometimes err, the authority which sought counsel is not held guilty of presumption, and the man who believed his advisers is not so much to be blamed as those with whom he agreed in their error.

On coming out from Chapter the sisters should apply themselves to suitable tasks, reading or chanting or handiwork until Terce. After Terce the Mass shall be said, and to celebrate this one of the monks shall be appointed priest for the week. If numbers are large he must come with a deacon and subdeacon to serve him with what is necessary or to perform their own office. Their coming in and going out must be so arranged as to be unseen by the sisters. If more have been needed, arrangements shall be made for them too and, if possible, provision so that the monks never miss divine offices in their own monastery because of the nuns' masses.

If the sisters are to take communion, one of the older priests must be chosen to administer it to them after Mass, but the deacon and subdeacon must first withdraw, to remove any risk of temptation. Three times at least in the year the whole convent must communicate, at Easter, Pentecost and the Nativity of the Lord, as it was ordained by the Fathers for the laity also. For these communions they must prepare themselves in the following way: three days before they should all make their confession and do suitable penance, and by three days of fasting on bread and water and repeated prayer, purify themselves humbly and fearfully, taking to themselves those terrible words of the Apostle:

> It follows that anyone who eats the bread or drinks from the cup of the Lord unworthily will be guilty of desecrating the body and blood of the Lord. A man must test himself before eating his share of the bread and drinking from the cup. For he who eats and drinks unworthily eats and drinks judgement on himself if he does not discern the body of the Lord. That is why many of you are feeble and sick and a number have died. But if we judged ourselves we should not be judged at all.[124]

After Mass they should return again to their work until Sext and not waste any time in idleness; everyone must do what she can and what is right for her. After Sext they should have lunch, unless it is a fast-day, when they must wait until None, and in Lent even until Vespers. But at no time must the convent be without reading, which the abbess may end when she wishes by saying 'Enough', and then they should all rise at once to render thanks to God. In summer they should rest in their dormitory after lunch until None, and after None return to work until Vespers. Immediately after Vespers they should eat and drink, and then, according to the custom of the season, they should go to Collation:[125] but on Saturday, before Collation, they should be made clean by washing of the feet and hands. The abbess should also participate in this rite along with the sisters on duty for the week in the kitchen. After Collation they are to come at once to Compline, and then retire to sleep.

As regards food and clothing, the opinion of the Apostle must be followed, in which he says, 'As long as we have food and something to wear let us rest content.'[126] That is, necessities should be sufficient and superfluous things not sought. They should be allowed whatever can be bought cheaply or easily obtained and taken without giving offence, for the Apostle avoids only what foods will offend his own or his brother's conscience, knowing that it is not the food which is at fault but the appetite for it.

The man who eats must not hold in contempt the man who does not, and he who does not eat must not pass judgement on the man who does ... Who are you to pass judgement on someone else's servant? ... He who eats has the Lord in mind when he eats, since he gives thanks to God; and he who abstains has the Lord in mind no less, and he too gives thanks to God ... Let us therefore cease judging one another, but rather make this judgement: that no obstacle or stumbling-block be placed in a brother's way. I know on the authority of the Lord Jesus that nothing is unclean in itself, only if a man considers a particular thing unclean ... The kingdom of God is not eating and drinking but justice, peace and joy in the Holy Spirit ... Everything is pure in itself, but anything is bad for the man who by his eating causes his brother to fall. It is good to abstain from eating meat or drinking wine, or doing anything which causes your brother's downfall.[127]

And after the offence to his brother he goes on to speak of the offence to himself of a man who eats against his own conscience: 'Happy is the man who does not bring judgement upon himself by what he approves. But a man who has doubts is guilty if he eats, because his action does not arise from his conviction, and anything which is not from conviction is sin.'

For in all that we do against our conscience and against our beliefs we are sinning; and in what we test by the law which we approve and accept, we judge and condemn ourselves if we eat those foods which we discriminate against or exclude by the law and set apart as unclean. So great is the testimony of our conscience that this more than anything accuses or excuses us before God. And so John writes in his First Letter: 'Dear friends, if our conscience does not condemn us, then we can approach God with confidence, and obtain from him whatever we ask, because we keep his commandments and do what he approves.'[128] It was therefore well said by Paul in the passage above that 'Nothing is unclean in the eyes of Christ, but only for the man who considers a thing unclean,' that is, if he thinks it impure and forbidden to him. (Indeed, we call certain foods unclean which according to the Law are clean, because the Law in forbidding them to its own people may still offer them publicly to those outside the Law. Hence 'common' women are unclean, and common things which are offered publicly are cheap or less dear.) And so the Apostle asserts that no food is 'common' or unclean in the eyes of Christ because the law of Christ forbids nothing except, as is said, to remove offence to one's own conscience or another's. On this he says elsewhere, 'And therefore if food be the downfall of my brother, I will never eat meat any more, for I will not be the cause of my brother's downfall.' 'Am I not a free man? Am I not an apostle?'[129] – as if he were to say, Have I not the freedom which the Lord gave to the apostles, to eat whatever I like or to take alms from others? For when the Lord sent out the apostles, he said in a certain passage: 'Eating and drinking what they have,'[130] and thus made no distinction between kinds of food. Noting this, the Apostle is careful to say that any kind of food, even if it is the food of unbelievers and consecrated to idols, is permitted to Christians and only the giving of offence in food is to be avoided:

> There are no forbidden things, but not everything does good. Nothing is forbidden me, but not everything helps to build the community. Nobody should look to his own interests, but the other man's. You may eat anything sold in the meat-market without raising questions of conscience; for the earth is the Lord's and everything in it. If an unbeliever invites you to a meal and you care to go, eat whatever is put before you without raising questions of conscience. But if someone says to you, 'This food has been offered in sacrifice to idols,' then, out of consideration for him who told you and for conscience's sake, do not eat it – not your conscience, I mean, but the other man's ... Give no offence to Jews or Greeks or to the Church of God.[131]

From these words of the Apostle it is plain that nothing is forbidden us which we can eat without offence to our own or another's conscience. We eat without offence to our own conscience if we are sure that we are keeping to that course of life whereby we can be saved, and without offence to another's if we are believed to be living in a manner leading to salvation.

We shall indeed live in this manner if we permit everything necessary to our nature while avoiding sin, and if we are not over-confident of our strength so as to bind ourselves by profession to a rule of life too heavy for us, under which we may fall: and the higher the degree of our profession, the heavier the fall would be. Such a fall, and such a foolish vow of profession, Ecclesiastes forestalls, when he says: 'When you make a vow to God do not be slow to pay it, for he has no use for unbelievers and foolish promises. Pay whatever you owe. Better not vow at all than vow and fail to pay.'[132] On this hazard too the Apostle advises, saying: 'It is my wish that younger widows shall remarry, have children, preside over a home, and give no opponent occasion for slander. For there have already been some who have taken the wrong turning and gone to the devil.'[133] Out of consideration for the nature of youth's frailty, he sets the remedy of a freer way of life against the risk of attempting a better one, and advises us to stay in a lowly position lest we fall from a high one.

Following him St Jerome also instructs the virgin Eustochium: 'But if those who are virgins may not be saved on account of other faults, what shall become of those who have prostituted the members of Christ and turned the temple of the Holy Spirit into a brothel? It would have been better for mankind to undergo matrimony, tread level ground, than to aim at the heights and fall into the depths of hell.' And if we search through all the words of the Apostle we shall never find that he allowed a second marriage except to women. To men he preaches continence. 'If anyone was circumcised before he was called, he should not disguise it.' And again, 'If you are free of a wife, do not seek one.'[134] Moses, on the other hand, was more indulgent to men than to women, and allowed one man several wives at the same time, but not one woman several husbands; and he punished the adulteries of women more severely than those of men. 'A woman,' says the Apostle, 'if her husband dies is free from the law of her husband, so that she does not commit adultery if she consorts with another man.'[135] And elsewhere, 'To the unmarried and to widows I say this: It is a good thing if they stay as I am myself, but if they cannot control themselves, they should marry. Better be married than burn with desire.' Again, 'The wife, if her husband is dead, is free to marry whom she will, as long as it is in the Lord. But she will be happier if she stays in accordance with my advice.'[136] Not only does he allow a second marriage to the weaker sex but he does not venture to set a limit to the number, simply permitting them to take other husbands when theirs are dead. He fixes no limit to their marriages, provided that they are not guilty of fornication. They should marry often rather than fornicate once, and pay the debts of the flesh to many rather than once be prostituted to one: such payment is not wholly free from sin, but lesser sins are permitted so that greater may be avoided.

No wonder, then, that what has no sin at all is allowed them lest they commit sin; that is, foods which are necessary and not superfluous. For, as we said, the food is not to blame but the appetite, when pleasure is taken in what is not permitted, and forbidden things are desired and sometimes shamelessly snatched, which causes very serious offence.

But what amongst all the foods of men is so dangerous, injurious and contrary to our religion or to holy quiet as wine? The wisest of men well understood this when he particularly warns us against it, saying:

Wine is reckless, and strong drink quarrelsome. No one who delights in these will be wise . . . Who will know woe, as his father will, and quarrels, brawls, bruises without cause and bloodshot eyes? Those who linger late over wine, and look for ready-mixed wine. Do not look on wine when it glows and sparkles in the glass. It goes down smoothly, but in the end it will bite like a snake and spread venom like a serpent. Then your eyes will see strange sights, and your mind utter distorted words; you will be like a man sleeping in mid-ocean, like a drowsy helmsman who has lost his rudder, and you will say: 'They struck me and it did not hurt, dragged me off and I felt nothing. When I wake up I shall turn to wine again . . .'

Again:

Do not give wine to kings, O Lemuel, never to kings; there is no privy counsel where drinking prevails. If they drink they may forget what they have decreed and neglect the pleas of the poor for their sons.[137]

And in Ecclesiasticus it says, 'A drunken workman will never grow rich; carelessness in small things leads little by little to ruin. Wine and women rob the wise of their wits and are a hard test for good sense.'[138]

Isaiah, too, passes over all other foods and mentions only wine as a reason for the captivity of his people. 'Shame on you,' he says, 'who rise in the morning to go in pursuit of liquor and drinking until evening, when you are heated with wine. At your feasts you have harp and lute, tabor and pipe and wine, but have no eyes for the work of the Lord. Shame upon you, mighty drinkers, violent mixers of drinks.'[139] Then he extends his lament from the people to priests and prophets, saying,

These too are fuddled with wine and bemused with drinking. Priest and prophet are stupid with drinking; they are sodden with wine, bemused with liquor; they do not recognize the true visionary and have forgotten justice. Every table is covered with vomit and filth that leaves no clean spot. Whom shall the prophet teach knowledge? Whom shall he compel to listen and understand?[140]

The Lord says through Joel, 'Wake up, you drunkards, and weep for the sweet wine you drink.'[141] Not that he forbids wine when necessary, for the Apostle recommends it to Timothy 'for the frequent ailments of your stomach'[142] – not ailments only, but frequent ones.

Noah was the first to plant a vineyard, still ignorant perhaps of the evil of drinking, and, when drunk, exposed his bare thighs, because with wine comes the shame of lechery. When mocked by his son he put a curse on him and bound him by a sentence of servitude, something we know was never done before. Lot was a holy man, and so his daughters saw that he could never be led into incest except through drunkenness. And the holy widow believed that Holofernes in his pride could never be tricked and brought low except by this device. The angels who visited the patriarchs of old and were hospitably received by them took food, we are told, but not wine. Elijah too, the greatest and first of our leaders, when he had retired to the wilderness was brought bread and meat for food by the ravens morning and evening, but not wine. The children of Israel also, we read, were fed in the desert mainly on the delicate flesh of quails, but neither received wine nor wished for it.[143] And those repasts of loaves and fishes wherewith the people were sustained in the wilderness are nowhere said to have included wine. Only a wedding, where incontinence is permitted, was granted the miracle of the wine which promotes sensuality.[144] But the wilderness, the proper habitation of monks, knew the benefit of meat rather than wine. Again, the cardinal point in the law of the Nazirites whereby they dedicated themselves to God forbade only wine and strong drink.[145] For what strength or virtue remains in the drunken? Thus not only wine, but anything which can intoxicate, we read, was also forbidden to the priests of old. And so Jerome, in writing to Nepotian about the life of the clergy, and highly indignant because the priests of the Law abstain from all strong drink and so surpass our clergy in abstinence, says:

> Never smell of wine, lest you hear said of you those words of the philosopher: 'This is not offering a kiss but proffering a cup.' The Apostle condemns priests who are given to drink and the Old Law equally forbids it: 'Those who serve the altar shall not drink wine and strong drink.' By 'strong drink' in Hebrew is understood any drink which can intoxicate, whether produced by fermentation, or from apple juice, or from honeycomb which has been distilled into a sweet, rough drink, or when the fruit of the date-palm is pressed into liquid, or water is enriched with boiled grain. Whatever intoxicates and upsets the balance of the mind, shun it like wine.

According to the Rule of St Pachomius, no one shall have access to wine and liquor except in the sickroom.[146] Which of you has not heard that wine in any form is not for monks, and was so greatly abhorred by the monks of old that in their stern warnings against it they called it Satan? And so we read in the *Lives of the Fathers* that:

Certain people told abba Pastor that a particular monk drank no wine, to which he replied that wine was not for monks.

And further on:

Once there was a celebration of the Mass on the Mount of abba Antony, and a jar of wine was found there. One of the elders took a small vessel, carried a cupful to abba Sisoi and gave it to him. He drank once, and a second time he took it and drank, but when it was offered a third time he refused, saying 'Peace, brother, do you not know it is Satan?'

It is also said of abba Sisoi:

His disciple Abraham then asked, 'If this happens on the Sabbath and the Lord's Day in church, and he drinks three cups, is that too much?' 'If it were not Satan,' the old man replied, 'it would not be much.'

St Benedict had this in mind when he allowed wine to monks by special dispensation, saying:

Although we read that wine is never for monks, in our times it is impossible to persuade monks of this.

It is not surprising, then, that if wine is strictly denied to monks, St Jerome absolutely forbids it to women, whose nature is weaker in itself, though stronger as regards wine. He uses strong words when instructing Eustochium, the Bride of Christ, on the preserving of her virginity:

And so, if there is any counsel in me, if my experience is to be trusted, this is my first warning and testimony. The Bride of Christ must avoid wine like poison. It is the first weapon of demons against youth. Greed does not make her waver nor pride bolster her up nor ambition seduce her in the same way. We can easily forgo the other vices, but this is a foe shut up within us. Wherever we go we carry the enemy with us. Wine and youth are the twin fires of lust. Why throw oil on the flame, why add the fuel of fire to the burning body?[147]

And yet it is well known from the evidence of those who write about physic that wine has much less power over women than men. Macrobius Theodosius, in the seventh book of his *Saturnalia*, gives a reason for this:

Aristotle says that women are rarely intoxicated, but old men often. Woman has an extremely humid body, as can be known from her smooth and glossy skin, and especially from her regular purgations which rid the body of superfluous humours. So when wine is drunk and merged with so general a humidity, it loses its power and does not easily strike the seat of the brain when its strength is extinguished.

Again:

A woman's body which is destined for frequent purgations is pierced with several holes, so that it opens into channels and provides outlets for the moisture draining away to be dispersed. Through these holes the fumes of wine are quickly released.

On what grounds, then, should monks be allowed what is denied to the weaker sex? What madness it is to permit it to those to whom it can do more harm while denying it to others! Nothing could be more foolish than that religion should not abhor what is so contrary to religion and takes us furthest away from God, nothing more shameless than that the abstinence of Christian perfection should not shun what is forbidden to kings and priests of the Law or, rather, should especially delight in it. For who does not know that today the interests of the clergy in particular, and also of the monks, revolve round the cellars, to see how they can fill them with different varieties of wine, and how to brew with herbs, honey and spices so that the more pleasurably they drink, the more easily they make themselves drunk, and the more they are warmed by wine, the more they incite themselves to lust? What error, or rather, what folly is this, when those who bind themselves most stringently by their profession of continence make less preparation for keeping their vow, and even do what makes it least likely to be kept? Though their bodies are confined to the cloister their hearts are filled with lust and minds on fire for fornication. In writing to Timothy the Apostle says: 'Stop drinking nothing but water; take a little wine for your digestion, for your frequent ailments.' Timothy is allowed a little wine for his ailments because it is clear that when in good health he would take none.

If we profess the apostolic life and especially vow to follow the way of repentance, if we preach withdrawal from the world, why do we particularly delight in what we see to be wholly contrary to our purpose and more delectable than any food? St Ambrose in his detailed description of repentance condemns nothing in the diet of the penitent except wine. 'Does anyone think,' he asks, 'that repentance exists where there is still ambition for high position, pouring out of wine and conjugal enjoyment of sexual union? Renunciation of the world can more easily be found among those who have kept their innocence than among those who have done fitting penance.'[148] Again, in his book *On Renouncing the World* he says: 'You renounce it well if your eye renounces cups and flagons lest it becomes lustful in lingering over wine.' Wine is the only form of nutriment he mentions in this book, and he says that we renounce the world well if we renounce wine, as if all the pleasures of the world depend on this alone: nor does he say 'if the palate renounces the taste of it' but 'if the eye renounces the sight', lest it be captivated by lust and delight in what it often sees. Hence the words of Solomon which we quoted above: 'Do not look on wine when it glows and sparkles in the glass.' But what, pray, are we to say when we have flavoured it with honey, herbs or different spices so as to enjoy its taste as well as the sight of it, and then want to drink it by flagons?

St Benedict was compelled to grant indulgence for wine, saying, 'Let us agree at least on this, that we should drink temperately, not to satiety, for "wine robs even the wise of their wits".' If only our drinking could stop at satiety and not be carried on to the greater sin of excess! St Augustine, too, in setting up monasteries for clerks and writing a Rule for them, says: 'Only on the Sabbath or on the Lord's Day, as the custom is, those who want to may take wine.'[149] This was out of reverence for the Lord's Day and its vigil, the Sabbath, and also because at that time the brothers scattered amongst the cells were gathered together; as when in the *Lives of the Fathers* St Jerome says, when writing of the place he named The Cells, 'They stay each in his own cell, but on the Sabbath and the Lord's Day they assemble in Church, and there see themselves restored to each other as if in heaven.'[150] This indulgence was therefore surely suitable at a time when they met together and could enjoy some relaxation, and feel as well as say 'How good it is and how pleasant for brothers to live together!'[151]

But if we abstain from meat, what a reproach it is to us if we eat everything else to excess, if we procure varied dishes of fish at vast expense, mingle the flavours of pepper and spices, and, when we are drunk on neat wine, go on to cups of herb-flavoured liquor and flagons of spiced drink! All this is to be excused by abstinence from ordinary meat provided that we do not guzzle in public – as if the quality rather than excess of food were to blame, although the Lord forbids us only dissipation and drunkenness,[152] that is, excess in food and drink, not the quality. St Augustine takes note of this, for his fears are all for wine, no other form of nourishment, and he draws no distinction between kinds of food when he says briefly what he believes to be sufficient abstinence: 'Subdue your flesh by fasting and by abstinence from food and drink as far as your health permits.'[153] If I am not mistaken, he had read this passage of St Athanasius in his exhortation to monks: 'Let there be no fixed measure of fasts for the willing, but let these last as long as possible, without being prolonged by effort, and except on the Lord's Day, if vowed they should be solemnly observed.'[154] In other words, if they are undertaken by vow they should be devoutly carried out, except on the Lord's Day. No fasts are fixed in advance but are to last as far as health permits, for it is said that 'He regards solely the capacity of nature and lets it set its own limit, knowing that there is failure in nothing if moderation is kept in everything.'[155] And so we should not be relaxed in our pleasures more than is right, like the people nourished on the germ of wheat and the purest wine, of whom it is written, 'He grew fat, he grew bloated and unruly';[156] nor should we succumb, famished and wholly defeated by excessive fasting, and lose our reward by complaining, or glory in our singularity. This Ecclesiastes foresees when he says: 'The righteous man perishes in his righteousness. Do not be over-righteous nor wiser than is necessary, lest you are bewildered';[157] that is to say, do not swell with pride in your own singularity.

Let discretion, the mother of all the virtues, preside over zeal and look carefully to see on whom she may lay which burdens, that is, on each according to his capacity, following nature rather than putting pressure on it, and removing not the habit of sufficiency but the abuse of excess, so that vices are rooted out but nature is unharmed. It is enough for the weak if they avoid sin, although they may not rise to the peak of perfection, and sufficient also to dwell in a corner of Paradise if you cannot take your seat with the martyrs. It is safe to vow in moderation so that grace may add more to what we owe; for of this it is written, 'When you have carried out all your orders you should say "We are servants and worthless; we have done only what it was our duty to do." '[158] 'The Law,' says the Apostle, 'can bring only retribution: only where there is no law can there be no breach of law.' And again, 'In the absence of law, sin is dead. There was a time when, in the absence of law, I was alive, but when the commandment came, sin sprang to life and I died. The commandment was meant to lead to life, but in my case it led to death, because sin found its opportunity in the commandment, seduced me, and through the commandment killed me.'[159]

Augustine writes to Simplician: 'By being prohibited desire has increased, it has become sweeter and so deceived me.'[160]

Similarly, in the *Book of Questions*, number 83: 'The persuasiveness of pleasure towards sin is more urgent when there is prohibition.' Hence the poet says,

Always we seek the forbidden and desire what is denied.[161]

Let him pay heed to this with reverence, who wishes to bind himself under the yoke of any rule, as though by obedience to a new law. Let him choose what he can, fear what he cannot. No one is held liable under a law unless he has accepted its authority. Think carefully before you accept it, but once you have done so, keep it. What was voluntary before afterwards becomes compulsory. 'There are many dwelling places,' says the Truth, 'in my Father's house.'[162] So too there are many ways whereby we may come to them. The married are not damned, but the continent are more easily saved. The rulings of the holy Fathers were not given us simply so that we can be saved, but so that we can be saved more easily and be enabled to devote ourselves more purely to God. 'If a virgin marries,' says the Apostle, 'she has done no wrong. But such people will have trouble in the flesh, and my aim is to spare you.' Again:

The unmarried and virgin woman cares for the Lord's business; her aim is to be holy both in body and spirit. But the married woman cares for worldly things and her aim is to please her husband. In saying this I have no desire to keep you on a tight rein; I am thinking simply of your own good, of what is seemly, and of your freedom to wait upon the Lord without distraction.[163]

The time for this to be most easily done is when we withdraw from the world in body too, and shut ourselves in the cloisters of monasteries lest we are disturbed by the tumult of the world. Not only he who receives but he who makes a law should take care not to multiply transgressions by multiplying restrictions. The Word of God came down to earth and curtailed the word on earth. Moses said many things, and yet, in the words of the Apostle, 'The Law brought nothing to perfection.'[164] He did indeed say many things, which were so burdensome that the apostle Peter declares that no one can endure his precepts: 'Men and brothers, why do you provoke God, laying on the shoulders of these converts a yoke which neither we nor our fathers were able to bear? No, we believe that it is by the grace of the Lord Jesus that we are saved, and so are they.'[165]

Christ chose only a few words to give the apostles moral instruction and teach the holiness of life and the way of perfection. He set aside what was austere and burdensome and taught sweetness and light, which for him was the sum of religion. 'Come to me,' he said, 'all you whose work is hard, whose load is heavy, and I will give you relief. Bend your necks to my yoke, and learn from me, for I am gentle and humble-hearted, and your souls will find rest. For my yoke is pleasant to bear and my load is light.'[166]

We often treat our good works as we do the business of the world, for many in their business labour more and gain less, and many outwardly afflict themselves more but inwardly make less progress in the sight of God, who regards the heart rather than works. The more they are taken up with outward things, the less they can devote themselves to inner ones; and the more they shine out amongst men, who judge by externals, the greater the fame they seek among them, and the more easily they are led astray by pride. The Apostle deals with this error when he firmly belittles works and extols justification by faith: 'For if Abraham was justified by works, then he has a ground for pride, but not before God. For what does Scripture say? "Abraham put his faith in the Lord and that faith was counted as righteousness."' And again: 'Then what are we to say? That Gentiles, who made no effort after righteousness, nevertheless achieved it, a righteousness based on faith; whereas Israel made great efforts after a law of righteousness but never achieved it. Why was this? Because their efforts were not based on faith, but (as they supposed) on works.'[167] They clean the outside of the pot or dish but pay little heed to cleanliness inside, they watch over the flesh more than the soul, and so are fleshly rather than spiritual.

But we who desire Christ to dwell in the inner man by faith, think little of outward things which are common to the sinner and the chosen; we heed the words 'I am bound by vows to thee, O God, and will redeem them with praise of thee.'[168] Moreover, we do not practise that outward abstinence prescribed by the Law, which certainly confers no righteousness. Nor does the Lord forbid us anything in the way of food except dissipation and drunkenness, that is, excess; and he was not ashamed to display in himself what he has allowed to us, although many of those present took offence and sharply rebuked him. With his own lips he says: 'John came neither eating nor drinking, and they say "He is possessed." The Son of Man came eating and drinking, and they say, "Look at him! a glutton and a drinker." '[169] He also excused his own disciples because they did not fast like the disciples of John, nor when they were about to eat did they bother much about bodily cleanness and hand-washing. 'The children of the bridegroom', he said, 'cannot be expected to mourn when the bridegroom is with them.' And elsewhere, 'A man is not defiled by what goes into his mouth but by what comes out of it. What comes out of the mouth has its origins in the heart, and that is what defiles a man; but to eat without first washing his hands, that cannot defile him.'[170]

Therefore no food defiles the soul, only the appetite for forbidden food. For as the body is not defiled except by bodily filth, so the soul can only be defiled by spiritual filth. We need not fear anything done in the body if the soul is not prevailed on to consent. Nor should we put our trust in the cleanliness of the flesh if the mind is corrupted by the will. Thus the whole life and death of the soul depends on the heart, as Solomon says in Proverbs: 'Guard your heart more than any treasure, for it is the source of all life.'[171] And according to the words of the Truth we have quoted, what defiles a man comes from the heart, since the soul is lost or saved by evil or good desires. But since soul and flesh are closely conjoined in one person, special care must be taken lest the pleasure enjoyed by the flesh leads the soul to comply, and when the flesh is overindulged it grows wanton, resists the spirit and begins to dominate where it should be subject. However, we can guard against this if we allow all necessities but, as we have often said, cut off completely any excess, and so not deny the weaker sex any use of food while forbidding all abuse of it. Let everything be permitted but nothing consumed beyond measure. 'For everything,' says the Apostle, 'that God created is good, and nothing is to be rejected when it is taken with thanksgiving, since it is hallowed by God's own word and prayer. By offering such advice as this to the brethren you will prove a good servant of Jesus Christ, bred in the precepts of our faith and of the sound instruction which you have followed.'[172]

Let us therefore, with Timothy, follow the teaching of the Apostle, and, in accordance with the words of the Lord, shun nothing in food except dissipation and drunkenness; let us moderate everything so that we sustain weak nature in every way but do not nurture vices. Whatever can do harm by excess must be the more strictly moderated, for it is better and more praiseworthy to eat in moderation than to abstain altogether. Thus St Augustine, in his book *On the Good of Marriage*, when he deals with bodily sustenance, says that 'A man makes no good use of these things unless he can also abstain from them. Many find it easier to abstain and not use at all than to be moderate so as to use well. But no one can use wisely unless he can also restrain himself from using.' St Paul also said of this practice, 'I know both what it is to have plenty and what it is to suffer need.'[173] To suffer need is the lot of all men, but to know how to suffer it is granted only to the great. So too, any man can begin to have plenty, but to know how to have plenty is granted only to those whom plenty does not corrupt.

As regards wine, then, because (as we said) it is a sensual and turbulent thing, and so entirely opposed both to continence and to silence, women should either abstain altogether, in God's name, just as the wives of the Gentiles are forbidden it through fear of adultery, or they should mix it with enough water to make it satisfy their thirst and benefit their health while not being strong enough to hurt them. This we believe can be done if at least a quarter of the mixture is water. It is indeed very difficult when drink is set before us to make sure that, as St Benedict ordered, we do not go on drinking to satiety. And so we think it safer not to forbid satiety and run the risk of breaking a rule, for it is not this, as we have often said, which is culpable, but excess. The preparation of wine mixed with herbs for medicinal purposes or even the drinking of neat wine is not to be forbidden, so long as the convent in general never takes these, but they are drunk separately by the sick.

Fine wheat flour we absolutely forbid; whenever the sisters use flour, a third part at least of coarser grain must be mixed with it. And they must never enjoy bread hot from the oven, but eat only what has been baked at least one day before. As for other foods, the abbess must see that, as we said above, what can be cheaply bought or easily obtained shall meet the needs of their weaker nature. For what could be more foolish than to buy extras when our own resources are sufficient, or to look outside for superfluous things when we have everything necessary to hand? We are taught this necessary moderation and discretion not so much by human as by angelic example, or even by that of the Lord himself, and should therefore know that for meeting the needs of this life we should not seek particular kinds of food but rest content with what we have; for the angels fed on meat set before them by Abraham, and the Lord Jesus refreshed a hungry multitude with fishes found in the wilderness. From this we are surely to learn that we are to eat meat or fish without distinguishing between them, and to take especially what is without offence of sin and is freely available, and consequently easier to prepare and less costly.

And so Seneca, the chief exponent of poverty and continence, and of all the philosophers the greatest teacher of morals, says:

> Our motto, as we all know, is to live according to nature. It is against nature for a man to torment his body, to hate simple cleanliness and seek out dirt, to eat food which is not only cheap but disgusting and revolting. Just as a craving for dainties is a token of extravagance, avoidance of what is familiar and cheaply prepared is madness. Philosophy calls for simple living, not a penance, and a simple way of life need not be a rough one. This is the standard I approve.[174]

Gregory too, in the thirtieth book of his *Morals*, when teaching that in forming men's character we should pay attention to the quality of our minds, not of our food, and distinguishing between the temptations of the palate, said: 'One moment it seeks more delicate food, another it desires its chosen dishes to be more scrupulously prepared.' Yet often what it craves is quite humble, but it sins even more by the very heat of its immense desire.

The people led out of Egypt fell in the desert because they despised manna and wanted meat, which they thought a finer food. And Esau lost the birthright of the firstborn because he craved with burning desire for a cheap food, lentils, and proved with what an appetite he longed for it by preferring it to the birthright he sold. Not the food but his appetite is at fault. And so we can often be blameless when we take more delicate foods but eat humbler fare with a guilty conscience. The Esau we spoke of lost his rights as firstborn for a dish of lentils, while Elijah in the desert maintained his bodily strength by eating meat.[175] Thus our old enemy, knowing that it is not food but the desire for food which is the cause of damnation, brought the first man into his power not with meat but by an apple, and he tempted the second not with meat but with bread.[176] Consequently the sin of Adam is often committed when plain and ordinary food is taken, and those things are to be eaten which the needs of nature require, not those which desire for eating suggests. But we crave with less desire for what we see is not so costly, but more plentiful and cheaper to buy: for example, the ordinary kind of meat which is much more strengthening than fish for a weak nature, and is less expensive and easier to prepare.

The use of meat and wine, like marriage, is considered to lie between good and evil, that is, it is indifferent, although the marriage tie is not wholly free from sin, and wine brings more hazards than any other food. Then if a moderate consumption of wine is not forbidden to religion, what have we to fear from other foods, so long as moderation is maintained? If St Benedict declares that wine is not for monks, and yet is obliged to allow it by special dispensation to the monks of his time when the fervour of the early Christian charity was cooling off, why should we not allow women other things which up to now no vow has forbidden them? If the Pontiffs themselves and the rulers of the Holy Church, if indeed monasteries of clerks are even allowed to eat meat without offence, because they are not bound by any profession of abstinence, who can find fault if women are allowed this too, especially if in other respects they submit to a much stricter discipline? 'It is sufficient for a pupil to be like his master',[177] and it seems over-severe if what is allowed to monasteries of clerks is denied to convents of women.

Nor should it be counted as insignificant if women, who are subject to other monastic restrictions, are not inferior in observance to religious laymen in this one indulgence of meat, especially since, as Chrysostom bears witness: 'Nothing is lawful to the lay clerk which is not also lawful for the monk, with one exception, intercourse with a wife.'[178] St Jerome too, judging the religion of clerks to be not inferior to that of monks, says, 'As though whatever is said against monks did not redound on clerks, who are the fathers of monks.'[179] And who does not know that it is against all good sense if the same burdens are imposed on the weak as on the strong, if equally strict abstinence is enjoined on women as on men? If anyone demands authority for this beyond the evidence of nature, let him consult St Gregory on this point too. For this great Ruler and Doctor of the Church gives considered instruction to the other Doctors on this matter in the twenty-fourth chapter of his *Pastoral*: 'And so men should be admonished in one way, women in another, for heavy burdens may be laid on men, and great matters exercise them, but lighter burdens on women, who should be gently converted by less exacting means.' What matters little in the strong is thought important in the weak. And although this permission to eat ordinary meat gives less pleasure than eating the flesh of birds or fishes, St Benedict does not forbid us these either; the Apostle also distinguishes between different kinds of flesh, and says, 'All flesh is not the same; there is flesh of men, flesh of beasts, of birds and of fishes, all different.'[180] Now the law of the Lord assigns the flesh of beasts and of birds to sacrifice, but not that of fish, so no one may suppose that eating fish is purer in the eyes of God than eating meat. Fish is indeed more of a hardship to the poor, being dearer, since it is in shorter supply than meat, and less strengthening for weak nature; so that on the one hand it is more of a burden and, on the other, gives less help.

We therefore, considering both the resources and nature of mankind, forbid nothing in the matter of food, as we said, except excess, and we regulate the eating of meat as of everything else in such a way that the nuns can show greater abstinence with everything allowed them than monks do with certain things forbidden. And so we would make it a rule for the eating of meat that the sisters do not take it more than once a day, different dishes must not be prepared for the same person, and no sauces may be added separately; nor may it ever be eaten more than three times a week,[181] on the first, third and fifth days, whatever feast-days intervene. For the more solemn the feast, the more dedicated should be the abstinence which celebrates it; this is warmly recommended to us by the famous doctor Gregory of Nazianzus in Book III *On Lights* or *The Second Epiphany*, where he says: 'Let us celebrate a feast-day not by indulging the belly but exulting in the spirit.' And in Book IV *Of Pentecost and The Holy Spirit*, 'This is our feast-day,' he says, 'let us store away in the soul's treasure-house something perennial and everlasting, not things which perish and melt away. Sufficient for the body is its own evil; it needs no richer matter, nor does the insolent beast need more lavish food to make it more insolent and violent in its demands.'[182] And so the feast-day should rather be kept spiritually, as St Jerome, Gregory's disciple, says in his letter about accepting gifts, where there is this passage: 'Thus we must take special care to celebrate the day of festival with exultation of spirit rather than abundance of food, for it is palpably absurd to honour by over-indulgence a martyr whom we know to have pleased God by his fasting.'[183] Augustine *On the Medicine of Penitence* says: 'Consider all the thousands of martyrs. Why do we take pleasure in celebrating their birthdays with vile banquets and not in following the example of their lives in honest ways?'

Whenever the convent has a meatless day, the nuns are to be allowed two dishes of vegetables, to which we are willing for fish to be added. But no costly condiments may be used in the food in the convent, and the sisters must content themselves with the produce of the country where they live. Fruit, however, they should eat only for supper. But as medicine for those who need it, we never forbid herbs or root vegetables, or any fruits or other similar things to appear on the table. If there happens to be any pilgrim nun staying as a guest and present at a meal, she should be shown the courtesy of charity by being offered an extra dish and, if she wishes to share this, she may. She and any other guests should sit at the high table and be served by the abbess, who will then eat later with those who wait at table. If any of the sisters wishes to mortify the flesh by a stricter diet, on no account may she do so except by way of obedience, but on no account shall this be refused her if her reason for wanting it seems sound and not frivolous, and her strength is sufficient to bear it. But no one must ever be permitted to go out of the convent for this reason, nor spend a whole day without food.

They must never use fat for flavouring on the sixth day of the week, but be content with Lenten food, and by their abstinence share the suffering of their bridegroom on that day. But one practice, common in many monasteries, is not only to be forbidden but strictly abhorred, that is, the habit of cleaning and wiping the hands and knives on some of the bread which is left uneaten and kept for the poor, so that in wishing to spare the tablecloths they pollute the bread of the poor, or indeed, the bread of him who treats himself as one of the poor when he says: 'Anything you did for one of my brothers here, however humble, you did for me.'[184]

As regards abstinence at fasts: the general ruling of the Church should be sufficient for them. We do not venture to burden them in this beyond the observance of religious laymen, nor dare to set their weakness above the strength of men. But from the autumn equinox until Easter, when the days are short, we believe one meal a day should be enough and, as the reason for this is not religious abstinence but seasonal shortness, here we make no distinction between kinds of food.

Costly clothes, which Scripture utterly condemns, must be absolutely banned. The Lord warns us especially against them, and condemns the pride in them of the rich man who was damned, while by contrast he commends the humility of John. St Gregory draws attention to this in his Sixth Homily on the Gospels:

> What does it mean to say 'Those who wear fine clothes are to be found in palaces'[185] unless to state in plain words that those men who refuse to endure hardships fight not for a heavenly but an earthly kingdom, and by devoting themselves only to outward show, seek the softness and pleasure of this present life?

And in his Fortieth Homily he says:

> There are some who do not think that the fashion of fine and costly garments is a sin. But surely if it were not blameworthy, the Word of God would never say so explicitly that the rich man who was tormented in hell had been clothed in satin and purple. For no one seeks special garments except for vainglory, in order to appear more worthy of esteem than his fellows; from vainglory alone is costly clothing sought. This is proved by the fact that no one cares to wear costly clothes where others cannot see him.

The First Letter of Peter warns lay and married women against the same thing:

> In the same way you women must accept the authority of your husbands, so that if there are any of them who disbelieve the Gospel they may be won over, without a word being said, by observing the chaste and reverent behaviour of their wives. Your beauty should reside, not in outward adornment – the braiding of the hair, or jewellery, or dress – but in the inmost centre of your being, the ornament of a gentle, quiet spirit, which is of value in the sight of God.[186]

And he rightly thought that women rather than men should be warned against this vanity, for their weak minds desire more strongly what enables extravagance to find fuller expression in them and through them. But if lay women are to be forbidden these things, what care must be taken by women dedicated to

Christ? Their fashion in dress is that they have no fashion and, whoever wants fashion, or does not refuse it if offered, loses the proof of her chastity. Any such person would be thought to be preparing herself not for religion but for fornication, and be judged not a nun but a whore. Moreover, fashion itself is the badge of the pimp and betrays his lewd mind, as it is written: 'A man's clothes and the way he laughs and his gait reveal his character.'[187]

We read that the Lord, as we said above, praised and commended the cheapness and roughness of John's clothing rather than of his food. 'What did you go out to see in the wilderness?' he asked. 'A man clad in fine clothes?' For there are times when the serving of costly food can usefully be conceded, but none for the wearing of costly clothing. Indeed, the more costly such clothing is, the more carefully it is preserved and the less useful it is – it is more of a burden to its purchaser, and being so fine it is more easily damaged and provides less warmth for the body. Black clothes are most fitting of all for the mournful garb of penitence, and lambs' wool the most suitable for the brides of Christ, so that even in their habits they can be seen to wear, or be told to wear, the wool of the Lamb, the bridegroom of virgins.

Their veils should not be made of silk but of dyed linen cloth, and we would have two sorts of veil, one for the virgins already consecrated by the bishop, the other for those not to be consecrated. The veils of the former should have the sign of the Cross marked on them, so that their wearers shall be shown by this to belong particularly to Christ in the integrity of their virginity, and as they are set apart from the others by their consecration, they should also be distinguished by this marking on their habit which shall act as a deterrent to any of the faithful against burning with desire for them. This sign of virginal purity the nun shall wear on the top of her head, marked in white thread, and she shall not presume to wear it before she is consecrated by the bishop. No other veils shall bear this mark.

They should wear clean undergarments next to the skin, and always sleep in them; nor do we deny their weak nature the use of soft mattresses and sheets. But each one must sleep and eat alone. No one should dare to be indignant if the clothing or anything else passed on to her by someone else is made over to another sister who has greater need of them; but she should look on it as an occasion for rejoicing when she enjoys the benefit of having given something as an act of charity, or sees herself as living for others and not only for herself. Otherwise she does not belong to the sisterhood of the holy society, and is not free of the sacrilege of having possessions.

It should be sufficient, we think, for them to wear an undergarment and woollen gown, with a cloak on top when the cold is very severe. This they can also use as a coverlet when lying in bed. To prevent infestation by vermin and allow accumulation of dirt to be washed away, all these garments will have to be in pairs, precisely as Solomon says in praise of the capable and provident housewife, 'She has no fear for her household when it snows, for all her servants are wrapped in two cloaks.' These cloaks must not be made so long as to hang down below the ankles and stir up dust, and the sleeves must not extend beyond the length of the arms and hands. Their feet and legs must be protected by shoes and stockings, and they are never to go barefoot on account of religion. On their beds a single mattress, bolster, pillow, blanket and sheet should suffice. They should wear a white band on their heads with the black veil over it, and because of their close-cropped hair a cap of lambs' wool may be worn if needed.

Excess must be avoided not only in diet and clothing but also in buildings or any possessions. In buildings excess is plain to see when they are made larger or finer than necessary, or if we adorn them with sculpture or paintings so as to set up palaces fit for kings instead of dwelling-places for the poor. 'The Son of Man,' says Jerome, 'has nowhere to lay his head, but you are measuring out vast porches and spacious roofs.'[188] When we take pleasure in costly or beautiful equipment the emptiness of pride is displayed as well as excess; and when we multiply herds of animals or earthly possessions, mounting ambition extends to outward things, and the more possessions we have on earth, the more we are obliged to think of these and are called away from contemplation of heavenly things. And although we may be enclosed in cloisters in the body, the mind still loves things outside, has an urge to pursue them, and dissipates itself in all directions with them. The more we possess which can be lost, the greater the fear which torments us, and the more costly these are, the more they are loved and ensnare the wretched mind with ambition to have them.

And so every care must be taken to set a firm limit to our household and our expenditure, and beyond what is necessary not to desire anything, receive any offering or keep what we have accepted. Whatever is over and above our needs we possess by robbery, and are guilty of the deaths of all the poor whom we could have helped from the surplus. Every year then, when the produce has been gathered in, sufficient provision must be made for the year, and anything left over must be given, or rather, given back to the poor.

There are some who lack foresight, and though their harvest is poor are pleased to think they have a large household, but when harassed by the responsibility to provide for it, they go begging without shame, or extort forcibly from others what they do not have themselves. Several abbots of monasteries we see to be like this. They boast of the numbers in their community and care more about having many sons than about having good ones; and they stand high in their own eyes if they are held to be higher than many. To draw these numbers under their rule they make smooth promises when they should preach harsh words, and easily lose as backsliders those whom they take in indiscriminately with no previous test of faith. Such men, I think, the Truth rebuked in the words: 'Alas for you, for you travel over sea and land to win one convert; but when you have won him, you make him twice as fit for hell as yourselves.'[189] They would surely boast less of their numbers if they sought to save souls instead of counting them, and presumed less on their strength when giving an account of their rule.

The Lord chose only a few apostles, and one of those he chose fell so far away that the Lord said of him: 'Have I not chosen you twelve? Yet one of you is a devil.'[190] And as Judas was lost to the apostles, so was Nicholas to the deacons; then when the apostles had gathered together no more than a few, Ananias and Sapphira his wife earned sentence of death.[191] Indeed, many of his disciples had previously fallen away from the Lord himself, and few stayed with him. The road which leads to life is narrow, and few set foot on it, but by contrast the road that leads to death is wide,[192] with plenty of room, and many choose to go that way. For as the Lord testifies elsewhere, 'Many are invited but few are chosen,' and according to Solomon, 'The number of fools cannot be counted.'[193] And so whoever rejoices in the large numbers of those beneath him should fear lest, in the words of the Lord, few are to be found chosen, and he himself by unduly increasing the numbers of his flock shall be less capable of watching over them; so that the words of the Prophet may rightly be applied to him: 'You increased their numbers but gave them no joy of it.'[194] Such men as boast of numbers, and are often obliged to meet their own needs and those of their people by going out and returning to the world to run round begging, involve themselves in bodily rather than spiritual cares, and incur disgrace instead of winning glory.

This is indeed all the more shameful in the case of women, for whom it seems less safe to be out in the world. And so whoever desires to live quietly and virtuously, to devote himself to the divine offices and be held as dear to God as to the world, should hesitate to gather together those for whom he cannot provide; for his own expenses he should not rely on other men's purses, and he should watch over the giving, not the seeking of alms. The Apostle and great preacher of the Gospel had authority from the Gospel to accept gifts for his expenses, but he worked with his hands so that he would not appear to be a burden to anyone nor detract from his glory.[195] How bold and shameless then are we, whose business is not preaching but lamenting our sins, if we go begging! How are we to support those whom we have thoughtlessly brought together? We also often break out into such madness that being ignorant of preaching ourselves, we hire preachers and lead around with us these false apostles, carrying crosses and phylacteries of relics to sell these or other such figments of the devil to guileless and foolish Christians, and we promise them whatever we believe will enable us to extort money. How far our Order and the very preaching of the divine Word is debased by such shameless cupidity, which seeks what is its own and not of Jesus Christ, is known, I think, to all.

Consequently abbots themselves or those who appear to have authority in monasteries take themselves off to pester the secular powers and the courts of the world, and have already learned to be courtiers rather than monks. They woo the favour of men by any device, they have grown accustomed to gossiping with men instead of communing with God; they read St Antony's warning often but to no purpose, ignoring it or hearing it without paying heed: 'As fish die, if they linger on land so too do monks, if they linger outside the cell or stay among men of the world and are released from their vow of quiet. So it is necessary for us to hurry back to the cell like fishes to the sea, lest by lingering outside we forget to care for what is within.'[196]

The author of the monastic Rule, St Benedict himself, also paid serious attention to this; he wished abbots to be active inside their monasteries and to keep careful watch over their flock, and he openly taught it in his writings and by his own example. For when he had left his brothers and gone to visit his holy sister, and she wished to keep him for one night at least, he frankly declared that it was quite impossible for him to stay outside his cell. In fact he did not say 'we cannot' but 'I cannot', because the brothers might do so by his leave, but he could not, except by revelation from the Lord, as afterwards came to pass. And so when he came to write the Rule, he made no mention of the abbot's but only of the brothers' going out of the monastery, and he made careful provision for the abbot's continual presence by laying down that on the vigils of Sundays and feast-days, the Gospel and what follows it[197] should be read by the abbot alone. And when he rules that the abbot's table shall always be shared with pilgrims and guests, and that whenever there are no guests he shall invite to it any of the brothers he likes, leaving only one or two of the other brothers with the rest,[198] he evidently implies that at mealtimes the abbot should never be absent from the monastery, nor leave the ordinary bread of the monastery to his subordinates as if he were one of those accustomed to the delicate fare of princes. Of such men the Truth says: 'They make up packs too heavy to carry and pile them on men's shoulders, but will not raise a finger to lift the load themselves.' And elsewhere, of false preachers, 'Beware of false prophets who come to you . . .'[199] They come of themselves, says the Truth, not sent by God, nor waiting to be summoned. John the Baptist, the first of us monks, to whom the priesthood came by inheritance, went out only once from the city to the wilderness, leaving his priestly for a monastic life and the cities for solitude. The people went out to him, he did not go in to the people. When he was so great that he was believed to be Christ and could correct many things in the cities, he was already in that bed from which he was ready to answer to the knocking of the Beloved: 'I have slipped off my dress: must I put it on again? I have washed my feet: must I soil them?'[200]

Whoever therefore wishes to learn the secret of monastic quiet must be glad to have a narrow bed and not a wide one. From the wider bed, as the Truth says, 'one will be taken, and the other left'.[201] But we read that the narrow bed belongs to the bride, that is to the contemplative soul which is more closely joined to Christ, and clings to him with the strongest desire. None, we read, have been left who lay on this, and the bride herself says of it: 'By night on my narrow bed I sought him whom my soul loves.'[202] She also refuses or fears to rise from this bed, but answers, as we said above, to the knocking of the Beloved. For she believes that the dirt she fears will soil her feet is only outside it.

Dinah went out to see alien women and was defiled.[203] And as it was foretold by his abbot to Malchus, that captive monk, and he afterwards found out for himself, the sheep which leaves the sheepfold is soon exposed to the bite of the wolf. So let us not assemble a crowd in which we look for an excuse, or rather, a compelling reason for going out and making money for others with detriment to ourselves; like lead which is melted in the furnace so that silver may be saved. We must rather beware lest lead and silver alike are consumed in the burning furnace of temptation. The Truth, men argue, says: 'The man who comes to me I will never turn away.'[204] Nor do we want to turn away those who have been admitted, but to be careful about admitting them, lest when we have taken them in we have to turn ourselves away on their account. For the Lord himself, we read, did not turn away anyone once admitted, but rejected some who offered themselves; to a man who said 'Master, I will follow you wherever you go,' he replied 'The foxes have holes . . .'[205]

He also warns us strictly to consider first the necessary cost when we think of doing something. 'Would any of you think of building a tower without first sitting down and calculating the necessary cost, to see whether he can afford to finish it? Otherwise, if he has laid the foundation and then is unable to finish, all onlookers will laugh at him. "There is the man," they will say, "who started to build and could not finish."'[206] It is a great thing if a man is able to save even himself alone, and dangerous for him to provide for many when he is scarcely able to keep watch over himself. No one is in earnest about keeping watch unless he has been cautious in granting admission, and no one perseveres in an undertaking like the man who takes time and forethought over making a start. In this indeed women show greater forethought, because their weakness is less able to bear heavy burdens, and is most in need of quiet to cherish it.

It is agreed that Holy Scripture is a mirror of the soul, in which anyone who lives by reading and advances by understanding perceives the beauty of his own ways or discovers their ugliness, so that he may work to increase the one and remove the other. Reminding us of this mirror, St Gregory says in the second book of his *Morals*: 'The Holy Scripture is set before the mind's eye as if it were a mirror in which our inward face may be seen reflected. For there we see our beauty or recognize our hideousness, there we perceive how far we have advanced and how distant we are from advancing.' But whoever looks at a Scripture which he does not understand is like a blind man holding a mirror to his eyes in which he is unable to see what sort of man he is; nor does he look for the instruction in Scripture for which alone it was composed. Like an ass before a lyre, he sits idly before the Scripture, and has bread set before him on which he does not break his fast, when he cannot see into the word of God by understanding it himself, nor have it opened to him by another's teaching, and so has no use for the food which does him no good.

Hence the Apostle, in a general exhortation to us to study the Scriptures, says: 'For all the ancient scriptures were written for our instruction, so that from the message of endurance and comfort the scriptures bring us, we may derive hope.' And elsewhere: 'Be filled with the Holy Spirit; speak to yourselves in psalms, hymns and spiritual songs.'[207] For a man speaks to himself or with himself who understands what he is saying, or by his understanding reaps the benefit of his words. To Timothy he says: 'Until I arrive, devote yourself to public reading, to exhortation and to teaching.' And again:

But for your part, stand by the truths you have learned and are assured of. Remember from whom you learned them; remember that from early childhood you have been familiar with the sacred writings which have power to lead you to salvation through faith in Christ Jesus. Every inspired scripture has its use for teaching the truth and refuting error, for correction and instruction in righteousness, so that the man who belongs to God may be perfected and equipped for good work of any kind.[208]

And when he is exhorting the Corinthians to understand Scripture so that they may be able to explain what others say of it, he says:

Make love your aim and spiritual gifts your aspiration and, above all, the gift of prophecy. The man who uses the language of ecstasy is talking to God, not man, but by prophesying he can build up the Church. And so he who speaks in the language of ecstasy must pray for the power to interpret it. I will pray with inspiration, I will pray too with my intelligence: I will sing hymns with inspiration and with intelligence. Otherwise, if you praise God with the language of inspiration, who will take the place of the plain man? How will he say Amen to your thanksgiving when he does not know what you are saying? True enough, you give thanks, but the other's faith is not built up. Thank God I am more gifted in ecstatic utterance than you, but in church I would rather speak five intelligible words for your instruction than ten thousand in the language of ecstasy. Brothers, do not be childish in your thoughts; be as innocent of evil as small children but grown men in your thinking.[209]

A man who 'speaks in the language of ecstasy' is one who forms words with his lips but does not give help with his intelligence by explaining them. But one who prophesies or interprets in the same way as the prophets, who are called 'seers', that is, 'understanders', understands the things he says so that he can explain them. The former prays or sings with inspiration but forms his words only by breathing and pronouncing them, without applying the understanding of his mind. When we pray with inspiration, that is, we form words only by breathing and pronouncing them, and what the mouth speaks is not conceived in the heart, our mind does not benefit as it should by prayer so as to be moved and fired towards God by its understanding of the words. And so the Apostle adjures us to seek this maturity in words, so that we may not, like children, only know how to speak them, but may also have a sense of the meaning in them; or else, he argues, our praying and hymn-singing does no good.

Following him, St Benedict says: 'Let us sing the psalms so that mind and voice may be in harmony.'[210] The Psalmist too tells us to 'Sing hymns with understanding', so that the words we speak do not lack the savour and seasoning of meaning, and with him we can truthfully say to the Lord, 'How sweet are thy words in my mouth,' and elsewhere, 'He will take no pleasure in a man's flute,'[211] for the flute gives out sounds for the gratification of pleasure, not for understanding by the mind. And so men are said to sing well to the flute but not to please God in doing so, because they delight in the melody of their singing but nothing can be built on its meaning. And how, asks the Apostle, can Amen be said after thanksgiving in church if no one understands what is prayed for, whether the object of the prayer is good or not?

For we often see in church how many simple and illiterate people pray by mistake for things which will bring them harm rather than benefit; for example, in the words 'that we may so pass through temporal things that we lose not things eternal', many are easily confused by the similarity in sound, so that either they say 'that we lose things eternal' or 'that we admit not things eternal'.[212] The Apostle is well aware of this hazard, when he asks: 'Otherwise, if you praise God with the language of inspiration,' (that is, you form the words of thanksgiving only by breathing their sound and do not instruct the mind of the listener in their meaning) 'who will take the place of the plain man?' That is, who among the congregation whose duty it is to respond, will be sure of not making a response which an ordinary man cannot or should not make? 'How will he say Amen' when he has no idea whether you are invoking a curse or a blessing? Finally, if the sisters have no understanding of Scripture, how will they be able to instruct each other by word, or even to explain or understand the Rule, or correct false citations from it?

And so we very much wonder what prompting of the enemy brought about the present situation in monasteries, whereby there is no study there on understanding the Scriptures, but only training in singing, which is no more than the forming of words without understanding them: as if the bleating of sheep were more useful than the feeding of them. For the food of the soul and its spiritual refreshment is the God-given understanding of Scripture, and so when the Lord destined the prophet Ezekiel for preaching, he first fed him on a scroll, which immediately 'in his mouth became sweet as honey.' Of such food Jeremiah also writes that 'Young children begged for bread but there was no one to break it for them.'[213] He breaks bread for young children who reveals the meaning of letters to the simple, and these children beg for bread to be broken when they long to feed their souls on understanding the Scripture, as the Lord bears witness elsewhere: 'I will send famine on the land, not hunger for bread nor thirst for water, but for hearing the word of the Lord.'[214]

On the other hand, the old enemy has implanted in cloisters of monasteries a hunger and thirst for hearing the words of men and gossip of the world, so that by giving ourselves up to empty talk we may weary of the word of God, and the more so if we find it tasteless because it lacks the sweetness and savour of meaning. Hence the Psalmist, as we said above, cried: 'How sweet are thy words in my mouth, sweeter than honey on my lips,' and what this sweetness was he went on to say at once: 'From thy precepts I got understanding', that is, I gained understanding from God's precepts rather than men's, and was taught and instructed by them. Nor did he omit to state what was to be gained from such understanding, adding 'Therefore I hate every path of wrongdoing.' For many paths of wrongdoing are so plainly seen for what they are that they easily come to be hated and despised by all, but only through the word of God can we know every one of them so as to avoid them all. So it is also written that 'I treasure thy words in my heart, so that I may not sin against thee.'[215] They are treasured in the heart rather than sounded on the lips when we meditate and retain understanding of them, but the less we care about understanding, the less we recognize and shun these paths of wrongdoing, and the less we can guard ourselves against sin.

Such negligence is all the more reprehensible in monks who aspire to perfection, the more opportunities they have for being taught, when they have abundance of sacred books and enjoy the peace of quiet. Those monks who boast about the numbers of their books but find no time to read them are sharply rebuked by that elder in the *Lives of the Fathers*, who says: 'The prophets wrote books: and your forebears came after and did much work on them. Then their successors committed them to memory. But now comes the present generation, which has copied them on paper and parchment and put them back to stand idle on the shelves.' So too, abba Palladius in exhorting us to learn and also to teach, says: 'It behoves the soul which professes to live in accordance with the will of Christ either to learn faithfully what it does not know or to teach plainly what it knows.'[216] But if it is unwilling to do either, though well able, it suffers from the disease of madness. For boredom with learning is the beginning of a withdrawal from God, and how can a man love God when he does not seek that for which the soul always hungers? St Athanasius too, in his *Exhortation to Monks*, recommends the practice of learning or reading so highly that he even allows prayers to be interrupted for this. 'Let me trace the course of our life,' he says. 'First must come care for abstinence, endurance of fasting, perseverance in prayer and desire to read or, if there be any who are still illiterate, to listen in eagerness to learn. For these are the first cradle-songs, as it were, of suckling infants, in knowledge of God.' And a little later, after saying that 'Your prayers should be so assiduous that scarcely any interval should come between them,' he then adds: 'If possible, they should be interrupted only by intervals for reading.'

Nor would the apostle Peter give different advice. 'Be always ready to give an answer to all who ask you to account for your faith and hope.'[217] And the Apostle says: 'We have not ceased to pray for you, that you may be filled with knowledge of God's will in all wisdom and spiritual understanding.' And again, 'Let the message of Christ dwell in you in all richness and wisdom.'[218] In the Old Testament, too, the Word implanted in men a similar care for holy teaching. Thus David says, 'Happy is the man who does not take the wicked for his guide ... but his heart is set on the law of the Lord.' And to Joshua God says, 'This book of the law shall never leave your hands and you must ponder over it day and night.'[219]

Moreover, amongst these occupations the hazards of wrong-thinking often insinuate themselves, and although constant application may keep the mind intent on God, the gnawing anxiety of the world makes it restless. If one who is dedicated to the toil of the religious life must suffer this, frequently and painfully, the idle man is surely never free of it. St Gregory the Pope, in the nineteenth book of his *Morals*, says:

We deplore that the time has now come when we see many holding office in the Church who are either unwilling to perform what they understand or scorn to understand and recognize the very words of God. They close their ears to the truth and turn away to listen to fables, while 'they are all bent on their own ends, not on the cause of Jesus Christ'.[220] God's Scriptures are everywhere to be found and are set before men's eyes, but they refuse to read them. Scarcely anyone wants to understand what he believes.

And yet both the Rule of their own profession and the example of the holy Fathers exhort them to do so. Benedict in fact says nothing about the teaching and study of chanting, though he gives many instructions about reading, and expressly assigns times for this as he does for manual work.[221] In his provision for teaching composition or writing, amongst the essentials for which the monks must look to the abbot, he includes tablets and pens. And when amongst other things he orders that 'At the beginning of Lent all the monks shall receive a book each from the library, which they shall read through consecutively,' what could be more absurd than for them to give time to reading if they do not take pains to understand? There is a well-known saying of the Sage, 'To read without understanding is to misread'; and to such a reader the philosopher's reproach about the ass and the lyre is rightly applicable, for a reader who holds a book but cannot do what the book was intended for is like an ass sitting before a lyre.[222] Readers such as this would more profitably concentrate on what might be some use to them, instead of idly looking at the written letters and turning the pages, for in them we see the words of Isaiah clearly fulfilled:

All prophetic vision has become for you like the words of a sealed book. Give such a book to one who can read and say, 'Read this,' and he will answer, 'I cannot, for it is sealed.' Give it to one who cannot read and say, 'Read it,' and he will answer, 'I cannot read.' Then the Lord said: 'Because these people approach me with their mouths and honour me with their lips while their hearts are far from me and their fear of me is but a precept of men, learned by rote, therefore yet again I must strike awe into the hearts of these people with some great and resounding miracle. For the wisdom of their wise men shall vanish and the discernment of the discerning shall be lost.'[223]

In the cloister those are said to know letters who have learned to pronounce them; but as far as understanding them is concerned, those who admit they cannot read have a book given to them which is just as much sealed as it is for those whom they call illiterate. The Lord rebukes them, saying that they approach him with their mouths and lips rather than with their hearts because they are able to pronounce words after a fashion but are quite unable to understand them. Lacking knowledge of the Word of God, they follow in their obedience the custom of men, not the benefit of Scripture. Therefore the Lord threatens that even those who are reckoned learned and sit as doctors among them shall be blinded.

Jerome, the greatest doctor of the Church and glory of the monastic profession, in exhorting us to love of letters, says: 'Love knowledge of letters and you will not love the vices of the flesh':[224] and we have learned from his own testimony how much labour and expense it cost him to learn them. Amongst other things which he writes about his own studies for the purpose of instructing us by his example, he recalls in the following passage, addressed to Pammachius and Oceanus:

> When I was a young man I was on fire with a marvellous love of learning. I did not teach myself, as some men are rash enough to do, but I frequently heard Apollinaris at Antioch and sat at his feet for instruction in the Holy Scriptures. My hair was already flecked with grey and I should have been a teacher rather than a pupil, yet I went on to Alexandria and heard Didymus, to whom I am grateful for much, learning from him what I did not know. Men thought I had come to an end of learning, but I returned to Jerusalem and Bethlehem, and there I had Baraninas the Jew as my teacher – with what labour and expense! He taught at night, for he feared the Jews, and to me he was a second Nicodemus.[225]

Surely Jerome had stored away in his memory what he had read in Ecclesiasticus: 'My son, seek learning while you are young, and when your hair is white you will still find wisdom.'[226]

Thus his learning, not only from the words of Scripture but also through the example of the holy Fathers, has added to the wealth of tributes paid to the excellent monastery he founded one on its exceptional training in the Holy Scriptures: 'As for meditation on and understanding of the Holy Scriptures and also of sacred learning, never have we seen such a degree of training; you might suppose nearly every one of them to be a professional spokesman for sacred wisdom.'[227]

The Venerable Bede too, who had been received into a monastery as a boy, says in his *History of the English People*, 'From then on I have spent the rest of my life living in the same monastery and devoted myself entirely to studying the Scriptures. While I have observed monastic discipline and sung the daily offices in church, learning and writing have always been my delight.'[228] But those who are educated in monasteries today are so persistent in their stupidity that they are content merely with the sound of letters, pay no attention to understanding them, and care only to instruct the tongue, not the heart. They are openly rebuked in a proverb of Solomon: 'A discerning man seeks knowledge, but the stupid man feeds on folly,'[229] that is, when he takes pleasure in words he does not understand. Such men are the less able to love God and be warmed towards him, the further they keep themselves from understanding him and appreciating the Scripture that teaches us about him.

This situation we believe has arisen in monasteries mainly for two reasons: either because of jealousy on the part of the lay monks, or even of the abbots themselves, or through the empty chatter of idleness, to which we see present-day monastic cloisters much addicted. Men like this try to attach us along with themselves to earthly rather than spiritual things, and are like the Philistines who persecuted Isaac when he was digging wells, filled them in with heaps of earth and tried to keep water from him.[230] St Gregory explains this in the sixteenth book of his *Morals*: 'Often when we try to concentrate on the word of God we are more seriously troubled by the designs of evil spirits who scatter the dust of earthly thoughts in our minds, so that they may darken the eyes of our concentration and withhold the light of inward vision.' This the Psalmist had suffered greatly when he said, 'Go away, you evil-doers, and I will keep the commandments of my God,'[231] for he clearly meant that he could not keep the commandments of God when suffering in mind from the designs of evil spirits.

We understand that the same thing is meant by the wickedness of the Philistines during the work of Isaac, when they heaped earth in the wells he had dug. For we are surely digging wells when we penetrate deeply into the hidden meaning of Holy Scripture, and the Philistines secretly fill these up when they introduce the earthly thoughts of an impure spirit while we are looking towards higher things, and so take away the water of sacred learning which we have found. But no one can overcome these enemies by his own power, as we are told through Eliphaz: 'The Almighty shall be your defence against your enemies, and he will be your silver heaped up.'[232] That is, when the Lord has driven evil spirits away from you by his own power, the talent of the divine Word will shine more brightly in you. St Gregory, if I am not mistaken, had read the *Homilies* of the great Christian philosopher Origen on Genesis, and had drawn from Origen's wells what he now says about these wells. For that zealous digger of spiritual wells strongly urges us not only to drink of them but also to dig our own, as he says in the twelfth homily of his exposition:

Let us try also to do what Wisdom bids us, saying: 'Drink water from your own cistern and running water from your own spring. Let them be yours alone.'[233] Do you then try too, my listener, to have your own well and your own spring, so that you also when you take up a book of the Scriptures may start to show some understanding of it from your own perception and in accordance with what you have learned in church. Try too to drink from the spring of your own spirit. You have within you a source of living water, the open channels and flowing streams of rational perception, so long as they are not clogged with earth and rubbish. Try to dig your ground and clear the filth from your spirit, remove idleness and inertia from your heart. Hear what Scripture says: 'Hurt the eye and tears will flow; hurt the heart and you will make it sensitive.'[234] So clean your spirit and then someday you too may drink from your own springs and draw living water from your wells. For if you have received living water from Jesus and received it with faith, it shall become in you a source of water gushing out towards everlasting life.

In the following homily Origen also says of the wells of Isaac we spoke of:

> Those which the Philistines had filled with earth are surely men who close their spiritual understanding, so that they neither drink themselves nor allow others to drink. Hear the word of the Lord: 'Alas for you lawyers and Pharisees! You have taken away the key of knowledge; you did not go in yourselves, and did not permit those who wished to enter.'[235] But let us never cease from digging wells of living water, and by discussing new things as well as old, let us make ourselves like the teacher of the law in the Gospel, of whom the Lord said that he could 'produce from his store both old and new'.[236] Let us return to Isaac and dig with him wells of living water, even if the Philistines obstruct us; even if they use violence, let us carry on with our well-digging, so that to us too it may be said: 'Drink water from your own cisterns and your own wells.' And let us dig until our wells overflow with water in our courtyards, so that our knowledge of the Scriptures is not only sufficient for ourselves but we can teach others and show them how to drink. Let our flocks drink too, as the Prophet also says: 'Man and beast you will save, O Lord.'[237]

Later on Origen says:

> He who is a Philistine and knows earthly things, does not know where in the earth to find water, where to find a rational perception. What do you gain by having learning and not knowing how to use it, having speech but being unable to speak? That is like the sons of Isaac who dig wells all over the earth for living water.

You must not be like this, but refrain altogether from idle talk, while those of you who have been given the grace of learning must work to be instructed in the things which are God's, as it is written of the happy man: 'The law of the Lord is his delight, the law his meditation day and night.' And the profit which follows on his diligent application to the law of the Lord is added at once: 'And he will be like a tree planted by a watercourse,'[238] for a dry tree is also unfruitful, because it is not watered by the streams of the words of God. Of these streams it is written that 'Rivers of living water shall flow from his bosom,' and these are the streams of which the bride sings in the Canticles in praise of the bridegroom, describing him thus: 'His eyes are like doves beside brooks of water, bathed by the milky water as they sit by the flooding streams.'[239] You too, then, are bathed in milky water, that is, you are shining with the whiteness of chastity, and must sit like doves by these streams, so that by drawing from them draughts of wisdom you may be able both to learn and also to teach, and be like eyes showing a path to others, and not only seeing the bridegroom but able to describe him to others.

Of his special bride, whose glory it was to conceive him by the ear of the heart, we know it is written, 'But Mary treasured all these words and pondered over them in her heart.'[240] Thus the Mother of the Supreme Word, having his words in her heart rather than on her lips, pondered over them carefully as she considered each one separately and then compared them with each other, seeing how closely all agreed together. She knew that according to the revelation of the Law every animal is called unclean unless it chews the cud and divides the hoof. And so no soul is clean and pure unless by meditating to the best of its ability it chews the cud of God's teachings and shows understanding in obeying them, so that it not only does good things but does them well, that is, with right intention. For division of the hoof is the mind's ability to distinguish, about which it is written: 'If you offer rightly but do not divide rightly, you have sinned.'[241]

'Anyone who loves me,' says the Truth, 'will heed what I say.'[242] But who can heed the words or precepts of the Lord by obeying them unless he has first understood them? No one will be zealous in obedience unless he has been attentive as a listener, like that blessed woman of whom we read that she put everything else aside and sat at the Lord's feet listening to his words – and listened with the ears of understanding which he himself requires, saying, 'If you have ears to hear, then hear.'[243]

Yet if you are unable to be kindled to such fervour of devotion, you can at least in your love and study of sacred Scriptures model yourselves on those blessed disciples of St Jerome, Paula and Eustochium, for it was mainly at their request that the great doctor wrote so many volumes to bring enlightenment to the Church.[244]

ABELARD'S CONFESSION OF FAITH

Heloise my sister, once dear to me in the world, now dearest to me in Christ, logic has made me hated by the world. For the perverted, who seek to pervert and whose wisdom is only for destruction, say that I am supreme as a logician, but am found wanting in my understanding of Paul. They proclaim the brilliance of my intellect but detract from the purity of my Christian faith. As I see it, they have reached this judgement by conjecture rather than weight of evidence. I do not wish to be a philosopher if it means conflicting with Paul, nor to be an Aristotle if it cuts me off from Christ. For there is no other name under heaven whereby I must be saved. I adore Christ who sits on the right hand of the Father. I embrace in the arms of faith him who acts divinely in the glorious flesh of a virgin which he assumed from the Paraclete. And so, to banish fearful anxiety and all uncertainties from the heart within your breast, receive assurance from me, that I have founded my conscience on that rock on which Christ built his Church. What is written on the rock I will testify briefly.

I believe in the Father, the Son and the Holy Spirit; the true God who is one in nature; who comprises the Trinity of persons in such a way as always to preserve Unity in substance. I believe the Son to be co-equal with the Father in all things, in eternity, power, will and operation. I do not hold with Arius, who is driven by perverted intellect or led astray by demoniac influence to introduce grades into the Trinity, laying down that the Father is greater and the Son less great, forgetting the injunction of the Law, 'You shall not mount up to my altar by steps.'[1] He mounts up to the altar of God by steps who assigns first and second place in the Trinity. I bear witness that in everything the Holy Spirit is consubstantial and co-equal with the Father and the Son, and is he who, as my books often declare, is known by the name of Goodness. I condemn Sabellius, who, in holding that the person of the Father is the same as that of the Son, asserts that the Passion was suffered by the Father – hence his followers are called *Patripassiani*.

I believe that the Son of God became the Son of Man in such a way that one person is of and in two natures; that after he had completed the mission he had undertaken in becoming man he suffered and died and rose again, and ascended to heaven whence he will come to judge the living and the dead. I also declare that in baptism all offences are remitted, and that we need grace whereby we may begin on good and persevere in it, and that having lapsed we may be restored through penitence. But what need have I to speak of the resurrection of the body? I would pride myself on being a Christian in vain if I did not believe that I would live again.

This then is the faith on which I rest, from which I draw my strength in hope. Safely anchored on it, I do not fear the barking of Scylla, I laugh at the whirlpool of Charybdis, and have no dread of the Sirens' deadly songs.[2] The storm may rage but I am unshaken, though the winds may blow they leave me unmoved; for the rock of my foundation stands firm.[3]

LETTERS OF PETER THE VENERABLE AND HELOISE

PETER THE VENERABLE: LETTER (98) TO POPE INNOCENT II[1]

To the sovereign Pope Innocent, our special father, brother Peter, humble abbot of Cluny: obedience and love.

Master Peter, well known, I believe, to your Holiness, passed by Cluny recently on his way from France. We asked him where he was going. He replied that he was weighed down by the persecutions of those who accused him of heresy, a thing he abhorred, that he had appealed to papal authority and sought protection from it. We praised his intention, and urged him to make his way to that common refuge which we all know. We told him that apostolic justice has never failed anyone, be he stranger or pilgrim, and would not be denied him, and assured him that if he had real need of mercy he would find it with you.

In the meantime the lord abbot of Cîteaux arrived, and spoke with us and with him about a reconciliation between him and the abbot of Clairvaux, the reason for his appeal to you. We too did our best to restore peace, and urged him to go to Clairvaux with the abbot of Cîteaux. We further counselled him, if he had written or said anything offensive to orthodox Christian ears, to take the advice of the abbot of Cîteaux and of other wise and worthy men, curb his language and remove such expressions from his writings. This he did. He went and came back, and on his return told us that through the mediation of the abbot of Cîteaux he had made his peace with the abbot of Clairvaux and that their previous differences were settled. Meanwhile, on our advice, or rather, we believe, inspired by God, he decided to abandon the turmoil of schools and teaching and to remain permanently in your house of Cluny. We thought this a proper decision in view of his age and weakness and his religious calling, and believed that his learning, which is not altogether unknown to you, could be of benefit to our large community of brothers; we therefore granted his wish, and on condition that it is agreeable to your Holiness, we have willingly and gladly agreed that he shall remain with us who, as you know, are wholly your own.

And so I, your humble servant, beg you, your devoted community of Cluny begs you, and Peter himself begs this on his own part, through us, through your sons who bring this letter, and through these very words which he asked me to write: permit him to spend the remaining days of his life and old age, which perhaps will not be many, in your house of Cluny, so that no one's intervention shall be able to disturb or remove him from the home the sparrow has reached or the nest the turtle-dove is so happy to have found.[2] For the honour in which you hold all good men and the love you bear him, let the shield of your apostolic protection cover him.[3]

PETER THE VENERABLE: LETTER (115) TO HELOISE

To the venerable and greatly beloved sister in Christ, the abbess Heloise, brother Peter, humble abbot of Cluny: the salvation which God has promised those who love him.

I was happy to receive from your Grace the letter which you sent me recently[1] through my son Theobald, and took it with friendly sentiments towards the sender. I wanted to write back at once to express what was in my heart, but the persistent demands of the duties to which I am obliged to give up most, or rather, all of my time, made it impossible. Now at last there is a day's respite (scarcely that) from turmoil, when I can try to carry out my intention.[2] I thought that I should make haste to repay if only in words the affection for me I discerned in your letter, and previously from the gifts you sent me, and to show you how large a place in my heart is reserved for my love for you in the Lord. For in fact it is not only now that I begin to love you; I can remember having done so for a long time. I had yet not quite passed the bounds of youth and reached early manhood when I knew of your name and your reputation, not yet for religion but for your virtuous and praiseworthy studies. I used to hear at that time of the woman who although still caught up in the obligations of the world, devoted all her application to knowledge of letters, something which is very rare, and to the pursuit of secular learning, and that not even the pleasures of the world, with its frivolities and delights, could distract her from this worthy determination to study the arts. At a time when nearly the whole world is indifferent and deplorably apathetic towards such occupations, and wisdom can scarcely find a foothold not only, I may say, among women who have banished her completely, but even in the minds of men, you have surpassed all women in carrying out your purpose, and have gone further than almost every man.

Later on when, in the Apostle's words, 'It pleased God who had set you apart since you were in your mother's womb to call you through his grace,'[3] you turned your zeal for learning in a far better direction, and as a woman wholly dedicated to philosophy in the true sense, you left logic for the Gospel, Plato for Christ, the academy for the cloister. You removed the spoils from your vanquished foe, crossed the desert of life's pilgrimage with the treasures of Egypt, and set up a precious tabernacle to God in your heart. With Miriam you sang a hymn of praise as Pharaoh sank beneath the waves,[4] like her in days of old, you took up the tambourine of blessed mortification, so that your skill with it sent the strain of new harmonies to the very ears of God. Now you trod underfoot what at the start you wore down by perseverance through the grace of the Almighty – the head of the serpent, the old enemy who always lies in wait for women – and crushed it so that it will never dare to hiss against you again. You make and will continue to make a laughing-stock of the proud prince of the world, and him whom the divine voice, in the words of God himself on the lips of holy Job, calls 'the King of the sons of pride',[5] you will force to groan when he is enchained for you and the handmaids of God who live with you.

Truly a unique miracle, one to be exalted above all marvellous works, for him of whom the prophet says, 'No cedar in God's garden overshadowed it, and no firs could equal the height of its boughs'[6] to be overcome by the weaker sex, and the most powerful of archangels to fall before a frail woman! Such a combat brings supreme glory to the Creator, but to the Tempter the greatest ignominy. This contest proves to his shame that it was not only foolish but above all absurd for him to have aspired to equality with the sublime Majesty, when he cannot even sustain a brief conflict with a woman's weakness; while she, alone victorious, will justly receive for her brow a jewelled crown from the King of heaven, so that though she was weaker in the flesh, in the battle she fought she will appear the more glorious in her everlasting reward.

I say this not to flatter you, my sister, dearest in the Lord, but by way of encouraging you to awareness of the great benefit you have long enjoyed; so that you will be the more eager to preserve it with due care, and the holy women who serve the Lord with you, through God's grace conferred on you, may be fired by your word and example to join eagerly in the same struggle. For you are one of those animals in the vision of the prophet Ezekiel, woman though you are, and must not only burn like coal but glow like a lamp[7] and give light as well. You are indeed the disciple of truth, but in your duty towards those entrusted to you, you are the teacher of humility. For surely the teaching of humility and of all instruction in heavenly matters is a task laid on you by God, and so you must have a care not only for yourself but for the flock in your keeping; and being responsible for all shall receive a higher reward than theirs. Yes, the palm is reserved for you on behalf of the whole community, for, as you must know, all those who, by following your lead, have overcome the world and the prince of the world, will prepare for you as many triumphs and glorious trophies before the eternal King and Judge.

Moreover, it is not altogether exceptional amongst mortals for women to be in command of women, nor entirely unprecedented for them even to take up arms and accompany men to battle. For if there is truth in the saying:

Even from a foe it is right to learn,[8]

amongst the pagans it is recorded that Penthesilea, queen of the Amazons, often fought at the time of the Trojan War along with her army of Amazons,[9] who were women, not men, while from God's chosen people the prophetess Deborah is said to have roused Barach, a judge in Israel, against the heathen.[10] Why then should not virtuous women also march to battle against the armed foe, become leaders in the army of the Lord, if Penthesilea could fight the enemy with her own hand, in defiance of convention, and our Deborah roused, armed and spurred on the men of Israel to fight God's wars? Then when Jobin the King was defeated, Sisera his commander lay dead and the heathen army was destroyed, she sang at once the song she wrote in devout praise of God. For you and yours, after the victory granted by God's grace over a far more formidable foe, there will be a far more glorious song, which you will so rejoice to sing that ever afterwards you will continue to sing it and rejoice. Meanwhile you will be for the handmaids of God, your heavenly army, what Deborah was for the Jewish people; whatever happens, you will never break off the battle for which the reward is so high until victory is yours. And because the name of Deborah, as your learning knows, means 'bee' in the Hebrew tongue, you will be a Deborah in this respect too, that is, a bee. For you will make honey, but not only for yourself; since all the goodness you have gathered here and there in different ways, by your example, word, and every possible means, you will pour out for the sisters in your house and for all other women. In this brief span of our mortal life you will satisfy yourself with the hidden sweetness of the Holy Scriptures, as also your fortunate sisters by your public instruction, until, in the words of the prophet, on that promised day 'the mountains shall run with sweetness and the hills flow with milk'.[11] For though this is said of the time of grace to come, nothing prevents it from being applied to an hour of glory and, indeed, it is pleasanter to take it thus.

It would also be pleasant for me to talk with you like this for longer, both because I am delighted by your renowned learning, and far more because I am drawn to you by what many have told me about your religion. If only our Cluny possessed you, or you were confined in the delightful prison of Marcigny[12] with the other handmaids of Christ who are there awaiting their freedom in heaven! I would have preferred your wealth of religion and learning to the richest treasures of any kings, and would rejoice to see that noble community of sisters still further illuminated by your presence there. You too would have derived no small benefit from them, and would have marvelled to see the highest nobility and pride of the world trodden underfoot. You would see every kind of worldly luxury exchanged for a wonderful poverty of life, and the former impure vessels of the devil turned into spotless temples for the Holy Spirit. You would observe those young girls of God stolen, as it were, from Satan and the world, building high walls of virtue in the foundation of their innocence, and raising the summit of their blessed edifice to the very threshold of heaven. You would rejoice to see them in the flower of their angelic virginity united with chaste widows, all alike awaiting the glory of that great and blessed Resurrection, their bodies confined within the narrow walls of their house as if buried in a tomb of blessed hope. Yet since you may have all these joys, and perhaps greater things than these in the companions given you by God, it may be that nothing can be added as regards your zeal for holy matters; but our own community would be enriched by no small advantage, I think, from the addition of your own gracious gifts.

But although God's providence which dispenses all things has denied us your presence, we have still been granted that of him who was yours, him, I say, who is often and ever to be named and honoured as the servant and true philosopher of Christ, Master Peter, whom in the last years of his life that same providence sent to Cluny, and by doing so enriched her in his person with a gift more precious than any gold and topaz.[13] The nature and extent of the saintliness, humility and devotion of his life among us, to which Cluny can bear witness, cannot briefly be told. I do not remember seeing anyone, I think, who was his equal in conduct and manner: St Germain could not have appeared more lowly nor St Martin himself so poor. And although at my insistence he held superior rank in our large community of brothers, the shabbiness of his attire made him look the humblest of them all. I often marvelled, and when he walked in front of me with the others in the usual processional order, I almost stood still in astonishment that a man who bore so great and distinguished a name could thus humble and abase himself. And because some who profess the religious life want unnecessary extravagance even in the habits they wear, he was completely frugal in such matters, content with a simple garment of each sort, seeking nothing more.

He was the same as regards food and drink and anything for his bodily needs, and condemned by word and by his living example, for himself as well as for others, not merely what was superfluous, but everything except the barest necessities. His reading was continuous, his prayer assiduous, his silence perpetual, except when informal conference amongst the brothers or a public sermon addressed to them in assembly on sacred subjects compelled him to speak. He was present at the holy Sacraments, offering the sacrifice of the immortal Lamb to God whenever he could, and indeed, almost without interruption, after he had been restored to apostolic grace through my letter and efforts on his behalf. What more need I say? His mind, his speech, his work were devoted to meditation, to teaching and to profession of what was always holy, philosophic and scholarly.

In such a way this simple, upright man lived among us, fearing God and shunning evil; and in this way, I repeat, he stayed for some time, dedicating the last days of his life to God, until I sent him to Chalon to give him respite, since he was more troubled than usual from skin irritation and other physical ailments. I believed this would be a suitable place for him, near the city on the opposite bank of the Saône, because of its mild climate which is about the best in our part of Burgundy.[14] There he renewed his former studies, as far as his ill-health permitted, and was always bent over his books; and as it is said of Gregory the Great, he never let a moment pass without praying, reading, writing or composing.[15]

He was engaged on such holy occupations when the Visitor of the Gospels came to find him, and found him awake, not asleep like so many; found him truly awake, and summoned him to the wedding of eternal life as a wise, not a foolish virgin. For he brought with him a lamp full of oil, that is, a conscience filled with the testimony of his saintly life. As the time came for him to pay the common debt of humanity, the sickness from which he suffered worsened and quickly brought him to his last hour. Then he first professed his faith, afterwards confessed his sins, and indeed in so holy, devout and Christian a manner; with such eagerness of heart he received the viaticum for his journey and the pledge of eternal life, the body of our Lord and Redeemer; to him he commended his body and soul here on earth and for eternity with such true faith: as all his brothers in religion and the whole community of the monastery where the body of St Marcellus the martyr lies can bear witness.

Thus did Master Peter end his days. He who was known nearly all over the world for his unique mastery of knowledge and who won fame everywhere as a disciple of one who said 'Learn from me, for I am gentle and humble-hearted,'[16] steadfast in his own gentleness and humility, thus passed over to him, as we must believe. Him, therefore, venerable and dearest sister in the Lord, him to whom after your union in the flesh you are joined by the better, and therefore stronger, bond of divine love, with whom and under whom you have long served God: him, I say, in your place, or as another you, God cherishes in his bosom, and keeps him there to be restored to you through his grace at the coming of the Lord, at the voice of the archangel, and the trumpet-note of God descending from heaven. Remember him in the Lord, remember me too, if you are pleased to do so, and duly commend to the prayers of the sisters serving God with you the brothers of our community, and also the sisters throughout the world who, to the best of their ability, serve the same Lord as you.

HELOISE: LETTER (167)
TO PETER THE VENERABLE

To Peter, most reverend lord and father and venerable abbot of Cluny, Heloise, God's and his humble servant: the spirit of grace and salvation.

The mercy of God came down to us in the grace of a visit from your Reverence. We are filled with pride and rejoicing, gracious father, because your greatness has descended to our lowliness, for a visitation from you is a matter for great rejoicing even for the great. Others are well aware of the great benefits conferred on them by the presence of your sublimity but, for my own part, I cannot even formulate my thoughts, much less find words for what a benefit and joy your coming was to me. Our abbot and Lord, on the 16th November of the past year[1] you celebrated a Mass here in which you commended us to the Holy Spirit. In Chapter you fed us by preaching the word of God. You gave us the body of our master and so yielded up the privilege which belonged to Cluny. To me too, whom (unworthy as I am to be called your servant) your sublime humility has not disdained to address as sister in writing and speech, you granted a rare privilege in token of your love and sincerity: a trental of masses[2] to be said on my behalf by the abbey of Cluny after my death. You also said that you would confirm this gift in a letter under seal.

Fulfil then, my brother, or rather, my lord, what you promised to your sister, or I should say, to your servant. May it please you too to send me also under seal an open document containing the absolution of our master, to be hung on his tomb. Remember also, for the love of God, our Astralabe and yours,[3] so that you may obtain for him some prebend either from the bishop of Paris or in some other diocese. Farewell; may the Lord keep you, and sometimes grant us your presence.

PETER THE VENERABLE: LETTER (168) TO HELOISE

To our venerable and dearest sister in Christ, the handmaid of God, Heloise, guide and mistress of the handmaids of God, brother Peter, humble abbot of Cluny: the fullness of God's salvation and of our love in Christ.

I was happy, very happy, to read the letter from your Sanctity, where I learned that my visit to you was no transitory call, and which made me realize that I have not only been with you, but in spirit have never really left you. My stay, I see, was not one to be remembered as that of a passing guest for a single night, nor was I treated as 'a stranger and a foreigner among you', but as 'a fellow-citizen of God's people and member of God's household.'[1] Everything I said and did on that fleeting or flying visit of mine has remained so firmly in your holy mind and made such an impression on your gracious spirit that, to say nothing of my carefully chosen phrases on that occasion, not even a chance, unconsidered word of mine fell to the ground unheeded. You noted all, you committed all to your retentive memory in the warmth of your unbounded sincerity, as if all were the mighty, the heavenly, the sacrosanct words or deeds of Jesus Christ himself. You may have been prompted to remember them in this way by the injunctions on receiving guests in our common Rule, which belongs to us both: 'Let Christ be worshipped in them, who is received in their persons.'[2] Perhaps you were also reminded of the Lord's words concerning those given authority, though I have no authority over you: 'Whoever listens to you listens to me.'[3]

May I ever be granted this grace from you: that you will think me worthy to be remembered, and will pray for the mercy of the Almighty upon me, along with the holy community of the flock entrusted to your care. I am repaying you now as far as I can, for long before I saw you, and particularly since I have come to know you, I have kept for you in the innermost depths of my heart a special place of real and true affection. I am therefore sending you, now that I have left you, a ratification of the gift of a trental I made you in person, in writing and under seal, as you wished. I am also sending the absolution for Master Peter you asked for, similarly written on parchment and sealed. As soon as I have an opportunity, I will gladly do my best to obtain a prebend in one of the great churches for your Astralabe, who is also ours for your sake. It will not be easy, for the bishops, as I have often found, are apt to show themselves extremely difficult when occasions have arisen for them to give prebends in their churches. But for your sake I will do what I can as soon as I can.[4]

THE ABSOLUTION FOR PETER ABELARD[1]

I, Peter, Abbot of Cluny, who received Peter Abelard as a monk of Cluny, and gave his body, removed in secret, to the Abbess Heloise and the nuns of the Paraclete, by the authority of Almighty God and of all the saints, in virtue of my office, absolve him from all his sins.

TWO HYMNS BY ABELARD

SABBATO AD VESPERAS

O quanta qualia
  sunt illa sabbata,
quae semper celebrat
  superna curia
quae fessis requies,
  quae merces fortibus,
cum erit omnia
  deus in omnibus.

Vera Jerusalem
  est illa civitas
cuius pax iugis est
  summa iucunditas:
ubi non praevenit
  rem desiderium,
nec desiderio
  minus est praemium.

Quis Rex, quae curia,
  quale palatium,
quae pax, quae requies,
  quod illud gaudium,
huius participes
  exponant gloriae,
si quantum sentiunt
  possint exprimere.

VESPERS: SATURDAY EVENING[1]

How mighty are the Sabbaths,
  How mighty and how deep,
That the high courts of heaven
  To everlasting keep.
What peace unto the weary,
  What pride unto the strong,
When God in whom are all things
  Shall be all things to men.

Jerusalem is the city
  Of everlasting peace,
A peace that is surpassing
  And utter blessedness;
Where finds the dreamer waking
  Truth beyond dreaming far,
Nor is the heart's possessing
  Less than the heart's desire.

But of the courts of heaven
  And him who is the King,
The rest and the refreshing,
  The joy that is therein,
Let those that know it answer
  Who in that bliss have part,
If any word can utter
  The fullness of the heart.

Nostrum est interim
    mentem erigere
et totis patriam
    votis appetere,
et ad Jerusalem
    a Babylonia
post longa regredi
    tandem exsilia.

Illic, molestiis
    finitis omnibus,
securi cantica
    Sion cantabimus,
et iuges gratias
    de donis gratiae
beata referet
    plebs tibi, Domine.

Illic ex Sabbato
    succedit Sabbatum,
perpes laetitia
    sabbatizantium,
nec ineffabiles
    cessabunt iubili,
quos decantabimus
    et nos et angeli.

Perenni Domino
    perpes sit gloria,
ex quo sunt, per quem sunt,
    in quo sunt omnia.
ex quo sunt, Pater est,
    per quem sunt, Filius,
in quo sunt, Patris et
    Filii Spiritus.

But ours, with minds uplifted
  Unto the heights of God,
With our whole heart's desiring,
  To take the homeward road,
And the long exile over,
  Captive in Babylon,
Again unto Jerusalem,
  To win at last return.

There, all vexation ended,
  And from all grieving free,
We sing the song of Zion
  In deep security.
And everlasting praises
  For all thy gifts of grace
Rise from thy happy people,
  Lord of our blessedness.

There Sabbath unto Sabbath
  Succeeds eternally,
The joy that has no ending
  Of souls in holiday.
And never shall the rapture
  Beyond all mortal ken
Cease from the eternal chorus
  That angels sing with men.

Now to the King Eternal
  Be praise eternally,
From whom are all things, by whom
  And in whom all things be.
From whom, as from the Father,
  By whom, as by the Son,
In whom, as in the Spirit,
  Father and Son in one.

IN PARASCEVE DOMINI: III.
NOCTURNO

Solus ad victimam procedis, Domine,
morti te offerens quam venis tollere:
quid nos miserrimi possumus dicere
qui quae commisimus scimus te luere?

Nostra sunt, Domine, nostra sunt crimina:
quid tua criminum facis supplicia?
quibus sic compati fac nostra pectora,
ut vel compassio digna sit venia.

Nox ista flebilis praesensque triduum
quod demorabitur fletus sit vesperum,
donec laetitiae mane gratissimum
surgente Domino sit maestis redditum.

Tu tibi compati sic fac nos, Domine,
tuae participes ut simus gloriae;
sic praesens triduum in luctu ducere,
ut risum tribuas paschalis gratiae.

GOOD FRIDAY: THE THIRD NOCTURN[1]

Alone to sacrifice thou goest, Lord,
    Giving thyself to death whom thou hast slain.
For us thy wretched folk is any word,
    Who know that for our sins this is thy pain?

For they are ours, O Lord, our deeds, our deeds,
    Why must thou suffer torture for our sin?
Let our hearts suffer for thy passion, Lord,
    That sheer compassion may thy mercy win.

This is that night of tears, the three days' space,
    Sorrow abiding of the eventide,
Until the day break with the risen Christ,
    And hearts that sorrowed shall be satisfied.

So may our hearts have pity on thee, Lord,
    That they may sharers of thy glory be:
Heavy with weeping may the three days pass,
    To win the laughter of thine Easter Day.

Appendix
An Excerpt from the 'Lost Love
Letters' of Heloise and Abelard

These anonymous letters between a man and a woman, which exist in a single fifteenth-century copy, are argued by Constant Mews to be the letters which Heloise and Abelard first wrote to each other. Mews's arguments are discussed in the additional introduction on 'Abelard and Heloise in Today's Scholarship', pp. lxxv–lxxxii. These letters differ in style from the known letters of Abelard and Heloise, but this in itself does not show that they are inauthentic as the circumstances of their composition would have been so different. This excerpt gives a taste of an intriguing new problem in the history of Abelard and Heloise.

The text for letters 18–31 is taken from the translation by Neville Chiavaroli and Constant J. Mews, in Constant J. Mews, *The Lost Love Letters of Heloise and Abelard: Perceptions of Dialogue in Twelfth-Century France* (New York, 1999), pp. 201–15.

18

WOMAN An equal to an equal, to a reddening rose under the spotless whiteness of lilies: whatever a lover gives to a lover.

Although it is wintertime, yet my breast blazes with the fervour of love. What more? I would write more things to you, but a few words instruct a wise man. Farewell, my heart and body, and my total love.

19

MAN Indeed your words are few, but I made them many by re-reading them often. Nor do I measure how much you say, but rather how fertile is the heart from which comes what you say. Farewell, sweetest.

20

<MAN> The star turns around the pole, and the moon colours the night,
        But that star is fading that should be my guide.
        Now, if through the retreating shadows, my own star should appear,
        No longer will my mind know the darkness of grief.
        You to me are Lucifer, who must banish the night.
        Without you day is night to me, with you night is splendid day.

Farewell, my star, whose splendour never dies. Farewell, my greatest hope, in whom alone I find favour, and whom I never bring back to mind since you never slip from mind. Farewell.

21

WOMAN To her beloved, special from experience of the reality itself: the being which she is.

Since my mind is turning with many concerns, it fails me, pierced by the sharp hook of love ... Just as fire cannot be extinguished or suppressed by any material, unless water, by nature its powerful remedy, is applied, so my love cannot be cured by any means – only by you can it be healed. My mind is bothered by not knowing through what gift I can enrich you. Glory of young men, companion of poets, how handsome you are in appearance yet more distinguished in feeling. Your presence is my joy, your absence my sorrow; in either case, I love you. Farewell.

22

MAN To his jewel, more pleasing and more splendid than the present light, that man who without you is shrouded in dense shadow: what else except that you glory unfailingly in your natural brilliance.

Scientists often say that the moon does not shine without the sun, and that when deprived of this light, it is robbed of all benefit of heat and brightness and presents to humans a dark and ashen sphere. Surely the similarity of this phenomenon to you and me is very plain to see: for you are my sun, since you always illumine me with the most delightful brightness of your face and make me shine. I have no light that does not come from you and without you I am dull, dark, weak and dead. But, to tell the truth, what you do for me is even greater than what the sun does for the sphere of the moon. For the moon becomes more obscure the closer it gets to the sun, whereas the nearer I am brought to you and the closer I get, the more on fire I become. So much do I burn for you, that, just as you yourself have often noted, when I am next to you I become completely on fire and am burned right down to the marrow.

What then shall I offer in return to equal your innumerable benefits? Nothing, actually, because you transcend your sweetest words with the number of your actions and you have so surpassed them by the demonstration of your love that you seem to me poorer in words than in actions. Among other things that you possess in infinite number compared with other people, you have this distinction too, that, poor in words but rich in actions, you do more for a friend than you say; this is all the more to your glory since it is more difficult to act than to speak . . .

You are buried inside my breast for eternity, from which tomb you will never emerge as long as I live. There you lie, there you rest. You keep me company right until I fall asleep; while I sleep you never leave me, and after I wake I see you, as soon as I open my eyes, even before the light of day itself. To others I address my words, to you my intention. I often stumble over words, because my thought is far from them. Who then will be able to deny that you are truly buried in me? . . . Envious time looms over our love, and yet you delay as if we were at leisure. Farewell.

23

WOMAN To the sweetest protector of her soul, planted at the root of her caring love, she in whose love you are firmly established and in whose honeyed taste of love you are well founded: whatever is far from anger and hate.

Although I wanted to write back to you, the magnitude of the task, being beyond my powers, drove me back. Indeed I wanted to but could not, I began then grew weak, I persisted but collapsed, my shoulders buckling under the weight. The burning feeling of my spirit longed to do so but the weakness of my dried-up talent refused. I endured the numerous disputes and litigious arguments of both, and after weighing up rationally to which of the two I would rather yield, I was unable to decide. For the feeling of my spirit said: *'What are you doing, ungrateful woman? For how long do you keep me in suspense with long and*

surely undeserved silence? Does not the generous kindness and kind
generosity of your beloved stir you? Compose a letter full of thanks,
give the thanks which you owe for his abounding integrity. For a kind
act does not seem pleasing and welcome when many thanks are not
received.'

I thought that I ought to heed these arguments, and certainly I
wanted to heed them, but the dryness of my talent resisted, rebuking
the attempts of my temerity with the harsh whip of reproach, saying:
'Where are you rushing, you foolish and feeble woman? Where does
the unthinking intention of your hasty spirit throw you? Do you begin
to speak mighty words, though you are unskilled and have unrefined
lips? Surely you are no match for such matter so distinguished. For
anyone who assumes to praise anything at all must in the end divide it
into parts and with the utmost care weigh the qualities of each indi-
vidual part, honouring each one according to its merit with a suitable
tribute of praise; otherwise he who diminishes its brilliance by < ... >
description, its elegance with outrageous description, harms the object
to be praised. But from where will you get such ability in writing that
you might speak of great things worthily? Look at yourself and at the
task you are undertaking. Abundant and various are the benefits for
which you are preparing to give thanks in your writing. Why are you
tossed about by so many storms of deliberations? Look at your cold
and brutish breast, utterly lacking the salt of learning and so inflated
with the sluggishness of dense air. Draw in the sails of your audacity,
the skiff in which you are preparing to cross the imperious ocean,
quickly, for unless you take heed, you will drown.'

Suspended between this alternating encouragement and discourage-
ment, I have until now deferred the due act of thanks, yielding to the
advice of a mental capacity ashamed of its own ineptitude. I pray that
the excellence of divine amiability abundant in you will not blame me
for this, but rather, since you are the son of true sweetness, may the
virtue of mildness familiar to you flow over me even more. Indeed I
know and admit that from the treasures of your philosophy the greatest
amount of joys have flown and still flow over me, but, if I may speak
freely, still less than what would make me perfectly happy in this
regard. For I often come with parched throat longing to be refreshed
by the nectar of your delightful mouth and to drink thirstily the riches
scattered in your heart. What need is there for more words? With God
as my witness I declare that there is no one in this world breathing
life-giving air whom I desire to love more than you ... May this
farewell, my beloved, sweetly penetrate your inner marrow.

24

MAN To a soul brighter and dearer to me than anything the earth has produced, the flesh which that same soul causes to breathe and move: whatever I owe her through whom I breathe and move.

The abundant and yet insufficient richness of your letter provides me with the clearest evidence of two things, namely, your overflowing faith and love; hence the saying: 'From the fullness of the heart the mouth speaks.' . . . And yet I receive your letters so eagerly that for me they are always too brief, since they both satisfy and stimulate my desire: like someone who is suffering from fever – the more the drink relieves him, the hotter he feels. God is my witness that I am stirred in a new way when I look at them more carefully; in a new way, I say, because my spirit itself is shaken by a joyful trembling, and my body is transformed into a new manner and posture. So praiseworthy are your letters that they direct my sense of hearing to whatever place they wish.

You often ask me, my sweet soul, what love is – and I cannot excuse myself on grounds of ignorance, as if I had been asked about a subject unfamiliar to me. For that very love has brought me under its own command in such a way that it seems not to be external but very familiar and personal, even visceral. Love is therefore a particular force of the soul, existing not for itself nor content by itself, but always pouring itself into another with a certain hunger and desire, wanting to become one with the other, so that from two diverse wills one is produced without difference . . .

Know that although love may be a universal thing, it has nevertheless been condensed into so confined a place that I would boldly assert that it reigns in us alone – that is, it has made its very home in me and you. For the two of us have a love that is pure, nurtured, and sincere, since nothing is sweet or carefree for the other unless it has mutual benefit. We say yes equally, we say no equally, we feel the same about everything. This can be easily shown by the way that you often anticipate my thoughts: what I think about writing you write first, and, as I remember well, you have said the same thing about yourself. Farewell, and regard me with unfading love just as I do you.

25

WOMAN To her incomparable treasure, more delightful than all the pleasures of the world: blessedness without end and well-being without weakening.

I too have been considering with innate reflection what love is or what it can be by analogy with our behaviour and concerns, that which above all forms friendships, and, once considered, leads to repaying you with the exchange of love and obeying you in everything . . . If our love deserted us with so slight a force, then it was not true love. The plain and tender words which to date we have exchanged with each other were not real, but only feigned love. For love does not easily forsake those whom it has once stung. You know, my heart's love, that the services of true love are properly fulfilled only when they are continually owed, in such a way that we act for a friend according to our strength and not stop wishing to go beyond our strength.

This debt of true love, therefore, I shall endeavour to fulfil, but alas I am unable to do so in full. However, if the duty of greeting you according to my meagre talents is not enough, at least my never ending desire to do so may be of some merit in your estimation. For know this, my beloved, and know it truly, that ever since your love claimed for itself the guest chamber – or rather the hovel – of my heart, it has always remained welcome and day after day more delightful, without, as often happens, constant presence leading to familiarity, familiarity to trust, trust to negligence and negligence to contempt. Indeed, you began to desire me with much interest at the very beginning of our friendship, but with greater longing you strove to make our love grow and last. And so our spirit fluctuates according to how your affairs turn out, so that your joy I count as my gain and your misfortune my most bitter loss. But your fulfilling what you have begun does not seem the same to me as your increasing what you have completed, because in one case what is lacking is added, in the other what is completed is added on. And even if we show perfect kindness to everyone, we still do not love everyone equally; and what is general for everyone is made particular for certain people. It is one thing to sit at the table of a prince, another to be there in order to advise him, and a greater thing to be drawn out of love, rather than just to be invited to a gathering. So I owe you fewer thanks for not spurning me than for receiving me with open arms. Let me speak plainly to your resplendent mind and heart so pure. It is not a great thing if I love you, but rather a wicked thing if ever I shall forget you. Therefore, my dear, do not make yourself so scarce to your faithful friend. So far I have somehow been able to bear it, but now, deprived of your presence and stirred by the songs of birds and the freshness of the woods, I languish for your love. Surely I would have rejoiced in all these things if I had been able to enjoy your conversation and presence according to my will.

May God do for me such as I desire for you. Farewell.

26

MAN To his beloved not yet known, and still to be known more intimately, the young man who deep within yearns to probe the understanding of such a great good: may you always abound in such a secret and inexhaustible fountain of goodness, and through it never be without refreshment.

... How fertile with delight is your breast, how you shine with untouched beauty, body so full of moisture, indescribable scent of yours! Reveal what is hidden, uncover what you keep concealed, let that whole fountain of your most abundant sweetness bubble forth, let all your love release its abundance in me, and may you keep absolutely nothing from your most devoted servant, because I believe nothing has been done as long as I see something remaining. Hour by hour I am bound closer to you, just like fire devouring wood: the more devouring the more plentiful its fuel ... You glitter with perpetual light and inextinguishable brightness immortally. Farewell.

27

WOMAN To her eye: the spirit of Bezalel, the strength of the three locks of hair, the beauty of the father of peace, the depth of Ididia.

28

MAN To his beloved, firmly stored in eternal memory: whatever leads to that state in whose fullness nothing is lacking.

May prolonged cause for envy be given to those who envy us, and may they long pine away for our prosperity, since that is what they want. But it is not possible to separate you from me, even if the sea itself should flow between us; I will always love you, I will always carry you in my spirit. Nor should you be surprised that twisted jealousy should turn its eyes towards such a conspicuous and fitting friendship as ours, because if we were miserable, we could undoubtedly live among others however we liked without any malicious attention. Therefore let them backbite, let them drag us down, let them gnaw, let them waste away inside, let them derive their bitterness from our good things; you will still be my life, my breath, my restoration in difficulty and finally my complete joy. Farewell, you who make me fare well.

29

WOMAN Having given up everything, I take refuge under your wings, I submit myself to your rule, resolutely following you in everything. I can scarcely speak these sad words: 'Farewell'.

30

MAN May God be gracious to you, sweetest. I am your servant, most ready for your commands. Farewell.

31

<MAN> To his sweetest, his only remedy in every affliction: may you never have worries or be troubled by any affliction.

... Consider how much you would have achieved by your actual presence if you had such power when absent. Surely if I could have directed my gaze to your most delightful face just once, I would have felt no grief whatsoever ... Send me to the place in which lies my destiny, since it is completely within your power. Farewell and never stop faring well.

MAPS

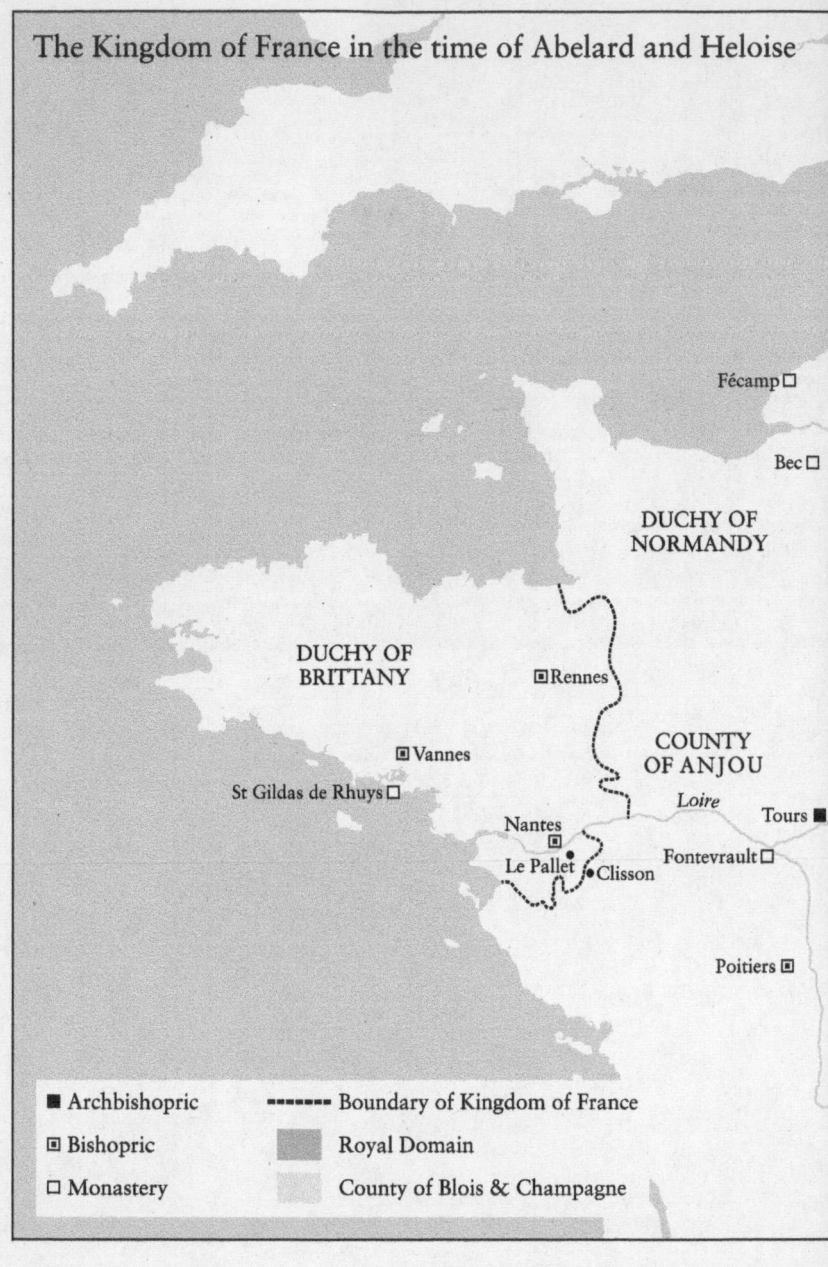

The Kingdom of France in the time of Abelard and Heloise

Fécamp ☐

Bec ☐

DUCHY OF NORMANDY

DUCHY OF BRITTANY

☒ Rennes

COUNTY OF ANJOU

☒ Vannes

St Gildas de Rhuys ☐

Loire

Tours ■

Nantes
☒
Le Pallet ● ● Clisson

Fontevrault ☐

Poitiers ☒

■ Archbishopric	------- Boundary of Kingdom of France
☒ Bishopric	Royal Domain
☐ Monastery	County of Blois & Champagne

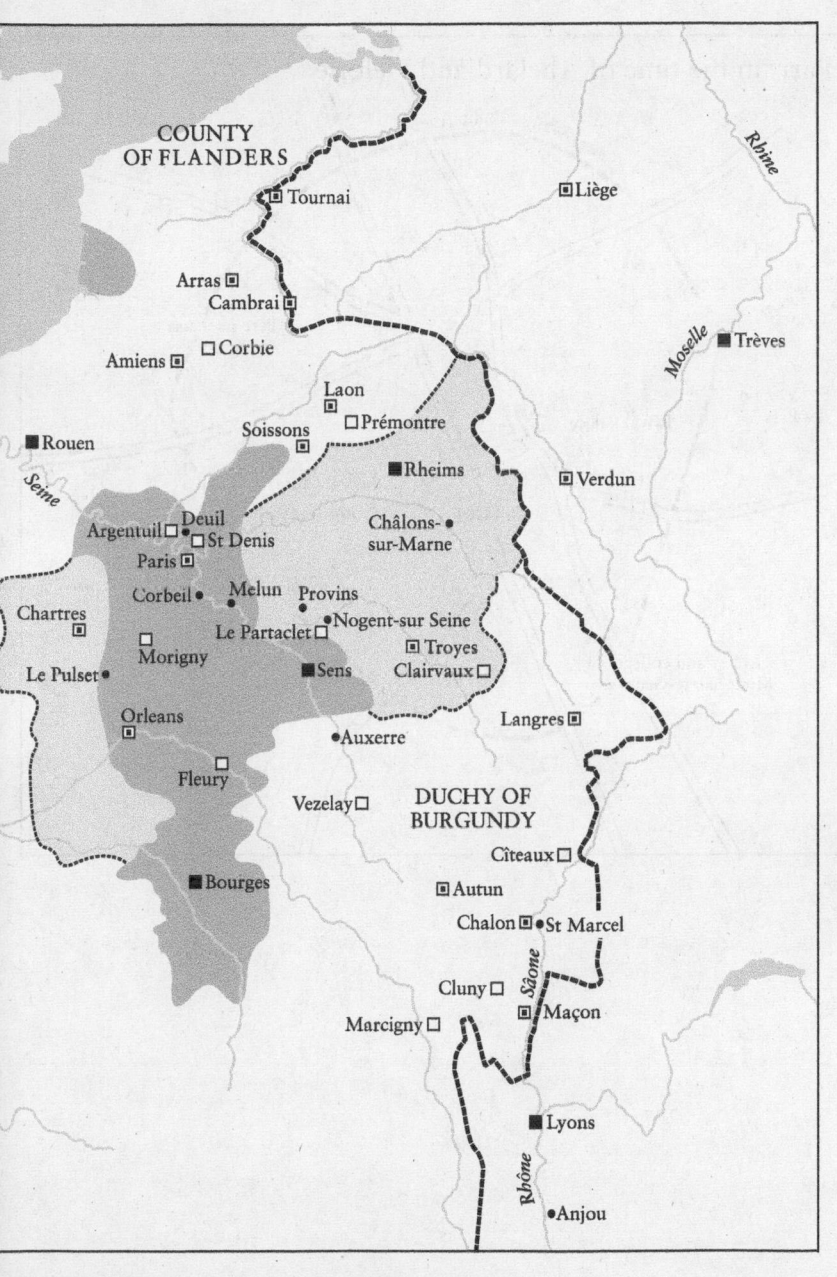

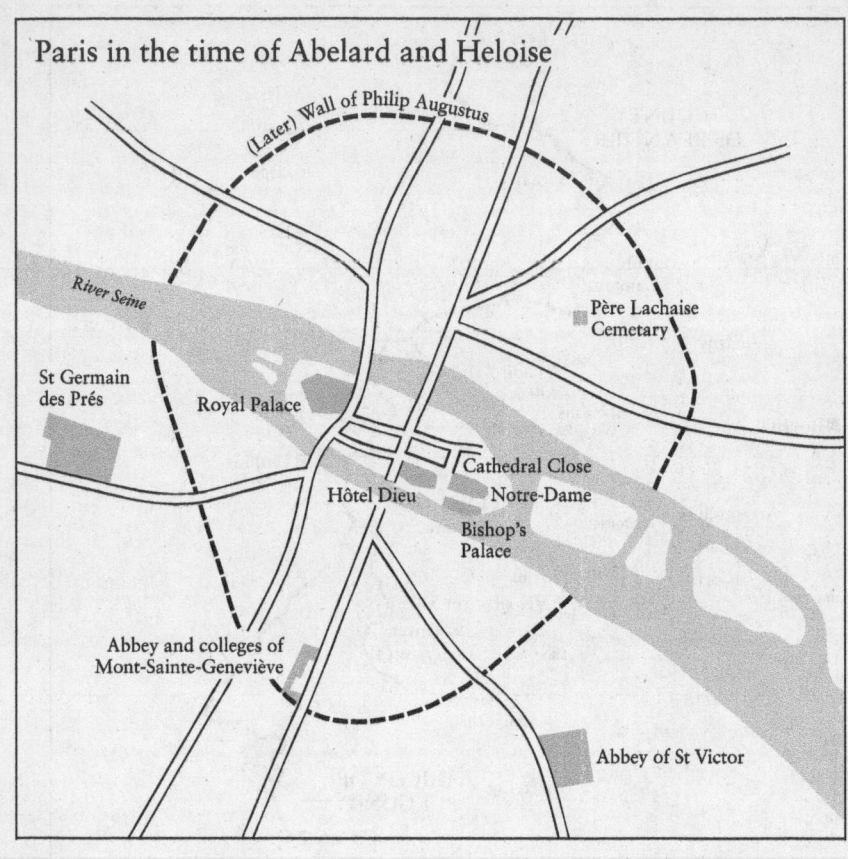

Paris in the time of Abelard and Heloise

(Later) Wall of Philip Augustus

River Seine

St Germain des Prés

Royal Palace

Père Lachaise Cemetary

Hôtel Dieu

Cathedral Close

Notre-Dame

Bishop's Palace

Abbey and colleges of Mont-Sainte-Geneviève

Abbey of St Victor

Notes
The Letters of Abelard and Heloise

LETTER I

HISTORIA CALAMITATUM

1. *Historia calamitatum . . . to bear*: The traditional title of *Historia calamitatum* and the third-person chapter-headings (omitted in this translation) were well known by Petrarch's time, though the best of the early manuscripts read *Abaelardi ad amicum suum consolatoria <epistula>* ('Abelard's letter of consolation to his friend'; the word in pointed brackets is lacking in the Latin). This version of the title and the opening paragraph indicate that however personal in content, this letter falls into one of the categories recognized by the art of rhetoric. The 'friend' who reappears as a fellow-monk in the closing paragraphs may be wholly imaginary, as part of the convention.

2. *Le Pallet*: Situated south of the river Loire, on the border between Brittany and Poitou, and on the road from Nantes to Poitiers (see the map at pp. 246–7). The remains of the castle there may date from Abelard's time. The Latin name *Palatium* for Le Pallet means 'the Palace', and this pun gave rise to Abelard's nickname of *Palatinus*: he was 'the man from the Palace', implying that he was a 'Palatine' or courtly nobleman. See M. T. Clanchy, *Abelard: A Medieval Life* (Oxford, 1997), pp. 130, 146–7.

3. *I was his first-born*: Abelard was probably born in 1079. His father, Berengar, was a Poitevin and not a Breton. His mother, Lucia, was presumably the heiress of the castle of Le Pallet which Berengar then acquired by marrying her. As the eldest son, Abelard stood to inherit this military position. Abelard had a sister and three brothers: for a tentative genealogy see: Brenda M. Cook, 'Abelard and Heloise', *Genealogists' Magazine* 26 (1999), pp. 205–11.

4. *Mars ... Minerva*: The Roman gods of war and of learning. Abelard uses them as literary metaphors.

5. *peripatetic philosopher ... the art of dialectic*: Abelard understood the Greek Peripatetics (the followers of Aristotle) to have been wandering scholars like himself, whereas in fact they took their name from the arcade (*peripatos*) where they 'walked about' while teaching. Abelard was nicknamed the *Peripateticus Palatinus* (the 'Palatine Peripatetic') because he was admired as the medieval Aristotle. 'Dialectic' meant training in argument through logic. Abelard had been taught by Roscelin, whom he does not mention here, presumably because he had been tried for heresy and he had attacked Abelard: see Introduction, p. xvi, and Clanchy, *Abelard*, pp. 292–5.

6. *William of Champeaux*: (*c.* 1070–*c.* 1120), archdeacon of Paris, head of the Cloister School of Notre-Dame, and then at the abbey of St Victor; in 1112 or 1113 bishop of Châlons-sur-Marne. He installed Bernard as abbot of Clairvaux and became a close friend. For Abelard's struggles with William, see Clanchy, *Abelard*, pp. 68–71, 83–4, and John Marenbon, *The Philosophy of Peter Abelard* (Cambridge, 1997), pp. 9–12, 110–14. See also note 9.

7. *Melun*: One of the residences of Philip I. None of Abelard's dates is precise; his school may have been set up as early as 1102. Corbeil was also a royal fief.

8. *For some years, being remote from France*: Abelard spent three or four years (*c.* 1105–*c.* 1108) at home; nothing further is known about this critical period in his life. He describes himself as 'remote from France' because 'France' in his time meant the area centred on Paris which was directly governed by the king.

9. *Canons Regular*: Their rule was based on that drawn up by St Augustine for secular clergy. It was intended to reform the cathedral clergy and to bridge the gap between scholars and monks (see also note 96). In *c.* 1105 William of Champeaux withdrew to the abbey of St Victor, just outside the walls of Paris, where he founded the very successful school of St Victor. The theologian Hugh of St Victor taught there 1115–41 and continued the school's opposition to Abelard.

10. *essence ... non-difference*: See Introduction, p. xvi, and Marenbon, *Philosophy of Peter Abelard*, p. 113.

11. *Isagoge*: (Meaning 'Introduction') by Porphyry, a Greek Neo-Platonist of the third century AD and pupil of Plotinus, was the elementary textbook which was used in Abelard's time as a way

into Aristotle's logic. It defined the basic terms in the Aristotelian system: things are categorized by 'genus', 'species' and 'properties' for example. See Marenbon, *Philosophy of Peter Abelard*, pp. 105ff.

12. *William's successor*: Not identified.

13. *Envy seeks . . . the summits*: Ovid, *De remedio amoris*, 1. 369.

14. *Mont-Sainte-Geneviève*: The site of the future university of Paris, it was on the outskirts of the city in Abelard's time (see point F on the map of Paris at p. 248). He was protected there by Stephen de Garlande, who was dean of the abbey of Sainte-Geneviève (see note 79). Abelard describes a three-cornered fight between himself at Mont-Sainte-Geneviève, William of Champeaux at St Victor (point H) and William's nominee at Notre-Dame (point A).

15. *Priscian*: Latin grammarian of the early sixth century AD, whose eighteen-book treatise on grammar (*Institutiones grammaticae*) was widely used in the Middle Ages.

16. *If you demand . . . my enemy*: Ovid, *Metamorphoses*, 13. 89–90. The meaning of this quotation is ambiguous, as Ajax killed himself in despair: see Clanchy, *Abelard*, p. 145.

17. *Anselm of Laon*: (c. 1055–c. 1117) was the master of the cathedral school at Laon from 1090 or earlier until his death. He was assisted by his brother, Ralph. Anselm (who should not be confused with his contemporary, the philosopher St Anselm, abbot of Bec and archbishop of Canterbury) was the most influential teacher of Christian doctrine and Scripture of his day. He was also very powerful in the city of Laon itself, as he was dean of the cathedral and chancellor. Abelard's account of him is prejudiced and misleading, as Anselm was at the height of his power in 1113 when Abelard arrived in Laon. Abelard may have been sent there by his patron, Stephen de Garlande, in order to topple Anselm (see Clanchy, *Abelard*, pp. 71–4).

18. *the fig tree which the Lord cursed . . . field of corn*: See Matthew 21:18–22; Lucan, *Pharsalia*, 1. 135–6.

19. *a session of Sentences*: 'Sentences' were written summaries or quotations giving the 'sense' of a master's teaching. Students might be permitted to copy these out and discuss them with the master. In his lectures a master like Anselm of Laon did a textual commentary on the Scriptures and also raised general questions arising from them. In 'a session of Sentences' the master might answer further questions concerning his lectures and permit the students to make notes. In his own commentaries on Scripture Abelard used the techniques which he had learned from Anselm.

20. *Alberic of Rheims and Lotulf of Lombardy*: Very little is known of Lotulf, who came from Novara. Alberic became archdeacon of Rheims in 1113 and ran the school there with Lotulf; in 1137 he was elected archbishop of Bourges. They were two of Abelard's main opponents at the Council of Soissons: see p. 20.

21. *forbade me to continue . . . in the place where he taught*: Anselm had the authority to expel Abelard from Laon because he held the offices of dean, chancellor and archdeacon. He was correct to argue that anything which Abelard taught at Laon might be attributed to him.

22. *the school . . . offered to me*: Abelard's official status at the cathedral school of Notre-Dame is obscure. He was not allocated a house in the precinct and neither is he recorded witnessing any documents as a canon. Possibly his teaching post was only provisional. This might explain why he says later 'I remained in possession' instead of categorically stating that he was the master of the school.

23. *'Knowledge breeds conceit' . . . the burning of the book*: 1 Corinthians 8:1. Abelard and Heloise both quote from the Bible very freely. Their own words have been translated when they are only approximate to the Latin of the Vulgate; otherwise the New English Bible, Knox or the Jerusalem Bible has been used. For the burning of Abelard's book, see p. 24.

24. *Heloise*: Heloise was probably illegitimate, as her father is never named. Possibly Fulbert was her father, but no medieval source says that. Why he wanted her to be so highly educated is unexplained; perhaps she was able to insist on this because she was so clever. What age she was when she met Abelard in *c.* 1115 is controversial: see Introduction, note 2 and 'The Letters of Abelard and Heloise in Today's Scholarship', p. lxxiv. The best biography is Enid McLeod, *Héloïse: A Biography* (1938; reprinted, London, 1971).

25. *songs . . . still popular and sung in many places*: Abelard's songs were almost certainly in Latin (rather than French); some of them may have found their way anonymously into the great thirteenth-century collection of secular Latin songs, the *Carmina Burana*: see Clanchy, *Abelard*, pp. 53, 133, 174, and David Wulstan, '*Novi modulaminis melos*: The Music of Heloise and Abelard', *Plainsong and Medieval Music* 11 (2002), p. 8.

26. *'We are . . . our ears'*: Jerome, *Epistulae*, 147. 10.

27. *happened to Mars and Venus*: They were found in bed together by her husband, Vulcan. The story was well known to Abelard

through the versions by Ovid in *Ars amatoria*, 2. 561ff. and *Metamorphoses*, 4. 169ff.

28. *removed her secretly ... whom she called Astralabe*: In Letter 5, p. 80, Abelard adds the detail that Heloise was disguised as a nun. The sister was probably the Denise or Dionysia who appears in the necrology of the Paraclete, as does Peter Astralabe or Astrolabe. Why Heloise named her son 'Astralabe' remains a mystery. The use of astralabes in the teaching of astronomy was coming into vogue, so this was the equivalent of naming a boy 'Computer' today. As astronomy combined with astrology, he was to be a child of destiny. The name may have been intended to echo Abelard's: the boy was 'Peter Astralabe' and his father was 'Peter Abelard'. Both 'Abelard' and 'Astralabe' were peculiar names.

29. *not to damage my reputation*: Abelard had to protect his reputation for celibacy because this was the standard which his predecessor, William of Champeaux, had established at the Notre-Dame cathedral school. Other canons were married and Abelard was not legally barred from marrying Heloise, as he was not a priest, but if he did so, the good name of his school would be damaged. Churches throughout Christendom funded students to go to the Paris schools to get an intellectual training in a rigorous religious setting. Masters and students were expected to live like monks: see Clanchy, *Abelard*, pp. 187–91.

30. *'Has your marriage ... from anxious care'*: I Corinthians 7:27–8, 32.

31. *St Jerome ... study of philosophy'*: *Contra Jovinianum*, 1. 47.

32. *'Philosophy is ... reject them'*: Seneca, *Epistulae ad Lucilium*, 72. 3.

33. *the name of monks*: Monachus ('monk') originally denotes one who chooses a solitary life. See also Letter 8, p. 138.

34. *Nazirites*: Their rule of life is described in Numbers 6. See also Judges 16:17 (Samson).

35. *the sons of the prophets ... as St Jerome bears witness*: See 2 Kings 4:1, 6:1; Jerome, *Epistulae*, 125. 7.

36. *Antiquities, the Pharisees, Sadducees and Essenes*: Josephus, *Antiquities*, 18. 1. 11; these Jewish ascetic or learned elites existed in the time of Christ.

37. *The Italian school ... a sage*: Augustine, *De civitate Dei*, 7. 2.

38. *Charybdis*: The legendary whirlpool in the straits of Messina which engulfed ships.

39. *'One day ... lead to rain"'*: Jerome, *Contra Jovinianum*, 1. 48.

These arguments appear in the same words in Abelard's *Christian Theology*, written in *c.* 1123. This suggests either that he borrowed them from Heloise's letter and reused them in his book, or that he found them for himself and added them to his version of her letter in *Historia calamitatum*.

40. *Argenteuil ... put it on*: The convent of Argenteuil had been endowed by royalty from Charlemagne onwards. By vesting Heloise as a nun, even without the veil signifying final vows, Abelard was signalling that he was divorcing her. Presumably he thought that Fulbert and her family were too weak to take reprisals against him.

41. *humiliation*: Fulk, prior of Deuil, gives another account of Abelard's castration: see Clanchy, *Abelard*, pp. 198–9.

42. *'Ye shall not ... the Lord'*: Leviticus 22:24; Deuteronomy 23:1.

43. *the Abbey of St Denis*: Like the convent of Argenteuil, the abbey was a royal foundation close to Paris. It enshrined the tomb of St Denis, the first bishop of Paris, who had been martyred by the Romans. By Abelard's time St Denis had become the patron saint of France and the abbey was the site of royal burials and coronations. Abelard was therefore entering the most prestigious abbey in France. The greatness of the abbey is described in detail by its abbot Suger, who was Abelard's contemporary: see Lindy Grant, *Abbot Suger of St Denis* (London, 1998).

44. *O noble husband ... gladly pay*: Lucan, *Pharsalia*, 8. 94.

45. *talent entrusted ... with interest*: See Matthew 25:15–30.

46. *retired to a cell*: This unidentified 'cell' of the abbey of St Denis was close either to Paris or to Nogent-sur-Seine: see Clanchy, *Abelard*, pp. 229–30.

47. *History of the Christian Church*: Eusebius, *Historia Ecclesiae*, 6. 8ff. For Origen's castration, see Peter Brown, *The Body and Society* (London, 1988), p. 168.

48. *two of them*: Presumably Alberic and Lotulf.

49. *occupying myself with secular literature*: This refers to the controversy in Abelard's time about whether monks should be contemplative or active. Monks should withdraw from the world; it was the business of the secular clergy and canons to deal with the laity. Hugh of St Victor argued that Abelard should be devoted to prayer and not to teaching, now that he had become a monk (see Clanchy, *Abelard*, pp. 229–30).

50. *a theological treatise on divine unity and trinity*: The title that Abelard gave to this book was *Theologia* (*Theology*), meaning in Greek 'discussion' (*logos*) about the nature of 'God' (*theos*).

He did not know Greek, but giving the book a Greek title made it look impressive. The book discusses the doctrine of the Trinity and whether non-Christians share this belief. (The revised edition was titled *Theologia Christiana*.)

51. *'blind guides of blind men'*: Matthew 15:14.
52. *Palestrina ... convene an assembly*: Praeneste in central Italy. Almost all that is known about Abelard's trial at Soissons sometime around 1121 is what he tells us here: see Clanchy, *Abelard*, pp. 295–305.
53. *'Our enemies are judges'*: Deuteronomy 32:31.
54. *"Here he is, speaking openly"*: John 7:26.
55. *'Whoever supposes ... beget itself'*: Augustine, *De Trinitate*, I. I.
56. *Geoffrey, bishop of Chartres*: Geoffrey of Lèves, Bishop of Chartres, 1115–49.
57. *his vine has spread ... to sea*: Cf. Psalm 80:8–12. The same phrase is applied to Abelard in the letter sent to Innocent II by the Council of Sens in 1140 or 1141.
58. *'Courage which ... mountain-peaks'*: Cf. Horace, *Odes*, II. 10. 11–12.
59. *'A false rumour ... his past'*: Jerome, *Epistulae*, 54. 13.
60. *'Does our ... the facts'*: John 7:51.
61. *Nicodemus*: The Pharisee who counselled that Jesus should be given a fair hearing (John 7:51). He was a secret supporter of Jesus (John 3:1–10) and assisted with his burial (John 19:39).
62. *approved by the authority of the Pope*: The argument that Abelard should have got his book approved probably refers to the precedent of St Anselm of Canterbury getting the approval of Pope Urban II in 1095 for his book against Roscelin, who had been Abelard's master: see M. T. Clanchy, 'Abelard's Mockery of St Anselm', *Journal of Ecclesiastical History* 41 (1990), pp. 15–16.
63. *Thierry by name*: This may have been the famous master Thierry of Chartres, who is associated with Abelard by Otto of Freising: see Clanchy, *Abelard*, p. 75. For his career see Peter Dronke, 'Thierry of Chartres', *A History of Twelfth-Century Western Philosophy* (Cambridge, 1988), pp. 358ff.
64. *not three Almighties, but one Almighty*: Thierry was quoting from the Athanasian Creed (see note 66). Abelard was probably charged at Soissons with teaching that only God the Father was omnipotent: see Constant J. Mews, 'The council of Sens (1141)', *Speculum* 77 (2002), pp. 359–60. For the doctrine of the Trinity, see Clanchy, *Abelard*, pp. 269–72.

65. '"*Are you such fools . . . Re-open the trial*"': Daniel 13:48–9
    (Vulgate). This is the story of Susanna, who was falsely accused
    of fornication by the elders, because they lusted after her.

66. *the Athanasian Creed*: Abelard was made to recite this particular
    creed because it defined the doctrine of the Trinity in detail. This
    creed was believed to have been written by St Athanasius, bishop
    of Alexandria, who died in 373; but it may not have been
    composed until the fifth century.

67. *the abbot of St Médard*: The abbey of St Médard specialized
    in disciplining monks. Abelard was handed over to the prior,
    St Goswin, who remembered him as 'that rhinoceros': see
    Clanchy, *Abelard*, pp. 147, 305, and Marenbon, *Philosophy of
    Peter Abelard*, p. 18.

68. *the lament of St Antony*: The Life of St Antony of Egypt (251?–
    356) by St Athanasius was well known because he was believed
    to be the first monk. The life describes how Antony was driven
    close to despair, even though he had withdrawn to the desert to
    live as a hermit, when he was assaulted by demons in the form of
    wild beasts.

69. *Bede, in his Commentary on the Acts of the Apostles*: Ch. 25.
    The English monk the Venerable Bede (673?–735), who is now
    famed for his *Ecclesiastical History of the English People*, was
    best known to medieval churchmen for his biblical commentaries.
    In this case, however, Bede's assertion about Dionysius the Areo-
    pagite (see following notes) is mistaken. Bede's evidence is there-
    fore irrelevant to Abelard's argument, but he purports here not
    to know this.

70. *the famous Areopagite*: The monks of the abbey of St Denis
    believed that their patron saint was Dionysius (or Denis in French)
    the Areopagite, the Athenian philosopher who had been con-
    verted by Paul himself, as described in Acts 17:19, 34. The monks
    believed that Dionysius had been bishop of Athens and had then
    gone to convert the Gauls, where he was martyred in Paris after
    becoming the first bishop there. Dionysius the Areopagite or
    St Denis was therefore the apostle of France.

71. *abbot Hilduin*: Hilduin (d. 840) established the fame of the abbey
    of St Denis. He knew enough Greek to make an outline in Latin
    of the theological works of Pseudo-Dionysius, a Christian Neo-
    Platonist who lived in Syria *c*. 500. Hilduin believed that in
    Pseudo-Dionysius he had discovered the philosophical works of
    Dionysius the Areopagite. Hilduin wrote the authoritative life of
    St Denis, which made one and the same person out of Dionysius

the Areopagite (converted by Paul), Pseudo-Dionysius (who lived *c.* 500) and Denis the apostle of the Gauls (who lived *c.* 250).

72. *the authority of Bede ... carried more weight with me*: Abelard was right to argue that Bede was generally a more reliable historian than Hilduin and that there was something suspicious about the accepted history of St Denis, but he was out of his depth because he did not know Greek. Abelard could not demonstrate (and probably he did not know) that Hilduin had conflated three saints named Dionysius/Denis from different centuries. Hilduin was correct, however, in refuting Bede's assertion that Dionysius the Areopagite had been bishop of Corinth.

73. *a traitor to the whole country*: Abelard was accused of being a traitor because St Denis was the patron of the French kingdom, whereas Abelard was not even a Frenchman but a Breton who had been accorded hospitality at St Denis. For example, in *The Song of Roland* (trans. Dorothy L. Sayers (Penguin Classics, 1957), chs 83–4, pp. 92–3), which dates from this time, Roland fights for Christendom, for France and for St Denis, and in 1124 King Louis VI headed his army with the banner of St Denis and saved France from a German invasion.

74. *nor did it much matter whether he was the Areopagite*: On the contrary, this mattered crucially to the monks of St Denis because their relics of the saint had to be authentic in order to work miracles. The shrine of St Denis was the source of the abbey's prestige and revenues from pilgrims. In *The Song of Roland*, Roland's sword Durendal is so strong because of the relics in its hilt, which include some of St Denis's hair (ch. 173, trans. Sayers, p. 141).

75. *He was ... delighted to seize the opportunity to destroy me*: Abbot Adam had in fact shown generosity to Abelard, first by accepting him as a monk after his castration and then by allowing him to return and continue his studies after he had been condemned as a heretic at the Council of Soissons in about 1121. Subsequently Abelard wrote Adam and the monks of St Denis a conciliatory letter, which concludes that Bede may have been mistaken: Letter XI, *Peter Abelard, Letters IX–XIV*, ed. Edmé R. Smits (Groningen, 1983), pp. 249–55.

76. *Count Theobald*: By gaining the protection of Count Theobald, Abelard had won the support of the most powerful ruler in France apart from the king. Theobald was the Count Palatine, and count of Blois, Chartres, Champagne, Provins and Meaux; in 1125 he acquired Troyes as well. He became the heir to the English crown

and the duchy of Normandy on the death of Henry I in 1135, but conceded his claim to his younger brother, Stephen, King of England (1135–54). Theobald was also the patron of St Bernard and he attended Abelard's second trial for heresy at Sens in 1140 or 1141, but he is not recorded to have given him protection then.

77. *Count Theobald . . . Provins*: Abelard was now a runaway monk subject to excommunication. Count Theobald may have protected him because he was frequently in dispute with the king of France. The priory in Provins where Abelard lived was probably the priory of St Ayoul.

78. *When his successor was appointed*: Abbot Adam of St Denis died in 1122 and was succeeded by the dynamic Abbot Suger: see Grant, *Abbot Suger of St Denis*, pp. 108ff.

79. *A certain Stephen*: Stephen de Garlande, King Louis VI's steward, chancellor and chief minister, 1108–27 and 1133–7. He was also archdeacon of the cathedral of Notre-Dame and dean of the church of Mont-Sainte-Geneviève, where Abelard had his school in Paris. The French historian Robert Bautier has plausibly argued that Stephen became Abelard's patron from the time when Abelard first arrived in Paris in *c*. 1100. By insulting the abbey of St Denis and fleeing to Count Theobald in about 1121, Abelard forfeited the long-standing royal protection which Stephen's patronage had given him. Stephen therefore brokered the deal described here whereby Abelard transferred from France to Champagne. (For Stephen's career, see Clanchy, *Abelard*, indexed references at p. 414.)

80. *built a sort of oratory*: Abelard's oratory or hermitage was on the banks of the river Ardusson, four miles south-east of Nogent-sur-Seine, in the parish of Quincey. The bishop was Hato of Troyes, friend and correspondent of both St Bernard and Peter the Venerable. See Clanchy, *Abelard*, pp. 237–40.

81. *'Lo, I . . . the wilderness'*: Psalm 55:7.

82. *'Death has . . . our windows'*: Jeremiah 9:21.

83. *Plato himself . . . muddy feet*: Diogenes Laertius, *Vitae philosophorum*, 6. 26. Diogenes the Cynic said that in doing so he trampled on Plato's pride, and Plato retorted that he showed pride of a different sort.

84. *The senses are like windows . . . their studies*: Jerome, *Contra Jovinianum*, 2. 8ff.

85. *'The sons . . . wild herbs'*: Jerome, *Epistulae*, 125. 7.

86. *'Remote as . . . my retreat'*: Jerome, *Quaestiones in Genesim*, 3. For 'as Quintilian says', see *Declamationes*, 13. 2.

87. *"Why, all ... after him"*: John 12:19.

88. *'not strong ... to beg'*: Luke 16:3.

89. *my pupils provided all I needed unasked*: In fact Abelard faced rebellion from his students, as described by Hilary of Orléans: see Clanchy, *Abelard*, pp. 240–41.

90. *I named it the Paraclete*: There were no precedents in the Latin Church for dedications to the Paraclete. By 'Paraclete' (*Paraclitus* in Latin transliterated from the Greek) is meant the 'Comforter' promised in John 14:16. Abelard's 'Confession of Faith' (p. 211) identifies the Paraclete with the generator of the Incarnation and hence with the doctrine of the Trinity. (For a fuller explanation, see Clanchy, *Abelard*, pp. 242–4.)

91. *'Praise be ... your Comforter"'*: 2 Corinthians 1:3–4; John 14:16.

92. *feast of Pentecost*: Acts 2:1ff.

93. *'But he ... to yourselves'*: 1 Corinthians 6:17, 19.

94. *Echo ... no substance*: Ovid, *Metamorphoses*, 2. 359.

95. *new apostles in whom the world had great faith*: Abelard is using here the rhetorical device recommended by Cicero of not naming his adversaries in order to draw the reader's attention to them. He calls them 'apostles' satirically because monastic reformers claimed to be reviving the life of the apostolic Church. Heloise calls them 'pseudo-apostles' (p. 47). To whom were Abelard and Heloise referring? The answer is almost certainly St Norbert and St Bernard (see also the following two notes). When Abelard was writing in 1132 or 1133, the world did indeed have great faith in Norbert and Bernard, as they were the churchmen who established Lothar III as Emperor and Innocent II as pope. Norbert was the imperial chancellor, responsible for Innocent II's crowning of Lothar III in Rome in 1133, and Bernard's preaching had been crucial in getting Innocent II recognized as pope. Possibly Abelard was frightened to name such powerful people and this is why he refers to them so obliquely. He had good reason to be frightened, as it was Bernard and Innocent II who condemned him as a heretic in 1140 or 1141 (Norbert had died in 1134).

96. *One of these boasted that he had reformed the life of the Canons Regular*: In 1115 Norbert, who had been the chaplain of the Emperor Henry V in 1110, challenged the clerical ownership of property and became an itinerant preacher. He regularized his position by founding the order of Premonstratensian Canons in 1121. They claimed to live by the 'rule' (Latin *regula*) of St Augustine and this is why Abelard describes them as 'Canons

Regular'. In a sermon (no. 33) in *c.* 1125, Abelard accused
Norbert and a 'co-apostle' of boasting that they could raise people
from the dead. This makes it likely that Norbert is one of the two
'new apostles' whom Abelard refuses to name in this letter. In
1126 Norbert left France to become archbishop of Magdeburg
with a mission to convert the pagans on Germany's eastern
frontier. (For a fuller explanation of the difference between
Canons Regular and monks, see Clanchy, *Abelard*, pp. 211–15,
and for Norbert see Marenbon, *The Philosophy of Peter Abelard*,
p. 20.)

97.   *the other the life of the monks*: St Bernard fits this description
because he claimed to reform monks of every sort and not only
his own monks of the abbey of Clairvaux or his own order of
Cistercians. In *c.* 1125 he published his 'Apologia for Abbot
William', which is an attack on the alleged ostentation and luxury
of non-Cistercian monks. Bernard was thought to be attacking
the Cluniac order in particular, but Abelard may have understood
this work as a personal attack on himself (see Clanchy, *Abelard*,
pp. 244–5). Abelard must have been hostile to Bernard as soon
as he became abbot of Clairvaux in 1115 because his patron was
Abelard's former master, William of Champeaux. Furthermore,
the 'Abbot William' to whom Bernard addressed his 'Apologia'
was William of St Thierry, who participated in Abelard's trial for
heresy at Soissons and initiated his second trial at Sens. (Extracts
from the 'Apologia for Abbot William' are translated by Pauline
Matarasso, *The Cistercian World* (Harmondsworth, 1993),
pp. 44–58.)

98.   *the heathen*: Abelard probably means the Moslems of Spain, who
tolerated Christians: see Clanchy, *Abelard*, pp. 245–6.

99.   *the lord of the district*: Conan III, duke of Brittany 1112–42, was
the patron of the abbey of St Gildas. This abbey housed the shrine
of the Celtic saint and scholar Gildas of Strathclyde. Abelard is
named as abbot in a charter of 1128: see Clanchy, *Abelard*,
pp. 242, 246–9, and Marenbon, *Philosophy of Peter Abelard*,
pp. 21–2.

100. *the Romans . . . drove St Jerome East*: St Jerome (*c.* 342–420) was
secretary for a time to Pope Damasus the First who encouraged his
revision of the Latin New Testament, but the hostility of the
Romans after the pope's death in 385 made him leave for Bethle-
hem along with Paula, Eustochium and other Roman ladies who
wished to live a studious, simple life under his direction.

101. *the language unknown to me*: The area around St Gildas was

Breton speaking, whereas Abelard's birthplace Le Pallet was south of the Loire and French-Occitan speaking: see Clanchy, *Abelard*, pp. 52–3, 247.

102. '*From the . . . in anguish*': Psalm 61:2.

103. *very powerful tyrant . . . Jews subject to tribute*: This 'tyrant' was probably not Duke Conan III but some local lord. Conan's authority was weak in the remoter parts of Brittany: see Clanchy, *Abelard*, p. 249. 'Jews subject to tribute' is used figuratively; Abelard would have seen Jews in Paris, but not in the Breton countryside.

104. '*Quarrels all . . . our heart*': 2 Corinthians 7:5.

105. '*There is . . . not finish*': Luke 14:30.

106. *belonged to his monastery by ancient right*: In 1129 Abbot Suger used forged charters to get possession of Argenteuil: see T. Waldman, 'Abbot Suger and the Nuns of Argenteuil', *Traditio* 45 (1985), pp. 239–72; McLeod, *Héloïse*, pp. 93–104; Grant, *Abbot Suger*, pp. 190–93; Constant Mews, *The Lost Love Letters of Heloise and Abelard* (New York, 1999), pp. 154–5.

107. *gathered there*: This was the first meeting of Abelard and Heloise after a separation of ten years.

108. *by charter*: Dated 28 November 1131: see Clanchy, *Abelard*, pp. 249–50, and Mary M. McLaughlin, 'Heloise the Abbess', in *Listening to Heloise*, ed. Wheeler, pp. 3, 12, note 16.

109. '*Before I . . . of heaven*': Jerome, *Epistulae*, 45. 2.

110. *concubines of King Ahasuerus*: See Esther 2:3.

111. *a eunuch of the Ethiopian Queen Candace . . . baptize*: Acts 8:26ff. More accurately, the NEB translates 'the Kandake, or Queen, of Ethiopia . . .' See also Letter 5, p. 88.

112. *Origen laid violent hands . . . History of the Church relates*: Eusebius, *Historia Ecclesiae*, 6.8, and see note 47 above.

113. '*A good name . . . great riches*': Proverbs 22:1.

114. "*For our aims . . . eyes of men*": 2 Corinthians 8:21.

115. *In his sermon . . . your neighbour*': Augustine, Sermon 355.

116. *To this end . . . own resources*': Augustine, *De Opere Monachorum*, 4. 5. 'After this he went journeying . . . own resources' is Luke 8:1–3.

117. *Leo the Ninth . . . intercourse with them*: Pope Leo IX (1048–54) started enforcing celibacy among the higher clergy. Abelard probably found this quotation in the treatise on canon law entitled *Panormia* (3, 15), which had been written in the 1090s by Ivo, bishop of Chartres. Abelard's reference to 'Parmenian' may be a confusion with the book title *Panormia*: see *Historia calamita-*

tum, ed. J. Monfrin (Paris, 1959), p. 103. 'Have I no right ... Cephas' is 1 Corinthians 9:5.

118. *'If this ... a sinner'*: Luke 7:39.

119. *the Lord's mother entrusted ... conversation of widows*: John 19:27 (see also Letter 8, p. 154); 3 Kings 17:10 (Apocrypha).

120. *Malchus ... with his wife*: Malchus was taken captive by the Saracens and forced to marry a woman who also wished to remain celibate.

121. *look after the women*: Acts 6:1–3.

122. *her head covered*: 1 Corinthians 11:5.

123. *abbesses and nuns ruling the clergy*: Abelard is referring to the great aristocratic nunneries, like Argenteuil and La Ronceray in Anjou, where the abbess acted as a territorial lord. By contrast, the new reformers' model was the Cluniac convent of Marcigny-sur-Loire, where the post of abbess was left vacant and the convent was administered by monks of Cluny.

124. *'Nothing is more intolerable than a rich woman'*: Juvenal, *Satires*, 6. 460. This quotation shows that Abelard was opposed to Heloise having much responsibility as an abbess: see Clanchy, *Abelard*, pp. 253–4.

125. *the curse of Cain*: Genesis 4:14.

126. *poison me – as happened to St Benedict*: The episode is told in the *Dialogues* of Gregory the Great, 2.3. Benedict was asked to leave his solitary life at Subiaco, east of Rome, to be abbot of a small monastery at Vicovaro, where the monks rebelled against his high standards and tried to poison him.

127. *during the very sacrifice of the altar*: Abelard must have been an ordained priest at this time, as he was celebrating Mass.

128. *special legate*: Probably Geoffrey, Bishop of Chartres.

129. *sword suspended by a thread over his own head*: The sword of Damocles; see Cicero, *Tusculanae Disputationes*, V. 20–21. Note the present tense; Abelard is still at the abbey of St Gildas.

130. *'As they ... its own'*: John 15:20, 18–19.

131. *'Persecution will come ... servant of Christ'*: 2 Timothy 3:12; Galatians 1:10.

132. *'They are ... rejected them'*: Perhaps an echo of Psalm 52, but the wording is very inexact.

133. *'"If I still ... servant of Christ'*: Jerome, *Epistulae*, 52. 13.

134. *'Thank God I have deserved ... with the rich"'*: Jerome, *Epistulae*, 45. 6, 14. 4; 'like a roaring lion ... to devour' is 1 Peter 5:8; and cf. 'He sits in ambush with the rich' to Psalm 10:8.

135. *'Thy will be done'*: Matthew 10 (the Lord's Prayer).

136. '*As we . . . love God*': Romans 8:28.
137. '*Whatever befalls the righteous man it shall not sadden him*':
     Proverbs 12:21: Vulgate version, reading *contristabit*. The NEB
     translates: 'No mischief shall befall the righteous.'

LETTER 2

HELOISE TO ABELARD

1. *Thank you . . . absent friend*: Seneca, *Epistulae ad Lucilium*, 40. 1.
2. *cry out*: Cf. Cicero, *In Catalinam*, 1. 8.
3. *built . . . upon another man's foundation*: Cf. Romans 15:20.
4. '*I planted . . . made it grow*': 1 Corinthians 3:6.
5. *turned to bitterness against you*: Cf. Jeremiah 2:21.
6. *cast pearls . . . before swine*: Matthew 7:6.
7. *And so in the precarious . . . when we had parted*: This sentence,
    often mistranslated as if it refers to the present and so suggesting
    that Abelard has never visited nor written to her at the Paraclete,
    has been used as evidence that the letters are a forgery because it
    contradicts what he says in the *Historia calamitatum* (p. 36). But
    the tense (*movit*) is past, translated here as 'I was troubled', and
    Heloise must be referring to his failure to help her by word before
    they separated and by letter after she had entered the convent.
    See McLeod, *Héloïse*, pp. 248–50.
8. *Aeschines Socraticus . . . of husbands*': He was a pupil of Socrates,
    and wrote several dialogues of which fragments survive. This is,
    however, no proof that Heloise knew Greek, as the passage was
    well known in the Middle Ages from Cicero's translation of it in
    De inventione, 1.31.
9. *the gift of composing and the gift of singing*: This passage about
    Abelard's poetic and musical gifts needs to be read in the original
    Latin because it uses technical terms. For example, 'the gift of
    composing' translates the Latin *dictandi gratia*, which literally
    means 'the grace of dictating'; the 'art of dictation' (*ars dictaminis*)
    was the usual way of describing the composition of prose or
    poetry. A good edition of Heloise's letter is that by Eric Hicks,
    La vie et les epistres Pierres Abaelart et Heloys sa fame (Paris,
    1991), where this passage is at p. 51, lines 188–96. See also the
    translation by L. Weinrich, 'Peter Abelard as a Musician', *Musical
    Quarterly* 55 (1969), pp. 296–7.
10. *It is not the deed . . . but the spirit in which it is done*: Cf.
    Introduction, p. xxii. This is the 'ethic of pure intention' held by

Heloise and Abelard and set out in his *Ethica* or *Scito te ipsum* (*Know yourself*): our actions must be judged good or bad solely through the spirit in which they are performed. See Clanchy, *Abelard*, pp. 84, 129, 278–81; Marenton, *Philosophy of Peter Abelard*, ch. 11; and Paul V. Spade, *Peter Abelard, Ethical Writings* (Indianapolis, 1995), pp. 12–14, 20–25.

11.   *Why ... have I been so neglected ... in absence*: This is not to be taken as contradicting Abelard's statement on p. 36 that he often visited the Paraclete, and had invited Heloise and her nuns to go there (either by letter or interview). Her complaint is that he never writes her a personal letter nor offers her help in her personal problems. In Letter 5, p. 79, he refers to her 'old perpetual complaint' to him, but he evidently will not be drawn into discussion.

12.   *Lot's wife turned back*: See Genesis 19:26.

13.   *Hell*: The Latin is *Vulcania loca*, Vulcan's regions, or Tartarus, and illustrates how Heloise's natural manner of expressing herself is classical.

14.   *grace in return for grace*: John 1:16.

LETTER 3
ABELARD TO HELOISE

1.   *Psalter you earnestly begged from me*: *Psalterium*, the Book of Psalms. This must have been some special type of Psalter, as the Latin Psalter was the commonest of all prayer books. Sister Benedicta Ward has suggested that it may have been in Hebrew or Greek. Or perhaps it may have been in French, like the Eadwine Psalter's translation. Possibly too, it was exceptionally illuminated, like Christina of Markyate's Psalter.

2.   *pray continually*: 1 Thessalonians 5:17.

3.   *'Let me alone ... my path'*: Exodus 32:10; Jeremiah 7:16, loosely quoted.

4.   *'Let me alone and ... threatened them'*: Exodus 32:10, Jeremiah 7:16; Exodus 32:14.

5.   *'He spoke, and it was'*: Psalm 33:9.

6.   *'In thy wrath remember mercy'*: Habbakuk 3:2.

7.   *Jephtha ... killed his only daughter*: Judges 11:30–39. See also Letter 7, p. 119. Abelard composed a lament for Jephtha's daughter (one of a set of six Laments), see Mary M. McLaughlin, 'Peter Abelard and the Dignity of Women', in *Pierre Abélard, Pierre le Vénérable* (Paris, 1975), p. 312, note 84.

8. *'member of his body . . . unto thee, O Lord'*: Cf. Ephesians 5:30; Psalm 101:1.

9. *'In that . . . no mercy'*: James 2:13.

10. *Psalmist himself considered . . . destruction of his house*: 1 Samuel 25:32ff.: the meeting of David and Abigail.

11. *'When two or three . . . my Father'*: Matthew 18:20, 19.

12. *'A good . . . and effective'*: James 5:16.

13. *homily of St Gregory*: The *Homilies on the Gospels* of Pope Gregory the Great (died 604) are sermons he preached to encourage monks.

14. *women have even received back their dead raised to life*: Hebrews 11:35 (Abelard quotes this a few sentences later). See also Letter 7, p. 122.

15. *by Elijah and his disciple Elisha . . . at her father's petition*: 1 Kings 17:17–23 and 2 Kings 4:32–5; Luke 7:11–15 (widow from Nain); John 11:1ff. (Lazarus); Mark 5:22ff.

16. *'A capable wife . . . gift from the Lord'*: Proverbs 12:4, 18:22, 19:14.

17. *'A good wife makes . . . a good life'*: Ecclesiasticus 26:1, 31.

18. *'the unbelieving . . . his wife'*: 1 Corinthians 7:14.

19. *when Clovis the king was converted . . . preaching of holy men*: Clovis (481–511), founder of the Merovingian House of France, was converted to Christianity after his victory over the Alamanni in 496; his wife Clotild, a princess of Burgundy, was already a Catholic and had long begged him to renounce his pagan ways. The story was well known from Gregory of Tours, *History of the Franks*, II. 29–31.

20. *'If the . . . he needs'*: Luke 11:8.

21. *Forsake me not . . . reach thee*: Psalms 38:21, 70:1 ('Make haste'), 102:1 ('hear my prayer . . . reach thee').

22. *O Lord, Father . . . my enemy gloats*: Cf. Ecclesiasticus 23:3; Psalm 35:2.

23. *bringing precious ointments*: See Mark 16:1.

24. *'The women . . . the Lord'*: Not in the Gospels. It is the antiphon for the Benedictus in the Roman Breviary for Holy Saturday. See also Letter 5, p. 85.

LETTER 4

HELOISE TO ABELARD

1. *deaconess*: It is not clear what Heloise means here by 'deaconess'. See Letter 7, p. 117: 'Those whom we now call abbesses they called deaconesses in former times.'
2. *precedence in order of address follows precedence in rank*: Heloise shows her knowledge of the rules for composing formal letters (*Dictamen* or *Ars dictandi*) which are found in several treatises from the eleventh century onwards: see *Three Medieval Rhetorical Arts*, ed. James J. Murphy (Berkeley, 1971).
3. *'Each day ... its own'*: Matthew 6:34.
4. *'Why is ... summon evil'*: Seneca, *Epistulae ad Lucilium*, 24. 1.
5. *May it be ... his fears*: Lucan, *Pharsalia* 2. 14–15.
6. *'But now ... of death'*: Proverbs 7:24–7.
7. *'I put ... her captive'*: Ecclesiastes 7:25–6.
8. *the Nazarite whose conception was announced by an angel*: Samson, in Judges 13:3.
9. *Solomon, wisest ... and writing*: 1 Kings 11:1–8.
10. *Job ... curse God*: Job 2:9–10.
11. *'I will speak out ... of soul'*: Cf. Job 10:1.
12. *'There are some ... accuses him'*: Gregory, *Moralia*, 9. 43.
13. *'I have ... known repentance'*: Ambrose, *De paenitentia*, 2.10.
14. *'Miserable creature ... this death'*: Romans 7:24.
15. *God ... searches our hearts and loins*: Psalm 7:10 (Vulgate).
16. *'Turn from evil and do good'*: Psalm 37:27.
17. *'O my people ... should take'*: Isaiah 3:12 (Vulgate).
18. *'Woe to ... catch souls'*: Ezekiel 13:18. This warns unscrupulous preachers not to make people feel comfortable in order to gain converts.
19. *'The sayings ... driven home'*: Ecclesiastes 12:11.
20. *'The heart of man ... to death'*: Jeremiah 17:9; Proverbs 14:12, 16:25.
21. *'Do not ... his lifetime'*: Ecclesiasticus 11:28.
22. *'Power comes to its full ... the rules'*: 2 Corinthians 12:9; 2 Timothy 2:5.
23. *'I confess ... pursue uncertainty'*: Jerome, *Contra Vigilantium*, 16. This letter breaks off without a valediction.

LETTER 5
ABELARD TO HELOISE

1. *'This is my reason . . . my Lord'*: Jerome, *Epistulae*, 22. 2. 'Lady' in Latin is *domina*. See also Letter 7, p. 117.
2. *'On your right stands the queen'*: Psalm 45:9.
3. *an Ethiopian . . . discoloured me'*: Numbers 12:1; Song of Solomon 1:5, 4, 6.
4. *truly widowed . . . charged to support*: 1 Timothy 5:16.
5. *'The women . . . the Lord'*: Not in the Gospels. See Letter 3, note 24.
6. *'his teeth whiter than milk'*: Genesis 49:12.
7. *'Persecution will . . . as Christians'*: 2 Timothy 3:12.
8. *'All the . . . is within'*: Psalm 44:14 (Vulgate).
9. *the foolish virgins . . . shut against them*: Matthew 25:1ff.
10. *'Night after . . . true love'*: Song of Solomon 3:1, but not a very apt quotation, as the context makes it clear that the 'bride' is longing for her lover on her solitary bed. (Radice's comment shows that she was unaware of the mystical interpretation of the Song of Solomon: see A. W. Astell, *The Song of Songs in the Middle Ages* (Ithaca, 1991).)
11. *the monastic life . . . beginning from Paul*: Jerome, *Vita Pauli primi eremitae*, 5.
12. *'No one adorns . . . can be seen'*: *Homilia in Lucam*, 40. 16. (In his copy Petrarch noted in the margin that Seneca said the same thing.)
13. *'But when . . . to your Father'*: Matthew 6:6.
14. *St Augustine . . . 'I am truth'*: Augustine, *De baptismo*, 3. 6. 9; cf. John 14:6.
15. *'But anyone . . . with him'*: 1 Corinthians 6:17.
16. *'And so in . . . or removed'*: See Letter 2, p. 48.
17. *rejoicing without weeping with those who weep*: Cf. Romans 12:15.
18. *'He who . . . be exalted'*: Proverbs 18:17; Luke 18:14.
19. *'We are . . . own praise'*: Jerome, *Epistulae*, 22. 24.
20. *She flees . . . be seen*: Virgil, *Eclogues*, 3. 65.
21. *unwary*: Latin *imprudentes*. The alternative reading is *impudentes* (wanton).
22. *your old perpetual complaint*: see Letter 2, note 11.
23. *God . . . has clearly shown himself kinder*: See Letter 4, p. 69.
24. *'The Lord takes thought for me'*: Vulgate only, the last verse of Psalm 39:18.

25. *lust . . . the greater sacraments*: Intercourse even between married couples was forbidden by the Church during Lent. See James A. Brundage, *Law, Sex, and Christian Society* (Chicago, 1987), p. 162.

26. *besought the Lord . . . not heard*: 2 Corinthians 12:7–8.

27. *castrated themselves . . . throw them away*: Matthew 19:12, 18:8.

28. *'The eunuchs . . . not perish'*: Isaiah 56:4–5.

29. *an ill-informed zeal*: Cf. Romans 10:2.

30. *declare how much . . . my soul*: Cf. Psalm 66:16.

31. *he named you Heloise, after his own name, Elohim*: The Old Testament uses the Hebrew word 'Elohim' to describe both the God of Israel and pagan gods. Abelard did not know Hebrew, but he would have known of 'Elohim' from glosses on the Latin Vulgate text. In fact the name 'Heloise' or 'Eloise' is of Old German origin in the form *Helewise*, where *hele* means 'hale' or 'well' and *wise* means 'wide' or 'strong'.

32. *'Women make . . . their faith'*: Ecclesiasticus 19:2.

33. *proved in the case . . . Solomon*: 1 Kings 11:1ff.

34. *to strike and convert Paul*: See Acts 9:3ff.

35. *'Whom the Lord . . . hates his son'*: Proverbs 3:12, Hebrews 12:6; Proverbs 13:24.

36. *'The Lord . . . shall arise'*: Cf. Nahum 1:9.

37. *'By your . . . your souls'*: Luke 21:19 (Vulgate).

38. *'Better be . . . a city'*: Proverbs 16:32.

39. *'A great crowd of people . . . is dry'*: Luke 23:27–31. Cf. this passage with Abelard's hymn translated on p. 235.

40. *'All you . . . my sorrow'*: Lamentations 1:12 (Vulgate).

41. *'They shall . . . first-born son'*: Zachariah 12:10.

42. *'God forbid . . . the world'*: Galatians 6:14.

43. *'There is . . . his friends'*: John 15:13.

44. *Pompey's reproach . . . And loved*: Lucan, *Pharsalia*, 8. 84–5. This is the nearest Abelard comes to a direct rebuke to Heloise for indulging in her memories.

45. *win his crown . . . kept to the rules*: Cf. 2 Timothy 2:5.

46. *'The beasts have rotted in their dung'*: Joel 1:17 (Vulgate).

47. *that blessed eunuch . . . his conversion*: Acts 8:26ff. See Letter 1, note 111. The passage the eunuch was reading was Isaiah 53:7–8.

48. *Prove us, Lord, and test us*: Psalm 26:2.

49. *'God keeps . . . sustain it'*: 1 Corinthians 10:13.

LETTER 6

HELOISE TO ABELARD

1. *To him who ... singularly his*: The manuscripts open with
    alternative readings: either *Suo specialiter* or *Domino specialiter*.
    Either reading could be correct, as the Latin *Domino* was abbrevi-
    ated to *Dno* and might then be mistaken for *Suo*. Heloise might
    well have written *Domino* ('To the lord'), as the word was fascin-
    atingly ambiguous. Was she dedicating her letter to Abelard as
    her 'lord' (as in the address of Letter 2), or 'to the Lord' (meaning
    that she now acknowledged her own dedication to God)? This
    ambiguity was subsequently exploited by Heloise in her final
    question (no. 42) in her *Problemata*. See Peter Dronke, *Women
    Writers of the Middle Ages* (Cambridge, 1984), p. 137; Linda
    Georgianna, 'Heloise's Critique of Monastic Life', in *Listening
    to Heloise*, ed. Wheeler, pp. 197, 212–13; Constant J. Mews,
    'Les lettres d'amour perdues d'Héloïse', in *Pierre Abélard, à
    l'aube des universités*, ed. Jean Jolivet and Henri Habrias (Nantes,
    2001), pp. 165–6.
2. *'A man's words ... the heart'*: Matthew 12:34.
3. *As one nail drives out another hammered in*: Cicero, *Tusculanae
    disputationes*, IV. 35. 75.
4. *At present the one Rule of St Benedict*: The Rule ascribed to
    St Benedict, who founded the abbey of Monte Cassino in *c*. 530,
    had been adapted over the centuries to all sorts of local needs,
    including those of nuns. But in the early 1100s reforming monks,
    headed by the Cistercians, insisted that only the original Rule of
    St Benedict was valid and there should be no local accretions or
    modifications. This is the context in which Heloise sets out here
    to demonstrate the inadequacy of the Rule alone as a guide for
    the conduct of nuns. (In general see C. H. Lawrence, *Medieval
    Monasticism*, 2nd edn. (London 1989), and the texts assembled
    by Matarasso, *The Cistercian World*.)
5. *cowls, drawers or scapulars*: The Rule of St Benedict, chapter 55.
    For a good modern translation, see *The Rule of St Benedict in
    Latin and English*, ed. Justin McCann (London, 1952).
6. *ruling ... start the hymn*: The Rule of St Benedict, chapter 11.
7. *drunkenness are ... to lechery*: Cf. Ephesians 5:18 (Vulgate).
8. *'It is difficult ... at table'*: Jerome, *Epistulae*, 117. 6.
9. *When wine ... to fire*: Ovid, *Ars amatoria* 1. 233–4, 239–40,
    243–4.

10. *to avoid contact with women of the world*: Jerome, *Epistulae*, 22. 16.

11. *'For if a man keeps . . . the same'*: James 2:10, 11.

12. *three readings of the Rule*: The Rule of St Benedict, chapter 58.

13. *virtues which exceed . . . among vices*: Jerome, *Epistulae*, 130. 11.

14. *Pastoral Rule*: Pope Gregory the Great's *Pastoral Rule*, written in the 590s, was the most influential set of regulations and advice for the secular clergy.

15. *done in moderation*: The Rule of St Benedict, chapter 48.

16. *he will accommodate . . . shrink from*: The Rule of St Benedict, chapters 2, 64. For the bruised reed see Isaiah 42:3. 'If I drive . . . single day' is Genesis 33:13.

17. *modification of regulations . . . before the rest*: The Rule of St Benedict, chapters 35–41, 36.

18. *'Everyone will . . . teacher's level'*: Luke 6:40.

19. *'My strength . . . in weakness'*: 2 Corinthians 12:9.

20. *Chrysostom reminds us*: St John Chrysostom's (*c.* 347–407) sermons and homilies, originally written in Greek for audiences in Antioch and Constantinople, begin to be quoted in the Latin West in the twelfth century because there was rich material in them for monastic reformers.

21. *'Be watchful in all . . . bodily appetites'*: Cf. Ephesians 6:18; Romans 13:14.

22. *marriage be honourable*: See Hebrews 13:4.

23. *'Because law can bring . . . multiply law-breaking'*: Romans 4:15; 5:20.

24. *'It is . . . for slander'*: 1 Timothy 5:14.

25. *'But if those . . . of hell'*: Jerome, *Epistulae*, 22. 6. See also Letter 8, p. 173.

26. *'Let her . . . from Christ'*: Augustine, *De bono viduitatis*, 9. 12.

27. *Aristotle says that women . . . wrinkled skin*: Macrobius Theodosius, *Saturnalia*, VII, 6. 16–17; 18. See also Letter 8, p. 178.

28. *'When you . . . our duty"'*: Luke 17:10.

29. *'But if . . . my return'*: Luke 10:35.

30. *love itself has grown cold*: Cf. Matthew 24:12. This pagan commonplace, a nostalgia for a Golden Age, would be known to Heloise through her classical reading, but it is equally common in the Middle Ages.

31. *'We have written down this Rule . . . protection of God'*: The Rule of St Benedict, chapter 73.

32. *whereas we read that the holy Fathers . . . clergy are*: Ibid., chapter 18.

33. *Wine is reckless ... wine again*: Proverbs 20:1, 23:29–35. See also Letter 8, p. 174.

34. *Do not give ... their sons*: Proverbs 31:4–5. See also Letter 8, p. 175.

35. *'Wine and women ... good sense'*: Ecclesiasticus 19:2. See also Letter 8, p. 175.

36. *Never smell of wine ... like wine*: Jerome, *Epistulae*, 52. 11. The philosopher is not identifiable. For the Apostle condemning priests who drink and 'Those who serve ... strong drink', cf. 1 Timothy 3:3 and Leviticus 10:9, respectively. See also Letter 8, p. 176.

37. *'Although ... of this etc.'*: The Rule of St Benedict, chapter 40. See also Letter 8, p. 177.

38. *Certain people told abba Pastor ... be much'*: *Vitae patrum*, V, 4. 31, 36, 37 (see also Letter 8, p. 177). The *Lives of the Fathers* is an anthology of biographies of the Desert Fathers, including St Antony of Egypt (see Letter 1, note 68). 'The *Lives of the Fathers* were second only to the Bible and the Rule of St Benedict in their influence on monasticism in the eleventh and twelfth centuries' (Giles Constable, *The Reformation in the Twelfth Century* (Cambridge, 1996), p. 160).

39. *damned and elect ... to the religious*: Cf. Letter 4, p. 70.

40. *the sum of the law and the object of what is commanded*: Cf. Romans 13:10; 1 Timothy 1:5.

41. *What room then is left ... gracious plan*: Romans 3:27–8, 4:2–3, 5.

42. *'The Kingdom of God ... your brother'*: Romans 14:17, 20–21.

43. *Peter was also trying to avoid giving such offence ... Galatians*: Galatians 2:11ff.

44. *'Certainly food does not commend ... in it'*: 1 Corinthians 8:8, 10:25–6.

45. *'Allow no one therefore ... of men'*: Colossians 2:16, 20–22.

46. *to eat any kind of food ... in the house*: See Luke 10:7.

47. *The Spirit says expressly ... have followed*: 1 Timothy 4:1–6.

48. *'Why is ... are not'*: Mark 2:18, referring to John the Baptist.

49. *Job's testing*: Job 1:8.

50. *'For John came neither ... own children'*: Matthew 11:18–19.

51. *perpetuate his race in Israel ... he had it*: Deuteronomy 25:5–10: Augustine means that a man could have the habit of continence though the Law forbade him to show it in practice. But the text quoted refers only to the brother-in-law of a widow.

52. *'the term was . . . who can'*: Galatians 4:4; Matthew 19:12, during a discussion of celibacy.

53. *Continence is a virtue not of the body . . . it untruthfully*: Augustine, *De Bono Conjugali*, chapters 25–7.

54. *apostles . . . pick the ears of corn*: Matthew 12:1ff.

55. *'To eat without first . . . adultery, murder'*: Matthew 15:19–20.

56. *'If a man looks . . . of God'*: Matthew 5:28; see 1 John 3:15 for 'Everyone who hates . . . of Christ and of God'.

57. *'who will judge . . . my gospel'*: Romans 2:16.

58. *modest offering of the widow . . . farthing*: See Mark 12:42–4.

59. *'The Lord . . . with favour'*: Genesis 4:4.

60. *'Keep yourself . . . to come'*: 1 Timothy 4:7–8.

61. *Jacob to provide . . . with Esau*: Genesis 27:6ff.

62. *'I have . . . thank-offerings'*: Psalm 56:12.

63. *'Do not look outside yourself'*: Persius, *Satires*, 1. 7.

64. *the insupportable yoke . . . Peter calls it*: see Acts 15:10. See also note 66 below.

65. *'Come to . . . is heavy'*: Matthew 11:28, 30.

66. *'My brothers . . . are they'*: Acts 15:7, 10–11.

67. *'If I am hungry . . . honour me'*: Psalm 50:12–15.

68. *'If any . . . full sense'*: 1 Timothy 5:16.

69. *the Lord provided his mother . . . to minister to devout women*: John 19:26–7; Acts 6:5 (see also Letter 1, p. 39).

70. *'A man who will not work . . . purpose of preventing idleness*: 2 Thessalonians 3:10; *The Rule of St Benedict*, chapter 48.

71. *But was not Mary sitting idle . . . day alone*: See Luke 10:39. See also Letter 8, p. 209. For 'burden and heat of the day', cf. Matthew 20:12.

72. *if they have to make material provision . . . the spirit*: Cf. 1 Corinthians 9:11.

73. *the tribe of Levi should have no patrimony . . . labour of others*: See Numbers 18:20–21.

74. *order the psalms differently, if it seemed better to do so*: The Rule of St Benedict, chapter 18. See also p. 101.

75. *reading the Gospel in the Night Office*: Cf. *The Rule of St Benedict*, chapter 11.

76. *after God you are the founder . . . of our community*: See Letter 2, p. 49, where the sentence appears in much the same form.

LETTER 7
ABELARD TO HELOISE

1. *summary ... quotations from Abelard*: The complete text is translated by C. K. Scott-Moncrieff in *The Letters of Abelard and Heloise* (London, 1925), and by Vera Morton and Jocelyn Wogan-Browne in *Guidance for Women in Twelfth-Century Convents* (Woodbridge, 2003). Abelard's letter is the most substantial and original contribution made in the Middle Ages to the debate about the ordination of women. But his arguments evoked no reactions, perhaps because they were too radical even for Heloise (she rarely called herself a 'deaconess', as he had wished). As so often, Abelard was on the losing side at a critical time; the canon lawyers of the twelfth century reaffirmed the rule of the Roman Church that women can have no holy orders like male priests.

2. *The widow Anna ... in St Luke's Gospel*: Luke 2:36, and see Alcuin Blamires, *The Case for Women in Medieval Culture* (Oxford, 1997), pp. 204–5, and Alcuin Blamires, 'Gender Polemic in Abelard's Letter "On the Authority and Dignity of the Nun's Profession"', in *The Tongue of the Fathers*, ed. Andrew Taylor and David Townsend (Philadelphia, 1998), pp. 138–9.

3. *"She has wrought ... on me"*: Mark 14:6, and see Blamires, *The Case for Women*, pp. 206–7.

4. *"My kingdom ... this world"*: John 18:36.

5. *as a memorial of her*: Mark 14:9.

6. *"There stood ... Mary Magdalene"*: John 19:25.

7. *prophesied long before by Job*: Job 19:20. Abelard's exegesis of this passage is explained by Blamires, 'Gender Polemic', pp. 147–8.

8. *'Go to my brethren ... my father'*: John 20:17. For female apostles (Latin *apostolae*), see Blamires, *The Case for Women*, pp. 110–12, 191–2; McLaughlin, 'Peter Abelard and the Dignity of Women', p. 296; and Katherine L. Jansen, *The Making of the Magdalen* (Princeton, 2000), pp. 62–3.

9. *"These all ... of Jesus"*: Acts 1:14.

10. *Paul 'seems openly ... Lord himself'*: Cf. 1 Corinthians 9:5, cited by Augustine, *De Opere Monachorum*, chapters 5–6, and see Blamires, *The Case for Women*, pp. 190–91.

11. *'And it came ... their substance'*: Luke 8:1–3, and see Blamires, *The Case for Women*, p. 30.

12. *multiplied among women . . . St Jerome*: Abelard depends here on the authority of St Jerome and Cassiodorus (*c.* 485–*c.* 580), who attest that the Jewish writer Philo of Alexandria (*c.* 20 BC–*c.* AD 50) described the piety of men and elderly women who lived like monks in Egypt.

13. *Miriam . . . spiritual chant in monastic congregations*: For Miriam and monastic chant, see Blamires, *The Case for Women*, p. 204.

14. *"Levitesses"*: See Blamires, 'Gender Polemic', p. 142 and notes 49, 50.

15. *'A widow . . . one man'*: 1 Timothy 5:9, and see note 19 below. See also Letter 8, p. 145.

16. *And Jerome explains . . . a good'*: The commentary on Paul, which Abelard cites here, was probably not in fact by Jerome.

17. *'The Son of Man . . . to minister'*: Matthew 20:28. For deaconesses, see McLaughlin, 'Peter Abelard and the Dignity of Women', pp. 298–301.

18. *Phebe of the church of Cenchrea . . . the Romans*: Romans 16:1.

19. *'Honour widows . . . widows indeed'*: 1 Timothy 5:3, and see Juanita F. Ruys, 'The Rhetorical Struggle over the Meaning of Motherhood in the Writings of Heloise and Abelard', in *Listening to Heloise*, ed. Bonnie Wheeler (New York, 2000), pp. 329–30.

20. *'Salute Rufus . . . and mine'*: Romans 16:13.

21. *'Unto the elect lady . . . one another'*: 2 John 1:1, 5.

22. *'After her . . . the king'*: Psalm 44:15–16 (Vulgate).

23. *Although women are the weaker sex . . . more perfect*: See Blamires, *The Case for Women*, pp. 134–6. Women as the 'weaker vessel' is 1 Peter 3:7.

24. *"The last . . . be last"*: Matthew 20:16.

25. *she was created in paradise . . . made outside*: See Blamires, *The Case for Women*, p. 104.

26. *the paradox . . . made outside*: Ambrose, *De Paradisis*, 4. 24.

27. *the courage of Deborah, Judith and Esther*: The stories of these three heroines are described in the Old Testament: in Judges 5, the Apocryphal Book of Judith and in Esther, respectively.

28. *the wicked king . . . the Law*: 2 Maccabees 7.

29. *'I know him not'*: Luke 22:57.

30. *the Lord has sanctified the female genitals . . . by circumcision*: See Blamires, *The Case for Women*, p. 107.

31. *Elizabeth, who prophesied . . . miraculous conception*: Luke 1:40–42.

32. *extend the gift of prophecy to the Gentiles as well, then the Sibyl*

should take centre stage: By the 'Gentiles' Abelard means pagans. The predictions of the ancient Greek and Roman female oracles, collectively known as the Sibyl, were treated as equivalents of the biblical prophecies because early Christian authorities such as Augustine interpreted them in this way, as Abelard describes here. He is, however, unique in arguing that the Sibyl was a greater prophet even than Isaiah.

33. *under Augustus Caesar in the time of Pollio's consulate*: The Emperor Augustus reigned from 27 BC to AD 14. The year of Pollio's consulate was believed to accord with the year of Christ's birth.

34. *'I know . . . all things'*: John 4:25. On the Samaritan woman, see John 4:6 ff., see also Blamires, *The Case for Women*, pp. 195–7, and Blamires, 'Gender Polemic', pp. 142–5.

35. *St Luke recalled . . . just man*: See Luke 23:27; Matthew 27:19.

36. *'Yea rather . . . keep it'*: Luke 11:28.

37. *"Now Jesus . . . and Lazarus"*: John 11:5, and see Blamires, *The Case for Women*, p. 203.

38. *Mary the Egyptian*: St Mary the Egyptian, who lived in the fifth century, was an actress and courtesan in Alexandria, who did penance and died as a hermit in Palestine.

39. *'I say . . . before you'*: Matthew 21:31.

40. *"the Lamb . . . he goeth"*: Revelation 14:4.

41. *Elijah's mantle . . . dry land*: See 2 Kings 2:8.

42. *"flamens"*: Roman priests dedicated to particular deities.

43. *'uni-virae' . . . other pagan deities*: Jerome, *Commentarium ad Galatas*, 3.6.

44. *'What am I . . . of divination'*: Jerome, *Contra Jovinianum*, 1. 41, and see Blamires, *The Case for Women*, p. 206, note 24.

45. *Vespasian is said to have healed the sick and St Gregory prayed for the soul of the emperor Trajan*: See Suetonius, *Lives of the Caesars*, chapter 7, and Paul the Deacon, *Life of Gregory the Great*, chapter 27.

46. *'because they . . . first faith'*: 1 Timothy 5:12, and see note 19 above.

47. *Jerome . . . such a great man as Augustine*: For Abelard's attitude to Jerome and Augustine, see Blamires, *The Case for Women*, p. 203, and Alcuin Blamires, 'No Outlet for Incontinence', in *Listening to Heloise*, ed. Wheeler, p. 296.

48. *'If all . . . venerable Paula'*: Jerome, *Epistulae*, 108. For Jerome's correspondence with women, see J. N. D. Kelly, *Jerome* (London, 1975), chapters 10, 11, 23.

49. 'There is ... deserted me': Jerome, *Epistulae*, 45. Abelard cites this with reference to himself in Letter 1, p. 36, when describing how he was vilified for rescuing Heloise from the closure of the convent of Argenteuil.
50. 'This man ... touches him': Luke 7:39.
51. *catechumen*: Person being instructed in Christianity who had not yet been received into the Church.

LETTER 8

ABELARD TO HELOISE

1. *spiritual temple of God which you are*: Cf. 2 Corinthians 6:16.
2. *Tully records in his Rhetoric*: Cicero, *De inventione rhetorica*, II. I.
3. *Greetings: Valete*. The valediction is suprising here, and has suggested to some that it marks the end of a separate short letter; but it may be intended to round off the formal introductory passage.
4. *to be ready with belts fastened, to forsake everything and to avoid idle talk*: Luke 12:35, 14:33 (see also note 8); Matthew 12:36.
5. 'The unmarried ... in spirit': 1 Corinthians 7:34.
6. 'Whoever listens ... rejects me': Luke 10:16.
7. 'What they ... their practices': Matthew 23:3.
8. 'Unless a man ... disciple of mine': Luke 14:33, 26.
9. 'If anyone ... with me': Luke 9:23.
10. 'I have ... sent me': John 6:38.
11. *takes it up himself ... to the world*: Cf. Galatians 6:14.
12. *The other Jesus ... your enemies*: Ecclesiasticus 18:30–31. The lesser Jesus is Jesus son of Sirach, the author of Ecclesiasticus named in its preface.
13. 'The whole ... his need': Acts 4:32, 35.
14. 'Far be ... may be': Augustine, *Retractiones*, 1, preface.
15. 'Where men ... is wise': Proverbs 10:19 (Vulgate).
16. 'At all times ... practise silence': *The Rule of St Benedict*, chapter 42.
17. 'All of us often ... deadly venom': James 3:2, 7, 5, 8.
18. 'A man ... is futile': James 1:26.
19. 'Like a city ... in speech': Proverbs 25:28.
20. *reply to Antony ... the ass*: *Vitae patrum*, V, 4. 1.
21. 'A woman ... be quiet': 1 Timothy 2:11–12.

22. *women are gossips and speak when they should not*: 1 Timothy 5:13.
23. *When we are careless ... softens anger'*: Gregory, *Moralia*, 7. 37. 'Letting out water starts quarrels' is Proverbs 17:14; 'Man's utterance ... runs deep' is Proverbs 18:4. 'He who ... softens anger' is Proverbs 26:10.
24. *Abba Macharius ... down alone*: *Vitae patrum*, V, 4. 27.
25. *'The harvest ... learn to keep silence*: Isaiah 32:17; *Vitae patrum*, V, 4. 7.
26. *the sons of the prophets ... the Jordan*: Jerome, *Epistulae*, 58. 5. Cf. Letter 1, p. 30.
27. *his forty days' fasting ... hidden places*: Matthew 4:2, 5:1, 17:1, 28:16; Acts 1:9.
28. *'Who has ... anything green'*: Job 39:5–8.
29. *'Consider the meaning ... a solitary'*: Jerome, *Epistulae*, 14.5.
30. *If you want to perform ... before the Lord*: Jerome, *Epistulae*, 58. 5. On the sons of Rechab, see Jeremiah 35:1ff.
31. *When abba Arsenius ... away dismayed*: *Vitae patrum*, V, 2. 3ff.
32. *'God knows ... with God'*: *Vitae patrum*, V, 17. 5.
33. *abba Simon ... started eating*: *Vitae patrum*, V, 8. 18.
34. *the hermit who, when he saw people ... he replied*: *Vitae patrum*, V, 12. 7.
35. *abba Moses ... a heretic'*: *Vitae patrum*, V, 8. 10.
36. *abba Pastor, who even refused ... her plea*: *Vitae patrum*, V, 8. 13.
37. *In the Life of St Martin ... with joy*: Not traced.
38. *'I have ... defile them'*: Song of Solomon 5:3.
39. *Obedientaries*: Small conventual establishments under the rule of a larger monastery.
40. *'Whoever sits ... the heart'*: *Vitae patrum*, V, 2. 3.
41. *'O desert ... the world'*: Jerome, *Epistulae*, 4. 10.
42. *provision should be made ... straying outside*: *The Rule of St Benedict*, chapter 66.
43. *'For its ... many rulers'*: Proverbs 28:2.
44. *You, Rome, have been ... a partner*: Lucan, *Pharsalia*, 1. 84–6, 89–93.
45. *abbot St Frontonius ... were born'*: *Vita Frontonii*, in *Vitae patrum*, I.
46. *'My brothers ... greater severity'*: James 3:1.
47. *No skill is learned ... your fellows*: Jerome, *Epistulae*, 125. 15.
48. *deaconess ... abbess*: Abelard often refers to the deaconess as a woman serving in the early Church; cf. Letter 7. He means here

that an abbess ('mother') must perform the same duties in the convent. He continues to use the term *diaconessa*, here translated as 'abbess' throughout.

49. *'Man's life on earth ... regimented army'*: Job 7:1; Song of Solomon 6:9 (Vulgate).

50. *A widow should not ... widows, etc.*: 1 Timothy 5:9–11. See also p. 163.

51. *'Their wives ... every way'*: 1 Timothy 3:11.

52. *'Woe betide the land ... brings understanding'*: Ecclesiastes 10:16 (Vulgate); Job 12:12.

53. *'Grey hair is a crown ... the Lord*: Proverbs 16:31; Ecclesiasticus 25:4–6.

54. *Speak, if you ... your elders*: Ecclesiasticus 32:4, 7–9.

55. *Lives of the Saints ... abbas or Fathers*: Some of the early books of the *Vitae patrum* are called *Verba seniorum*.

56. *the advice of the Apostle*: 1 Timothy 5.

57. *'set out to do and teach'*: Acts 1:1.

58. *'He is ... by words'*: Vitae patrum, V, 10. 75.

59. *the argument of St Antony ... of letters'*: Vitae patrum, I, 45.

60. *'Has not God ... his presence'*: 1 Corinthians 1:20, 27–9.

61. *accepted public correction from his fellow-apostle Paul*: Galatians 2:11.

62. *Lord often reveals ... the lesser man*: The Rule of St Benedict, chapter 3, reading *minori*. The alternative reading is *iuniori*, 'younger'.

63. *'A prophet ... native place'*: Matthew 13:57.

64. *'The conclusion of these ... a sin'*: Jerome, *Epistulae*, 14. 7.

65. *'Rob not ... the truth'*: Psalm 119:43.

66. *'God's word ... am speaking'*: Psalm 50:16–17.

67. *'I punish ... myself rejected'*: 1 Corinthians 9:27.

68. *'Physician, heal yourself'*: Luke 4:23.

69. *'If any man ... of Heaven'*: Matthew 5:19.

70. *It is the Lord ... the mighty*: Wisdom 6:4–7.

71. *'My son ... eyelids slumber'*: Proverbs 6:1–4.

72. *like a roaring lion ... to devour*: See 1 Peter 5:8 (quoted p. 151).

73. *'Have you daughters ... be defiled'*: Ecclesiasticus 7:24, 42:9.

74. *'Death comes ... our windows'*: Jeremiah 9:21.

75. *'Do not ... the soul'*: Matthew 10:28.

76. *'A lying ... the soul'*: Wisdom 1:11.

77. *'enjoy rich fare'*: Cf. Habakkuk 1:16.

78. *'The flooded ... his mouth'*: Job 40:18 (Vulgate).

79. *struck ... the four corners ... daughters*: See Job 1:19.

80. *'Those who . . . and robbers'*: John 10:8.
81. *'Nobody . . . Aaron was'*: Hebrews 5:4.
82. *'No one should . . . rooted out'*: Gregory, *Moralia*, 24. 25.
83. *'The just . . . accuse himself'*: See Letter 5, note 18, and p. 166.
84. *'A foolish . . . a friend'*: Cf. Proverbs 17:18.
85. *concerned about pilgrims and guests . . . entertain them*: The Rule of St Benedict, chapters 53, 56.
86. *'when the people . . . were satisfied'*: Cf. Lucan, *Pharsalia*, 9. 498ff.
87. *'Do not . . . and man'*: Ecclesiasticus 4:35, 10:7.
88. *'The Lord . . . of themselves'*: Ecclesiasticus 10:17, 32:1.
89. *'Never be . . . your sisters'*: 1 Timothy 5:1–2.
90. *'You did not . . . chose you'*: John 15:16.
91. *'You know . . . with you'*: Luke 22:25–6.
92. *'places of honour at feasts . . . be humbled'*: Matthew 23:6–7, 8–9, 12.
93. *'If a great . . . his invitation'*: Ecclesiasticus 13:9.
94. *lay monks: Conversi*, in a Benedictine house monks who had come late to monastic life and were not brought up in the cloister.
95. *Joseph was bidden . . . sleep with her*: See Matthew 1:20ff.
96. *'Woman's head . . . is God'*: 1 Corinthians 11:3.
97. *Shall the brother who presides . . . kept brief*: Cf. *Patrologia Latina*, ed. J.-P. Migne (Paris, 1855), Vol. 103, p. 551. 'Let all be done . . . order' is 1 Corinthians 14:40; 'Is my freedom . . . man's conscience' is 1 Corinthians 10:29; 'But I have . . . gospel of Christ' is 1 Corinthians 9:12.
98. *By common consent . . . their protection*: Article 11, *Concilia*, Vol. 10, ed. G. D. Mansi, p. 560.
99. *'there will . . . one shepherd'*: John 10:16.
100. *if she happens . . . take her place*: T. P. McLaughlin's text, adding *infirmaria* from the single manuscript containing this letter in full ('Abelard's Rule for Religious Women', *Mediaeval Studies* 18 (1956), pp. 241–92). The alternative reading means, 'if the abbess happens to be busy . . . the Chantress shall take her place'.
101. *'My son . . . all sin'*: Ecclesiasticus 39:9–10.
102. *For the anointing of the sick . . . James the apostle*: James 5:14.
103. *'I was . . . visited me'*: Matthew 25:36.
104. *'It is better to visit . . . is joy'*: Ecclesiastes 7:2, 4.
105. *'She seeks wool . . . her blessed'*: Proverbs 31:13, 19, 21, 27–8. See also p. 193.
106. *'For God loves a cheerful giver'*: 2 Corinthians 9:7.

107. *Judas abused ... keeping money back*: John 13:29; Acts 5:1–10.

108. *'A soft answer ... soothe enemies'*: Proverbs 15:1; Ecclesiasticus 6:5.

109. *'For you ... brothers' feet'*: *Vitae patrum*, VII, 4. 8.

110. *'I was ... me in'*: Matthew 25:35.

111. *'Through thy ... of thee'*: Cf. Psalm 5:7.

112. *rise at midnight ... laid down*: I.e. the Night Office and the seven offices of the day, Lauds, Prime, Terce, Sext, Nones, Vespers and Compline. *The Rule of St Benedict*, chapter 16. The prophet is David, in Psalm 119:62.

113. *a need to meditate ... also says*: *The Rule of St Benedict*, chapter 8. Note that the nuns must not follow the usual contemporary practice of reading aloud.

114. *However strict the discipline ... angels fell*: Augustine, *Epistulae*, 78. 8. On 'Noah's Ark ... holy mildness of his father', see Genesis 9:22 (Ham); Genesis 21:10 (Hagar and Ishmael); Malachi 1:3; Genesis 35:22 (Reuben and Bilhar, Jacob's concubine); 2 Samuel 13:1ff. (Amnon and his half-sister Tamar); 2 Samuel 15:1ff. (Absalom and David). 'Quarrels all ... forebodings within' is 2 Corinthians 7:5; 'There is no one here ... own ends' is Philippians 2:20–21.

115. *'Let the ... his filth'*: Cf. Revelation 22:11.

116. *'My son, do not spurn ... grieve you'*: Proverbs 3:11–12, 13:24, 19:25, 21:11, 26:23, 28:23; Hebrews 12:11; Ecclesiasticus 22:3, 30:1–2, 8–9.

117. *'He who ... commanded him'*: This is not in existing texts of the *Confessions*.

118. *'Whoever despises truth and presumes ... before custom'*: Augustine, *De baptismo*, 3. 5, 6, 7; 4. 5.

119. *'And certainly ... be abolished'*: Ivo of Chartres, *Decretum*, 4. 213.

120. *'Do not be ashamed to speak ... every deed'*: Ecclesiasticus 4:24, 30; 37:16.

121. *'The number of fools ... are chosen'*: Ecclesiastes 1:15; Matthew 22:14.

122. *Even from ... to learn*: Ovid, *Metamorphoses*, 4. 428. See also p. 219.

123. *'The people fares ill ... no regrets'*: Proverbs 11:14, 12:15; Ecclesiasticus 32:24 (Vulgate).

124. *It follows that ... at all*: 1 Corinthians 11:27–31.

125. *Collation*: The daily reading from the *Conferences* of John Cas-

sian before Compline, instituted by Benedict: *The Rule of St Benedict*, chapter 42.

126. *'As long ... rest content'*: 1 Timothy 6:8.

127. *The man who eats ... brother's downfall*: Romans 14:3ff. In the next sentence, 'Happy is the man ... is sin' is Romans 14:22–3.

128. *'Dear friends ... he approves'*: 1 John 3:21–2.

129. *'And therefore ... an apostle'*: 1 Corinthians 8:13, 9:1.

130. *'Eating and ... they have'*: Luke 10:7.

131. *There are no ... of God*: 1 Corinthians 10:23–9, 32.

132. *'When you ... to pay'*: Ecclesiastes 5:4–5.

133. *'It is ... the devil'*: 1 Timothy 5:14–15.

134. *'If anyone was circumcised ... seek one'*: 1 Corinthians 7:18, 27.

135. *'A woman ... another man'*: Romans 7:3.

136. *'To the unmarried ... my advice'*: 1 Corinthians 7:8–9, 39–40.

137. *Do not give ... their sons*: Cf. Proverbs 31:4–5.

138. *'A drunken ... good sense'*: Ecclesiasticus 19:1–2.

139. *'Shame on you ... of drinks'*: Isaiah 5:11–12, 22.

140. *These too ... and understand*: Isaiah 28:7–9.

141. *'Wake up ... you drink'*: Joel 1:5.

142. *'for the frequent ailments of your stomach'*: 1 Timothy 5:23. See also p. 179.

143. *Noah was the first ... wished for it*: Genesis 9:20 (Noah); Genesis 19:33–4 (Lot); Judith 12–13 (Holofernes); Genesis 18:1ff. (angels and Abraham (see also p. 186)); 1 Kings 17:1ff. (Elijah); Exodus 16:4ff. (Israelites fed in desert).

144. *repasts of loaves and fishes ... promotes sensuality*: Matthew 15:32ff.; John 2:1ff.

145. *law of the Nazarites ... strong drink*: See Numbers 6:3.

146. *Rule of St Pachomius ... the sickroom*: St Pachomius (c. 286–c. 346) was the first monk to organize the hermits of the Egyptian desert into a community with a written Rule. Abelard would know the text of this from the Latin translation by Jerome. The original version is lost.

147. *And so, if there ... burning body*: Jerome, *Epistulae*, 22.8.

148. *'Does anyone ... fitting penance'*: Ambrose, *De paenitentia*, 2. 10.

149. *'Only on ... take wine'*: From the fifth-century *Ordo monasterii*, the attribution of which to Augustine is doubtful.

150. *'They stay ... in heaven'*: *Patrologia Latina*, ed. Migne, Vol. 23, p. 444.

151. *'How good ... live together'*: Psalm 133:1.

152. *Lord forbids ... dissipation and drunkenness*: See Luke 21:34.

153. 'Subdue your . . . health permits': Augustine, *Epistulae*, 211. 8.
154. 'Let there . . . solemnly observed': This work is thought to be spurious.
155. 'He regards . . . in everything': Author unknown.
156. 'He grew . . . and unruly': Deuteronomy 32:15. The NEB gives 'and unruly' as the meaning of *recalcitravit* ('kicked').
157. 'The righteous . . . are bewildered': Ecclesiastes 7:15–16.
158. 'When you . . . to do"': Luke 17:10.
159. 'The Law . . . killed me': Romans 4:15, 7:8–11.
160. 'By being . . . deceived me': Augustine, *Ad Simplicianum*, 1. 1.
161. *Always we . . . is denied*: Ovid, *Amores*, III. 4. 17.
162. 'There are . . . Father's house': John 14:2.
163. 'If a virgin marries . . . without distraction: 1 Corinthians 7:28, 34–5.
164. 'The Law . . . to perfection': Hebrews 7:19.
165. 'Men and . . . are they': Cf. Acts 15:10–11.
166. 'Come to me . . . is light': Matthew 11:28–30.
167. 'For if Abraham . . . on works': Romans 4:2, 9:30–32.
168. 'I am . . . of thee': Psalm 56:12.
169. 'John came . . . a drinker"': Matthew 11:18–19.
170. 'The children of the bridegroom . . . defile him': Cf. Matthew 9:15; Matthew 15:11, 18, 20.
171. 'Guard your . . . all life': Proverbs 4:23.
172. 'For everything . . . have followed': 1 Timothy 4:4–6.
173. 'I know . . . suffer need': Philippians 4:12.
174. *Our motto . . . I approve*: Seneca, *Epistulae ad Lucilium*, 5. 4.
175. *Esau lost the birthright . . . eating meat*: Genesis 25:17ff.; 1 Kings 17:4 (Elijah).
176. *tempted the second . . . with bread*: The temptation of Jesus by the devil: Matthew 4:1–4.
177. 'It is . . . his master': Cf. Matthew 10:24.
178. 'Nothing is . . . a wife': Chrysostom, *Homilia* VII, in *Epistolam ad Hebraeos*.
179. 'As though . . . of monks': Jerome, *Epistulae*, 54.
180. *St Benedict does not forbid . . . all different*': *The Rule of St Benedict*, chapter 39, where the flesh of four-footed animals is allowed only to the sick and weak; 1 Corinthians 15:39.
181. *eating of meat . . . times a week*: For the question of meat-eating at the Paraclete, see Introduction, p. xxxiv and McLeod, *Héloïse*, pp. 220–23.
182. 'This is our feast-day . . . its demands': Cf. *Patrologia Graeca*, Vol. 36, pp. 358, 430: the works Abelard loosely names and

quotes are *Orationes*, 39 and 46. 'Books' must refer to the folios he used.

183. *'Thus we . . . his fasting'*: Jerome, *Epistulae*, 31.

184. *'Anything you . . . for me'*: Matthew 25:40.

185. *'Those who . . . in palaces'*: Matthew 11:8. See also p. 192.

186. *In the same . . . of God*: 1 Peter 3:1–4.

187. *'A man's . . . his character'*: Ecclesiasticus 19:30.

188. *'The Son of Man . . . spacious roofs'*: Matthew 8:20; Jerome, *Epistulae*, 14.

189. *'Alas for . . . as yourselves'*: Matthew 23:15.

190. *'Have I . . . a devil'*: John 6:70.

191. *Nicholas . . . sentence of death*: Acts 6:5, 5:1ff.

192. *road which leads to life . . . to death is wide*: Matthew 7:13.

193. *'Many are invited . . . cannot be counted'*: Matthew 22:14; cf. Ecclesiastes 1:15 (Vulgate).

194. *'You increased . . . of it'*: Isaiah 9:3 (Vulgate: the negative is in doubt).

195. *detract from his glory*: Cf. 1 Corinthians 9:14–15.

196. *'As fish . . . is within'*: *Vitae patrum*, V, 2. 1.

197. *what follows it*: I.e. the Lesser Litany and Collect.

198. *And when he rules . . . with the rest*: *The Rule of St Benedict*, chapter 56.

199. *'They make up . . . to you'*: Matthew 23:4, 7:15.

200. *'I have . . . soil them'*: Song of Solomon 5:3.

201. *'one will . . . other left'*: Luke 17:34.

202. *'By night . . . soul loves'*: Song of Solomon 3:1.

203. *Dinah went out . . . was defiled*: See Genesis 34:1–2.

204. *'The man . . . turn away'*: John 6:37.

205. *'Master, I . . . have holes'*: Matthew 8:19, 20.

206. *'Would any . . . not finish'' '*: Luke 14:28–30.

207. *'For all the ancient . . . spiritual songs'*: Romans 15:4; Ephesians 5:18–19.

208. *'Until I arrive . . . any kind*: 1 Timothy 4:13; 2 Timothy 3:14–17.

209. *Make love your aim . . . your thinking*: 1 Corinthians 14:1–2, 4, 13–20.

210. *'Let us . . . in harmony'*: *The Rule of St Benedict*, chapter 19.

211. *'Sing hymns with understanding . . . man's flute'*: Psalms 47:7, 119:103, 147:10. *Non in tibiis viri beneplacitum erit ei*. This is usually interpreted as 'takes no pleasure in a runner's legs', as the first half-verse refers to the strength of a horse. *Tibia* can mean both leg-bone and flute or pipe.

212. *that we lose not things eternal . . . that we lose things eternal . . . that we admit not things eternal*: I.e. instead of saying *ut non amittamus aeterna* some say *ut nos amittamus aeterna*, others *ut non* admittamus *aeterna*.

213. *'in his mouth . . . for them'*: Ezekiel 3:3: Lamentations 4:4.

214. *'I will . . . the Lord'*: Amos 8:11.

215. *'How sweet are thy words . . . against thee'*: Psalm 119:103–4, 11.

216. *'The prophets wrote books . . . it knows'*: *Vitae patrum*, V, 10. 114; V, 10. 67. *Fenestrae*, 'shelves', or rather alcoves like blind windows in walls. A twelfth-century example from an Augustinian abbey of Lilleshall, Shropshire, is shown in C. Brooke, *The Twelfth Century Renaissance* (London, 1969), fig. 14.

217. *'Be always . . . and hope'*: 1 Peter 3:15.

218. *'We have not ceased . . . and wisdom'*: Colossians 1:9, 3:16.

219. *'Happy is the man . . . and night'*: Psalm 1:1; Joshua 1:8.

220. *'they are . . . Jesus Christ'*: Philippians 2:21.

221. *instructions about reading . . . manual work*: The Rule of St Benedict, chapters 48 and 55.

222. *'To read without understanding . . . ass sitting before a lyre'*: Cato, whose apocryphal sayings were widely quoted in the Middle Ages. The Greek proverb about the ass and the lyre is quoted by Jerome.

223. *All prophetic vision . . . be lost'*: Isaiah 29:11–14.

224. *'Love knowledge . . . the flesh'*: Jerome, *Epistulae*, 125. 11.

225. *When I was . . . second Nicodemus*: Jerome, *Epistulae*, 84. 3.

226. *'My son . . . find wisdom'*: Ecclesiasticus 6:18.

227. *'As for . . . sacred wisdom'*: Rufinus, *Historia monachorum*, 21.

228. *'From then . . . my delight'*: *Historia ecclesiastica gentis Anglorum*, 5. 24.

229. *'A discerning . . . on folly'*: Proverbs 15:14.

230. *Philistines who persecuted Isaac . . . water from him*: See Genesis 26:15.

231. *'Go away . . . my God'*: Psalm 119:115.

232. *'The Almighty . . . heaped up'*: Job 22:25.

233. *'Drink water . . . yours alone'*: Proverbs 5:15, 17.

234. *'Hurt the . . . it sensitive'*: Ecclesiasticus 22:19.

235. *'Alas for . . . to enter'*: Luke 11:52.

236. *'produce from . . . and new'*: Matthew 13:52.

237. *'Man and . . . O Lord'*: Psalm 36:7.

238. *'The law of the Lord . . . a watercourse'*: Psalm 1:2–3.

239. *'Rivers of living water . . . flooding streams'*: John 7:38; Song of Solomon 5:12.

240. 'But Mary . . . her heart': Luke 2:19.
241. 'If you . . . have sinned': Cf. Genesis 4:7.
242. 'Anyone who . . . I say': John 14:23.
243. 'If you . . . then hear': Matthew 11:15. The woman is Mary (see Letter 6 and note 71).
244. Church: The letter breaks off abruptly without the formal ending of Letter 7.

ABELARD'S CONFESSION OF FAITH

1. 'You shall . . . by steps': Cf. Exodus 20:26.
2. deadly songs: Once more Abelard uses classical symbols, here as a means of expressing dilemmas and temptations. Cf. Letter 5, p. 81.
3. firm: This confession, moving in its simplicity and the fact that it is addressed to Heloise, is preserved only in an open letter by one of Abelard's pupils, Berengar of Poitiers, violently attacking Bernard and all Abelard's detractors at the Council of Sens. It is not known whether it was written shortly before or immediately after the Council, nor how Berengar came by it. He says it is a fragment, but it appears to be complete. Berengar's 'Apologia' is edited by R. M. Thomson, 'The Satirical Works of Berenger of Poitiers', Mediaeval Studies 42 (1980), pp. 111–33, and the 'Confession of Faith' in C. S. F. Burnett, 'Confessio Fidei ad Heloisam', Mittellateinisches Jahrbuch 21 (1986), pp. 152–3.

LETTERS OF PETER THE VENERABLE
AND HELOISE

PETER THE VENERABLE: LETTER (98)
TO POPE INNOCENT II

1. Letter (98) to Pope Innocent II: Radice's translation; this and the following three letters are numbered according to Giles Constable's The Letters of Peter the Venerable, 2 vols. (Cambridge, Mass., 1967).
2. the home the sparrow has reached . . . have found: Cf. Psalm 84:3.
3. him: This letter was written probably in July 1140 or 1141, after Abelard's condemnation by the Council of Sens, but before the

papal sentence of 16 July had reached France. It is the only evidence we have for the reconciliation between Abelard and Bernard of Clairvaux, and suggests that Peter the Venerable supported the overtures made by Abbot Rainald of Cîteaux rather than made the first move himself. The request was granted, as the next letter shows.

PETER THE VENERABLE: LETTER (115)
TO HELOISE

1. *sent me recently*: This letter does not survive.
2. *carry out my intention*: Abelard died on 21 April 1142, but as Peter the Venerable is known to have been travelling to Spain at the time, his reply must have been written in 1143 at the earliest.
3. *'It pleased . . . his grace'*: Galatians 1:15.
4. *With Miriam you sang . . . the waves*: See Exodus 15:19–20.
5. *'the King of the sons of pride'*: Cf. Job 41:34.
6. *'No cedar . . . its boughs'*: Ezekiel 31:8.
7. *one of those animals . . . glow like a lamp*: See Ezekiel 1:13.
8. *Even from . . . to learn*: Ovid, *Metamorphoses*, 4. 428. See also Letter 8, p. 169.
9. *Penthesilea . . . Amazons*: Probably known to Peter from Virgil's *Aeneid*.
10. *the prophetess Deborah . . . against the heathen*: See Judges 4:9ff.
11. *'the mountains . . . with milk'*: Joel 3:18.
12. *Marcigny*: Famous Cluniac nunnery in the diocese of Autun near Semur-en-Brionnais, which Peter's mother Raingard had entered after her husband's death about 1117. Cf. his Letter 53.
13. *enriched her . . . gold and topaz*: Cf. Psalm 119:127.
14. *Chalon . . . Burgundy*: This was the Cluniac priory of St Marcel (Marcellus) at Chalon-sur-Saône: See Clanchy, *Abelard*, pp. 262–3, 322.
15. *writing or composing*: In fact none of Abelard's known works can be dated to the eighteen months he spent at Cluny and St Marcel. See Introduction, p. xliii.
16. *'Learn from . . . humble-hearted'*: Matthew 11:29.

HELOISE: LETTER (167) TO PETER THE VENERABLE

1. *November of the past year*: I.e. November 1143. See Letter 115, p. 217, and note 2.
2. *trental of masses*: Series of thirty masses for the repose of a soul.
3. *Astralabe and yours*: Astralabe was born about 1118 and would now be twenty-six or twenty-seven. What the suggested connection was between him and Peter the Venerable is not clear, but see p. 227 and note 4.

PETER THE VENERABLE: LETTER (168) TO HELOISE

1. *'a stranger and a foreigner ... God's household'*: Genesis 23:4; Ephesians 2:19.
2. *'Let Christ ... their persons'*: *The Rule of St Benedict*, chapter 53.
3. *'Whoever listens ... to me'*: Luke 10:16.
4. *for your Astralabe ... as I can*: It is not known whether Peter the Venerable was successful on behalf of Astralabe, nor what became of him. He is never mentioned by Heloise in her letters to Abelard, and Abelard's only reference to him (outside Letter 1) is in the verses of advice addressed to him and thought to have been written about 1135. His death-day is recorded in the necrology of the Paraclete as 29 or 30 October, and he is named there as *Petrus Astralabius magistri nostri Petri filius*, but no year is given. An Astralabe is on record as a canon of the Cathedral of Nantes in the year 1150, and another as abbot of a Cistercian abbey at Hauterive in the Swiss canton of Fribourg, but it is uncertain if either refers to him. See McLeod, *Héloïse*, pp. 253, 283–4.

THE ABSOLUTION FOR PETER ABELARD

1. *The Absolution for Peter Abelard*: The text is printed by Victor Cousin, *Petri Abaelardi opera*, 2 vols (Paris, 1849), Vol. 1, p. 717, who took it from the notes written by André Duchesne to the edition of the letters of Peter the Venerable published in Paris in 1614, but it cannot be traced in the records of the Paraclete.

TWO HYMNS BY ABELARD

SABBATO AD VESPERAS

1. *Vespers: Saturday Evening*: Translated by Helen Waddell, *Mediaeval Latin Lyrics*, 4th edn. (London, 1952), pp. 175–7. For J. M. Neale's version, see *The English Hymnal*, No. 465.

IN PARASCEVE DOMINI: III. NOCTURNO

1. *Good Friday: The Third Nocturn*: Translation by Waddell, *Mediaeval Latin Lyrics*, p. 179. This hymn was sung in the night office (Nocturns) of prayers on the evening of Good Friday.

Index

Abelard, Peter: birth and early education, xiii–xiv, 3, 249n; arrival at Paris, xv, 3–4; teaching at Melun and Corbeil, 4, 5; student at Laon, xvii, 7–8; head of Cloister School in Paris, xviii, xx, 8–9, 11, 66; meeting with Heloise, xixff., 9ff.; marriage, xix–xxiii, 13ff.; castration, xxiii, 17, 66, 69, 80–83; entry into abbey of St Denis, xxiii, 18–19; condemnation at Council of Soissons, xxiv, xl–xli 20ff., 47, 252n; at abbey of St Médard, 25ff.; founds oratory of the Paraclete, xxiv, xlv, xlvi, 28ff., 49; hands over the Paraclete to H., xxvii, 35ff., 264n; meets H. again, 35 and 261n; abbot of St Gildas, xxv, xxvii–xxix, 33ff.; writes *Historia calamitatum*, xiii, xxiv, xxviii–xxix; return to Paris, xxix, xxxvii, xl; letters to H., xxixff., liii–liv, 56ff., 72ff., 112ff., 130ff., clash with St Bernard, xxiv, xxxviiiff.; condemnation at Council of Sens, xliff., 285n; confession of faith, 211–12; enters Cluny, xlii–xliii, 215–16, 221–2; reconciliation with Bernard, xlii–xliii, 215; death at St Marcel, xliii, 223, 286n; burial at the Paraclete, xliv, xlv, 2; absolution for, xliv 227, 228; epitaphs on, xliii–xliv; as logician, xv–xvii, xviii, xxiv, xxxviii–xxxix, 5, 19, 211; as teacher, xvii–xviii, xix, xxiii–xxiv, xxix, 19–20, 28–30, 34–5; views on monastic reform, xxiv, xxxiii–xxxiv, xxxviii, 141, 183, 194, 195–6, 201, 206

works: Apologia, xlii, xlvi; *Confessio fidei*, xxxix, xlii, xliii, lxii, 211–12; *Dialogue between a Philosopher, a Jew and a Christian*, xl, xliii; *Ethica (Scito te ipsum)*, xl; *Hexameron*, xxxvii, xl, xliii; *Historia calamitatum*, xiii, xvi, xix, xxii–xxiv, xxvii–xxix, xlviiff., liii, lvin, lviin, lxiii–lxxi, 47, 249n, 254n, 263n, 287n; *Hymns*, xxxv–xxxvi, xl, lvn, 268n, 230–35; *Laments*, xxxvi, 264n; love lyrics and songs (lost), xviii, xix, 11, 52–3, 54–5, 252n, 263n *Problems of Heloise*, xxxv, 269n; *Sermons*, xxxvi, xl; *Sic et Non*, xxxix, xlvi, lxxxi; *Theologia*, xl, 9, 20ff., 254–5n; *Theologia Christiana*, xxii, xl, 254n; verses for Astralabe, xliii, 287n